POSTWAR AMERICA

A Student Companion

JOBS

OXFORD

Student Companions to American History

WILLIAM H. CHAFE, GENERAL EDITOR

POSTWAR AMERICA

A Student Companion

Harvard Sitkoff

Oxford University Press
New York

OXFORD
UNIVERSITY PRESS

Oxford New York
Athens Auckland Bangkok Bogotá Buenos Aires Calcutta
Cape Town Chennai Dar es Salaam Delhi Florence Hong Kong Istanbul
Karachi Kuala Lumpur Madrid Melbourne Mexico City Mumbai
Nairobi Paris São Paulo Singapore Taipei Tokyo Toronto Warsaw
and associated companies in
Berlin Ibadan

Published by Oxford University Press, Inc.
198 Madison Avenue, New York, New York 10016
www.oup.com

Library of Congress Cataloging-in-Publication Data
Sitkoff, Harvard
Postwar America: a student companion / Harvard Sitkoff
p. cm.
Includes bibliographical references and index
ISBN 0-19-510300-9
1. United States—History—1945- —Encyclopedias, Juvenile I. Title.
E740.7.S58 1999
973.92—dc21 98-34183

9 8 7 6 5 4 3 2 1

Printed in the United States of America
on acid-free paper

History research: Valerie Dunham, Michael Foley, Bill Jordan, and
Beth McDermott
Design: Sandy Kaufman
Layout: Valerie Sauers
Picture Research: Marty Baldessari, Christine Buese

On the cover: (top left) President John F. Kennedy; (top right) Government issue fallout shelter sign (1952); (bottom) The launching of the Spaceshuttle Columbia at Cape Canaveral, Florida

Frontispiece: Thousands of marchers gather at the Lincoln Memorial in Washington, D.C., on August 28, 1963, to hear Martin Luther King Jr.'s "I Have a Dream" speech.

CONTENTS

PREFACE

It is now clear that the half-century since the end of the Second World War constitutes a coherent historical period—one that continues today to shape who we are as individuals and what the United States is as a nation. Poised uncertainly at the start of a new millennium, we can look back on the last half-century and more of American life and try to make sense of its broad areas of consensus as well as its many conflicts, dramatic changes, and enduring continuities.

The entries that follow, inevitably selective and interpretive, reflect a number of interrelated principal themes. First and foremost is the pervasive impact of the cold war, the long period of superpower struggle that touched virtually every aspect of U.S. history since 1945, from international relations to race relations to sexual relations. It would bring death to young Americans in such countries as Korea and Vietnam, prove critical to unparalleled economic growth and prosperity in the United States, and tempt Americans to seek security in material abundance, mass culture, and suburban living.

Almost as vital in its consequences is the matter of social change, with its emphasis on the categories of gender, class, and race. In manifold ways, the grand protest movements by African Americans, women, gays, workers, and others produced a social landscape fundamentally different from the America of 1945. This occurred, of course, in a political context. Thus, many of the entries deal with legislation and judicial decisions, with the shifting fortunes of liberalism and conservatism, with passionate protestors and equally adamant defenders of tradition, with all that is conveyed by such terms as "McCarthyism" and "Watergate," as well as with the wrangles over changing work, population, and family patterns.

Rather than attempt to give equal weight to each decade since 1945, the entries in this volume mirror a view of what most critically influenced American life: proportionately more emphasis is given to the development of the cold war and its many ramifications, as well as to the reform and protest movements altering American society and its values, than to the past two decades, which have been marked largely by the end of the cold war and the resurgence of political and cultural conservatism.

Thus, the articles in this book have been selected to provide an account of the most vital developments and events in domestic politics, social and cultural change, and foreign affairs. They focus on the people who have had a significant impact on postwar American life; they highlight the key themes of the cold war, the ongoing struggle by women and minorities for equality and justice, and the shifting course of political movements and issues that define and decide the kind of society Americans choose for themselves; and, not least importantly, they also treat the fundamental demographic, economic, and technological developments that have transformed American society since 1945. I hope that these brief entries will answer some of the questions you have about the recent past. They will undoubtedly also raise new questions, which can be investigated through use of the many suggestions for further reading.

Any compilation such as this depends on the scholarship of the countless historians who have examined these matters. I am profoundly indebted to those whose works are cited in this volume as well as to others too numerous to mention. This book, moreover, owes much to the questions and comments from the many students in classes on the United States since 1945 that I have been teaching for more than 30 years. Finally, and most vitally, I have relied on the research and imagination of my wonderfully talented graduate assistants: Valerie Dunham, Michael Foley, Bill Jordan, and Beth McDermott. I dedicate this book to them, and to those who might read it and be inspired to become tomorrow's graduate students and professors of history.

HOW TO USE THIS BOOK

The articles in this *Companion* are arranged alphabetically, so you can look up words, ideas, or names as you come across them in other readings. You can then use the SEE ALSO listings at the end of the article to find entries about related subjects. Sometimes you may find that the *Companion* deals with information under a different article name than the one you looked up. The book will then refer you to the proper article. For example, if you look up Nuclear freeze movement, you will find the notation "SEE Antinuclear movement." If you cannot find a separate article on a particular subject, look in the index, which will guide you to the relevant articles. All people are listed alphabetically by last name; for example, the entry for Henry Kissinger is listed under K as Kissinger, Henry Alfred; Madonna is listed under M as Madonna.

You can also use this *Companion* topically, by reading all the articles about a particular aspect of U.S. history since 1945. Below are several groupings of topics around common themes.

Notable Individuals: There are articles on some of the people who made history in this period. They range from Abzug, Bella, to Wilkins, Roy, and list personal data about each, including, where relevant, the place and dates of birth and death, education, offices held, and other significant accomplishments. In many cases, a book, such as *The Naked and the Dead*, is listed under the author's name—Mailer, Norman; in others, where a book is historically especially important, it is listed by title—*The Other America*.

Riots and Demonstrations: When they have proved to be historically important, these events, such as the conflict in People's Park in Berkeley or the killings at Kent State University, are listed by place name—People's Park battle or Kent State University.

Cultural, Social, and Political Movements: These range from AIM, the American Indian Movement, to Feminism. Information about such broad movements as civil rights will be found under the general topic entry (civil rights) as well as such other specific ones as notable people (e.g., Lewis, John Robert); subgroups (e.g., Student Nonviolent Coordinating Committee); legislation (e.g., Voting Rights Act of 1965); and demonstrations (e.g., Sit-ins).

Congressional Legislation and Supreme Court Decisions: Important laws enacted by Congress and major Supreme Court rulings have their own entries, in addition to the topics they address, such as *Roe* v. *Wade* and Abortion issue, or the Taft-Hartley Act, and Labor Movement of 1954. Also see individual justices; for example, O'Connor, Sandra Day, or Warren, Earl.

Foreign Policy: Information on the affairs of the United States abroad is dealt with in national strategies and ideologies (such as Containment doctrine or Détente), specific conferences and peace talks (Geneva Conference of 1954 or Camp David peace talks), key individuals (Powell, Colin Luther, or Vandenberg, Arthur) and organizations (Atomic Energy Commission or Sandinistas), military actions (Persian Gulf War or Tet offensive), and major disputes and conflicts (Iran-Contra affair or Bosnia, United States and).

Core Concepts: This category of subjects defines and discusses major ideas and concepts central to the history of the United States since 1945, including the Fair Deal, Conservatism, Consumer culture, Keynesian economics, and Terrorism.

Further Reading: To help you find out more about a specific topic or subject, important recent books are listed at the conclusion of most entries. More general sources and broad overviews appear in the FURTHER READING guide at the end of the book.

Abortion issue

A legal and widespread practice in the United States until the 19th century, abortion remained commonplace, although driven underground, in the last part of the 19th century and in the first half of the 20th century. In the 1950s various women's and civil liberties groups, as well as some doctors, began to call for the repeal of laws that made abortion a crime.

In the 1960s the feminist movement made a woman's control over her body, including the right to terminate an unwanted pregnancy, a central demand of modern feminism. In response to these changed public attitudes, several states repealed or modified their anti-abortion statutes. By 1970, in New York, where laws banning abortion had been struck down, one fetus was being aborted for every two live births. In most states, however, abortions continued to be banned entirely or were severely restricted. The Supreme Court changed that situation by ruling in the 1973 case of *Roe* v. *Wade* that women, as part of their constitutional right to privacy, could freely choose to abort a fetus in the first three months (trimester) of pregnancy. States were given the right to restrict second-trimester abortions only in the interest of a woman's safety. During the third trimester, the law protects a fetus that is "viable" (able to survive outside the womb). This means that the woman's life or health must be endangered in order to abort the pregnancy.

The *Roe* decision did not settle the issue for Americans, however. Opponents of the ruling (particularly the Roman Catholic Church and many evangelical and fundamentalist Protestants) squared off against *Roe* supporters (a broad coalition of Americans led by feminist organizations) in the political arena. Frequently, a person's position on abortion became a test of his or her qualification to hold office.

Calling for legalized abortion, pro-choice demonstrators march in front of St. Patrick's Cathedral in New York City in 1967 to protest the Catholic Church's stance against the procedure.

Both the "right to life" and the "pro choice" sides ferociously argued their positions when a challenge to the *Roe* decision came before the U.S. Supreme Court in 1989. In its decision in *Webster* v. *Reproductive Health Services* that year, the Supreme Court upheld its basic ruling in *Roe* by a 5-to-4 vote but also supported a Missouri law prohibiting public employees and facilities from counseling women on abortion or performing abortions in cases where the woman's life was not in danger.

In another 5-to-4 decision, the Court in *Planned Parenthood of Southeastern Pennsylvania* v. *Casey* (1992) again reaffirmed the constitutionality of *Roe* while also upholding the right of states to regulate abortion, as long as the regulations did not present an "undue burden" on women seeking the procedure.

Operation Rescue—one of the most dramatic groups in the right-to-

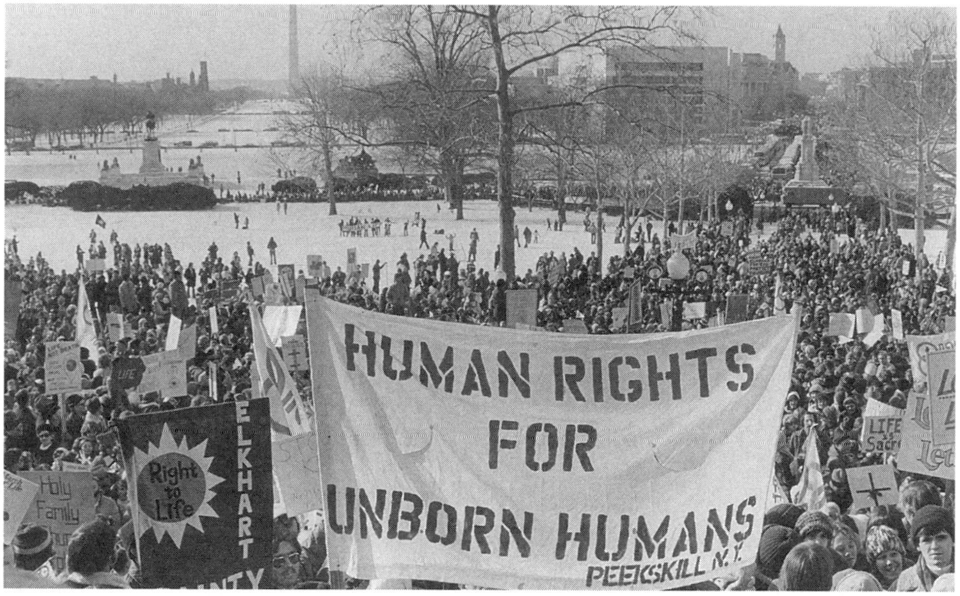

In 1978 supporters of the right-to-life movement gather in Washington, D.C., to protest abortion, which was legalized by the 1973 Roe *v.* Wade *decision of the Supreme Court.*

life, or anti-abortion, movement—organizes "rescues" at abortion clinics, where members protest and often block the entrances. The 1990s have seen the movement turn more violent with clinic bombings, harassment of patients, and the murder of doctors and clinic staff. The pro-choice movement has countered the violence of Operation Rescue through federal legislation—the 1994 Freedom of Access to Clinic Entrances Act—that bans the use of force, threats, or blockades in order to interfere with access to health care, including abortion. The Supreme Court has upheld this act. Because of the physical threat to doctors, nurses, and clinic staff, however, the number of physicians performing abortions has continued to decline; by 1996 84 percent of the counties in the United States did not have even one abortion provider.

Because of the legal, religious, and ethical questions surrounding abortion, it has remained an important and highly charged issue in American politics, affecting every Presidential campaign since the 1970s. In 1995 Henry Foster, President Bill Clinton's nominee for surgeon general, was rejected by the Senate for having performed legal abortions during his medical career. Given the uncompromising positions of those on both sides of the debate, it is unlikely that this issue will be resolved in the political arena any time soon.

SEE ALSO

Feminism; *Roe* v. *Wade* (1973); Sexual revolution

FURTHER READING

Colker, Ruth. *Abortion & Dialogue: Pro-Choice, Pro-Life, and American Law.* Bloomington: Indiana University Press, 1992.

Craig, Barbara Hinkson, and David M. O'Brien. *Abortion and American Politics.* Chatham, N.J.: Chatham House, 1993.

Guernsey, Joann B. *Abortion: Understanding the Controversy.* Minneapolis, Minn.: Lerner, 1993.

Luker, Kristin. *Abortion and the Politics of Motherhood.* Berkeley: University of California Press, 1984.

Martin, William. *With God on Our Side: The Rise of the Religious Right in America.* New York: Broadway, 1997.

Petchesky, Rosalind Pollack. *Abortion and Woman's Choice: The State, Sexuality and Reproductive Freedom.* Boston: Northeastern University Press, 1990.

Petchesky, Rosalind Pollack. *Sexuality and Reproductive Freedom.* Boston: Northeastern University Press, 1990.

Roleff, Tamara L., ed. *Abortion: Opposing Viewpoints.* San Diego, Calif.: Greenhaven Press, 1997.

Staggenborg, Suzanne. *The Pro-Choice Movement: Organization and Activism in the Abortion Conflict.* New York: Oxford University Press, 1991.
Tompkins, Nancy. *Roe v. Wade: And the Fight over Life and Liberty.* Danbury, Conn.: Franklin Watts, 1996.
Tribe, Lawrence H. *Abortion: The Clash of Absolutes.* New York: Norton, 1992.

Abstract expressionism

The most original and influential movement in American art history, abstract expressionism developed in New York City after World War II. The attention it garnered at a 1951 exhibit at the Museum of Modern Art soon caused New York to eclipse Paris as the capital of the art world. Characterized by a total absence of representational figures or scenes (that is, the absence of people, houses, trees, rooms, furniture, mountains, or other identifiable objects), abstract expressionism relied solely on color, line, and form to convey emotions and ideas. The best-known artists associated with the movement include Jackson Pollock, Willem de Kooning, and Mark Rothko.

Jackson Pollock, one of the country's most influential abstract expressionist painters, demonstrates his drip technique of painting in 1956.

FURTHER READING

Anfam, David. *Abstract Expressionism.* London: Thames & Hudson, 1990.
Leja, Michael. *Reframing Abstract Expressionism: Subjectivity and Painting in the 1940s.* New Haven, Conn.: Yale University Press, 1997.
Polcari, Stephen. *Abstract Expressionism and the Modern Experience.* Cambridge, England: Cambridge University Press, 1993.
Ross, Clifford, ed. *Abstract Expressionism: Creators and Critics: An Anthology.* New York: Abrams, 1990.

Abzug, Bella S.

- *Born: July 24, 1920, Bronx, N.Y.*
- *Accomplishments: Founded Women Strike for Peace, 1961; U.S. Representative (Democrat–N.Y.), 1971–76*
- *Died: Mar. 31, 1998, New York, N.Y.*

Famous for wearing dashing hats, Bella Abzug was an activist for a variety of liberal causes in the 1960s, particularly the women's rights, civil rights, and antiwar movements. A leader in the feminist movement, Abzug cochaired the President's National Advisory Committee on Women from 1977 to 1979, after leaving the U.S. House of Representatives. In 1980 she returned to private legal practice and wrote several books on women and politics, including *Bella! Ms. Abzug Goes to Washington* (1972) and *Gender Gap: Bella Abzug's Guide to Political Power for American Women* (1984).

SEE ALSO

Feminism

FURTHER READING

Faber, Doris. *Bella Abzug*. New York: Lothrop, 1976.

Acheson, Dean G.

- *Born: Apr. 11, 1893, Middletown, Conn.*
- *Accomplishments: Assistant Secretary of State, 1941–49; Secretary of State, 1949–53*
- *Died: Oct. 12, 1971, Sandy Spring, Md.*

A product of Groton, Yale, and Harvard Law School, Dean Acheson played a leading role in developing the communist containment policy that guided U.S. foreign policy for the four decades known as the cold war that followed World War II.

First as undersecretary of state in President Harry Truman's administration and then as successor to the ailing George Marshall as secretary of state, Acheson painted a stark picture of the dangers of Soviet political ambition. To counter what was seen as the Soviet Union's efforts to take over governments that were friendly to the United States, Acheson convinced the President and Congress to use U.S. money and arms to stop the spread of communism (a policy called the Truman Doctrine). He also played a leading role in the efforts to assist European economic recovery (the Marshall Plan), reunify Germany, and create a U.S. military

President Harry S. Truman (left) shakes hands with his Secretary of State, Dean Acheson. Acheson was instrumental in developing Truman's cold war policy.

alliance with the Western European nations (the North Atlantic Treaty Organization, or NATO).

Acheson became a target of Republican criticism after communists led by Mao Zedong took control of China in 1949. Accusations that he had allowed the communist victory in China grew louder during the Korean War (1950–53) and as a result of his loyal defense of his friend Alger Hiss, a State Department employee accused in 1948 of spying for the Soviet Union. Senator Joseph McCarthy particularly relished ridiculing the "Red Dean," describing Acheson as a "pompous diplomat in striped pants, with a phony British accent."

After his retirement, Acheson served as an unofficial advisor to Presidents John Kennedy and Lyndon Johnson. He remained a hard-line "cold warrior," ever concerned that U.S. appeasement would encourage communist aggression. He demanded air strikes against Soviet missiles being installed in Cuba in 1962 and initially strongly supported the U.S. escalation of the war in Vietnam. Not until after the Tet offensive in 1968 did Acheson conclude that the United States should seek a negotiated settlement of the conflict in Vietnam.

SEE ALSO

Cold war; Containment doctrine; Korean War; Marshall Plan; North Atlantic Treaty Organization (NATO); Truman Doctrine; Truman, Harry S.

FURTHER READING

Acheson, Dean G. *Present at the Creation: My Years at the State Department.* New York: Norton, 1969.

Brinkley, Douglas, ed. *Dean Acheson and the Making of U.S. Foreign Policy.* New Haven, Conn.: Yale University Press, 1992.

Chace, James. *Acheson: The Secretary of State Who Created the American World.* New York: Simon & Schuster, 1998.

Leffler, Melvyn. *A Preponderance of Power: National Security, the Truman Administration, and the Cold War.* Stanford, Calif.: Stanford University Press, 1992.

Smith, Gaddis. *Dean Acheson.* New York: Cooper Square, 1972.

Acquired immune deficiency syndrome (AIDS)

Sometimes referred to as "the plague of the 20th century," acquired immune deficiency syndrome (AIDS) was first diagnosed in the United States in 1981. The disease spread quickly, causing 200,000 deaths in the United States alone by September 1993. By that time, an additional 1 million Americans had become infected with the human immunodeficiency virus (HIV), the virus that causes AIDS.

Medical science has had no luck in finding a cure for the disease or a vaccine against the virus. Despite much misinformation spread throughout the 1980s, it is now known that HIV is transferred only through bodily fluids. Most cases of AIDS can be traced to sexual contact with an infected person or to the sharing of syringes during intravenous drug use, but it can be transmitted through blood transfusions. Today there are tests of blood supply.

The disease was first associated with homosexuals, and because of a fear of homosexuals (called homophobia), as well as a lack of understanding of the disease, prejudice against AIDS patients was rampant in the 1980s. Ryan White, a young hemophiliac from Florida whose family suffered much abuse when he contracted AIDS from injections to treat his blood disease, became a prominent advocate of AIDS awareness in this country. White's illness and death also brought attention to the problem of pediatric AIDS. By the mid-1990s it was estimated that 15,000 children were infected with HIV in the United States, and that AIDS had become the seventh leading cause of death in American children.

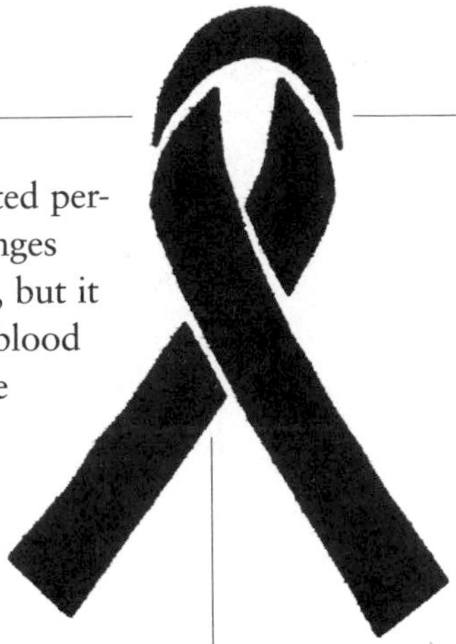

The red ribbon is a symbol of support for people with AIDS. It was created in 1991 by the Visual AIDS Artists' Caucus and first seen at the Tony Awards that year. The red symbolizes love, blood, and passion; ribbons are a symbol of compassion and support.

Celebrity athletes who had the disease, including Earvin "Magic" Johnson and Arthur Ashe, also came forward to help educate Americans about AIDS. Increased public awareness and "safe sex" campaigns have slowed the spread of the disease, and medicines like AZT (azidothymadine) have helped prolong the lives of those infected. But with no cure or vaccine in sight, AIDS remains one of the leading causes of premature death for Americans.

SEE ALSO

Gay liberation movement; Sexual revolution

FURTHER READING

Check, William A. *AIDS.* Broomall, Pa.: Chelsea House, 1998.

Corea, Gena. *The Invisible Epidemic.* New York: HarperCollins, 1992.

Schoub, B. D. *AIDS & HIV in Perspective: A Guide to Understanding the Virus and Its Consequences.* New York: Cambridge University Press, 1994.
Shilts, Randy. *And the Band Played On: Politics, People, and the AIDS Epidemic.* New York: St. Martin's Press, 1987.

Affirmative action

Affirmative action is a policy that allows race and gender to be considered among other factors in decisions on hiring, promotion, public contracting, and public school admissions. The program had its roots in President John F. Kennedy's 1961 executive order requiring federal contractors not to discriminate in hiring practices. Title VII of the Civil Rights Act of 1964 and President Lyndon B. Johnson's Executive Order 11246 in 1965 committed the federal government to actively enforcing equality of opportunity. Johnson's action required federal agencies to adopt, hire, and promote individuals without regard to race, color, religion, or national origin. Sex discrimination was later banned also.

By the early 1970s, however, federal agencies and courts were requiring employers to meet specific numerical guidelines as proof of compliance with equal opportunity rules, a practice that some opponents of affirmative action say amounts to racial and sexual quotas that give unfair advantages to minorities. Affirmative action has become widespread in university admissions and hiring at corporations with federal contracts, as well as at state and local governmental agencies.

Opposition to affirmative action increased in the late 1970s as some whites charged "reverse discrimination." In the *Bakke* v. *Board of Regents of California* decision of 1978, the Supreme Court outlawed quotas but allowed the use of race and sex as "positive factors" in hiring and college admissions. Affirmative action programs suffered a series of setbacks in the mid-1990s as politicians began to call for their end. In July 1995 the University of California Board of Regents voted to end affirmative action in that state's institutions of higher education, and Governor Pete Wilson ceased all state preference programs under his control.

SEE ALSO

Bakke v. *Board of Regents of California* (1978); Civil rights movement; Supreme Court

FURTHER READING

Bergmann, Barbara R. *In Defense of Affirmative Action.* New York: Basic Books, 1996.
Guernsey, Joann Bren. *Affirmative Action: A Problem or a Remedy?* Minneapolis, Minn.: Lerner, 1997.
Skrentny, John David. *The Ironies of Affirmative Action.* Chicago: University of Chicago Press, 1996.

African Americans

The experiences of black servicemen who fought in World War II convinced many of the African Americans who came home from Europe and the Pacific that the contradictions in their lives had to be battled and changed; when they returned from fighting for other people's rights they were not willing to have none of their own. Over the course of the next 20 years there were extraordinary changes in American society, fueled by the courage and determination of the African Americans who often faced fear, physical assault, humiliation, and even death to win better lives for themselves and their children.

By the end of the war U.S. society had begun to change. Threats of a march on Washington had led President Franklin D. Roosevelt to issue an order banning employment discrimination in war-related industries in 1941; in 1943 simmering distrust between blacks and whites had exploded in a race riot in Detroit; and southern blacks continued their exodus to the north. In 1945 Jackie Robinson, a gifted baseball player who displayed not only athletic prowess but astonishing self-control as well, became the first African American to play in the major leagues. Branch Rickey, manager of the Brooklyn Dodgers, gave Robinson a chance; in 1949 Robinson won the National League's Most Valuable Player award.

In the South the Jim Crow laws under which African Americans had lived, which pushed them to the backs of buses, confined their children to segregated and clearly inferior schools, denied them the right to register to vote, and humiliated them constantly in their daily lives by not even allowing them such basic freedoms as the right to sit at a counter and order lunch, were repeatedly challenged and eventually repealed. In 1954 attempts at desegregating public schools culminated in the Supreme Court's *Brown v. Board of Education* ruling, which found that separate schools were inherently unequal and that segregation was not legal. The case was argued before the Supreme Court by a brilliant African-American lawyer, Thurgood Marshall, who would go on to become the first black Supreme Court justice. A young African-American veteran, Robert Williams, wrote in a memoir that "my inner emotions must have been approximate to the Negro slaves' when they first heard about the Emancipation Proclamation."

A crowd gathers in Philadelphia in 1950 to honor African Americans who died in World War II.

However, the rights that the Supreme Court had granted in theory still had to be claimed by the people. In many towns and small cities across the South, African-American schoolchildren, with the support of their parents and the rest of the community, went to previously all-white schools in an atmosphere of overt hostility and physical threat as the state and federal governments dithered over protecting them. One of the most dramatic of the school desegregation battles was fought in Little Rock, Arkansas. Television audiences across the country watched as the nine teenagers chosen to desegregate Central High School walked past crowds of screaming white people, their faces contorted with hate, and local policemen stood back, unwilling or unable to help. This was one of the first ongoing stories covered by television, and no doubt the strength of the images it broadcast, along with the novelty of the medium, helped convince people across America that desegregation was necessary. Eventually, President Dwight D. Eisenhower did send federal troops to Little Rock, and eight of the nine teenagers managed to complete the school year they had begun there.

More courageous acts by large numbers of people caused the end of desegregation in the South. Once Rosa Parks refused to give up her seat on a bus in Montgomery, Alabama, in 1955, 95 percent of the community supported the boycott that followed and refused to ride the buses until they were desegregated. College students in Greensboro, North Carolina, sat at a lunch counter day after day, being verbally and then physically assaulted, until eventually public accommodations were desegregated. And hundreds of people went to church rallies, to marches, and eventually to jail. Many people modeled themselves after Mohandas Gandhi and his idea of nonviolent direct action, which combines courage and self-control. The method worked for Gandhi in India, and it worked in the South as well.

The fight for voting rights culminated in the Freedom Rides through Mississippi in the summer of 1964, when about 1,000 volunteers—most of them from the North, about three-quarters of them white, and about 300 of them women—came to help register black voters. Three of them were murdered and their bodies hidden that summer—James Chaney, an African American from Mississippi, and Andrew Goodman and Michael Schwerner, two white New Yorkers. The publicity given the killings and the eventual discovery of their decomposed bodies helped more people outside the South understand the importance of the cause to which the three had given their lives.

Challenging times often produce leaders who prove to be up to the challenge; many such African-American leaders emerged during the 20 years after the war, including Martin Luther King, Jr., Rosa Parks, John Lewis, James Meredith, Robert Moses, Fannie Lou Hamer, and Malcolm X. There were also organizations that were influential; chief among them were the National Association for the Advancement of Colored People (NAACP); the Nation of Islam (NOI); the Southern Christian Leadership Council (SCLC); and the Student Nonviolent Coordinating Committee (SNCC).

African-American music and literature flourished during the postwar period. James Baldwin, Ralph Ellison, and Richard Wright wrote with anger and clarity about their experiences as black men; each man, with his own distinctive voice, provided inspiration for the generation of writers who followed. Black music, which was a powerful way of expressing the emotions of the communities from which it sprang, became increasingly electric and complex as it moved North and became increasingly mainstream. The blues went from being played on one guitar to small groups to big bands to become rhythm and blues; jazz became increasingly sophisticated as musicians developed the style known as bebop.

By 1968, when Martin Luther King, Jr., was assassinated in Memphis, enormous changes had transformed the lives of African Americans. By then many black people had moved to the cities of the North, where they faced a new set of challenges.

Nineteen sixty-eight was a year of chaos and violence. There were race riots and shoot-outs between police and black activists, the war in Vietnam and growing opposition to it was further poisoning the atmosphere, and the

Douglas Wilder, the first African American to be elected governor of any state, takes the oath of office to become the governor of Virginia in January 1990.

assassination of Robert Kennedy that year added to the feeling of a world gone out of control. It was in 1968 that the Kerner Commission, charged with examining race relations, found that there was a widening gulf between blacks and whites. The commission, most of whose members were liberals, reported that racism was endemic to U.S. society, attributable not to bad behavior but to a structural sickness.

During the 1970s changes in the global economy led to the loss of industrial jobs and so to massive unemployment and poverty among African Americans, and to the growth of single-parent households. The black middle class expanded during that time, but the gap between the middle class and everyone else widened as well.

At the beginning of the 1970s African Americans began to win political victories. They began with low-level municipal elected positions, but soon were well represented in big-city mayors' offices throughout the country—beginning with the election of Tom Bradley in Los Angeles in 1973; Carl Stokes in Cleveland and Richard Hatcher in Gary, Indiana, both in 1975; then Harold Washington in Chicago in 1983, and more recently David Dinkins in New York in 1988.

In 1971 black members of Congress formed the Congressional Black Caucus, and in 1972 some 8,000 African Americans (3,000 of them official delegates) attended the first convention of the National Black Political Assembly, called the Gary Convention after the Indiana town that hosted it. The convention passed a statement declaring that "the American system does not work for the masses of our people, and it cannot be made to work without radical, fundamental changes." The people who had been to the convention left energized by the vision they shared; unfortunately, that vision was abandoned a bit at a time, whittled down by the outside world. However, at the 1972 Democratic Convention Shirley Chisholm, a representative from Brooklyn who was the first black woman elected to Congress, entered the contest for the Presidential nomination; she earned 150 votes before she was defeated by the eventual candidate, George McGovern. Another African-American member of Congress, Barbara Jordan of Texas, a stirring orator and a woman of great presence, sat on the House Judicial Committee as it held hearings on the impeachment of President Richard Nixon.

Jesse Jackson, an ordained Baptist minister who is also a prominent social activist, ran for President in 1984 and again in 1988. Although he did not win the election, he did have enough support to be seen as a power broker; his Rainbow Coalition brought together a range of people, including black and Hispanic activists, environmentalists, and feminists, as he challenged all Americans to dream of a better, more democratic, more colorblind America.

The second African-American to become a Supreme Court justice, Clarence Thomas, won confirmation of his nomination to fill the seat of the retiring Justice Thurgood Marshall in 1991. Unlike Marshall, Thomas was controversial in the black community, because despite his race he was a conservative Republican who made clear his disdain for affirmative action and for most of the leadership of the civil rights movement. Since his appointment, Thomas has voted just as his detractors feared and his supporters hoped he would, providing a consistently conservative voice on the Court.

SEE ALSO

Baldwin, James; Black Muslims; *Brown* v. *Board of Education of Topeka, Kansas* (1954); Civil rights movement; Ellison, Ralph; Freedom rides; Hamer, Fannie Lou Townsend; Kerner Commission (National Advisory Commission on Civil Disorders); King, Martin Luther, Jr.; Little Rock, Arkansas, desegregation crisis (1957); Malcolm X (Malcolm Little); Meredith, James Howard; Moses, Robert Parris; Montgomery bus boycott (1955–56); National Association for the Advancement of Colored People (NAACP); Robinson, Jackie; Southern Christian Leadership Conference (SCLC); Student Nonviolent Coordinating Committee (SNCC); Supreme Court

FURTHER READING

Branch, Taylor. *Parting the Waters: America in the King Years, 1954–63*. New York: Viking, 1993.

Branch, Taylor. *Pillar of Fire: America in the King Years, 1963–65*. New York: Simon & Schuster, 1999.

Bullard, Sara. *Free at Last: A History of the Civil Rights Movement and Those who Died in the Struggle*. New York: Oxford University Press, 1993.

Harding, Vincent, Robin D. G. Kelley, and Earl Lewis. *We Changed the World: African Americans 1945–1970*. New York: Oxford University Press, 1997.

Kelley, Robin D. G. *Into the Fire: African Americans Since 1970*. New York: Oxford University Press, 1996.

Jones, Jacqueline. *The Dispossessed: American's Underclasses from the Civil War to the Present*. New York: Basic Books, 1992.

Terkel, Studs. *Race: How Blacks and Whites Think and Feel About the American Obsession*. New York: New Press, 1992.

Agnew, Spiro

- *Born: Nov. 9, 1918, Baltimore, Md.*
- *Accomplishments: Governor of Maryland (Republican), 1966–68; Vice President, 1969–73*
- *Died: Sept. 18, 1996, Berlin, Md.*

Spiro Agnew served as governor of Maryland before Richard Nixon chose him to be his Vice Presidential running mate in the 1968 election. Despised by many liberals for his attacks on critics of the Nixon administration, Vice President Agnew was popular, however, with Americans who believed in conservative family values and longed for more law and order rather than the turbulence of the late 1960s. He accused antiwar protestors of being "encouraged by an effete corps of impudent snobs." In speeches for Republican candidates in the off-year elections of 1970, Agnew blamed America's ills on "nattering nabobs of negativism," "vicars of vacillation," "pusillanimous pussyfooters," and "hopeless, hysterical hypochondriacs of history."

A 1971 investigation by the U.S. attorney for Maryland resulted in Agnew's indictment on bribery and conspiracy charges because of kickbacks he had taken while serving as a Baltimore County executive and governor. After plea bargaining by his lawyers, the Justice Department dropped the charges of bribery and conspiracy, and Agnew pleaded *nolo contendere*—no contest—to charges of tax evasion.

On October 10, 1973, Agnew became the first Vice President to resign from office. He was fined $10,000 and placed on a three-year probation. He soon took up residence in California as an international businessman. President Nixon nominated House minority leader Gerald Ford to replace Agnew as Vice President.

SEE ALSO

Nixon, Richard Milhous

FURTHER READING

Agnew, Spiro T. *Go Quietly . . . Or Else.* New York: Morrow, 1980.

Cohen, Richard, and Jules Witcover. *A Heartbeat Away: The Investigation and Resignation of Vice President Spiro T. Agnew.* New York: Viking, 1974.

AIDS

SEE Acquired immune deficiency syndrome (AIDS)

Ali, Muhammad (Cassius Clay)

- *Born: Jan. 17, 1942, Louisville, Ky.*
- *Accomplishments: Golden Gloves champion, 1959, 1960; Olympic gold medalist, 1960; heavyweight boxing champion, 1964–67, 1974–78, 1978–79*

Boxing champ Muhammad Ali, a hero to American boys, visits a children's hospital in 1963.

Despite being barred from his sport for three years during the prime of his career, prizefighter Muhammad Ali was one of the world's most recognizable sports figures in the 20th century.

Born Cassius Clay, the 1960 Olympic gold medalist changed his name in 1963 after joining the Nation of Islam, a black Muslim group. The following year he knocked out Sonny Liston to win the world professional heavyweight championship. Three years later, after nine successful title defenses, boxing officials stripped him of his title and banned him from boxing for having resisted induction into the U.S. Army and for speaking out against the Vietnam War. "I ain't got nothing against them Viet Congs," Ali declared.

After a three-year legal battle, the Supreme Court ruled that Ali was a conscientious objector and should be allowed to box again. In 1970 Ali began a long comeback, culminating in his underdog win against champion George Foreman in 1974. Before his retirement in 1979, Ali lost and regained the title one more time. Ali, who has suffered from Parkinson's disease since 1984, appeared at the 1996 Summer Olympics in Atlanta to light the flaming cauldron that signals the start of the Games.

SEE ALSO

Black Muslims

FURTHER READING

Early, Gerald Lyn, ed. *The Muhammad Ali Reader.* Hopewell, N.J.: Ecco, 1998.
Gorn, Elliott J., ed. *Muhammad Ali, the People's Champ.* Urbana: University of Illinois Press, 1995.
Hauser, Thomas. *Muhammad Ali: His Life and Times.* New York: Simon & Schuster, 1992.
Remnick, David. *King of the World: The Rise of Muhammad Ali.* New York: Random House, 1998.

Alliance for Progress

Fearful that widespread poverty was making Latin America ripe for Fidel Castro–style communism, President John F. Kennedy proposed the Alliance for Progress, an economic and social program designed to raise the living standards of Latin Americans, to that region's ambassadors on March 13, 1961. Formalized by an agreement between 22 Latin American countries and the United States at Este, Uruguay, in August 1961, the *Alianza para el Progreso* promised $100 billion in U.S. aid over 10 years to promote political democracy, economic growth, and social reform.

Like the Peace Corps, the Alliance for Progress was an innovation to win "the hearts and minds" of developing nations and to work a "peaceful revolution" in Latin America's social structure. But Kennedy seemed more concerned with appearing "tough" against communism and proving his mettle than in promoting reform, and the expenditures for the Alliance for Progress never matched its expectations. By 1970 Latin America was worse off than it had been in 1961. The Alliance for Progress was eventually taken over, on a greatly reduced scale, by the United Nations Economic Commission for Latin America and the Caribbean.

With aid from the Alliance for Progress, farmers in Venezuela work together and share their new equipment on a cooperative farm.

FURTHER READING

Levinson, Jerome, and Juan de Onis. *The Alliance That Lost Its Way; A Critical Report on the Alliance for Progress.* Chicago: Quadrangle Books, 1970.
Scheman, L. Ronald. *The Alliance for Progress: A Retrospective.* New York: Praeger, 1988.

American Indian Movement (AIM)

In 1968 a group of militant Chippewa Indians in Minnesota started the American Indian Movement (AIM), calling for self-determination for American Indian tribes—initially just the Chippewa—and cash payments by the U.S. government for lands AIM considered stolen from the Indians. It also established armed patrols to combat police brutality.

Soon joined by Indians from other tribes, the group began a campaign of confrontational protest in 1969 by occu-

pying Alcatraz Island near San Francisco. AIM members also occupied the Washington office of the federal Bureau of Indian Affairs in 1972 and a trading post at Wounded Knee, South Dakota, the site of a 19th-century U.S. Army massacre of Indians in 1973.

AIM's protests drew attention to the dire plight of American Indians and influenced the federal government to end its policy of dismantling Indian reservations and relocating Indian inhabitants to nonreservation cities and towns (a policy called "reservation termination"). At the same time, the U.S. government gave more control of Indian affairs back to the tribes.

The movement still exists, although it is not as active as it was during the 1970s. It has local and regional chapters throughout the United States and Canada.

SEE ALSO

Native Americans; Wounded Knee (1973)

FURTHER READING

Matthiessen, Peter. *In the Spirit of Crazy Horse.* New York: Viking, 1992.

Stern, Kenneth. *Loud Hawk: The United States Versus the American Indian Movement.* Norman: University of Oklahoma Press, 1995.

American Indians

SEE Native Americans

Americans for Democratic Action (ADA)

In 1947, in response to the formation of the Progressive party led by Presidential candidate Henry Wallace, a prominent group of liberals founded the Americans for Democratic Action (ADA) to formulate and support liberal domestic and foreign policies. Its organizing committee included such notables as former First Lady Eleanor Roosevelt, theologian Reinhold Niebuhr, labor leader Walter Reuther, and historian Arthur Schlesinger, Jr.

Unlike the Progressive party, the ADA aggressively denounced communism, making it the most respectable institution of the left in the 1950s and 1960s. Over the years, it supported many progressive candidates and causes, and worked for liberal legislation through public education and lobbying. In the late 1960s, however, its popularity and influence declined rapidly.

SEE ALSO

Liberalism

FURTHER READING

Gillon, Steven. *Politics and Vision: The ADA and American Liberalism, 1947–1985.* New York: Oxford University Press, 1987.

Hamby, Alonzo. *Liberalism and Its Challengers: From F.D.R. to Bush.* New York: Oxford University Press, 1992.

Anticommunism

Communism was based broadly on the ideas of Karl Marx and first practiced by the Bolsheviks in Russia after their successful revolution in 1917. In theory, it promoted the equitable distribution of economic goods and state ownership of the means of production. However, for most Americans it came to mean the violent takeover of the state by the proletariat and the establishment of an anti-religious society. In 1919–20 increased immigration and the resulting xenophobia, the growth of labor unions and a rash of labor strikes, and violence against public officials in the United States combined to feed fears of bolshevism. This led to the paranoia known as the Red Scare and an anticommunist crusade. Immigration officials cracked down on foreigners, and employers used heavy-handed tactics to break strikes. Concern about communism then diminished until the years immediately after World War II, when it reached the point of near hysteria. At this time, the expansion of communism into Eastern Europe, the Soviet Union's development of an atomic bomb, the communist victory in China, and the stalemated Korean War re-ignited anticommunist sentiment in the United States. These developments provided fertile ground for the idea of a communist conspiracy within the United States to explain the crises abroad. At home, meanwhile, the Truman administration began to review the loyalty of government employees and to bar people it thought might be communists from government jobs, and partisan Republicans made a great point of stressing the perceived communist leanings of some Democratic appointees. Many people were blacklisted and lost their jobs; some had been members of the communist party and some had not. The sensational hearings held by Republican senator Joseph McCarthy in the early 1950s were the climax of the second Red Scare, but McCarthy went too far; by 1954 he was finished as a politician and the Red Scare lost its grip on the American people.

SEE ALSO

Army–McCarthy hearings (1954); Cold war; Korean War; McCarthyism

FURTHER READING

Caute, David. *The Great Fear*. New York: Simon & Schuster, 1978.
Fried, Richard. *Nightmare in Red*. New York: Oxford University Press, 1990.
Navasky, Victor. *Naming Names*. New York: Viking, 1980.

Antinuclear movement

The acceleration of the nuclear arms race between the Soviet Union and the United States throughout the 1950s, and the heightened concern over the health hazards caused by radioactive fallout from hydrogen-bomb tests, led in the 1960s and 1970s to an especially strong antinuclear movement and a series of public protests against the continuation of nuclear testing and the spread of nuclear weapons.

It helped produce a Test Ban Treaty in 1963 between the United States and the Soviet Union, halting atmospheric nuclear tests, and the Nuclear Nonproliferation Treaty of 1968, signed by 153 nations, that attempted to prevent the spread of nuclear weapons among participating countries. The treaty's major weakness is that several important countries have not signed it, including France, China, and India.

There have been many successes in the antinuclear movement in recent years. The Intermediate Nuclear Forces (INF) Treaty negotiated between the Soviet Union and the United States in 1988 called for a withdrawal of medium-range nuclear missiles from Europe. The Strategic Arms Reduction Treaty (START), covering the long-range nuclear weapons of the United States and the former Soviet Union, was finally ratified by the U.S. Senate after many stalled negotiations in 1991. It set a timetable and goals for the reduction of long-range missiles.

FURTHER READING

Daley, Michael J. *Nuclear Power: Promise or Peril?* Minneapolis, Minn.: Lerner, 1996.

Ellsberg, Daniel. "Manhattan Project II." *The Progressive* (August 1993): 28–32.

Meyer, David S. *A Winter of Discontent: The Nuclear Freeze and American Politics.* Westport, Conn.: Greenwood, 1990.

Antiwar movement

Not long after the 1963 Nuclear Test Ban Treaty seemed to remove much of the need for a strong peace movement, a new, more powerful antiwar movement began to emerge because of events in Indochina. Lyndon Johnson's marked escalation of the Vietnam War in 1965 met with almost immediate protest. In the next few years a new movement evolved, one that represented a merging of the efforts of dozens of organizations with roots in the Old and New Left such as the National Mobilization Committee to End the War in Vietnam, Students for a Democratic Society (SDS), Weathermen, and the Youth International Party (Yippies). More importantly, however, the antiwar movement grew into a mass effort based on grass-roots participation.

Peaceful demonstrations aimed at raising the consciousness of the nation and building political pressure to end the war grew in size from 20,000 marchers in Washington in 1965 to nearly 500,000 in 1969. In 1965 teach-ins were held on campuses from Berkeley, California, to Columbia University in New York City. In 1970 nationwide campus strikes to protest the war were marred by tragedies such as the one at Kent State University in Ohio, where state National Guardsmen killed four people at a student protest against the U.S. invasion of Cambodia.

For many, participating in marches led to civil disobedience and willful violation of Selective Service laws (the Selective Service administered the military draft). Many protestors eventually became disillusioned as the war raged on, and the movement fragmented after 1969 as some members became increasingly radical and others drifted away. It is not yet clear to historians exactly how the antiwar movement affected the course of the war, but it is obvious to them that the effect was strong.

Protesters gather in New York City's Bryant Park to call for an end to U.S. involvement in the Vietnam war. The coffin in the center represents the dead in Vietnam.

SEE ALSO

Hayden, Thomas ("Tom"); Kent State University, killings at (1970); National Mobilization Committee to End the War in Vietnam; New Left; Students for a Democratic Society (SDS); Vietnam War; Weathermen; Youth International party (Yippies)

FURTHER READING

Bundy, McGeorge. *Danger and Survival.* New York: Random House, 1988.

DeBenedetti, Charles. *An American Ordeal: The Antiwar Movement of the Vietnam Era.* Syracuse, N.Y.: Syracuse University Press, 1990.

Wells, Tom. *The War Within: America's Battle Over Vietnam.* Berkeley: University of California Press, 1994.

Zaroulis, Nancy, and Gerald Sullivan. *Who Spoke Up? American Protest Against the War in Vietnam, 1963–1975.* Garden City, N.Y.: Doubleday, 1984.

Arab oil embargo

Resenting the United States for its longtime support of Israel, and to retaliate for the aid given to Israel in the Yom Kippur War of 1973, Arab leaders in December 1973 imposed an embargo, or a halt, on shipments of oil to the United States and its allies, such as Japan and countries in western Europe. The Organization of Petroleum Exporting Countries (OPEC), then controlled by Arab oil-producing states, raised its charges to $11.65 per barrel—387 percent higher than before the war. The embargo lasted until March 1974, and oil prices remained high for many years after.

In the United States, the embargo caused a heightened sense of national vulnerability, greater reliance on nuclear power, the lowering of thermostats and speed limits, and runaway inflation. Retail prices increased 11 percent in 1974 and wholesale prices rose 18 percent, sparking a decade of economic decline and uncertainty.

SEE ALSO

Energy crisis; Middle East–U.S. relations

FURTHER READING

Adelman, M. A. *The Genie Out of the Bottle: World Oil Since 1970.* Cambridge, Mass.: MIT Press, 1995.

Yergin, Daniel. *The Prize: The Epic Quest for Oil, Money, and Power.* New York: Simon & Schuster, 1991.

Arms race

The arms race began when the United States dropped the first atomic bomb on Hiroshima, Japan, on August 6, 1945. President Harry Truman's administration had hoped that the U.S. atomic monopoly would force the Soviet Union to be more cooperative in organizing the post–World War II peace. Those hopes were shattered when the Soviet Union successfully tested its own atomic bomb in 1949. Shortly thereafter, the United States began a crash program to develop a more powerful "super" weapon, the hydrogen bomb, which was first tested in 1952.

Uncle Sam is almost knocked off his feet as Sputnik I*—representing Soviet scientific progress—flies by overhead. In response to the launching of the Soviet satellite, the United States pushed the development of its own scientific programs and increased its weapons production.*

President Dwight Eisenhower, always budget conscious, speeded up the arms race in the 1950s by his preference for nuclear weapons over conventional ones. He felt that nuclear weapons gave "more bang for the buck." Eisenhower's response to the Soviets' orbiting a man-made satellite named *Sputnik* in 1957, reflecting his administration's view of technology as central to ending Communist expansion, was to authorize the development of intercontinental ballistic missile (ICBM) systems, further pushing the pace of the U.S. nuclear weapons program, as did John Kennedy's firm anticommunist foreign policies. This in turn prompted the Soviet Union to expand its nuclear weaponry further. New, more powerful warheads and faster, more accurate delivery systems came into being, creating greater instability and the prospect of a devastating nuclear war.

Despite efforts at détente, or the relaxation of tensions, beginning in 1972 new technology advanced the arms race between the United States and the Soviet Union. In the relaxation of tension, and the various nuclear treaties signed with the Soviet Union, the proliferation of high-tech delivery systems and the increasing number of countries with nuclear weapons have raised the arms race to new levels of sophistication and menace. The continuing spread of nuclear arms technology around the world has made the control of such weapons even more difficult.

SEE ALSO

Atomic bomb; Détente; Hydrogen bomb; Nuclear arms control

FURTHER READING

Craig, Paul P. *The Nuclear Arms Race: Technology and Society.* New York: McGraw-Hill, 1990.

Denardo, James. *The Amateur Strategist: Intuitive Deterrence Theories and the Politics of the Nuclear Arms Race.* New York: Cambridge University Press, 1995.

Powaski, Ronald. *March to Armageddon: The United States and the Nuclear Arms Race.* New York: Oxford University Press, 1987.

Sherry, Michael S. *The Rise of American Air Power: The Creation of Armageddon.* New Haven, Conn.: Yale University Press, 1987.

Army–McCarthy hearings (1954)

For 35 days, from April to June 1954, more than 20 million Americans tuned in to view the televised hearings of Senator Joseph McCarthy's investigation of alleged communist infiltration of the U.S. Army. McCarthy called for these hearings in retaliation against the army for having drafted one of his top aides, David Schine.

Stunned viewers watched as McCarthy bullied and browbeat witnesses and constantly interrupted others while they were speaking (shouting "point of order, Mr. Chairman, point of order!"). McCarthy's badgering turned the nation against him. In June McCarthy accused one of the young lawyers for the army of being a homosexual. Joseph Welch, the chief counsel for the army, responded: "Until this moment, Senator, I think I really never gauged your cruelty or your recklessness. . . . Have you no sense of decency, sir?" Welch had spoken for the nation. In December the Senate voted 67 to 22 to censure McCarthy. His witch hunt, which had ruined reputations and trampled constitutional rights, was over.

SEE ALSO

Anticommunism; McCarthyism; McCarthy, Joseph

Asian Americans

In 1945 the Asian-American population was still relatively small; foreign-born Asians were legally considered to be "aliens ineligible to citizenship" so many Asians who had lived in the United States for most of their lives still were not technically Asian Americans. In 1943 Chinese immigrants were allowed to become naturalized citizens, in 1946 that right was extended to Filipinos and Asian Indians, and in 1952 all ethnic and racial bars to naturalization were dropped. The experiences of Asian Americans in the United States until the end of World War II were often hard; the Chinese faced racial prejudice, and the Japanese who lived on the West Coast were interned in camps by a U.S. government that reacted to the Japanese attack on Pearl Harbor by doubting the loyalty of all ethnic Japanese in the United States.

After the war, however, the situation began to change. The internees were released from the camps; some went home while others went on to establish new lives in other places. Many people were badly hurt by the experience and their wounds took decades to heal. In 1952, however, Congress finally lifted the restrictions that kept Asian immigrants from becoming citizens, and by 1965 about 46,000 Japanese Americans had taken advantage of the opportunity. In 1988 Congress authorized a payment of $20,000 to each surviving internee, and each payment came with a letter of apology signed by the President.

In the postwar period many Japanese Americans prospered. Several politicians reached high levels: in 1959 Daniel Inouye of Hawaii became the first Asian American to be elected to the House of Representatives; later he became the first Japanese American to become a senator. Patsy Mink, also of Hawaii, was the first Asian-American woman to serve in the

The oath of citizenship ceremony, such as this one performed in 1962, is the final step taken by immigrants before they become American citizens. Large numbers of Asian, especially Japanese, Americans took advantage of the opportunity to become citizens once the government lifted its ban in 1953.

House, and George Ariyoshi was governor of that state. Norman Mineta, who had been in an internment camp during the war, was elected to Congress from California; California sent S. I. Hayakawa to the Senate. Many Japanese Americans became successful, high-earning professionals, artists, scientists, athletes, and performers; the austere elegance of Japanese style, the low-fat tastiness of Japanese food, and the serenity perceived as being available to followers of Japanese religion, particularly Zen Buddhism, were admired by many non-Asian Americans. In fact, Japanese Americans soon became stereotyped as a model minority.

Chinese immigrants had begun to arrive in the United States before many Japanese came, but until the end of World War II most of the immigrants had been men. That changed with the end of the war; nearly 90 percent of new Chinese immigrants were women. As a group Chinese Americans prospered; as the society around them shed much of the prejudice that had hemmed them in, many Chinese Americans joined the middle class. New immigrants continued to enter the country, many from places such as Hong Kong and Taiwan, many already well educated. Today a larger percentage of Chinese Americans than members of any other ethnic group have college degrees. Many Chinese Americans entered high-tech fields—An Wang, the founder of Wang Laboratories, who became not only a scientist but a major philanthropist as well, is a good example —while others became writers, filmmakers, artists, scientists, and architects. After 1965, when immigration laws relaxed again, the new immigrants conformed to a different pattern, however; they were more likely to be unskilled and to take the sort of low-wage jobs that no one else wants. These new Chinese Americans, following the patterns set by earlier immigrants, assume that they, too, will achieve success one day.

Two events that greatly affected Asian Americans were the Immigration Reform Act of 1965 and the end of the Vietnam War in 1975. The changes to immigration law removed quotas that had favored emigrants from western Europe, and floods of Asian immigrants streamed into the United States. Asian Indians, Filipinos, and Koreans began coming to the United States in large numbers. Most of the Indians who immigrated after 1965 are Hindu, most live in the New York metropolitan area, and many are well-educated professionals. Filipinos had had a presence in the United States since early in the 20th century, but it was fairly small. It was not until after 1965 that large numbers of Filipinos immigrated; this wave was mainly made up of professionals, many of them in health-care fields. There had not been many Koreans in the United States until 1953, but with the end of the Korean War the community began to build; it was augmented by the many immigrants newly free to move to the United States beginning in 1965.

The end of the Vietnam War brought many people from southeastern Asia to the United States; unlike early immigrants many of them were refugees. Cambodians, Laotians, Hmong, and Vietnamese refugees all have established communities in the United States. Many of them are poor and came here not able to speak English; many of them had had very little contact with Western culture and very little understanding of Western life before they crossed the Pacific. They are still adjusting to the United States, and few of them have been here long enough for observers to make many generalizations about their eventual place in American life.

SEE ALSO

Immigration Reform Act of 1965; Vietnam War

FURTHER READING

Hoobler, Dorothy, and Thomas Hoobler. *The Chinese American Family Album.* New York: Oxford University Press, 1994.

Hoobler, Dorothy, and Thomas Hoobler. *The Japanese American Family Album.* New York: Oxford University Press, 1996.

Takaki, Ronald. *Strangers from a Different Shore.* Boston: Back Bay, 1998.

Takaki, Ronald. *Strangers at the Gate Again: Asian American Immigration After 1965.* Broomall, Pa.: Chelsea House, 1995.

Tateishi, John, and Roger Daniels. *And Justice for All: An Oral History of the Japanese-American Detention Camps.* Seattle: University of Washington Press, 1999.

Atomic bomb

Nuclear fission, the process of harnessing an uncontrolled nuclear explosion's destructive force, was first discovered in Germany in 1938. Worried that Germany might develop an atomic bomb, Albert Einstein and other scientists urged President Franklin D. Roosevelt to establish a research program into atomic weaponry. Fearful of what might occur if Adolf Hitler got such a bomb first, Roosevelt gave his approval to establish what was code named the Manhattan Project in 1942. The U.S. Army assumed full control of the Manhattan Project. More than 125,000 people and $2 billion were allocated to fashioning what Secretary of the Army Henry Stimson called "the most terrible weapon ever known in human history."

While the United States was engaged in World War II, the first successful detonation of an atomic blast occurred at Alamogordo, New Mexico, on July 16, 1945. The test gave President Harry S. Truman confidence that this secret awesome weapon might shock Japan into surrendering before a U.S. invasion of the Japanese home islands became necessary. Truman also believed that U.S. possession of atomic weapons might push the Soviet Union into letting the Eastern European nations choose their own democratically elected governments after the war.

After warning Japan to surrender unconditionally or face "prompt and utter destruction," Truman ordered the military to drop an atomic bomb if Japan did not surrender by August 3. It did not, and on August 6 the bomber

Japanese industrial worker Hiromichi Matsudo took this photograph from the outskirts of Nagasaki 20 minutes after the U.S. bomb destroyed most of that city.

Enola Gay dropped a uranium bomb on Hiroshima, incinerating much of the city and killing more than 70,000 people. Many more would subsequently die of radiation poisoning.

Three days later, after Japan still refused to surrender, a U.S. plane exploded a plutonium bomb over Nagasaki, killing 40,000 and injuring more than 60,000. On August 14, Japan accepted the United States's terms of surrender. World War II was over and the nuclear age had begun.

SEE ALSO
Arms race

FURTHER READING

Black, Wallace B., and Jean F. Blashfield. *Hiroshima and the Atomic Bomb.* Parsippany, N.J.: Silver Burdett Press, 1993.
Hersey, John. *Hiroshima.* New York: Knopf, 1948.
Rhodes, Richard. *The Making of the Atomic Bomb.* New York: Simon & Schuster, 1986.
Sherwin, Martin J. *A World Destroyed: Hiroshima and the Origins of the Arms Race.* New York: Vintage, 1987.
Skates, John Ray. *The Invasion of Japan, Alternative to the Bomb.* Columbia: University of South Carolina Press, 1994.
Steins, Richard. *The Postwar Years: The Cold War and the Atomic Age (1950–1959).* Fairfield, Iowa: Twenty First Century Books, 1993.
Walker, Samuel J. *Prompt and Utter Destruction: Truman and the Use of Atomic Bombs Against Japan.* Chapel Hill: University of North Carolina Press, 1997.
Young, Robert. *Hiroshima: Fifty Years of Debate.* Parsippany, N.J.: Silver Burdett, 1994.

Atomic Energy Commission (AEC)

Established by the Atomic Energy Act of 1946 as an independent agency of the federal government, the five-member civilian Atomic Energy Commission (AEC) was given the authority to develop and control both military and civilian uses of atomic energy.

As revised in 1954, the Atomic Energy Act permitted private enterprises to develop civilian uses of atomic energy and gave the AEC regulatory powers over the private nuclear energy industry. Because of the potential for conflict of interest in the AEC's dual tasks of regulating and promoting the use of nuclear power, Congress enacted the 1974 Energy Reorganization Act, replacing the AEC with the Nuclear Regulatory Commission and the Energy Research and Development Administration.

FURTHER READING

Ford, Daniel. *The Cult of the Bomb: The Secret Papers of the Atomic Energy Commission.* New York: Simon & Schuster, 1982.
Hewlett, Richard, and Oscar Anderson. *A History of the United States Atomic Energy Commission.* University Park: Pennsylvania State University Press, 1962.

Baby boom

The prosperity and optimism that characterized the post–World War II United States sparked an intense interest in family and "normalcy," which in turn created a most unusual generation of Americans, the "baby boomers." The baby boom consisted of the generation of children fathered by veterans returning to civilian life at the end of World War II. The U.S. population rose by an incredible 20 million people from 1940 to 1950. In 1957 alone, a baby was born every 7 seconds. Medical advances made during the war decreased infant

Young men attend a parenting class to prepare them for fatherhood. Returning from World War II, veterans were eager to start a family and have a "normal" life.

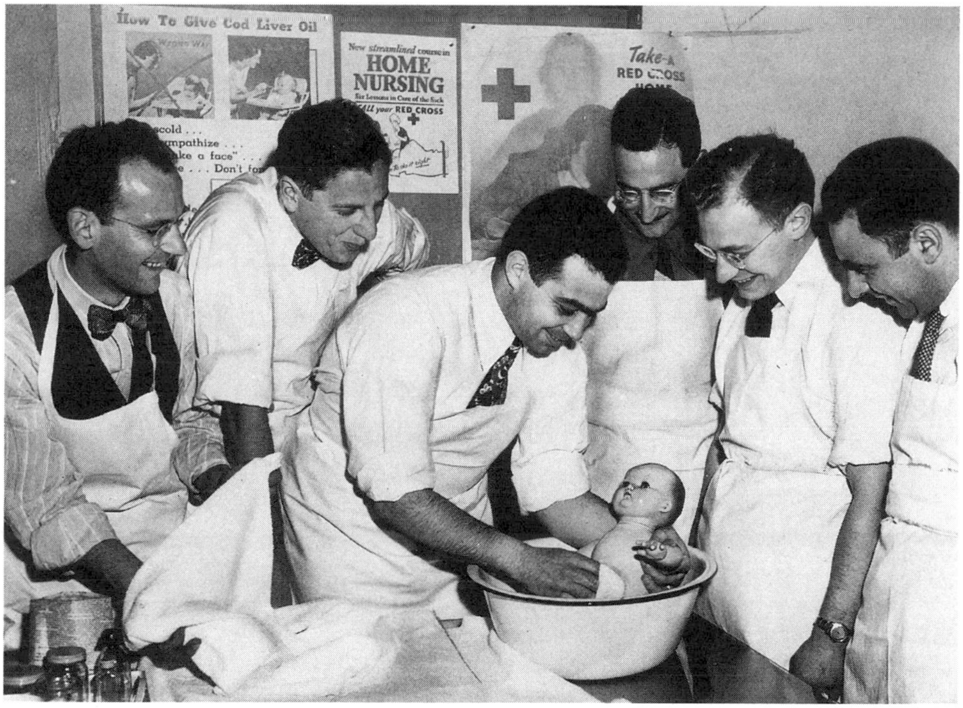

mortality rates considerably while increasing life expectancy, which rose from 65.9 years in 1945 to 70.9 years in 1970.

During the baby boom years, the family was seen as the strength of the United States, and traditional child-rearing practices came under intense discussion. Parents turned to Dr. Benjamin Spock, the pediatrician and author of the best-selling *Common Sense Book of Baby and Child Care* (1946), for guidance on how best to raise their children. He advised parents to consider their children's needs as well as their own; for example, he was an early advocate of on-demand rather than on-schedule feeding of newborns. At first Spock reinforced the common belief that motherhood was a full-time job, although later he retreated somewhat from that position. On shows such as "Leave It to Beaver" and "Ozzie and Harriet," television presented its own vision of the "perfect" 1950s American family, in which clean-cut children came home to an orderly house after school, did their homework, and had dinner with both parents once Dad arrived from the office.

The baby boom generation, raised by parents who had lived through the Great Depression and World War II, buffeted by the emotions evoked by the war in Vietnam, the antiwar movement, the sexual revolution, and feminism, grew up to become the hippies of the 1960s and later the "Me Generation" of the 1970s and yuppies (young urban professionals) of the 1980s. Because there are so many baby boomers (they have been compared to a mouse moving through the digestive system of a snake!) they have affected the culture around them as they have moved through life. As they enter their retirement years beginning early in the third millennium, they will most likely force some changes in the way medical and social services are delivered to the elderly.

SEE ALSO

Hippies; Spock, Benjamin; Television; Yuppies

FURTHER READING
Jones, Landon Y. *Great Expectations: America and the Baby Boom Generation.* New York: Ballantine, 1981.
May, Elaine Tyler. *Homeward Bound: American Families in the Cold War Era.* New York: Basic Books, 1988.
May, Elaine Tyler. *Pushing the Limits: American Women 1940–1961.* New York: Oxford University Press, 1998.
Owram, Doug. *Born at the Right Time: A History of the Baby-Boom Generation.* Toronto: University of Toronto Press, 1996.
Rukeyser, William S. "Let's Do the Hobble: The Generation that Won't Go Away." *Atlantic Monthly* (July 1995): 16–18.

Baker v. *Carr* (1962)

In the *Baker* v. *Carr* decision, the Supreme Court ruled that federal courts have the power to oversee the way states create districts (called apportionment) for their houses of representatives and senates. The case arose when the state of Tennessee neglected to change the boundaries of its legislative districts in response to a growing population. A voter, Charles Baker, sued state officials, arguing that urban voters were underrepresented in comparison to rural voters. A U.S. district court ruled against the plaintiff, saying the court could not overrule the legislature. In a 6-to-2 decision, the Supreme Court overturned the ruling and gave federal courts jurisdiction over apportionment. Calling *Baker* v. *Carr* "the parent case of the one man, one vote doctrine," Chief Justice Earl Warren later considered it one of the most important decisions of his tenure; it was just as wrong to dilute a citizen's vote by means of unfair legislative apportionment as it was to deny the right to vote on the basis of race, sex, or creed.

SEE ALSO
Civil rights movement; Supreme Court; Warren Court

FURTHER READING
Graham, Gene. *One Man, One Vote: Baker v. Carr and the American Levellers.* Boston: Little Brown, 1972.
Grofman, Bernard. *Voting Rights, Voting Wrongs: The Legacy of Baker v. Carr.* New York: Priority Press, 1990.

Bakke v. *Board of Regents of California* (1978)

In the *Bakke* case the Supreme Court ruled against the use of fixed quotas in university admissions to increase the number of disadvantaged students from certain minority groups, such as African Americans, Latinos, and Native Americans. The case came before the court after Allan Bakke, a white man, sued the Board of Regents for denying him admission to the University of California at Davis medical school. Bakke charged that an affirmative action program, under which 16 of 100 openings were set aside for racial minority members, was unconstitutional and that he had been passed over in favor of less qualified students. In a 5-to-4 decision, the U.S. Supreme Court ordered Bakke admitted to Davis, ruling that inflexible racial quotas were unconstitutional but that race could be taken into consideration as a factor in admissions policies.

SEE ALSO
Affirmative action; Supreme Court

FURTHER READING
Schwartz, Bernard. *Behind Bakke.* New York: New York University Press, 1988.
Sindler, Alan P. *Bakke, DeFunis, and Minority Admissions: The Quest for Equal Opportunity.* New York: Longman, 1978.
Wilkinson, J. Harvie, III. *From Brown to Bakke: The Supreme Court and School Integration, 1954–1978.* New York: Oxford University Press, 1981.

Baldwin, James

- *Born: Aug. 2, 1924, New York, N.Y.*
- *Accomplishments: Novelist; essayist; civil rights activist*
- *Major works:* Go Tell It on the Mountain *(1953),* Notes of a Native Son *(1955),* Giovanni's Room *(1956),* The Fire Next Time *(1963),* Going to Meet the Man *(1965),* If Beale Street Could Talk *(1989),* Nobody Knows My Name: More Notes of a Native Son *(1993)*
- *Died: Nov. 30, 1987, St.-Paul-de-Vence, France*

James Baldwin, one of the major African-American writers and thinkers of the twentieth century, wrote about his own life and about the lives of other African Americans. His life was strongly influenced by his childhood as the stepson of a harsh man who appeared not to like him very much, by the church to which he escaped and which he later criticized and left, and by his homosexuality, which he accepted when he was young. His first book, *Go Tell It on the Mountain,* was strongly autobiographical.

Baldwin's life, like the lives of other African Americans, was also deeply affected by the racism of the society around him, and this racism provided him with another theme that ran throughout his writing. He left the United States to live in France in 1957 (he returned to the United States and lived for short periods in other European countries) but he prophesied the violent racial upheavals of the 1960s in *The Fire Next Time.* Baldwin argued that the United States's history of brutal oppression had built up a reservoir among blacks of frustration, "rage, hatred and murder, hatred for white men so deep that it . . . made all love, all trust, all joy impossible." Unless African Americans were given equal treatment and all the rights of citizenship, Baldwin warned, whites could expect retaliation.

Although James Baldwin moved to France in the late 1950s, he continued to write about America. "The responsibility of a writer," he said, "is to excavate the experience of the people who produced him."

In the late 1970s Baldwin began returning to the United States frequently to lecture and teach; he continued to do so for the rest of his life. He never stopped writing about racism and the failure of democracy in the United States to provide racial justice to African Americans.

SEE ALSO

Black power; Detroit race riot (1967); Race riots; Watts riot (1965)

FURTHER READING

Baldwin, James. *Collected Essays: Notes of a Native Son, Nobody Knows My Name, The Fire Next Time, No Name in the Street, The Devil Finds Work, Other Essays.* Edited by Toni Morrison. New York: The Library of America, 1998.

Baldwin, James. *The Fire Next Time.* New York: Dial Press, 1963.

Chametzky, Jules, ed. *Black Writers Redefine the Struggle: A Tribute to James Baldwin: Proceedings of a Conference at the University of Massachusetts at Amherst* [April 22,1989]. Amherst: University of Massachusetts Press, 1989.

Ball, George

- *Born: Dec. 21, 1909, Des Moines, Iowa*
- *Accomplishments: Undersecretary of state for economic affairs, 1961–66; ambassador to the United Nations, 1968*
- *Died: May 26, 1994, New York, N.Y.*

Among the advisors to Presidents John Kennedy and Lyndon Johnson, Undersecretary of State George Ball stood almost alone in holding the view that sending U.S. forces to Vietnam would result in disaster. Ball, recalling the defeat of the French in difficult terrain there, suggested that "once on the tiger's back, we cannot be sure of picking the place to dismount."

In the spring and summer of 1965, Ball vehemently urged President Johnson to resist escalating hostilities in Vietnam, but to no avail. Johnson, however, armed with the Gulf of Tonkin Resolution, which gave him a congressional mandate to use force to repel attacks against U.S. forces, ordered the bombing of North Vietnam and authorized a U.S. troop buildup that would exceed 500,000 men. Ball later resigned in protest.

SEE ALSO

Gulf of Tonkin Resolution (1964); Johnson, Lyndon Baines; Vietnam War

FURTHER READING

Ball, George. *The Past Has Another Pattern: Memoirs.* New York: Norton, 1982.

Bill, James A. *George Ball: Behind the Scenes in U.S. Foreign Policy.* New Haven, Conn.: Yale University Press, 1997.

Small, Melvin. *Johnson, Nixon, and the Doves.* New Brunswick, N.J.: Rutgers University Press, 1988.

Bay of Pigs

President John Kennedy's passion for decisive action in foreign affairs and fear of a growing closeness between Fidel Castro's Cuba and the Soviet Union led him to approve a Central Intelligence Agency (CIA) plan, originally conceived under President Dwight Eisenhower, to invade Cuba. On April 17, 1961, some 1,500 anti-Castro exiles, who had fled Cuba for the United States, landed at the Bay of Pigs on Cuba's southern coast. It was hoped that their arrival would foster a general wave of revolt against the government, ultimately resulting in the overthrow of Castro.

Fidel Castro, as usual shown with a cigar wedged in his mouth, easily survived the invasion at the Bay of Pigs, as he has survived every subsequent attempt to topple him.

Almost everything, however, that could go wrong did go wrong. The first air strike by U.S. planes failed to destroy most of Castro's planes and alerted him to the imminent attack. Kennedy then canceled the second air strike planned to accompany the invasion, fearing it would expose the U.S. involvement. United States landing craft sank on coral reefs, and a drop of parachutists missed its target. Pinned down on the beach and exposed to enemy fire, the invaders pleaded for air support, but Kennedy again refused. After 114 members of the exile brigade had lost their lives, the remaining 1,189 surrendered to Castro.

The debacle made Kennedy leery of relying on the advice of top CIA officials and military brass, but he remained committed to getting rid of Castro and utilizing the CIA and Special Forces (elite guerrilla warfare units) to undermine unfriendly governments abroad.

SEE ALSO

Cuban missile crisis (1962); Kennedy, John Fitzgerald

FURTHER READING

Higgins, Trumbull. *The Perfect Failure: Kennedy, Eisenhower, and the CIA at the Bay of Pigs*. New York: Norton, 1987.

Paterson, Thomas G. *Contesting Castro: The United States and the Triumph of the Cuban Revolution.* New York: Oxford University Press, 1994.

Wyden, Peter. *Bay of Pigs: The Untold Story.* New York: Simon & Schuster, 1979.

Beat movement

The Beat movement was a literary movement of the 1950s centered in the coffeehouses of New York and San Francisco. Jack Kerouac's novel *On the Road* (1957) and Allen Ginsberg's poem "Howl" (1956) are its highlights.

Known primarily for experimentation with various drugs and freewheeling sexual adventures, the Beats attracted college-aged, educated people reacting against middle-class society. Although they were the main critical voice of the "silent generation" (the conservative, conformist students of the 1950s), the Beats and their Beatnik followers sought to escape from American society rather than to change it. As Jack Newfield, a New York journalist, stated in *A Prophetic Minority* (1966), "The Beats may have been rebels without a cause, but theirs was the only rebellion in town."

SEE ALSO

Ginsberg, Allen; Kerouac, Jack

FURTHER READING

Charters, Ann. *The Portable Beat Reader.* New York: Penguin, 1992.

Cook, Bruce. *The Beat Generation.* New York: Scribners, 1971.

Hickey, Morgen. *The Bohemian Register: An Annotated Bibliography of the Beat Literary Movement.* Lanham, Md.: Scarecrow, 1990.

Kherdian, David, ed.. *Beat Voices: An Anthology of Beat Poetry.* New York: Henry Holt, 1995.

McClure, Michael. *Scratching the Beat Surface.* San Francisco: North Point, 1982.

Beatles, the

- *Albums:* Meet the Beatles *(1964),* Help *(1965),* Sgt. Pepper's Lonely Hearts Club Band *(1967),* The White Album *(1968),* Yellow Submarine *(1969),* Abbey Road *(1969),* Let It Be *(1970)*

The Beatles, a rock-and-roll group from Liverpool, England, inspired a wave of unprecedented mania among the teenage population when they brought their lively and upbeat music to the United States in 1964. Borrowing from folk music and rhythm and blues, the so-called Fab Four, led by the

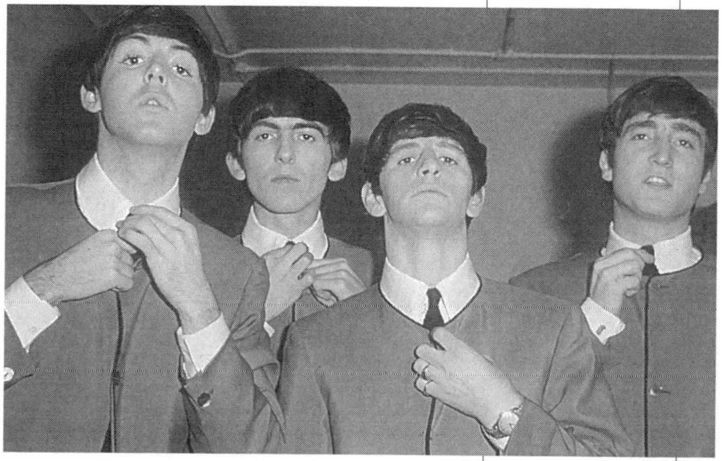

The Beatles in 1963, the year before they made their first appearance in the United States. They were still clean-cut then; their psychedelic phase was still to come.

prolific songwriting team of John Lennon and Paul McCartney, cranked out a steady stream of No. 1 hits throughout the rest of the decade while reflecting the mood of their generation. They moved quickly beyond lighthearted love songs like "I Want to Hold Your Hand" to numbers that celebrated drugs (such as "Lucy in the Sky with Diamonds") and the counterculture and advocated social protest.

SEE ALSO

Counterculture

FURTHER READING

Assayas, Michka, and Claude Meunier. *The Beatles and the Sixties*. New York: Henry Holt, 1997.

Beatles, the. *The Complete Beatles*. Edited by Todd Lowry. Milwaukee, Wis.: Hal Leonard, 1993.

Davis, Andy. *The Beatles Files*. New York: BHB International, 1998.

Martin, Marvin. *The Beatles: The Music Was Never the Same*. Danbury, Conn.: Franklin Watts, 1996.

Miles, Barry. *The Beatles: A Diary*. New York: Music Sales Corp., 1998.

Norman, Philip. *Shout! The Beatles in Their Generation*. New York: Simon & Schuster, 1981.

Berlin, blockade of

The wartime agreement reached at Yalta in 1945 by Britain, the Soviet Union, and the United States divided Germany as well as the city of Berlin into four separate occupation zones. But the agreement included no arrangements for American, French, or British access to Berlin, which was set deep in the Soviet zone of East Germany. And after the war, relations between the Soviets and the West steadily deteriorated, leading to the cold war.

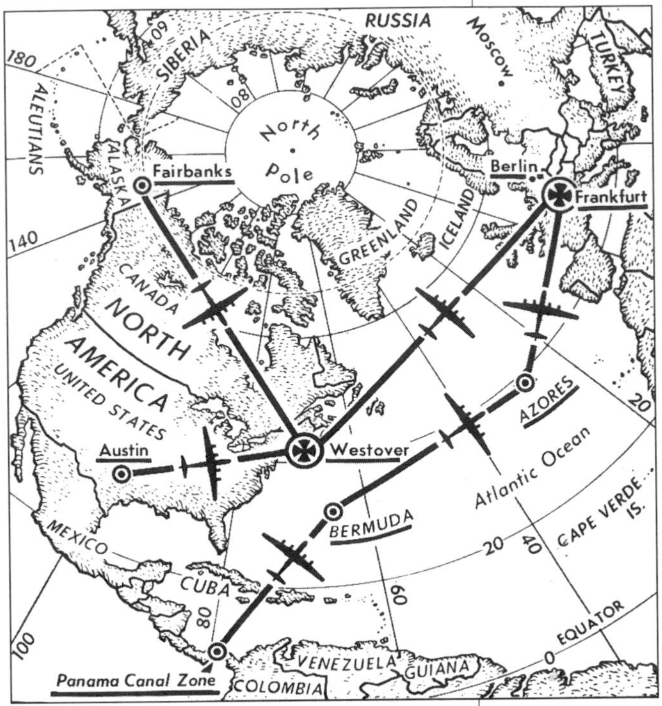

This map shows the routes used by the U.S. Air Force in transporting supplies to Berlin during the Soviet blockade. Planes left from Fairbanks, Alaska, and Austin, Texas, as well as the Canal Zone.

In June 1948, the Soviets, angry at the increasing Western commitment to establish a unified, capitalist West German nation, blocked all rail and highway routes through the Soviet zone into Berlin. Determined neither to abandon Berlin nor have the U.S. army shoot its way into the blockaded city, President Harry Truman ordered a massive airlift to provide the 2 million Berliners in the Western zones with the necessities to survive. The Berlin airlift lasted for 321 days, and some 272,000 flights delivered thousands of tons of supplies each day. On May 12, 1949, the Soviets suddenly reopened the borders, signaling the failure of the blockade.

SEE ALSO

Cold war; Truman, Harry S.; Yalta Conference

FURTHER READING

Clay, Lucius D. *Decision in Germany*. New York: Doubleday, 1950.

Collier, Richard. *Bridge across the Sky: The Berlin Blockade and Airlift 1948–49*. New York: McGraw-Hill, 1978.

Berlin Wall

Comparing U.S. troops in the divided city of Berlin to "a bone stuck in the throat," Soviet Premier Nikita Khrushchev threatened to bypass the United States in early 1961 to sign a separate peace agreement with East Germany that would imperil Western rights in Berlin. In June 1961, Khrushchev renewed his ultimatum to the Western powers: unless the four-power city of Berlin were unified under East German control and Western troops were removed, the Soviet Union would sign a separate peace treaty with the German Democratic Republic (GDR), formally ending the hostilities of World War II and ceding to that government control over land and air access to Berlin.

President Kennedy refused to budge. Claiming that Berlin was "the great testing place of Western courage and will," he significantly increased U.S. defense spending and forces in Europe.

Meanwhile, as the crisis intensified, the flow into West Berlin of refugees fleeing the economically depressed and restrictive conditions of East Germany dramatically increased. In a surprise move, Khrushchev signed a peace treaty with East Germany that did not affect the American role in Berlin, and on August 13, 1961, the communists erected a wall around the Soviet zone of the city, shutting off the flow of refugees to the West and destroying any hopes of reunifying Germany. With the collapse of the Soviet Union, however, the Berlin Wall, the preeminent symbol of the cold war and of the communist denial of personal freedom, came tumbling down in November 1989. Germany was reunited within a year.

SEE ALSO

Cold war; Kennedy, John Fitzgerald

FURTHER READING

Spencer, William. *Germany Then and Now.* Danbury, Conn.: Franklin Watts, 1994.

Symynkywicz, Jeffrey B. *Germany: United Again.* Parsippany, N.J.: Silver Burdett, 1995.

In 1962, West Germans hoist themselves up to peer over the Berlin Wall. Built in 1961, the wall continued to divide the people of the city, and their two ways of life, until 1989.

Berrigan, Daniel

- *Born: May 9, 1921, Virginia, Minn.*
- *Accomplishments: Jesuit priest and antiwar activist*

A Jesuit priest and former chaplain at Cornell University, Daniel Berrigan first came to prominence in the antiwar movement in 1968 as a member of the Catonsville Nine, who were accused of burning hundreds of Selective Service records in Maryland with homemade napalm. (The Selective Service administered the military draft.) After their conviction, the nine men (including Daniel's brother Philip) refused to surrender for imprisonment. Daniel Berrigan—who was also accused by FBI director J. Edgar Hoover of planning to kidnap Presidential advisor Henry Kissinger and to blow up the underground heating system for federal buildings in Washington, D.C.—remained a fugitive the longest, four months, until the FBI captured him in August 1970.

An award-winning poet, Berrigan wrote a play based on the trial of the Catonsville Nine and other books about his experiences as a fugitive and in prison. He and his brother remained active in the antinuclear movement of the 1980s and 90s.

SEE ALSO

Antiwar movement

FURTHER READING

Berrigan, Daniel. *The Dark Night of Resistance.* Garden City, N.Y.: Doubleday, 1971.

Berrigan, Daniel. *The Trial of the Catonsville Nine.* Boston: Beacon Press, 1970.

Birmingham civil rights demonstrations (1963)

A series of civil rights demonstrations in Birmingham, Alabama, in 1963 won the support of most Americans and forced President John F. Kennedy to take action on behalf of the protestors. Martin Luther King, Jr., had organized

In Birmingham, firefighters turn their hoses against peaceful civil rights demonstrators.

a series of marches, sit-ins, and pray-ins on Good Friday. Birmingham police commissioner Eugene ("Bull") Connor responded by arresting the peaceful demonstrators. When schoolchildren reinforced the ranks of the protestors, Connor used even more confrontational tactics, ordering his officers to turn high-pressure fire hoses, cattle prods, and attack dogs on the demonstrators.

Appearing on national news programs, these events pricked the nation's conscience and won support for the civil rights movement. President Kennedy worked behind the scenes to convince the city's leaders to end segregation in public facilities and discrimination in hiring practices. Later in the year he defined civil rights as a "moral issue" and proposed a major civil rights bill to Congress.

SEE ALSO

Civil rights movement; King, Martin Luther, Jr.

FURTHER READING

Garrow, David, ed. *Birmingham, Alabama, 1956–1963: The Black Struggle for Civil Rights*. Brooklyn, N.Y.: Carlson, 1989.

Black Muslims

Founded in 1931 in Detroit by Wallace D. Fard, the Lost-Found Nation of Islam in the Wilderness of North America was taken over in 1934 by his disciple Elijah Poole, who changed his name to Elijah Muhammad. Teaching that blacks (*Negro* was rejected as a slave term) were the original creation of Allah and that whites were evil mutants who would eventually destroy themselves, Muhammad urged blacks to prepare themselves to rule by "waking up, cleaning up, standing up." He demanded that members of his sect observe strict rules of personal behavior and self-discipline and rejected the goal of integration with whites. In fact, Muhammad called on blacks to remain altogether separate from "white devils," and he sought to enhance black self-esteem and racial pride through the study of black history.

Elijah Muhammad and his son Wallace pose in front of a portrait of Nation of Islam founder Wallace D. Fard. Muhammad took over the leadership in 1934 and called for self-discipline among blacks and separation from whites.

Much of the Nation's recruitment energy went into converting black prison inmates. The most famous of these, Malcolm X, became Muhammad's leading spokesman. A brilliant orator, Malcolm X rejected the integrationist and nonviolent stand of the civil rights movement. Malcolm X's assassination in 1965 by Black Muslims in retaliation for his break with Elijah Muhammad, and subsequent attempts to discredit his mentor, led to a split within the organization. However, since the 1960s, the Nation of Islam has maintained its organizational strength, and Elijah Muhammad's loyalists eventually regrouped under Louis Farrakhan. Although this controversial figure is frequently accused of anti-Semitism, he gained international attention in 1995 by organizing a "Million-Man March" in Washington, D.C., to demonstrate the unity of African Americans and the commitment of black men to family values.

SEE ALSO

Black nationalism; Malcolm X (Malcolm Little)

FURTHER READING

Banks, William H. *The Black Muslims.* Broomall, Pa.: Chelsea House, 1996.
Essien-Udom, E. U. *Black Nationalism: A Search for an Identity in America.* Chicago: University of Chicago Press, 1962.
Lincoln, C. Eric. *The Black Muslims in America.* 3rd ed. Trenton, N.J.: Africa World Press, 1973.
Raboteau, Albert J. *African-American Religion.* New York: Oxford University Press, 1999.

Black nationalism

Black nationalism, a philosophy that exalted black cultural expression, pride in blackness, and often separation from white society, has been an important current within African-American intellectual history since the 19th century, when some free blacks advocated emigration to Africa.

Frustrated by violence, discrimination and the slow progress in gaining rights at the start of the 20th century, some African Americans had lost hope of ever achieving equality in the United States. Led by Jamaican-born Marcus Garvey, black nationalists advocated the creation of a new African-American nation—a black homeland in Africa. In 1914 Garvey founded the Universal Negro Improvement Association (UNIA) to encourage African-American economic independence and to organize his "Back to Africa" cause. His movement declined after he was jailed for mail fraud in 1925 in connection with his fund-raising activities (though he was later pardoned by President Coolidge), but his beliefs have influenced other African American leaders throughout the century. Since 1945 few African-Americans have supported a return to Africa, but many have espoused other aspects of black nationalism inspired by Garvey, including group solidarity, racial separatism, and ethnic pride.

The most visible agent of black nationalism has been the Nation of Islam and its adherents, including the outspoken and controversial Malcolm X, who converted to Islam in prison and was assassinated in 1965. Malcolm called on blacks to separate themselves from "white devils" and defend themselves "by any means necessary." Malcolm's ideas spread beyond the Black Muslims and influenced the "black power" movement. A variety of activist groups adopted nationalism of different sorts in the later 1960s, from the Black Panthers, who sought to gain black power "through the barrel of a gun" to soul singer James Brown, who affirmed black pride by singing, "Say it loud—I'm black and I'm proud." Influenced by black nationalism, members of other racial and ethnic minority groups, including Native Americans and Chicanos, adopted similar positions.

SEE ALSO

Black Muslims; Black power; Malcolm X (Malcolm Little)

FURTHER READING

Carmichael, Stokely, and Charles V. Hamilton. *Black Power: The Politics of Liberation in America.* New York: Random House, 1967.

Deburg, William L. Van. *New Day in Babylon: The Black Power Movement and American Culture*. Chicago: University of Chicago Press, 1992.

Black Panther party

Two college students formed the Black Panther party in 1966 in Oakland, California, to provide social-welfare programs for poor blacks and advocate self-defense against police brutality. Huey Newton and Bobby Seale gained national attention for their organization by arming the group's members and engaging in a series of high-profile confrontations with police.

Newton liked to quote Chinese communist leader Mao Zedong, saying that "power comes through the barrel of a gun." Like other advocates of "black power" in the late 1960s who rejected the nonviolent and integrationist goals of more moderate civil rights leaders, the Panthers were frustrated by the slow pace of racial progress, continued white violence against peaceful civil rights demonstrators, and the grinding poverty found in urban ghettos.

The Black Panther party, a militant organization, also ran programs in poor African American neighborhoods that distributed food, provided children with healthcare, and gave people hope. In this 1970 poster, the rage often felt by party members is clear.

SEE ALSO

Black nationalism; Black power

FURTHER READING

Foner, Philip S., ed. *The Black Panthers Speak*. 1970. New York: Da Capo, 1995.
Newton, Huey, with J. Herman Blake. *Revolutionary Suicide*. New York: Harcourt Brace Jovanovich, 1973.
Seale, Bobby. *A Lonely Rage: The Autobiography of Bobby Seale*. New York: Times Books, 1978.

Black power

In the mid-1960s, "black power" became the slogan of militant blacks who rejected the nonviolence of Martin Luther King, Jr., and the moderate goals of the early civil rights movement. Stokely Carmichael, the firebrand elected to head the Student Nonviolent Coordinating Committee in 1966, popularized the black power slogan that summer during the civil rights protest march to Jackson, Mississippi. Carmichael rejected SNCC's initial commitment to nonviolence and integration, saying, "The only way we gonna stop them white men from whippin' us is to take over. We been saying freedom for six years and we ain't got nothin'. What we gonna start saying now is Black Power!" Carmichael was replaced as head of the SNCC by the even more militant H. Rap Brown in 1967.

Black power grew out of frustrations caused by the limited progress of the civil rights movement, desperation at

After taking over the Cornell University student union in 1969, armed black students negotiated with the administration for the creation of a black studies program. The students took control after enduring attacks and discrimination by white students.

the poverty most blacks suffered, urban race riots beginning in 1964, and the powerful ideas of Malcolm X, a black Muslim who rejected integration and advocated self-defense. Those who adopted the black power slogan ranged from the Black Panthers, who sought to gain black power "through the barrel of a gun," to those who took pride in their African roots and racial heritage. The black power movement heightened the self-esteem of many African Americans and spurred mainstream civil rights leaders to focus attention on the economic plight of the black urban underclass.

SEE ALSO

Black nationalism; Black Panther party; Carmichael, Stokely; Malcolm X (Malcolm Little); Student Nonviolent Coordinating Committee (SNCC)

FURTHER READING

Brown, H. Rap. *Die Nigger Die!* New York: Dial, 1969.

Carmichael, Stokely, and Charles V. Hamilton. *Black Power: The Politics of Liberation in America.* New York: Random House, 1967.

Kelley, Robin D. G. *Into the Fire.* New York: Oxford University Press, 1996.

Wright, Nathan, Jr. *Black Power and Urban Unrest.* New York: Hawthorne Books, 1967.

Bosnia, United States and

Civil war in Bosnia, pitting Croats against Serbs against Bosnian Muslims, erupted with force in 1991. These closely related ethnic groups, three of the many that had lived together in Yugoslavia under the rule of Marshall Tito, resumed their historical enmities once his death led to the country's breakup. While President Bill Clinton was concentrating on domestic issues in 1992, Americans witnessed the atrocities, starvation, and wreckage in the Balkans nightly on television, especially after Serbian forces launched murderous campaigns of "ethnic cleansing" (exterminating other ethnic groups).

In the spring of 1993, Clinton sought to intervene by using NATO troops, but western European governments refused to put their ground forces at risk and Americans were uneasy about committing their troops in a centuries-old conflict that few understood or considered vital to the national security of the United States. Not wanting to repeat the mistakes of Vietnam or endanger his reelection chances, Clinton did nothing as the Serbs overran Muslim enclaves such as Srebrenica in 1995 and menaced U.N.-designated "safe areas," including Bosnia's capital, Sarajevo.

Late in 1995, however, Clinton ordered U.S. troops to Bosnia to enforce a truce that the warring parties had agreed to in meetings held in Dayton, Ohio. Although the presence of troops and the conditions set forth by the Dayton treaty have provided the region with peace, they offer little hope of a united future. Ethnic divisions remain strong among the Muslims, Serbs, and Croats, and among other ethnic groups in the region as well, and can be seen in the Serbian attempt in 1999 to evict ethnic Albanians from their homes in the province of Kosovo.

SEE ALSO

Clinton, William Jefferson ("Bill")

FURTHER READING

Cohen, Roger. *Hearts Grown Brutal: Sagas of Sarajevo.* New York: Random House, 1998.

Bretton Woods Conference

By calling together the Allied nations to meet at Bretton Woods, New Hampshire, in mid-1944, the United States sought to create a structure that would promote worldwide economic cooperation, as well as new markets and trade for itself in the postwar years, and thus prevent a recurrence of the Great Depression of the 1930s. To this end, the meeting established two new international organizations that would help rebuild Europe and stabilize world currency: the International Bank for Reconstruction and Development (the World Bank), with $7.6 billion in initial funding, and the International Monetary Fund, with $7.3 billion.

Representatives of 43 nations meet in Bretton Woods, New Hampshire, to discuss "an enduring program of future economic cooperation and peaceful progress."

FURTHER READING

Schild, Georg. *Bretton Woods and Dumbarton Oaks: American Economic and Political Post-War Planning in the Summer of 1944.* New York: St. Martin's, 1995.
Van Dormael, Armand. *Bretton Woods: Birth of a Monetary System.* New York: Holmes & Meier, 1978.

Bricker Amendment (1951)

Conservative Republican John Bricker of Ohio, who had been the Republican Vice Presidential candidate in 1944, won a Senate seat in 1946. Bricker was angered by the secret diplomacy between President Franklin D. Roosevelt and the Soviet Union's Joseph Stalin at Teheran and

Senator John Bricker and a supporter stand behind some of the many petitions sent to him in support of his constitutional amendment to limit the treaty-making powers of the President. The Senate rejected his proposal.

Yalta, where they coordinated wartime strategy and made plans for the postwar world, and by Roosevelt's failure to consult Congress. Bricker proposed a constitutional amendment in 1951 that would give Congress "power to regulate all executive and other agreements with any foreign power or international organization."

Although the amendment was favored by a large part of the public, the Democratic leadership blocked its consideration by Congress in 1951. Three years later, President Dwight Eisenhower convinced the Senate to reject the proposal. Eisenhower opposed Bricker's amendment because it diminished a President's ability to conduct foreign policy; he said that the amendment's supporters "had lost all their brains."

FURTHER READING

Tanenbaum, Duane. *The Bricker Amendment Controversy: A Test of Eisenhower's Political Leadership.* Ithaca, N.Y.: Cornell University Press, 1988.

Brown v. *Board of Education of Topeka, Kansas* (1954)

In one of the most important rulings of the 20th century, the Supreme Court unanimously found racial segregation of schools to be unconstitutional. In *Brown* v. *Board of Education of Topeka, Kansas,* the Court overturned the so-called "separate but equal" decision of the 1896 *Plessy* v. *Ferguson* case, which upheld racial segregation. "Separate educational facilities are inherently unequal," the Court stated in 1954, because they deprive the plaintiffs of "the equal protection of the laws guaranteed by the Fourteenth Amendment."

The court accepted the argument of the plaintiffs, presented by Thurgood Marshall of the National Association for the Advancement of Colored People (NAACP), that segregating children "solely because of their race generates a feeling of inferiority as to their status in the community that may affect their hearts and minds in a way unlikely ever to be undone."

The *Brown* case had begun when Linda Brown, a black student, sued to force the Topeka public schools to allow her to attend a white school, arguing that walking to a more distant black school would have been a hardship. After several courts had ruled against her, the case reached the Supreme Court, where it was consolidated with similar cases from South Carolina, Delaware, and Virginia. The Supreme Court's decision meant that the education system of the entire South—and some northern cities—was unconstitutional.

In a related case a year later, known as *Brown II,* the court ruled that schools must be desegregated "with all deliberate speed." Border states and the District of Columbia quickly complied with the ruling, but the rest of the South refused, and President Dwight D. Eisenhower did not force the states to desegregate their schools. White schools remained separate in the entire Deep South as of the

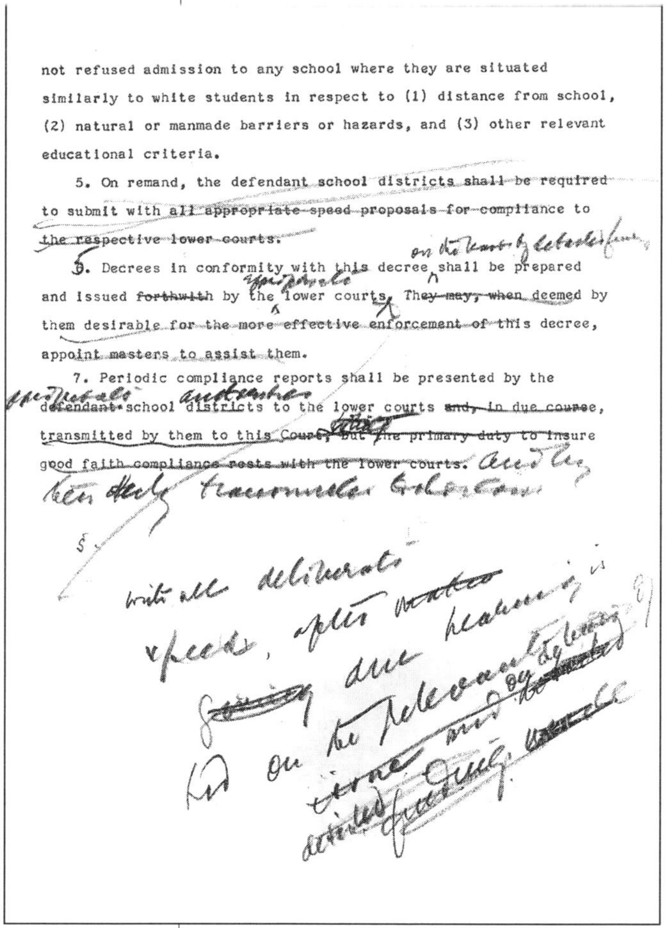

not refused admission to any school where they are situated similarly to white students in respect to (1) distance from school, (2) natural or manmade barriers or hazards, and (3) other relevant educational criteria.

5. On remand, the defendant school districts shall be required to submit with all appropriate speed proposals for compliance to the respective lower courts.

6. Decrees in conformity with this decree shall be prepared and issued forthwith by the lower courts. They may, when deemed by them desirable for the more effective enforcement of this decree, appoint masters to assist them.

7. Periodic compliance reports shall be presented by the defendant school districts to the lower courts and, in due course, transmitted by them to this Court, but the primary duty to insure good faith compliance rests with the lower courts.

In Justice Felix Frankfurter's draft of the decree implementing the Brown *decision, handwritten notes show some significant changes. In item 6, a change was made to say that ending school segregation should be made "with all deliberate speed," but many segregationists still resisted complying.*

end of 1956. It was not until later that progress began to be made toward desegregation.

SEE ALSO

Civil rights movement; Marshall, Thurgood; National Association for the Advancement of Colored People (NAACP); Supreme Court

FURTHER READING

Gaillard, Frye. *The Dream Long Deferred.* Chapel Hill: University of North Carolina Press, 1988.

Kluger, Richard. *Simple Justice.* New York: Vintage, 1977.

Tushnet, M. V., B. M. Henson, and R. R. Olney. *Brown v. Board of Education: The Battle for Integration.* Danbury, Conn.: Franklin Watts, 1996.

Wilkinson, J. Harvie, III. *From Brown to Bakke: The Supreme Court and School Integration, 1954–1978.* New York: Oxford University Press, 1981.

Brzezinski, Zbigniew

- *Born: Mar. 28, 1928, Warsaw, Poland*
- *Accomplishments: Director, National Security Council, 1977–81*

A Polish-born political scientist, Zbigniew Brzezinski was appointed director of the National Security Council by President Jimmy Carter in 1977. Brzezinski deeply mistrusted the Soviets and took a hard-line anticommunist position on most foreign policy issues.

In contrast, Carter's secretary of state, Cyrus Vance, advocated a more conciliatory policy toward the Soviet Union and the continuation of détente, or a lowering of international tensions. Carter moved back and forth between these opposing positions for most of his term. In the end, however, Brzezinski won. When Americans were taken hostage at the U.S. Embassy in Iran in 1979, Brzezinski argued for a military rescue, while Vance opted for diplomacy.

Carter eventually listened to Brzezinski and ordered a helicopter rescue that failed, killing eight Americans. Vance resigned in protest and Carter, after the January 1980 Soviet invasion of Afghanistan, adopted Brzezinski's tough stance toward Moscow. He cut off grain and technology sales to the Soviet Union, boycotted the 1980 Summer Olympics in Moscow, and withdrew the SALT II agreement (an arms-reduction treaty) from the Senate while increasing defense spending.

SEE ALSO

Carter, James Earl, Jr. ("Jimmy"); Iranian hostage crisis (1979); Vance, Cyrus

FURTHER READING

Brzezinski, Zbigniew. *The Grand Chessboard: American Primacy & Its Geostrategic Imperatives.* New York: Basic Books, 1997.

Brzezinski, Zbigniew. *Power and Principle: Memories of the National Security Advisor, 1977–1981*. New York: Farrar, Straus & Giroux, 1983.

Buchanan, Patrick J.

- *Born: Nov. 2, 1938, Washington, D.C.*
- *Accomplishments: Conservative talk show host; candidate for Republican Presidential nomination, 1992, 1996*

A hard-line conservative who wrote speeches for Vice President Spiro Agnew, served as White House director of communications under President Ronald Reagan, and then became a popular TV commentator, Pat Buchanan unsuccessfully challenged President George Bush for the Republican nomination in 1992. Buchanan again tried to win the nomination in the 1996 contest but dropped out of the primary race after a string of losses to Robert Dole, despite receiving strong support in the New Hampshire primary. Buchanan campaigned both times on a platform that opposed abortion, gay rights, illegal immigrants, feminism, and other threats to "family values." He enjoyed enthusiastic support from the Christian Right, but moderate Republicans saw him as too extreme and divisive.

SEE ALSO

Conservatism; Moral Majority

Buckley, William F., Jr.

- *Born: Nov. 24, 1925, New York, N.Y.*
- *Accomplishments: Founder and editor of* National Review *magazine; host of TV talk show "Firing Line"*

A conservative Catholic editor and writer, William Buckley, Jr., gained national attention with the publication of his first book, *God and Man at Yale* (1951). Written only a year after he graduated from that university, the book attacked the liberal bent of American colleges and the diminishing significance of religion and philosophy in the curriculum.

William F. Buckley, Jr., spreads his arms wide as he appeals for votes in his run for the New York City mayor's office. He was the nominee of the Conservative party.

Four years later, Buckley established the highly intellectual *National Review,* a monthly magazine whose "new conservatism" approved of McCarthyism, assailed the Supreme Court under Chief Justice Earl Warren, and criticized the moderate policies of President Dwight Eisenhower's administration. Buckley remained editor in chief of the *National Review,* the leading organ of conservative opinion, until his retirement in 1990.

In 1965 Buckley unsuccessfully ran for mayor of New York City, receiving almost 12 percent of the vote. Although he has never held political office, Buckley has had a significant influence on politics through his magazine and through "Firing Line," a television program that he hosts. Impressing even opponents with his wit and intellectual rigor, Buckley's was the most respected voice in the postwar conservative movement.

SEE ALSO

Conservatism

FURTHER READING

Buckley, William F. *Nearer, My God: An Autobiography of Faith*. New York: Doubleday, 1997.

Burger, Warren

- *Born: Sept. 17, 1907, St. Paul, Minn.*
- *Accomplishments: Assistant attorney general, Civil Division, Justice Department, 1953–56; U.S. Court of Appeals judge for District of Columbia, 1956–69; Chief Justice of the United States, 1969–86*
- *Died: June 25, 1995, Washington D.C.*

Although he served as chief justice of the United States for 17 years, Warren Burger left no distinctive imprint on the Court. President Richard M. Nixon nominated Burger, a judge on the court of appeals for the District of Columbia circuit, in 1969 in the hope that the conservative chief justice would lead the Court to the right.

Although the court did move to a more conservative position on some issues, it did not reverse the liberal rulings of the Earl Warren Court on freedom of speech, separation of church and state, and the right to privacy. The Burger Court also upheld affirmative action (with some limitations), opposed school segregation based on race, and strengthened the legal rights of women, most notably with the *Roe* v. *Wade* decision of 1973, which guaranteed a woman's right to an abortion.

Burger retired after the fall session of 1985, having presided over a deeply divided Court that he had been unable to lead effectively.

SEE ALSO

Supreme Court; Warren Court; Warren, Earl

FURTHER READING

Schwartz, Herman, ed. *The Burger Years: Rights and Wrongs in the Supreme Court, 1969–1986*. New York: Viking, 1987.

Bush, George Herbert Walker

- *Born: June 12, 1924, Milton, Mass.*
- *Accomplishments: U.S. Representative (Republican–Tex.), 1967–71; ambassador to the United Nations, 1971–73; chief of United States liaison office in China, 1974–75; director of Central Intelligence Agency, 1976–77; Vice President, 1981–89; 41st President of the United States, 1989–93*

The presidency of George Bush was marked by a string of foreign policy successes but little activity on the domestic front. Despite high popularity ratings throughout much of his term, he lost his bid for reelection in 1992 when he refused to take action to end an economic recession and voters perceived him to be out of touch with the concerns of average people.

George Bush, the son of a U. S. senator from Connecticut, enlisted in the Navy during World War II. He was 19 years old when he became the Navy's youngest pilot. He flew 58 combat missions before he returned home. After the war Bush got married, graduated from Yale, moved to Texas, started a successful oil company, and became a politician. He won elections to the House of Representatives but he lost elections to the Senate. He was appointed to many offices by two Presidents, Richard Nixon and Gerald Ford; he was the chair of the Republican National Committee, the United States ambassador to the United Nations, the head of the office that kept an open

President George Bush greets the troops in November 1990, during the Persian Gulf War.

relationship between the United States and China, and the head of the Central Intelligence Agency (CIA).

His unsuccessful bid for the 1980 Republican party Presidential nomination led to his selection as Ronald Reagan's running mate in the general election. As Vice President from 1981 to 1989, Bush proved a loyal member of the administration and presided over the White House crisis management team and a drug interdiction task force.

In the 1988 election, Bush and his Vice Presidential nominee, Dan Quayle, defeated Governor Michael Dukakis of Massachusetts, a lackluster campaigner, by 426 to 111 in the electoral college. Bush, who received 54 percent of the popular vote, embraced a conservative social agenda opposing gun control and abortion, while he promised to build a "kinder, gentler America." His most persistent campaign slogan, however, paraphrased a line from a popular movie: "Read my lips; no new taxes."

Constrained by heavy Democratic majorities in both the House and the Senate, Bush proposed few new laws or programs for the country. Instead he used his veto power to maintain things as they were and focused most of his energies on foreign affairs. Aided by his secretary of state, James Baker, Bush developed cordial relations and business ties with China, achieved arms control with the Soviet Union, pursued peace in Israel, and abandoned military pressures on the Soviet-backed Sandinista government in Nicaragua. Bush supported Soviet leader Mikhail Gorbachev's program of economic and political restructuring and in 1991 opposed the efforts of some Soviet republics to secede from the Soviet Union.

Bush did not hesitate to use military power to achieve his foreign policy objectives. He invaded Panama late in 1989, seized its dictator, Manuel Noriega, and placed him on trial for drug trafficking. (Noriega was convicted and sentenced to prison in 1992.)

The most momentous event of the Bush Presidency, however, began in August 1990, when troops from Iraq invaded and occupied the nearby kingdom of Kuwait. Bush organized an international blockade of Iraq, sent 400,000 U.S. troops to mass on the border between Saudi Arabia and Kuwait, and began to pressure Iraqi President Saddam Hussein, now isolated even from his Arab allies, to withdraw.

In January, determining that Saddam would not yield, Bush launched an air war on the Iraqi troops and the capital, Baghdad. On February 23, allied ground troops entered Kuwait and three days later the entire Iraqi army gave up, fleeing north or surrendering. Bush decided not to pursue the retreating forces and not to attempt to depose Saddam Hussein's regime.

Bush also used U.S. troops in late 1992 to provide protection for relief workers in famine-ravaged Somalia.

In domestic affairs, Bush signed a new Clean Air Act and a civil rights bill, an earlier version of which he had opposed, and appointed two justices to the Supreme Court, David Souter and Clarence Thomas. His most fateful domestic policy decision, however, may have been his budget agreement with congressional Democrats in 1990 to cut the skyrocketing federal deficit through a combination of spending cuts and tax increases. His breaking of the 1988 "no tax" campaign pledge would come back to haunt him during his reelection bid. Bush's problems were compounded in 1990 when recession struck.

Slow to admit that the economy was in trouble and unwilling to act to reverse the decline, the President seemed unconcerned with the suffering of his constituents. Bush's approval ratings, which had risen to an all-time high of 90 percent in the aftermath of the Gulf War against Iraq, began to decline as the economic situation worsened. Conservative commentator Patrick J. Buchanan entered the Republican primaries, and though Bush easily won the nomination, Buchanan won a surprising number of delegates and scored telling blows against the President from the party's disgruntled conservative wing.

In the November 1992 election, Bush lost to Arkansas governor Bill Clinton, thanks in part to Clinton's energetic and effective campaign style and the third-party candidacy of Ross Perot, who may have siphoned off votes from the Republicans. Since leaving the White House, Bush has lived in Houston, Texas, and remained aloof from public affairs.

SEE ALSO

Clinton, William Jefferson ("Bill"); Persian Gulf War; Reagan, Ronald Wilson

FURTHER READING

Duffy, Michael, and Dan Goodgame. *Marching in Place: The Status Quo Presidency of George Bush*. New York: Simon & Schuster, 1992.

Parmet, Herbert S. *George Bush: The Life of a Lone Star Yankee*. New York: Scribner, 1997.

Scowcroft, Brent, and George H. W. Bush. *A World Transformed*. New York: Knopf, 1998.

Smith, Jean E. *George Bush's War*. New York: Holt, Rinehart & Winston, 1992.

Byrnes, James Francis

- *Born: May 2, 1872, Charleston, S.C.*
- *Accomplishments: Secretary of State, 1945–47; governor of South Carolina (Democratic), 1951–55*
- *Died: Apr. 9, 1972, Columbia, S.C.*

Appointed secretary of state by President Harry Truman in 1945, James ("Jimmy") Byrnes accompanied the President to the Potsdam Conference and advised him that dropping the atomic bomb on Japan might "make Russia more manageable" and "put us in a position to dictate our own terms at the end of the war." But the United States's atomic monopoly did not change Soviet behavior, and Byrnes then hoped that economic pressures would force Stalin to make concessions. That strategy failed as well, and Byrnes could devise no other way for dealing with the Soviet Union. Truman lost confidence in Byrnes and grew irri-

U.S. Secretary of State James Byrnes addresses the delegates at the Paris Peace Conference in 1946. Twenty-one countries were represented at that conference.

tated by his patronizing manner; in 1947 Truman replaced Byrnes with George Marshall.

Byrnes was later elected governor of South Carolina. He denounced the Supreme Court's decision in *Brown* v. *Board of Education* (1954) and vowed that South Carolina would not integrate its public schools.

SEE ALSO

Truman, Harry S.

FURTHER READING

Byrnes, James F. *All in One Lifetime.* New York: Harper & Brothers, 1958.

Clements, Kendrick, ed. *James F. Byrnes and the Origins of the Cold War.* Durham, N.C.: Carolina Academic Press, 1982.

Messer, Robert L. *The End of an Alliance: James F. Byrnes, Roosevelt, Truman, and the Origins of the Cold War.* Chapel Hill: University of North Carolina Press, 1982.

Robertson, David. *Sly and Able: A Political Biography of James F. Byrnes.* New York: Norton, 1994.

Cambodia, bombing and invasion of

Soon after taking office as President, Richard Nixon, who as a candidate had promised "peace with honor" in Vietnam, ordered the covert, or secret, bombing of Vietcong havens of refuge in the eastern provinces of adjoining neutral Cambodia. To ensure secrecy, Air Force officials created an elaborate system of bogus flight reports. Two months later, when the *New York Times* began to report on the suspected bombings, Nixon ordered the FBI to wiretap the phones of several government officials and reporters in an effort to determine who had leaked the information. The secret bombings lasted 15 months and were not made public until 1972.

Meanwhile, on April 30, 1970, Nixon had announced a ground invasion of Cambodia, designed to hit Vietcong sanctuaries just over the border and shore up the new Cambodian government, which was being threatened by communist revolutionaries aided in part by North Vietnam. Nixon explained that the action was necessary to help his scheme of "Vietnamization" (the gradual process of handing the fighting of the war over to the South Vietnamese), but the U.S. public viewed it as an expansion of the war. As a result of this action, college campuses across the nation burst into protest. Four days after Nixon's announcement, four student protestors were killed at Kent State University by members of the Ohio National Guard.

SEE ALSO

Kent State University, killings at (1970); Vietnam War

FURTHER READING

Hall, Kari, and Rene Josh Getlin. *Beyond the Killing Fields.* Edited by Marshall Lumsden. New York: Aperture, 1992.

Shawcross, William. *Side-Show: Kissinger, Nixon, and the Destruction of Cambodia.* New York: Pocket Books, 1979.

President Jimmy Carter meets with Menachem Begin (left) and Anwar Sadat (right) at Camp David in Maryland. With the signing of the peace accords in 1978, Israel agreed to return captured territory to Egypt, and Egypt agreed to recognize Israel as a nation.

Camp David peace talks

At Camp David, the Presidential retreat in Maryland, President Jimmy Carter mediated talks between Israeli prime minister Menachem Begin and Egyptian president Anwar Sadat for two weeks in September 1978. The Camp David accord signed between Israel and Egypt led to a normalization of diplomatic relations between the two nations for the first time since 1948, when Israel was declared an independent state. In that accord's "Framework for the Conclusion of a Peace Treaty between Israel and Egypt," Israel agreed to return territory captured from Egypt in the Six-Day War of 1967, and Egypt recognized Israel as a nation, becoming the first Arab state to do so.

Israel also agreed to a gradual transition to autonomy for the West Bank and Gaza Strip Palestinians, but the other Arab states rejected the accords, and in 1981 Islamic extremists assassinated Sadat for negotiating with Israel. Despite its limited success in bringing peace to the Middle East, Camp David constituted the high point of Carter's presidency.

SEE ALSO

Carter, James Earl, Jr. ("Jimmy")

FURTHER READING

Quandt, William B. *Camp David.* Washington, D.C.: Brookings Institution, 1986.

Carmichael, Stokely

- *Born: June 21, 1941, Port of Spain, Trinidad*
- *Died: Nov. 16, 1998, Conakry, Guinea*
- *Accomplishments: Chairman of the Student Nonviolent Coordinating Committee, 1966–67; leader of the Black Panthers, 1967–69; writer*

Stokely Carmichael was a pivotal figure in changing the focus of the civil rights movement in the 1960s from nonviolent integrationism (with the goal of integrating African Americans into U.S. society) to an emphasis on black power (which stressed black self-reliance and separation from white society).

Born in Trinidad, Carmichael immigrated to the United States in 1952 and

In 1963, Stokely Carmichael meets with young African Americans at a rally in support of SNCC. Carmichael later went on to head the organization.

was attending Howard University in 1960 when he became involved in the civil rights movement. He participated in the Freedom Rides of 1961 and the Mississippi Freedom Summer in 1964, becoming a member of the Student Nonviolent Coordinating Committee (SNCC, pronounced "Snick"). Carmichael, however, gradually came to repudiate SNCC's emphasis on racial integration and nonviolent protest. He said blacks should eject whites from SNCC and use force to defend themselves against the attacks of violent racists. He was elected chairman of SNCC in 1966 and helped to lead the group away from nonviolence.

In 1967 he coauthored *Black Power,* a book outlining his radical black nationalist philosophy. Carmichael then briefly joined the Black Panther party, demanding self-determination for the black community. In 1968 he changed his name to Kwame Ture, and moved to Guinea to work for African empowerment.

SEE ALSO

Black nationalism; Black power; Civil rights movement; Student Nonviolent Coordinating Committee (SNCC)

FURTHER READING

Carmichael, Stokely, and Charles V. Hamilton. *Black Power: The Politics of Liberation in America.* New York: Random House, 1967.

Carson, Rachel

- *Born: May 27, 1907, Springdale, Pa.*
- *Accomplishments: Environmental scientist and activist; writer*
- *Died: Apr. 14, 1964, Silver Spring, Md.*

Rachel Carson is best known as the author of *Silent Spring* (1962). In it she argued that the pesticides used by farmers poisoned the very food they were intended to protect, killing many birds and fish as well. Carson contended that one pesticide in particular, DDT, made its way through the entire food chain, from plants to animals to humans. *Silent Spring* shocked many Americans, awakening them to the damaging effects of pesticides on the natural environment. In 1972 the federal government outlawed DDT.

Carson had studied genetics and zoology at Pennsylvania College for Women and at Johns Hopkins University. For many years she worked as a researcher at the U.S. Fish and Wildlife Service. She won many awards for her

Rachel Carson testifies before the Senate Government Operations subcommitte in 1963. The subcommittee was investigating the effects of pesticides on the environment.

writings about the environment, including the Literary Award of the Council of Women of the U.S.A. (1956), the Schweitzer Prize for Animal Welfare (1963), and the Conservationist Award from the National Wildlife Federation.

SEE ALSO

Environmental movement

FURTHER READING

Brodeur, Paul. "Legacy." *The New Yorker* (June 7, 1993): 114.
Carson, Rachel. *Silent Spring*. Boston: Houghton Mifflin, 1962.
Hynes, Patricia. *The Recurring Silent Spring*. New York: Pergamon, 1988.
Keene, Ann T. *Earthkeepers*. New York: Oxford University Press, 1994.
Lear, Linda J. *Rachel Carson: Witness for Nature*. New York: Holt, 1997.

Carter Doctrine

In his January 1980 State of the Union address, President Jimmy Carter declared that the oil of the Persian Gulf region was vital to U.S. national security; therefore, "an attempt by any outside force to gain control of the Persian Gulf region" would "be repelled by any means necessary, including military force."

The immediate target of the Carter Doctrine was the Soviet Union's invasion of Afghanistan on December 25, 1979, which the President termed "the gravest threat to peace" since World War II. The doctrine would later be invoked by President George Bush in his response to Iraq's invasion of Kuwait in August 1990. Bush termed the integrity of the Persian Gulf nations a vital American interest, vowed that "aggression will not stand," and dispatched U.S. planes and troops—in an operation called Desert Shield—to protect Saudi Arabia from an Iraqi attack.

SEE ALSO

Carter, James Earl, Jr. ("Jimmy"), Persian Gulf War

Carter, James Earl, Jr. ("Jimmy")

- *Born: Oct. 1, 1924, Plains, Ga.*
- *Accomplishments: Georgia state senator (Democrat), 1962–66; governor of Georgia, 1971–75; 39th President of the United States, 1977–81*

In 1976, in the shadow of the Watergate scandal, Americans elected Jimmy Carter, the ultimate Washington outsider, to become their President. A little-known peanut farmer and former governor of Georgia, Carter was a deeply moral and earnest man. He thus seemed to be the perfect unifying symbol for the nation. By 1980, however, the politics of morality were not suffi-

Jimmy Carter waves to his supporters at the Democratic National Convention in New York in 1980.

Former U.S. President Jimmy Carter, former Secretary of State James Baker, and former Costa Rica President Oscar Arias monitor the October 1996 national elections in Nicaragua for The Carter Center's Council of Freely Elected Heads of Government.

cient to control soaring interest rates and inflation, or to free U.S. hostages in Iran. Consequently, voters replaced him with Ronald Reagan.

As a state senator and governor in Georgia, Carter built a reputation for being progressive. He fought segregationists and promoted better race relations by increasing minority hiring in state agencies by 50 percent. At the same time, however, he had a poor relationship with the state legislature, leading many to think of him as arrogant and condescending. Such characterizations would reappear during his Presidency.

When Carter arrived in Washington, he immediately took steps to improve the image of the Presidency. On inauguration day, he walked with his wife and daughter from the Capitol to the White House, emphasizing his turning away from the pomp of the imperial presidency. Carter trimmed the White House staff by one third and gave televised addresses to the nation as he sat by the fireside, casually dressed in slacks and a cardigan sweater. He appointed an unprecedented number of women and minorities to positions in his administration. To his critics, Carter's term in office never amounted to more than a Presidency of gestures.

Domestically, Carter achieved some significant successes. He raised the minimum wage; ordered the creation of the Department of Energy; deregulated the airline, railroad, and trucking industries; established a "superfund" to clean up toxic waste sites; and persuaded Congress to divide the Department of Health, Education, and Welfare into two departments, one for education and the other for health and human services.

But Carter proved unable to solve deeper economic problems or alleviate the latest energy crisis. Moreover, his populist moral appeal had begun to wear thin. After one of his initiatives failed in Congress, Carter essentially blamed the American people, claiming that they were "suffering from a crisis of confidence." In an echo of his Georgia career, many people perceived this gesture as an arrogant attitude of moral superiority.

Carter's greatest achievements and failures came in foreign affairs. In 1977 he negotiated a set of unpopular Panama Canal treaties, which called for the United States to turn over operation of the canal to Panama by the year 2000. The treaties were only narrowly ratified in the Senate. Later, Carter brokered a peace agreement between Israel and Egypt called the Camp David accords. In addition, he signed the second Strategic Arms Limitation Treaty (SALT II) with the Soviet Union, which he later withdrew from consideration in the Senate when the Soviets invaded Afghanistan.

Carter made perhaps his most fateful decision in 1979 when he allowed the deposed shah of Iran to enter the United States for medical treatment. This touched off vehement anti-American demonstrations in Teheran and the seizure of 76 American hostages by Shiite militants, underscoring the post-Vietnam notion of a weakened United States. The most catastrophic blow hit Carter in April 1980, when he had to report to the American people that a failed attempt to rescue the hostages had resulted in the deaths of eight U.S. servicemen. Television news reports showed Iranians proudly displaying mangled helicopter equipment and the charred bodies of the American soldiers. The hostage crisis henceforth dominated all other foreign policy and played a significant role in Carter's electoral defeat that fall.

After leaving office Carter devoted himself to a new career of volunteerism. He opened the Carter Presidential Center in Atlanta, an organization dedicated to promoting worldwide human rights. He also monitored elections in numerous countries and with his wife, Rosalyn, became an active participant in Habitat for Humanity, an organization dedicated to providing adequate housing to poor people in the United States and around the world.

SEE ALSO

Camp David peace talks; Iranian hostage crisis (1979)

FURTHER READING

Bourne, Peter G. *Jimmy Carter.* New York: Scribner, 1997.

Carter, Jimmy. *Keeping Faith: Memoirs of a President.* New York: Bantam, 1982.

Carter, Jimmy. *Talking Peace: A Vision for the Next Generation.* New York: Puffin, 1995.

Glad, Betty. *Jimmy Carter: From Plains to the White House.* New York: Norton, 1980.

Hargrove, Erwin C. *Jimmy Carter as President: Leadership and the Politics of the Public Good.* Baton Rouge: Louisiana State University Press, 1988.

Morris, Kenneth. *Jimmy Carter, American Moralist.* Athens: University of Georgia Press, 1996.

Central Intelligence Agency (CIA)

An outgrowth of the Office of Strategic Services, the World War II–era spy agency, the Central Intelligence Agency (CIA) was established by the National Security Act of 1947. The CIA was empowered to gather and evaluate information on foreign countries, to engage in counterintelligence in order to thwart spying on the United States, and to engage in covert political activities.

Under director Allen Dulles (1953–61), the brother of Secretary of State John Foster Dulles, the CIA was involved in the overthrow of governments in Guatemala and Iran, the creation and defense of South Vietnam, the U-2 affair (involving secret high-altitude photo reconnaissance flights over the Soviet Union), plotting the Bay of Pigs invasion in Cuba, and attempted assassinations of that country's president, Fidel Castro.

Such operations, as well as questions concerning the CIA's role in the 1973 military overthrow of the Chilean

At a National Security Council meeting in 1976, CIA Director George Bush (left) points out evacuation routes for Americans in Lebanon, a country torn by civil war. President Gerald Ford (far right) and Henry Kissinger (to Ford's right) examine the map.

government and subsequent murder of its socialist president, Salvador Allende, led to congressional investigations. The inquiries revealed a history of CIA involvement in the domestic affairs of foreign powers. They also revealed that under director Richard Helms (1966–74) the agency illegally spied on and harassed Americans in the United States in direct violation of its charter.

In the 1980s, under director William J. Casey, the CIA became involved in controversies surrounding the Iran-Contra affair and the support of Panama's drug-trafficking strongman Manuel Noriega. It failed to predict the invasion of Kuwait by Iraq in 1990. In the 1990s it redirected its focus to the gathering of industrial and trade intelligence that would help the United States maintain its economic power.

SEE ALSO

Bay of Pigs; Dulles, Allen; Iran-Contra affair; U-2 crisis; Vietnam War

FURTHER READING

Bissell, Richard M., Jr. *Reflections of a Cold Warrior: From Yalta to the Bay of Pigs.* New Haven, Conn.: Yale University Press, 1996.

Ranelagh, John. *The Agency: The Rise and Decline of the CIA.* New York: Simon & Schuster, 1986.

Troy, Thomas F. *Wild Bill and Intrepid: Bill Donovan, Bill Stephenson, and the Origin of the CIA.* New Haven, Conn.: Yale University Press, 1996.

Chambers, Whittaker

- *Born: Apr. 1, 1901, Philadelphia, Pa.*
- *Accomplishments: Writer and editor; instigator of post–World War II communist "witch hunts"*
- *Died: July 9, 1961, Westminster, Md.*

In 1948, Whittaker Chambers, a senior editor at *Time* magazine and a former member of the Communist Party U.S.A., testified before the House Un-American Activities Committee (HUAC). There Chambers accused Alger Hiss, a government official who had served in the departments of agriculture and state, of having been a communist in the 1930s. To prove his charge, Chambers produced microfilm copies of incriminating government documents allegedly typed on a typewriter once owned by Hiss and hidden in a hollowed-out pumpkin. Chambers handed the so-called "Pumpkin Papers" over to HUAC member Richard M. Nixon, who later elicited an admission from Hiss that he had known

Whittaker Chambers, sitting before the microphone during a hearing before the House Un-American Activities Committee, accuses Alger Hiss (behind the table with his eyes closed) of having been a Communist.

Chambers after all. (Hiss had originally denied it.)

Hiss never admitted to being a communist, but he was convicted on two counts of perjury and sentenced to five years in jail. Chambers published his autobiography, *Witness,* in 1948 and later wrote for the conservative *National Review.*

SEE ALSO

House Un-American Activities Committee (HUAC); McCarthyism; Nixon, Richard Milhous

FURTHER READING

Chambers, Whittaker. *Witness*. New York: Random House, 1952.

Goodman, Walter. *The Committee: The Extraordinary Career of the House Committee on Un-American Activities*. New York: Farrar, Straus & Giroux, 1968.

O'Reilly, Kenneth. *Hoover and the Un-Americans: The FBI, HUAC, and the Red Menace*. Philadelphia: Temple University Press, 1983.

Tanenhaus, Sam. *Whittaker Chambers: A Biography.* New York: Random House, 1997.

Weinstein, Allen. *Perjury: The Hiss–Chambers Case*. New York: Knopf, 1978.

Chavez, Cesar

- *Born: Mar. 31, 1927, Yuma, Ariz.*
- *Accomplishments: Labor and civil rights activist; founder, United Farm Workers, 1962.*
- *Died: Apr. 23, 1993, San Luis, Ariz.*

Cesar Chavez led a movement of migrant agricultural workers in the 1960s, using strikes and national boycotts of farm products to force concessions from employers. The son of migrant farm workers himself, Chavez got his start in labor organizing in the Community Service Organization (CSO) of San Jose, California, in the 1950s.

In 1962 Chavez resigned as director of the CSO for all of California and Arizona in order to lead the United Farm Workers Organizing Committee. That group's activities after 1965, including consumer boycotts of nonunion grapes and lettuce (nonunion produce are crops

Cesar Chavez marches in a demonstration with California farm workers in 1968.

that have been picked by nonunion workers), became the most successful labor actions taken by farm workers ever. Thereafter, Chavez became a symbol of Mexican-American ethnic consciousness as well as the voice of workers' rights. His success with the United Farm Workers galvanized other Latinos to press for fuller equality in all aspects of American life.

SEE ALSO

Chicanos; Hispanic Americans; Labor movement; United Farm Workers of America (UFW)

FURTHER READING

Castillo, Richard Griswold del, and Richard A. Garcia. *Cesar Chavez: A Triumph of Spirit*. Norman: University of Oklahoma Press, 1995.

Fodell, Beverly. *Cesar Chavez and the United Farm Workers*. Detroit: Wayne State University Press, 1974.

Horowitz, George. *La Causa: The California Grape Strike*. New York: Macmillan, 1970.

Chicago Seven

In the wake of the violent upheaval on the streets of Chicago during the 1968 Democratic National Convention, the U.S. attorney general charged antiwar demonstrators Rennie Davis, Dave Dellinger, John Froines, Tom Hayden, Abbie Hoffman, Jerry Rubin, Bobby Seale, and Lee Weiner with conspiracy to incite, organize, promote, and encourage antiwar riots in Chicago during the convention. The trial that followed dominated the news from September 1969 to February 1970, when the jury found five of the defendants guilty.

The case attracted the nation's attention as much for the unconventional dress and unruly behavior of the defendants in court—behavior designed to provoke and make a mockery of the legal process—as for the rulings of Judge Julius Hoffman, who held Bobby Seale bound and gagged in the courtroom and made no secret of his efforts to influence the jury against the defense. Bobby Seale represented himself at this trial—his codefendants were represented by William Kunstler, who became well known for representing left-wing clients until his death in 1995—and eventually his behavior caused his case to be declared a mistrial. This turned the group that had once been called the Chicago Eight into the Chicago Seven.

SEE ALSO

Democratic National Convention (Chicago, 1968); Hayden, Thomas ("Tom"); New Left; Youth International party (Yippies)

FURTHER READING

Schultz, John. *The Chicago Conspiracy Trial*. Rev. ed. New York: Da Capo, 1993.

Chicanos

In the late 1960s, young Mexican Americans, who had been inspired by the efforts of Cesar Chavez to fight for social and economic justice for farm workers, began to demand that others refer to Mexican American men as Chicanos and women as Chicanas—a Mexican Spanish abbreviation of *Mexicanos* that expressed pride in their ethnic heritage. Groups such as Alianza Federal de Mercedes (Federal Alliance of Land Grants) and La Raza Unida (the United People party) adopted the designation as part of a campaign to foster ethnic pride. They also demanded education in the Spanish language and the teaching of Chicano culture in public schools and universities. The Brown Berets of California (militant Chicanos who modeled themselves on the Black Panthers) began to use the slogan "brown power" to highlight their desire for control of their own communities.

SEE ALSO

Chavez, Cesar; Hispanic Americans

FURTHER READING

Hoobler, Dorothy and Thomas. *The Mexican American Family Album*. Oxford University Press, 1994.
Marin, Marguerite. *Social Protest in an Urban Barrio: A Study of the Chicano Movement, 1966–1974*. Lanham, Md.: University Press of America, 1991.
Muñoz, Carlos, Jr. *Youth, Identity, Power: Chicano Movement*. New York: Verso, 1989.
Sanchez, George J. *Becoming Mexican American: Ethnicity, Culture, and Identity in Chicano Los Angeles, 1900–1945*. New York: Oxford University Press, 1995.
Stavans, Ilan. *Bandido: Oscar "Zeta" Acosta and the Chicano Experience*. New York: HarperCollins, 1995.

China–U.S. relations

After World War II the United States tried, unsuccessfully, to mediate the Chinese civil war between the Nationalist forces of Chiang Kai-shek and the communists led by Mao Zedong. When negotiations failed, the United States supported the Nationalists. But U.S. dollars could not stem the "red tide" of communism. By the end of 1949, Chiang's regime had collapsed and then formed an exile government on the island of Taiwan (Formosa). The United States refused to recognize Mao's communist People's Republic of China, and within a year Chinese and U.S. troops would be battling in Korea, following the invasion of South Korea by China's ally North Korea.

Tensions continued in the 1960s as the Chinese assisted the Vietminh and the North Vietnamese in their war with South Vietnam and the Americans. At the same time, the United States continued to veto the admission of "Red China" to the United Nations and to bar its allies from trading with China. President Richard Nixon, however, recognized that the normalization of relations with China might help the United States bring the Vietnam War to an end and also widen the rift between the Chinese and the Soviets.

When Nixon's national security advisor Henry Kissinger began secret talks with China, Mao also saw an opportunity to check the Soviets and end China's isolation. Accordingly, in February 1972 Nixon flew to Beijing and became the first U.S. President to visit the most populous country in the world since 1879, when a retired Ulysses Grant had gone to China.

Nixon's visit ended more than two decades of hostility between China and the United States and began the process of normalizing relations between the two nations, which quickened with the death of Mao Zedong in 1976 and the desire of his successor, Deng Xiaoping, for closer links with the United States. On January 1, 1979, President Jimmy Carter restored full diplomatic relations with the People's Republic, permitting extensive academic, cultural, economic, and scientific exchanges.

A decade later, improved relations between China and the United States received a jolt when the Chinese army brutally crushed a pro-democracy rally in Beijing's Tiananmen Square, killing hundreds of unarmed students and jailing many more. President George Bush's administration protested vigorously and curtailed diplomatic contacts but refrained from breaking diplomatic relations or canceling trade agreements with China.

Similarly, despite China's continuing repression of dissidents, its human-rights abuses, and its unfair trade practices, President Bill Clinton's administration extended "most favored nation" trading status to China. By the mid-1990s, China had become the fourth-largest trading partner with the United States, and the continuation of that commerce guided U.S. policy toward China and led Clinton to visit there in 1998.

SEE ALSO

Korean War; Nixon, Richard Milhous; Vietnam War

FURTHER READING

Chang, Gordon. *Friends and Enemies: The United States, China, and the Soviet Union, 1948–1972.* Stanford, Calif.: Hoover Institution Press, 1989.
Iriye, Akira. *The Cold War in Asia: A Historical Introduction.* Englewood Cliffs, N.J.: Prentice Hall, 1974.
Madsen, Richard. *China and the American Dream: A Moral Inquiry.* Berkeley: University of California Press, 1995.

Chisholm, Shirley

- *Born: Nov. 30, 1924, New York, N.Y.*
- *Accomplishments: New York state assemblywoman (Democrat), 1964–68; U.S. Representative (Democrat–N.Y.), 1969–83; candidate for Democratic Presidential nomination, 1972*

The first African-American woman to run for her party's nomination for President and to be elected to the House of Representatives, Shirley Chisholm fought in Congress for the rights of women and minorities, an Equal Rights Amendment to the Constitution, application of the minimum wage to domestic workers, and federal funding of day care.

Congresswoman Shirley Chisholm announces that she is a candidate for the Democratic Presidential nomination in 1972.

Chisholm served in the New York State Assembly from 1964 to 1968, when she was elected to represent New York's 12th Congressional District. She served in that position until 1983. She won 152 votes for the Democratic Presidential nomination at the party's 1972 national convention. Chisholm came out of retirement in 1993 to serve as President Bill Clinton's ambassador to Jamaica.

FURTHER READING

Chisholm, Shirley. *The Good Fight.* New York: Harper & Row, 1973.
Chisholm, Shirley. *Unbought and Unbossed.* Boston: Houghton Mifflin, 1970.
Duffy, Susan. *Shirley Chisholm: A Bibliography of Writings by and About Her.* Metuchen, N.J.: Scarecrow Press, 1988.

Civil Rights Act of 1964

The Civil Rights Act of 1964, signed into law by President Lyndon B. Johnson, was a major turning point in the quest of African Americans for equal treatment under the law. Its numerous titles, or sections, struck down a network of laws that had historically kept black people, especially in the South, from voting, using public accommodations, and receiving equal treatment under the law.

Title I of the act restricted the use of literacy tests and poll taxes (a tax on adults of voting age that had prevented most blacks from voting) Titles II and III outlawed certain types of segregation and discrimination in hotels, restaurants, and other public accommodations. Title IV furthered the cause of school desegregation. Titles VII and VIII outlawed discrimination by employers with more than 100 workers and established the Equal Employment Opportunity Commission (EEOC) to investigate violations and enforce the law. Other titles established procedures for the federal government to enforce civil rights laws and updated court procedures.

President Lyndon Johnson addresses the nation before signing the Civil Rights Act on July 2, 1964. Attorney General Robert Kennedy is seated in the front row on the left; Senator Hubert Humphrey is in the front row in the center, and Martin Luther King, Jr., is at the far right.

SEE ALSO

Civil rights movement; Johnson, Lyndon Baines; King, Martin Luther, Jr.

FURTHER READING

Harvey, James C. *Black Civil Rights During the Johnson Administration.* Jackson: University Press of Mississippi, 1973.
Stern, Mark. *Calculating Visions: Kennedy, Johnson and Civil Rights.* New Brunswick, N.J.: Rutgers University Press, 1992.
Whalen, Charles, and Barbara Whalen. *The Longest Debate: A Legislative History of the 1964 Civil Rights Act.* Cabin John, Md.: Seven Locks Press, 1985.

Civil rights movement

Although African Americans had been agitating for civil rights since before the Civil War, developments in the 1940s and 1950s permitted revolutionary advancements in the struggle for black equality in the United States. The civil rights movement became one of the most successful grassroots political movements of all time and has provided inspiration for other peoples' movements around the world.

A series of developments during and after World War II led to rising expectations among blacks that they would gain full citizenship rights in the United States. American leaders had promoted the war as a struggle against the racism of the Nazi regime; an influential study by Gunnar Myrdal, *An American Dilemma,* had called attention to the contradiction between American ideals and the treatment of blacks in the United States; and in 1948 President Harry S. Truman formally ordered the desegregation of the U.S. armed forces.

The spark that ignited the civil rights movement, however, came in 1954, when the Supreme Court ruled that school segregation was unconstitutional in the case of *Brown* v. *Board of Education of Topeka, Kansas.* The Court unanimously overturned the so-called "separate but equal" decision of *Plessy* v. *Ferguson* (1896), which had upheld racial segregation. "Separate educational facilities are inherently unequal," the Court stated in its decision. The Court later called for desegregation "with all deliberate speed," and although the border states and the District of Columbia quickly complied with the ruling, the rest of the South resisted.

The *Brown* ruling had raised black expectations for equality, but when segregation and discrimination persisted, blacks, sometimes in conjunction with whites, began to form new organizations and adopt new tactics, such as direct confrontation, civil disobedience, and nonviolent protest.

Children hurl insults at a black family moving into a white neighborhood in Folcroft, Pennsylvania, in 1963. All over the country, blacks faced harassment as they fought for their civil rights.

Black demonstrators in 1963 marched in Birmingham, Alabama, until police officers ordered fire trucks to hose them down. Despite such tactics, blacks continued their nonviolent protests around the country, culminating in the March on Washington on August 28, 1963.

The first salvo in the new campaign was fired by blacks in Montgomery, Alabama, where, as elsewhere throughout the South, blacks were forced to sit at the back of public buses and give up seats to any white passenger who was standing. In December 1955, seamstress Rosa Parks refused to give up her seat to a white man and was arrested. Black leaders in the city organized a year-long boycott, which ended in the desegregation of the buses.

Martin Luther King, Jr., an eloquent 26-year-old black minister, received national attention as the leader of the Montgomery bus boycott and emerged as the leading figure of the civil rights movement. King developed a philosophy of nonviolent civil disobedience based on the teachings of Indian pacifist Mohandas Gandhi and the American transcendentalist writer Henry David Thoreau, among others. King urged his followers to respond to even brutal attacks with love. "If we are arrested every day," King said, "don't ever let anyone pull you so low as to hate them. We must use the weapon of love." By loving their enemies, black protestors would win them over.

The tactic of passive resistance proved extremely effective. It was adopted by newly formed civil rights organizations, including King's Southern Christian Leadership Conference (SCLC) and the Student Nonviolent Coordinating Committee (SNCC). It won support from a majority of Americans who, over the next several years, watched nightly news films of peaceful black protestors being brutalized and arrested by white police officers and racist counterdemonstrators. In 1963 a horrified nation watched as Birmingham, Alabama, police commissioner Eugene ("Bull") Connor turned police dogs, high-pressure fire hoses, and cattle prods on peaceful demonstrators.

Black college students became involved in the civil rights movement in 1960 after a group of students organized a sit-in at the whites-only Woolworth's lunch counter in Greensboro, North Carolina. The demonstrations eventually spread to other cities and led to the desegregation of many of the lunch counters.

Students who had participated in the demonstrations and members of the SCLC, including longtime activist Ella Jo Baker, formed SNCC in 1960. This organization adopted passive resistance, but less out of ideological commitment than as an effective tactic.

In the spring of 1961, the Congress of Racial Equality (CORE), an older civil rights group, organized a series of "freedom rides" to travel through the Deep South and test the Supreme Court rulings that had banned segregation on interstate bus routes and segregated facilities in bus terminals. The freedom riders were attacked by white mobs in Alabama, drawing national attention to and support for their cause, and forcing President John Kennedy to use U.S. marshals to protect the riders.

Kennedy again used federal troops in the fall of 1962, this time to force Governor Ross Barnett to admit a black student, James Meredith, to the University of Mississippi. In June 1963 Kennedy forced Governor George Wallace to admit two black students to the University of Alabama. These events, along with the brutal treatment of protestors in Birmingham in the spring of 1963, the peaceful nature of the demonstrations, and the constant television coverage, won support for civil rights among northern voters and damaged the nation's image abroad. Kennedy was forced to act, and in a televised address in June he publicly supported civil rights. A week later he proposed a comprehensive civil rights bill.

The high point of the civil rights movement occurred on August 28, 1963, when 250,000 Americans converged on Washington to hear civil rights orations, including King's famous "I Have a Dream" speech. In his sonorous voice King repeatedly sounded his refrain, calling America to share his dream of a better world in which "little black boys and black girls will be able to join hands with little white boys and white girls as sisters and brothers."

Despite the many successes of King and others in the years leading up to 1963, the pace of progress still seemed slow to a majority of blacks, who remained locked in poverty in both the cotton fields of the Deep South and northern urban ghettos. Their lives had not been significantly touched by the slow but steady legal reforms in southern locales or, even later, by the great advances that occurred when President Lyndon B. Johnson signed the Civil Rights Act of 1964 and the Voting Rights Act of 1965. Together these measures outlawed segregation in public accommodations, obstacles to the right to vote, and discrimination in employment, and they provided means for federal enforcement.

All these measures again raised expectations for progress. Yet when most blacks remained mired in poverty, many began to express their frustration. From 1964 to 1968, the nation experienced a series of "long, hot summers" during which African Americans, mostly in northern and western cities, acted out their rage in hundreds of riots in which they attacked police, burned buildings, and looted stores.

The frustration was also apparent among some leaders of the civil rights movement, including Stokely Carmichael, leader of SNCC, who in 1966 abandoned nonviolence in favor of "black power." As he said, "The only way we gonna stop them white men from whippin' us is to take over." His successor, H. Rap Brown, called on blacks to arm themselves. He and other advocates of armed self-defense—including Black Muslim leader Malcolm X, and Bobby Seale and Huey Newton, who formed the Black Panthers in Oakland, California, in 1966—repudiated King's policy of nonviolence as unrealistic. "Don't be trying to love that honky to death," Brown said. "Shoot him to death."

As the movement shifted in the late 1960s from the rural South to the urban North, from nonviolence to black power, and from the clear-cut issue of legal discrimination to the more complicated matter of economic deprivation, it began to lose much of the support it had won from white Americans. Images of peaceful protestors being sprayed by fire hoses were now replaced by films of urban rioters.

In 1968 George Wallace won 14 percent of the vote in his third-party bid for the Presidency, picking up substantial support in the North. Meanwhile, Federal Bureau of Investigation agents harassed and infiltrated civil rights organizations in a campaign to destroy them, and Martin Luther King was gunned down by an assassin in 1968. By the end of the decade the movement had lost its most effective leader and most of its momentum. In the years since the 1960s, race relations in the United States have remained problematic, marked by conflict over poverty programs, affirmative action, and crime.

Still, the movement had accomplished much, and it became a model for other movements, including the crusade against the Vietnam war, feminism, and the struggles of other ethnic minorities. In addition, it has inspired activists all over the world. During the Tiananmen Square pro-democracy uprising in China in 1989, for example, protestors could be heard singing the civil rights anthem "We Shall Overcome."

SEE ALSO

Affirmative Action; Black Power; *Brown* v. *Board of Education of Topeka, Kansas* (1954); Carmichael, Stokely; Congress of Racial Equality (CORE); Freedom Rides; Johnson, Lyndon Baines; King, Martin Luther, Jr.; Sit-ins (1960–61); Southern Christian Leadership Conference (SCLC); Student Nonviolent Coordinating Committee (SNCC)

FURTHER READING

Allen, Zita. *Black Women Leaders of the Civil Rights Movement.* Danbury, Conn.: Franklin Watts, 1996.

Archer, Jules. *They Had a Dream: The Civil Rights Struggle from Frederick Douglass to Marcus Garvey to Martin Luther King and Malcolm X.* New York: Puffin, 1996.

Bloom, Jack. *Class, Race, and the Civil Rights Movement.* Bloomington: Indiana University Press, 1987.

Branch, Taylor. *Parting the Waters: America in the King Years, 1954–63.* New York: Simon & Schuster, 1988.

Branch, Taylor. *Pillar of Fire: America in the King Years, 1963–65.* New York: Simon & Schuster, 1998.

Bullard, Sara. *Free at Last.* New York: Oxford University Press, 1993.

Dornfeld, Margaret. *The Turning Tide: From the Desegregation of the Armed Forces to the Montgomery Bus Boycott (1948–1956).* Broomall, Pa.: Chelsea House, 1995.

Garrow, David. *Bearing the Cross: Martin Luther King, Jr., and the Southern Christian Leadership Conference.* New York: Morrow, 1986.

Hampton, Henry, et al. *Voices of Freedom: An Oral History of the Civil Rights Movement from the 1950s through the 1980s.* New York: Bantam, 1990.

Harding, Vincent, Robin D. G. Kelley, and Earl Lewis. *We Changed the World: African Americans, 1945–1970.* New York: Oxford University Press, 1997.

Marable, Manning. *Race, Reform and Rebellion: The Second Reconstruction in Black America from 1945 to 1982.* Jackson: University Press of Mississippi, 1984.

Myers, Walter Dean. *Now Is Your Time!: The African-American Struggle for Freedom.* New York: HarperCollins, 1992.

Powledge, Fred. *Free at Last: The Civil Rights Movement and the People Who Made It.* New York: Harper, 1991.

Senna, Carl. *The Black Press and the Struggle for Civil Rights.* Danbury, Conn.: Franklin Watts, 1994.

Sitkoff, Harvard. *The Struggle for Black Equality, 1954–1992.* New York: Hill & Wang, 1993.

Williams, Juan. *Eyes on the Prize: America's Civil Rights Years, 1954–1963.* New York: Penguin, 1987.

Clean Air Act (1963)

The rise in environmental awareness in the 1960s prompted Congress to pass the Clean Air Act in 1963. This law regulated automotive and industrial emissions. As the number of cars increased and smog and pollution became serious problems in densely populated areas, regulation of car emissions became increasingly strict. Congress passed amendments to the Clean Air Act in both 1970 and 1990, setting goals for the reduction of sulfur dioxide emissions and carbon monoxide in the atmosphere, requiring stricter controls on automobile exhaust and the use of cleaner fuels, applying specific emissions standards to hundreds of utilities, and granting extensive powers to the Environmental Protection Agency to set and enforce acceptable levels for toxic chemicals in the air.

SEE ALSO

Environmental movement

FURTHER READING

Bailey, Christopher J. *Congress and Air Pollution: Environmental Policies in the United States.* New York: St. Martin's, 1998.

Bryner, Gary C. *Blue Skies, Green Politics: The Clean Air Act of 1990.* Washington D.C.: Congressional Quarterly, 1993.

Cleaver, Eldridge

- *Born: Aug. 31, 1935, Wabbaseka, Ark.*
- *Accomplishments: African-American protest leader; writer; Black Panther party leader*
- *Died: May 1, 1998, Los Angeles, Calif.*

As information minister of the Black Panther party in the late 1960s, Eldridge Cleaver provided one of the most militant voices of protest in the black struggle for equality. Cleaver, who had spent much of his youth in prison, symbolized the disillusionment of blacks and the radicalization of the civil rights movement, especially after the publication of his best-selling book *Soul on Ice* in 1968. He called for "total liberty for black people or total destruction for America." Following a shootout with Oakland, California, police in 1968, Cleaver fled the country. After seven years of exile (spent mainly in Communist countries), he returned to the United States, where he was able to negotiate a sentence of community service for the Oakland incident. Explaining that he had become disenchanted with communism and radical politics, Cleaver radically altered his views and turned to conservatism and evangelism in the late 1970s. He remained a supporter of right-wing politics until his death in 1998.

SEE ALSO

Black Panther party; Black power

FURTHER READING

Cleaver, Eldridge. *Soul on Ice.* New York: McGraw-Hill, 1968.

Scheer, Robert, ed. *Eldridge Cleaver: Post-Prison Writing and Speeches.* New York: Random House, 1969.

Clifford, Clark

- *Born: Dec. 25, 1906, Fort Scott, Kans.*
- *Accomplishments: Secretary of Defense, 1968–69*
- *Died: Oct. 11, 1998, Bethesda, Md.*

Clark Clifford served as an advisor to every Democratic President from Harry Truman to Jimmy Carter. His most prominent role in the government came in 1968, when he became Lyndon Johnson's new secretary of defense, replacing Robert McNamara. In the wake of the Tet offensive, Clifford formed a task force to reappraise U.S. policy in Vietnam in light of General William Westmoreland's request for an additional 206,000 troops. He questioned Pentagon officials about the need for additional troops and about the prospects of winning the war. Ultimately, he concluded that "the military course we were pursuing was not only endless, but hopeless."

Clifford urged Johnson to change the direction of U.S. policy and propose negotiations. He suggested that the President call a meeting of the "wise men," a group of elder statesmen whom Johnson had relied on for advice before. The "wise men" agreed with Clifford and urged Johnson to end the war. Persuaded, Johnson took the first steps by stopping all bombing of North Vietnam and refusing Westmoreland's request for additional troops.

After leaving his career in government, Clifford had a lucrative career as a lawyer. In his final years, however, he faced charges of fraud, conspiracy, and bribe-taking in the well-publicized Bank of Credit and Commerce International (BCCI) scandal. Before his death, he and his law partner, Robert Altman, reached a settlement with the Federal Reserve Board.

SEE ALSO

Vietnam War

FURTHER READING

Clifford, Clark, with Richard Holbrooke. *Counsel to the President.* New York: Random House, 1991.

Frantz, Douglas. *Friends in High Places: The Rise and Fall of Clark Clifford.* Boston: Little, Brown, 1995.

Clinton, William Jefferson ("Bill")

- *Born: Aug. 19, 1946, Hope, Ark.*
- *Government service: Governor of Arkansas (Democrat), 1979–81, 1983–92; 42nd President of the United States, 1993–*

The first baby boomer to serve as President, Bill Clinton grew up in Arkansas with his mother, Virginia, his alcoholic and sometimes violent stepfather, Roger Clinton, and his stepbrother, Roger, Jr. Despite family turmoil, as a teenager Bill Clinton played tenor saxophone in a jazz band, volunteered in nonprofit organizations, served as

William Jefferson—more often known to voters and headline writers as Bill—Clinton posed for a formal photograph early in his first term.

junior class president, and graduated fourth in his class.

During a trip to Washington in 1963, he shook hands with President John F. Kennedy and shortly thereafter decided to embark on a career in politics. After working as an intern for Senator J. William Fulbright during his college years at Georgetown University, Clinton won a Rhodes scholarship to Oxford University. While in London in 1969 he organized two protests against the Vietnam War, a fact that caused him some political embarrassment during his run for the Presidency.

Clinton worked with his future wife, Hillary Rodham, in George McGovern's Presidential campaign in 1972. After attending Yale Law School, he taught constitutional law at the University of Arkansas Law School from 1974 to 1976. He lost a bid for the U.S. House of Representatives in 1974 but was elected Arkansas attorney general in 1976 and governor in 1978. After enacting unpopular gasoline tax and automobile registration fee increases, he became the youngest ex-governor in U.S. history, losing his reelection bid in 1980.

Clinton returned to office in 1983 and remained governor until he became President. During the 1980s, his major accomplishment was the implementation of a sweeping education reform act, which required competency testing for teachers. After considering and rejecting a run for the Presidency in 1988, Clinton delivered the nominating speech for Michael Dukakis at the Democratic National Convention that year. The speech was widely panned for its dull subject matter, excessive length, and uninspiring delivery.

Undaunted, Clinton launched his bid for the 1992 Democratic nomination in the spring of 1991. After fending off charges of extramarital affairs, marijuana smoking, and avoiding the draft, Clinton defeated his primary opponents. These charges continued to dog him throughout the general election campaign as President George Bush tried to make an issue of Clinton's "character." Nevertheless, thanks to a weak economy, tireless and effective campaigning, and the third-party candidacy of Ross Perot (who took votes from Bush), Clinton won 370 votes in the electoral college, comfortably defeating Bush, who won only 160.

The new administration got off to a poor start, however, when Clinton sought to overturn a ban on gays in the armed forces and then backed off in the face of strong opposition. The incident disappointed both liberals, who lamented the President's lack of commitment to civil rights, and conservatives, who charged that Clinton was too liberal on social issues.

Clinton next turned his energies to winning passage of a budget that focused on deficit reduction and education reform. The budget reduced the projected federal deficit for 1995 from $284 to $171 billion. It included a proposal to "make work pay" by allowing newly employed welfare recipients to retain Medicaid benefits. Clinton also expanded the Head Start program, which prepares preschoolers from low-income families for grade school; signed "Goals 2000," which provides grants to local school districts; and established a national service program, which provides financial aid for college students in exchange for community service.

Clinton succeeded in pushing significant anticrime legislation through Congress, including the "Brady bill," which imposed a five-day waiting period for the purchase of a handgun. A $30 billion crime bill paid for hiring police officers, building new prisons, and extending the death penalty to more than 50 crimes. The bill also placed a ban on 19 types of assault weapons.

Clinton also won passage of two hotly debated free-trade measures. The North American Free Trade Agreement (NAFTA) reduced trade barriers among the United States, Canada, and Mexico, while the General Agreement on Tariffs and Trade (GATT) promised to resolve trade disputes and reduce protectionism (taxes on imports called tariffs) in world trade.

The most ambitious undertaking of Clinton's first term was his attempt to provide health insurance for all Americans. Drawn up by a committee headed by Hillary Rodham Clinton, the complicated Health Security Act went before Congress in the fall of 1993. Under the plan, an estimated 40 percent of currently insured Americans would have paid higher premiums and employers would have been required to pay 80 percent of employees' health premiums. Assailed by lobbyists for insurance companies and the medical community and attacked in slick political ads on television, the proposal languished in congressional committees and never came to a vote.

The defeat of his health-care proposal marked a low point in Clinton's tenure, but he suffered a greater defeat in the fall of 1994, when congressional Republicans handed the Democrats a crushing defeat in the midterm elections. Running on House minority leader Newt Gingrich's "Contract with America," which proposed tax cuts, tougher crime laws, a balanced budget amendment, and congressional term limits, the Republicans took control of both branches of the legislature for the first time since the 1940s.

After the election, Clinton moved to the right on many issues and adopted a more modest domestic program while focusing more intensely on foreign policy issues. He successfully portrayed congressional Republicans as extreme and mean spirited, helped by a widespread perception that their agenda had been set by business lobbyists. Meanwhile, he positioned himself as a reasonable moderate, dedicated to preserving popular programs.

Clinton was also helped by favorable developments in foreign policy. Criticized early in his administration for "waffling" on the diplomatic front, particularly in Somalia and in Bosnia (where ethnic conflict between Muslims, Catholics, and Greek Orthodox Bosnians exploded into civil wars), the administration then scored a string of foreign policy successes. Clinton used economic sanctions to restore democratic government to Haiti after a brutal military takeover; deterred an invasion of Kuwait by sending 36,000 troops to the Persian Gulf in response to an Iraqi troop buildup on the Kuwaiti border; avoided a confrontation with North Korea over nuclear weapons; helped to further peace in Northern Ireland and Israel; and, after two years of indecision, brokered a settlement to the conflict in Bosnia.

Still, Clinton's foreign policy achievements were fragile. The peace in Bosnia was threatened by attempts to resolve charges of war crimes, and peace accords in Northern Ireland and Israel were set back by the renewal of extremist terrorism.

Slow-simmering but potentially explosive scandals also threatened Clinton's reelection. He faced a sexual harassment suit and numerous investigations into the Whitewater real estate investment that he and his wife had made in the 1980s. Just as a Senate investigation of the affair was about to close in June 1996, without having made any damaging revelations, a federal jury found the Clintons' Whitewater partners James and Susan McDougal guilty in a case involving the land deal.

Even in the face of these developments, Clinton was able to win reelection to a second term by handily defeating his Republican rival, former Senator Bob Dole of Kansas. Then came one of the most incredible, topsy-turvy years in American politics, which would end with Clinton being the first and only elected President to be impeached—and with his popularity with the American public reaching new heights. It began with allegations in January 1998 that Clinton had carried on a sexual affair from 1995 to 1997 with a young White House intern, Monica Lewinsky, and had lied about it and urged others to lie about it in the sexual harassment case brought against him by Paula Jones. The President publicly denied all the allegations; White House aides questioned the motives and the credibility of those making charges against Clinton and those investigating him; and the President's job rating started to rise. Seven months later, Lewinsky, after being granted immunity, admitted to the grand jury inquiring into the matter that she and the President had carried on a sexual affair in the White House. Faced with Lewinsky's reversal the President also changed his story in testimony to the grand jury in August. He now admitted to the grand jury, and to the public, that he had had an inappropriate relationship with Ms. Lewinsky. He said he had misled but that he had not lied to the grand jury and to the public. He expressed regret but did not apologize, blaming the mess on the Special Prosecutor and a partisan GOP. At this point, even some of the leading Democrats in Congress termed his behavior "reprehensible," "immoral," and "disgraceful," and called for a public rebuke.

Once again, however, the actions of Clinton's opponents saved him. The public release in September of Special Prosecutor Kenneth Starr's tawdry, sexually explicit report recommending impeachment disgusted most Americans as much as what the President did. The airing of Clinton's videotaped testimony to the grand jury, showing the President being repeatedly pressed to reveal the most intimate details of the relationship between him and Lewinsky, also stirred some sympathy for the President. Then the haste with which the House Judiciary Committee and later the full House voted, largely along party lines, to conduct an impeachment inquiry seemed to many an unwarranted act of vengeful partisanship. Public opinion polls indicated that while a clear majority deplored the President's personal conduct and believed that he had lied and obstructed justice, they did not think his actions constituted "high crimes and misdemeanors" and did not want him removed from office. Indeed, with the economy doing better than at any time since the 1950s, the crime rate falling, and the stock market soaring, some two-thirds of those polled consistently rated Clinton's moderate-centrist Presidency highly. In November the voters delivered a blow to the Republicans, maintaining the Democratic numbers in the Senate and giving the Democrats five additional seats in the House. For the first time since 1934, a President's party had gained seats in a midterm election, causing Speaker Newt Gingrich, Clinton's main antagonist, to give up his leadership post and announce his retirement from Congress.

It appeared as if the public had spoken, and the Republicans would heed its voice. But defying the election results and public opinion, in December the vindictive Judiciary Committee and then

Bill Clinton's wife, Hillary Rodham Clinton, and their daughter Chelsea on safari in Africa in 1997. Mrs. Clinton, a successful lawyer, became a new kind of First Lady as she continually and visibly wrestled with defining the role of President's wife.

the full House of Representatives approved articles of impeachment alleging that Clinton had lied under oath before a grand jury and that he had obstructed justice in a federal civil rights action by seeking to cover up evidence of his affair with Lewinsky. A dispirited Senate, knowing full well that the Republicans could not muster the two-thirds vote necessary to convict and remove the President from office, went through the motions of a trial. The anticlimax came on February 12, 1999; with all 45 Democrats sticking with the President, the Senate voted 50–50 on the count of obstruction of justice and 55–45 against the charge of perjury. Clinton had again vanquished his political enemies. It was the ultimate victory of the "Comeback Kid" in a career marked by seemingly miraculous political resurrections. The first Democrat since FDR to win two full terms in office, Clinton could take credit for a balanced budget, welfare reform, free trade, the end of inflation, negligible unemployment, and booming prosperity. But as tainted as he was talented, whether William Jefferson Clinton will be remembered as more than a joke about sordid sex remains in doubt. Primarily the consequence of his own conduct, aided and abetted by scurrilous prosecutorial tactics and mean-spirited partisanship, his legacy may be the further decline of the moral authority of the Presidency and an increase in the cynicism of Americans toward the entire political system and political process.

SEE ALSO

Bush, George Herbert Walker; Fulbright, J. William

FURTHER READING

Drew, Elizabeth. *On the Edge: The Clinton Presidency.* New York: Simon & Schuster, 1995.

Maraniss, David. *First in His Class: The Biography of Bill Clinton.* New York: Simon & Schuster, 1996.

Morris, Roger. *Partners in Power: The Clintons and Their America.* New York: Holt, 1996.

Stewart, James B. *Blood Sport: The President and His Adversaries.* New York: Simon & Schuster, 1996.

Cold war

In 1947 columnist Walter Lippmann coined the term *cold war* to describe the conflict and competition, short of direct military engagement, between the United States and the Soviet Union following the end of World War II. The United States had been opposed to the Bolshevik Revolution in Russia in 1917, but during World War II the United States and the Soviet Union allied against Nazi Germany and Japan. Disagreements over postwar plans, however, renewed mutual suspicions. Having lost more than 20 million people in World War II and suffered two invasions by Germany in 30 years, Soviet leader Joseph Stalin wanted to control Poland, establish a buffer zone in Eastern Europe, dominate the Balkans, and crush Germany's capacity to make war.

Stalin's refusal to abandon Soviet dominance of Eastern Europe was matched by President Harry Truman's unwillingness to concede Soviet supremacy outside Russia's own borders. To that end Truman insisted on self-determination for Poland, equal economic access to Eastern Europe for the United States, and the rebuilding of Western Europe to serve as a hub in world affairs, with Germany at its center. Despite the U.S. monopoly on atomic weapons, Stalin ignored Truman's demands, took control of Poland, and sealed off his Eastern European satellites from Anglo-American influence and trade, creating what Winston Churchill called an "iron curtain" across the eastern half of Europe.

In February 1947 the British-controlled monarchy in Greece was being threatened by communist-led insurgents and a financially weak Britain was forced to cease aid. Truman decided to provide massive assistance to Greece and Turkey, which were then being pressured by the Soviets for access to the Mediterranean Sea, and when he requested the funds from Congress, he used the opportunity to rally American support for the emerging conflict with the Soviet Union. Known as the Truman Doctrine, the President's declaration that it was the United States's duty to protect "free" peoples against "totalitarian" regimes committed the United States, in theory, to the role of global policeman. A month later, the Truman administration proposed the Marshall Plan, a program of economic assistance for European recovery.

When Stalin had threatened in 1946 that there could be no lasting peace with capitalism, U.S. State Department officer and counselor of the American embassy in Moscow George Kennan responded that the only answer to Stalin was "a long-term, patient but firm and vigilant containment of Russian expansive tendencies." Along with Stalin's mistrust of the West and his obsession with Soviet security, Kennan's containment policy and Truman's rhetoric set the course for the cold war.

In 1948 Western Europe found itself rebuilding, courtesy of $12 billion that the United States pumped into Europe as part of the Marshall Plan. Fearing that Germany would again be strong, Stalin shut off western access to Berlin, located deep in the Soviet zone of East Germany. The city itself was divided and controlled by the four postwar powers: the Soviet Union, the United States, Britain, and France. Instead of risking a military confrontation, Truman decided to airlift supplies over the blockade into West Berlin during 1948–49. Stalin backed down but responded with an economic plan for Eastern Europe similar to that of the Marshall Plan. Stalin also surprised Truman in 1949 by successfully testing an atomic bomb, ending the U.S. atomic monopoly.

The continuing fear of a Soviet assault on Western Europe fostered support for a strong West German state and a collective security alliance. In 1949 the United States, Britain, and France approved the establishment of the Federal Republic of Germany, and joined other Western European nations and Canada to form the North Atlantic Treaty Organization (NATO), a military alliance that proclaimed that an attack on any member would be considered an attack against all. Early in 1950 Truman ordered the development of the hydrogen bomb and approved a report of his National Security Council advocating a massive U.S. military buildup to counter the Soviet Union's "design for world domination."

The hostility between Moscow and Washington also led to the division of Asia into contending military and economic camps. And when North Korean troops swept across the 38th Parallel to invade South Korea on June 25, 1950, Truman acted as if it were Soviet-directed aggression, a test of the containment policy and U.S. will. He quickly won United Nations approval for a "police action" against the aggressor, ordering U.S. troops to fight the North Koreans. The war would go on for three years and cost the United States more than 54,000 American lives, 100,000 other casualties, and some $54 billion. It ended in a cease-fire that restored the demarcation line between the two Koreas to where it had been prior to the conflict. It also speeded up the use of the Security Council report and the transformation of containment into a general global policy.

President Dwight Eisenhower sought the same cold war ends as Truman, but by different means. Ever budget conscious, Eisenhower cut the federal budget and reduced military spending by one-third. Instead of relying on conventional forces, Eisenhower preferred to use the threat of nuclear war as a deterrent, feeling that nuclear weapons offered "more bang for the buck." Eisenhower's secretary of state, John Foster Dulles, defined this policy as "massive retaliation," stressing the free world's ability to "retaliate, instantly, by means and at places of our own choosing." Eisenhower also used the Central Intelligence Agency to overthrow governments that were leaning toward communism in Iran in 1953 and in Guatemala in 1954, and sent troops to Lebanon in 1958 to ensure its pro-American stance.

In turn, Soviet premier Nikita Khrushchev increased Soviet power by creating the Warsaw Pact (an East European version of NATO), developing his own hydrogen bomb, enlarging the Soviet nuclear stockpile ("more rubble for the ruble"), and assisting in wars of national liberation in the poorer countries of the world (often referred to during the time of U.S.–Soviet confrontation as the Third World, because these countries sided with neither the United States nor the Soviet Union).

In 1961 Khrushchev had a wall built around the Soviet sector of Berlin to stop Germans from leaving communist East Germany, and in 1962 his government secretly placed nuclear missiles in Cuba. The two superpowers, in Secretary of State Dean Rusk's phrase, stood "eyeball to eyeball" in the fall of 1962 as President John F. Kennedy confronted Khrushchev about the missiles in Cuba. After days of standing on the brink of war, Khrushchev and Kennedy came to an agreement in which Khrushchev pledged to pull the missiles out of Cuba

Soviet premier Nikita Khrushchev, beaming proudly (left), presents President Dwight Eisenhower with a model of the Sputnik *satellite as Vice President Richard Nixon looks on. The launch of* Sputnik, *the first man-made satellite, spurred Eisenhower to create NASA and to try to outpace Soviet scientific achievements during the cold war.*

in return for Kennedy's promise not to invade Cuba as he had in 1961 during the Bay of Pigs affair.

During the 1960s, the United States's cold war focus shifted to Vietnam. Attempting to prevent the North Vietnamese communists from unifying Vietnam under their rule, which Americans feared would then lead to communist takeovers of other nations in Asia (called at the time the "domino theory"), the United States first sought to help South Vietnam remain noncommunist and when that failed directly intervened militarily to save South Vietnam. The effort would prove to be the United States's longest war and costliest defeat: some 58,000 U.S. dead and more than 300,000 wounded; at least $150 billion spent and a weakened U.S. economy; and an embittered generation, greater domestic problems, and a divided nation left in confusion.

Détente, or the deliberate effort to ease tensions between the superpowers, was established, although only for a short time, in 1972, when President Richard Nixon went to Moscow and signed the Strategic Arms Limitation Treaty (SALT I), which limited the number of strategic nuclear weapons allowed to both countries. Nixon also visited the People's Republic of China, beginning the process of normalizing U.S.–Chinese relations. Tensions in the Middle East, Chile, Iran, and Angola, however, strained relations between the Soviet Union and the United States, and the two powers continued to seek advantages over each other. When President Ronald Reagan took office in 1981, the thaw begun by Nixon in 1972 had chilled considerably.

Reagan promised to fight the Soviet "Evil Empire" at every turn and spent $2.2 trillion for the military in eight years to do so. By 1985 hostilities between the two powers rivaled those of the late 1940s, and conditions might very well have worsened if Mikhail Gorbachev had not assumed power in Moscow that year. Gorbachev, in an attempt to save the Soviet economy from collapse, began to ease tensions with the United States and within the Soviet Union through *perestroika* (economic restructuring) and *glasnost* (openness). In 1989 Gorbachev pulled Soviet troops out of Afghanistan and announced that the "postwar period is over."

In 1989–90, the end came for most communist regimes in the Eastern bloc, the Berlin Wall was torn down, and Germany was reunited. When Gorbachev was replaced by Boris Yeltsin on December 25, 1991, the Soviet Union officially ceased to exist. After 45 years, the cold war had come to an end. But it had fundamentally changed the United States, and the long shadow of the cold war continued to influence the United States's most basic institutions.

SEE ALSO

Berlin, blockade of; Berlin Wall; Containment doctrine; Cuban missile crisis of 1962; Détente; Eisenhower, Dwight David; Kennan, George F.; Kennedy, John Fitzgerald; Korean War; Marshall Plan; Nixon, Richard Milhous; North Atlantic Treaty Organization (NATO); Truman, Harry S.; Truman Doctrine; Vietnam War

FURTHER READING

Ambrose, Stephen. *Rise to Globalism.* New York: Penguin, 1993.

Gaddis, John L. *The Long Peace: Inquiries into the History of the Cold War.* New York: Oxford University Press, 1987.

Gormly, James. *The Collapse of the Grand Alliance, 1945–1948.* Baton Rouge: Louisiana State University Press, 1987.

Hyland, William. *The Cold War Is Over.* New York: Random House, 1990.

Leffler, Melvyn P. *A Preponderance of Power: National Security, the Truman Administration, and the Cold War.* Stanford, Calif.: Stanford University Press, 1992.

McCormick, Thomas J. *America's Half-Century: United States Foreign Policy in the Cold War.* Baltimore, Md.: Johns Hopkins University Press, 1989.

Communist Control Act of 1954

In the same month that the Senate began investigations into the alleged misconduct of the nation's most outspoken anticommunist, Senator Joseph McCarthy, the Senate and the House passed the Communist Control Act of 1954, in effect making membership in the Communist party illegal. Illustrative of the strong bipartisan consensus to root out communism from American society, the legislation passed unanimously in the Senate and by a 265-to-2 vote in the House. The fear of communism and the desire to purge the nations of its influences persisted long after McCarthy's downfall that year. In this extension of the Internal Security Act of 1950, legislators determined that those found to have "knowingly and willfully" joined the party would be subject to imprisonment and fines.

SEE ALSO
Internal Security Act of 1950; McCarthyism

Computers

In ways that initially could not even be imagined, the development of the electronic computer—and the technological revolution that it spawned—fundamentally changed the American economy and society. The new era dawned in 1944 with the Mark I calculator, an electromechanical computer designed to decipher Axis codes in World War II, developed by scientists working at International Business Machines Corporation (IBM) and at Harvard University. Two years later, the Mark I's successor, ENIAC, an electronic computer intended for artillery calculations, could perform 1,000 times faster.

In 1947, Bell Labs produced the first solid-state miniaturized components, called transistors, which ended reliance on radio tubes and facilitated the microprocessor revolution. In the 1960s, the silicon microchip introduced even speedier and more startling advances in computers, heralding the shift in the United States from heavy manufacturing to such high-tech industries as genetic engineering, fiber optics, lasers, and robotics.

Popular Mechanics magazine boldly predicted in 1949 that "computers in the future may weigh no more than 1.5 tons." It is now easy to walk into a computer store and stroll out carrying a laptop that weighs in at under three pounds. As computers got smaller, faster, and smarter, sales of electronic computers rose from 20 in 1954 to more than 1,000 in 1957 and 2,000 in

Dr. J. Presper Eckert, Jr. demonstrates the ENIAC computer that he coinvented. ENIAC was faster than Mark I, but was still too difficult to program and had too small a memory to be as useful to a general public as today's computers.

1960. By 1965, sales of computing equipment approached $3 billion and by 1970 this figure doubled again. Then, in the mid-1970s, Steven Jobs and Stephen Wozniak built a prototype of a personal computer (PC) in their garage, founded Apple Computers, and made *Fortune* magazine's list of the top 500 corporations faster than any company in history. IBM introduced its first PC in 1981 and the numbers in use rose quickly from less than 2 million to more than 65 million in 1991.

The impact of the computer on American life accelerated and showed no signs of slowing as the 20th century neared its close. Many students took computers rather than typewriters to college, and looked for library books in electronic databases rather than in card catalogs; their parents routinely expected computerized supermarket scanners to calculate their grocery bills while keeping store inventory, and computerized automated teller machines (ATMs) to let them conduct their banking transactions virtually anywhere in the world. In the 1990s, moreover, it became increasingly common for many Americans in what futurist Alvin Toffler called the "electronic cottage" to communicate by e-mail; to shop on the Internet; to travel with laptop or notebook computers; to work from home, in their pajamas if they want to, avoiding traffic and disruptions as they telecommute; to schedule themselves using ever-smaller handheld electronic gadgets; to respond to the beeps and vibrations of their computerized pagers and cellular telephones; and to do their own desktop publishing.

Among other consequences, the replacement of slower mechanical processes with faster computerized ones generated a rapid rise in productivity, and the subsequent need for fewer workers, a phenomenon termed "technological unemployment." Computerization also promoted greater concentration of ownership in industry. Often only the largest corporations could afford the latest, most sophisticated, and most expensive technology, thus forcing smaller corporations out of the market. The greatest fortunes of the late 20th century, moreover, went to the men and women who capitalized on the constantly expanding market for computers and computer services. By far the wealthiest man in America in the 1990s was William Gates, the youthful founder and president of Microsoft, a software company whose operating systems served the vast majority of the world's computers. Gates, however, was only the most successful among the many Americans who earned great fortunes from the computer revolution.

SEE ALSO

Gates, Bill; Internet, The; World Wide Web

FURTHER READING

Ceruzzi, Paul. *A History of Modern Computing*. Cambridge, Mass: MIT Press, 1998.

Levy, Steven. *Insanely Great: The Life and Times of Macintosh, the Computer That Changed Everything*. New York: Viking, 1994.

Northrup, Mary. *American Computer Pioneers*. Springfield, N.J.: Enslow, 1988.

Ritchie, David. *The Computer Pioneers*. New York: Simon & Schuster, 1986.

Wulforst, Harry. *Breakthrough to the Computer Age*. New York: Scribner, 1982.

Congress of Racial Equality (CORE)

In 1942, black and white members of the Fellowship of Reconciliation, a pacifist organization, formed the Congress of Racial Equality (CORE). In

Black and white workers joined together in CORE to register voters and participate in freedom rides. At this office, the sign at left refers to three civil rights workers who were killed in Mississippi.

1955 CORE members went to the South to train volunteers in the techniques of nonviolent protest against segregation and other forms of racism. The group was led by seminary students, including James Farmer, who became head of the organization in 1961 and went on to become a prominent leader of the civil rights movement.

At first the group used sit-ins, freedom rides, and civil disobedience in its efforts to end segregation. Next, in the early 1960s, it concentrated on voter registration in the South. Later, by the mid-1960s, as members became pessimistic about the likelihood of true integration, it focused on achieving political power for blacks and also was active in the antiwar movement.

CORE still exists, though it has been only sporadically active in the fight for civil rights in the 1990s.

SEE ALSO

Civil rights movement; Freedom rides; Sit-ins (1960–61)

FURTHER READING

Farmer, James. *Lay Bare the Heart: The Autobiography of the Civil Rights Movement.* New York: Arbor House, 1985.

Meier, August, and Elliot Rudwick. *CORE, A Study in the Civil Rights Movement: 1942–1968.* New York: Oxford University Press, 1973.

Consciousness-raising groups

In the late 1960s and early 1970s, small groups of women held regularly scheduled meetings where they would share intimate details of their lives with each other. These women, who were mainly fairly young, middle to upper middle class, well educated, and white, found that when they discussed their lives and their feelings common patterns emerged. Most of them shared experiences of oppression that they realized came from being female in a male-dominated society, and from that realization came the idea that "the personal is political"; in other words, that experiences that seem to be deeply personal often have roots in the surrounding culture and thus do not have to be repeated if the relationships and assumptions from which they develop could be changed.

Consciousness-raising groups grew out of the civil rights and antiwar movements, and had an important effect on the newly re-emerging feminist movement. They flourished for a short time but then withered, the victim of their own ideology. Because participants tried to avoid the kind of hierarchy that they thought represented the male world they did not want to have leaders, but without the kind of organization that leadership represents the groups fell apart. However, from the groups came many new insights into how relationships between men and women and between women and other women could be improved.

SEE ALSO

Feminism

FURTHER READING

Boston Women's Health Book Collective. *Our Bodies, Ourselves.* New York: Simon & Schuster, 1973.

Echols, Alice. *Daring to Be Bad: Radical Feminism in America, 1967–75.* Minneapolis: University of Minnesota Press, 1989.

Shreve, Anita. *Women Together, Women Alone: The Legacy of the Consciousness-Raising Movement.* New York: Viking, 1989.

Conservatism

After suffering more than a decade of diminished prestige and power during the popular Presidency of Franklin D. Roosevelt, conservatives unleashed their frustrations at the end of World War II. Postwar conservatives were staunchly anticommunist and sought to return federal–state relations and the powers of the Presidency to their pre–Franklin Roosevelt state.

Even before the anticommunist hysteria created by Senator Joe McCarthy in 1950, conservatives urged the United States to take a tough stance against the expansion of Soviet communism and demanded that reputed communists in Harry Truman's administration, indeed in all walks of American life, be exposed and removed from positions of power. But after two decades of depression and war, most Americans were ready for the normalcy that characterized the years of Dwight Eisenhower's Presidency and preferred a middle-of-the-road politics that shunned both the right and the left.

Conservatism did not become prominent in the postwar United States until Barry Goldwater captured the Republican Presidential nomination in 1964. His militant followers, particularly the young political activists influenced by the *National Review* and its

President Ronald Reagan, a champion of conservatism, points out how the tax bill for the average American family would keep growing unless Congress cut taxes. Millions of Americans agreed with him.

editor, William Buckley, disdained the 1950s political spirit of compromise and sought a religiously oriented American society of self-regulating individuals. They particularly appealed to Americans who had supported McCarthyism and opposed the civil rights movement, who were disturbed by the cold war stalemate and the centralized decision making of an expanding federal government. Going further to the right, Robert Welch founded the John Birch Society in 1958 to combat a perceived infiltration of communism into American life. It sought the abolition of the graduated income tax and Social Security system, withdrawal of the United States from the United Nations, and the impeachment of Chief Justice of the United States Earl Warren.

Conservatism triumphed in the late 1960s as a majority of Americans reacted angrily to the violence of race riots and a sharply rising crime rate, to the drugs and sexuality associated with the counterculture, to an alleged lack of patriotism in the antiwar movement, and to what conservatives saw as extreme demands made by liberals, student radicals, militant feminists, and proponents of black power.

A "New Right" emerged, a cultural conservatism stressing social and moral issues and demanding a restoration of "traditional values." As New Right leader Paul Weyrich explained: "We talk about issues people care about, like gun control, abortion, taxes, and crime. Yes, they're emotional issues, but that's better than talking about capital formation." Thus Jerry Falwell's Moral Majority, one of many groups merging evangelical Christianity and political action, campaigned against what conservatives called "secular humanism" in the schools (teachings that were not rooted in the Bible), the rising rates of abortion and divorce, and what they saw as a pervasiveness of pornography, sex, and violence in the mass media.

In 1980 the unabashedly conservative Ronald Reagan won the Presidential race by attacking the legacy of liberal ideals from Franklin Roosevelt's New Deal programs and Lyndon Johnson's Great Society. Reagan's platform of deregulation, tax cuts, traditional values, and militant patriotism and anti-communism rang sweetly in the ears of millions of usually Democratic blue-collar and middle-class Americans, as well as normally conservative Republicans. His success in enacting much of his agenda, the "Reagan Revolution," swelled the ranks of conservatism and defined the issues for much of the politics of the 1990s.

Yet, by the 1990s, conservatism no longer had the ability to bring different groups together that it had in the heyday of Ronald Reagan. The movement was racked by conflict between those primarily concerned with economic matters and the more radical conservatives associated with the Christian Coalition and with politicians such as Pat Buchanan. Nonetheless, conservatism continued, despite the 1992 and 1996 elections of Democrat Bill Clinton, to garner support on many social issues. Fueled by Republican Newt Gingrich's "Contract with America" and ongoing debates over equal opportunity measures such as affirmative action, conservatism remained a powerful force in the politics of the 1990s.

SEE ALSO

Abortion issue; Affirmative action; Agnew, Spiro; Buckley, William F., Jr.; Bricker Amendment (1951); Buchanan, Patrick J.; Gingrich, Newton L. ("Newt"); Goldwater, Barry; John Birch Society; Liberalism; McCarthy, Joseph; Moral Majority; Reagan, Ronald Wilson; Wallace, George Corley

FURTHER READING

Crawford, Alan. *Thunder on the Right: The "New Right" and the Politics of Resentment.* New York: Pantheon, 1981.

Falwell, Jerry, ed. *The Fundamentalist Phenomenon: The Resurgence of Conservative Christianity.* Garden City, N.Y.: Doubleday, 1981.

Hodgson, Godfrey. *The World Turned Right Side Up: A History of the Conservative Ascendancy in America.* Boston: Houghton Mifflin, 1997.

Hoeveler, J. David. *Watch on the Right: Conservative Intellectuals in the Reagan Era.* Madison: University of Wisconsin Press, 1991.

Rothenberg, Randall. *The Neoliberals: Creating the New American Politics.* New York: Simon & Schuster, 1984.

Consumer culture

The affluence and productivity of the 1950s produced a U.S. culture strongly influenced by a desire for consumer goods. As the gross national product skyrocketed from $318 billion to $488

Commerce defies every wind •
outrides every tempest • invades every zone •
SHIPS FOR VICTORY

A World War II propaganda poster proclaims the virtues of commerce and consumerism. Conditioned by such messages to think of commerce as a point of national pride and the boon of the free world, Americans were primed to begin the rampant consumerism of the postwar period.

Now transistors replace tubes in Color TV
10 solid state modules like this eliminate hundreds of chances for human error...bring a whole new standard of reliability to color television.
This is America's most advanced Color TV—with solid state devices replacing all tubes but one, and innovations for reliability, tuning ease, and color reproduction not available on other color sets today.
Separate circuits that work without tubes are contained in 10 solid state modules like the one shown above. This construction principle, using solid state electronics, is designed for maximum operating reliability. It eliminates hundreds of chances for human error in manufacture, and is specified in virtually all space electronics and computer systems.
It was engineered to make the TV repair man a stranger at your house. Yet, reliable as it is, we made it simple to maintain. If anything ever goes wrong with any module, your service man can remove the old and plug in a new one in minutes.
There's more: Motorola's Visi-Trak tuning is easier to fine-tune right than black and white. You get instant sound and an automatically color-purified picture in about 5 seconds.
See it at your Motorola dealer's.
MOTOROLA
Leading through Creativity in Electronics
TIME NOV 3 1967
Motorola brings you America's first all-transistor Color TV

A color TV was just one of the many items that people were able to afford during the economic boom of the postwar years. Technology, too, was booming, as consumers benefited from scientific advances; it is not an accident that the television displays a picture of a rocket heading up into space.

billion in the 1950s, Americans had increased wealth and more products available for purchase. Companies tripled their budgets on advertising to convince Americans of their need for products they had never seen before. The first credit card, Diners Club, was released in 1950, helping Americans spend more on luxury goods, such as power lawn mowers, air conditioners, and cars. In the 1950s, Americans bought 58 million new cars alone.

The consumerism of the 1950s was rejected by both the Beat movement and the counterculture that followed in the 1960s. Hippies, for example, expressed their contempt for the consumer culture by wearing torn army surplus clothing. The consumer culture made a serious comeback in the 1980s, however. The yuppie (young urban professional) generation found a renewed interest in luxury items, such as imported luxury cars and home gym equipment. During the booming prosperity of the 1990s, Americans spent more than ever before, buying more and more powerful computers, home entertainment centers, fur coats, and ever-larger sports utility vehicles.

SEE ALSO

Beat movement; Hippies; Yuppies

FURTHER READING

Galbraith, John Kenneth. *The Affluent Society.* Boston: Houghton Mifflin, 1958.

Ritzer, George. *The McDonaldsization of Society: An Investigation into the Changing Character of Contemporary Social Life.* Thousand Oaks, Calif.: Pine Forge Press, 1996.

Schor, Juliet. *The Overspent American: Upscaling, Downshifting, and the New Consumer.* New York: Basic Books, 1998.

Containment doctrine

The key foundation of U.S. foreign policy during much of the cold war, the containment doctrine was based on an article that George F. Kennan wrote under the pseudonym "X" for the journal *Foreign Affairs* in 1947. The goal of containment was to stop communists from taking over governments in parts of the world considered important to the security of the United States. During the 45 years of the cold war, this included most countries in the world.

Containment was achieved by regional military pacts such as NATO, the selective distribution of foreign aid, secret CIA operations, and the threat of nuclear war. Although Kennan originally intended containment to be limited to select, strategic areas, U.S. foreign policymakers often misinterpreted his doctrine to mean containing the Soviets at every point, strategic or not.

SEE ALSO

Cold war; North Atlantic Treaty Organization (NATO)

FURTHER READING

Acheson, Dean G. *Present at the Creation: My Years at the State Department.* New York: Norton, 1969.

Hixon, Walter. *George F. Kennan: Cold War Iconoclast.* New York: Columbia University Press, 1989.

Kennan, George F. *George F. Kennan and the Origins of Containment, 1944–1946: The Kennan-Lukacs Correspondence.* Columbia: University of Missouri Press, 1997.

Council of Economic Advisors (CEA)

The Council of Economic Advisors (CEA), established by the Employment Act of 1946, is a part of the Executive Office of the President. The mission of the three-member council is to achieve "maximum employment, production, and purchasing power" for the United States. The CEA is to advise the President on economic issues and prepare the annual economic report of the President. The CEA has been influential in shaping the economic programs of all Presidents. In 1993, during Bill Clinton's administration, Laura D'Andrea Tyson became the first woman to be named chairperson of the CEA.

Counterculture

Many of the disillusioned young people of the 1960s replaced the values of their parents and "the Establishment" with the "sex, drugs, and rock and roll" associated with the counterculture. Historian Theodore Roszak coined the term *counterculture* to describe "a culture so radically disaffiliated from the mainstream assumptions of our society that it scarcely looks to many as a culture at all, but takes on the alarming appearance of a barbarian intrusion."

In Washington, D.C., in 1967, members of a communal house sit around a makeshift table made of boards and milk cartons to share food and ideas.

The counterculture grew out of the Beat movement of the 1950s, but it went much further in scope. Its adherents rejected the conformity and materialism of the 1950s, expressing their contempt by wearing tie-dyed shirts, old torn clothes bought from army-navy surplus stores, and shaggy beards and unkempt long hair; by establishing "crash pads" for runaways, free medical clinics, and "underground" newspapers; and by violating taboos against easy sex and illicit drugs.

The music of the 1960s reflected the counterculture's celebration of "peace and love." Such musical groups as the Grateful Dead; Jefferson Airplane; Big Brother and the Holding Company; and Crosby, Stills, and Nash performed to hundreds of thousands at events like the 1967 San Francisco Bay Area "Human Be-In," also known as "A Gathering of the Tribes," and the 1969 Woodstock Festival of Life in

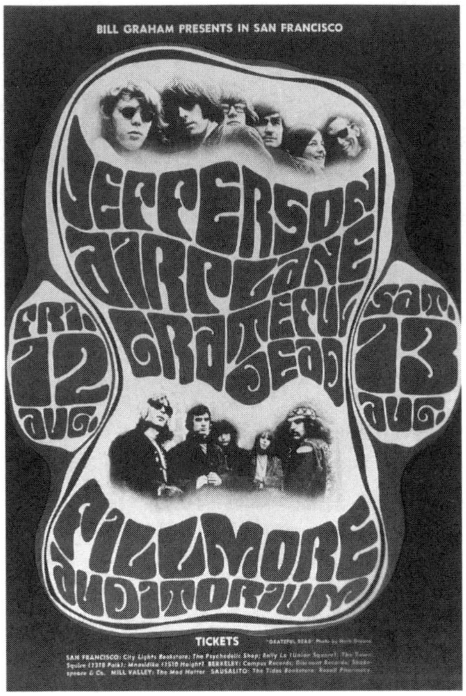

A poster advertises a concert of Jefferson Airplane and the Grateful Dead at the Fillmore in San Francisco. Music, particularly folk-like protest songs and electronic rock played by these two groups, was an important part of the counterculture.

New York State. Often viewed as the pinnacle of the counterculture, the Woodstock festival attracted more than 400,000 young people who endured three days of rain and mud, and openly engaged in drug use and sexual activity with surprisingly little violence. By 1969, however, such hippie meccas as Haight-Ashbury in San Francisco and the East Village in New York City overflowed with crime, violence, and an epidemic of serious drug problems. The end of the 1960s saw the end of the counterculture.

SEE ALSO

Beat movement; Drugs; Grateful Dead; Haight-Ashbury; Hippies; Rock and roll; Sexual revolution; Woodstock Festival (1969)

FURTHER READING

Berger, Bennett. *The Survival of a Counterculture.* Berkeley: University of California Press, 1981.

Bloom, Alexander. *Takin' It to the Streets.* New York: Oxford University Press, 1995.

Dickstein, Morris. *Gates of Eden: American Culture in the Sixties.* New York: Basic Books, 1977.

Rossman, Michael. *The Wedding Within the War.* Garden City, N.Y.: Anchor, 1971.

Cox, Archibald

- *Born: May 17, 1912, Plainfield, N.J.*
- *Accomplishments: Professor of law, Harvard University, 1946–61, 1965–84; Solicitor General of the United States, 1961–65; Watergate special prosecutor, 1973*

Forced by public pressure to name an independent special prosecutor to investigate the Watergate break-in and subsequent cover-up, in May 1973 Attorney General Elliot L. Richardson named Archibald Cox, a Harvard Law School professor. Working closely with a federal grand jury, Cox subpoenaed the recordings of conversations and meetings that Richard Nixon had secretly taped in the Oval Office.

Nixon refused to release the tapes and ordered Cox fired. The two highest officials in the Justice Department resigned rather than carry out Nixon's order; the third, Robert Bork, fired Cox on October 20, 1973. A firestorm of protest swept the nation, and Washington was deluged with telegrams condemning what was known as the "Saturday Night massacre." Nixon then had to allow the appointment of another special prosecutor, Leon Jaworski, who continued to press for the tapes that ultimately revealed Nixon's role in the cover-up and compelled the President to resign.

SEE ALSO

Nixon, Richard Milhous; Richardson, Elliot Lee; Watergate

FURTHER READING

Gormley, Ken, and Elliot Richardson. *Archibald Cox: Conscience of a Nation.* Reading, Mass.: Addison-Wesley, 1997.

Kutler, Stanley. *The Wars of Watergate: The Last Crisis of Richard Nixon.* New York: Knopf, 1990.

Cuban missile crisis of 1962

Just months after John F. Kennedy was inaugurated as President in 1961, he faced his first foreign policy crisis. A mounting fear of the communist presence in Cuba had led Kennedy to approve a CIA plan, originally conceived during Dwight Eisenhower's administration, to invade Cuba. In mid April 1961, some 1,500 anti-Castro exiles landed at the Bay of Pigs on Cuba's southern coast. It was hoped that their arrival would foster a general wave of revolt against the government, ultimately resulting in the overthrow of Fidel Castro. The invasion failed and Kennedy accepted the blame. But he did not halt his plans to oust Castro, leading to a major crisis in October 1962.

The Soviet Union had been sending military supplies to Castro since the Bay of Pigs invasion, and in the summer of 1962 Soviet premier Nikita Khrushchev ordered the construction of medium-range ballistic missile sites and the placement of missiles in Cuba. On October 14, American U-2 reconnaissance planes photographed a launchpad being built in Cuba that could fire missiles with a range of 1,000 miles. Still smarting from the Bay of Pigs disaster, believing his own credibility was at stake, and under pressure from Republicans for failing to depose Castro, Kennedy reacted strongly.

On October 22, Kennedy went on television to denounce the Soviets' "clandestine, reckless, and provocative threat to world peace" and to announce that the United States was imposing a "strict quarantine on all offensive military equipment" being shipped to Cuba. Placing U.S. military forces on full alert, Kennedy warned Khrushchev that any missile launched on any nation in the Western Hemisphere would be regarded as an attack against the United States, which would facilitate a full retaliation against the Soviet Union. The President insisted that Khrushchev remove the missiles immediately under United Nations supervision.

A 1962 aerial photograph reveals where the Soviet Union had placed missiles in Cuba. When President John Kennedy insisted that the Soviets remove the missiles, the world was pushed to the brink of a nuclear war.

With the two superpowers on the brink of nuclear war, Khrushchev first responded by calling the U.S. naval blockade "outright banditry" and ordering Soviet technicians to continue working on the launchpads while Soviet ships steamed toward the blockade. Meanwhile, unaware that Soviet forces in Cuba already possessed functioning missiles and the authority to use tactical nuclear weapons, U.S. troops assembled in Florida, ready to invade Cuba. B-52 bombers armed with nuclear warheads took to the skies, and 200 naval ships patrolled the

Caribbean. This was the closest the two superpowers had ever come to nuclear war, and the whole world waited to see who would blink first.

Suddenly, on October 26, Khrushchev sent a long and emotional letter to Kennedy. Recognizing the futility of nuclear annihilation, Khrushchev agreed to remove or destroy the weapons in Cuba if Kennedy would withdraw the blockade and promise not to invade Cuba. Before the United States could respond to the premier's proposal, Kennedy received a more belligerent message from Khrushchev raising the stakes. Perhaps under pressure from his own military, Khrushchev said he would take out the missiles in Cuba only when the Americans removed their missiles from Turkey. Ironically, Kennedy had earlier ordered the removal of those missiles, but due to a bureaucratic foul-up they were still in Turkey.

That same day, a U.S. U-2 reconnaissance plane was shot down over Cuba. To remove the missiles in Turkey now was not an option for Kennedy, who was concerned with prestige and appearances. The possibility of nuclear war continued. Then the President's younger brother, Attorney General Robert Kennedy, suggested that Kennedy ignore Khrushchev's second letter and respond favorably to the first proposal. Kennedy took the suggestion and sent an appropriate letter to Khrushchev, promising the United States would not invade Cuba.

War was avoided and a chastened Kennedy and Khrushchev agreed to install a hot line between the White House and the Kremlin so that the two superpowers could communicate instantly in future crises. In the summer of 1963 the two nations began a tentative step-by-step relaxation of tensions and signed a treaty outlawing atmospheric and undersea nuclear testing, ushering in the first round of a new phase of the cold war—détente.

SEE ALSO

Bay of Pigs; Cold war; Kennedy, John Fitzgerald

FURTHER READING

Beschloss, Michael. *The Crisis Years: Kennedy and Khrushchev, 1960–1963.* New York: HarperCollins, 1991.

Chayes, Abram. *The Cuban Missile Crisis.* New York: Oxford University Press, 1974.

Fursenko, Aleksandr, and Timothy Naftali. *One Hell of a Gamble: Khrushchev, Castro, and Kennedy, 1958–1964.* New York: Norton, 1997.

May, Ernest R., and Philip D. Zelikow, ed. *The Kennedy Tapes: Inside the White House During the Cuban Missile Crisis.* Cambridge, Mass.: Harvard University Press, 1997.

Patterson, Thomas G. *Contesting Castro: The United States and the Triumph of the Cuban Revolution.* New York: Oxford University Press, 1994.

Daley, Richard J.

- *Born: May 15, 1902, Chicago, Ill.*
- *Accomplishments: Illinois state representative (Democrat), 1936–38; Illinois state senator, 1939–46; Cook County clerk, 1950–55; Mayor of Chicago, 1955–76*
- *Died: Dec. 20, 1976, Chicago, Ill.*

One of the last of the big-city political bosses, Richard J. Daley served as mayor of Chicago from 1955 to 1976; during that time he became a national figure in the Democratic party. His administration promoted urban renewal and overhauled the corrupt Chicago police department. Daley is most remembered, however, for his role as host to the 1968 Democratic National Convention.

Daley had vowed that as long as he was mayor there would be law and order, but demonstrations by antiwar protestors and unrestrained attacks on them by riot-helmeted police led to massive disorder in Chicago, fracturing the Democratic party, which helped elect Republican Richard M. Nixon as President. Although Connecticut senator Abraham Ribicoff accused Daley of allowing the Chicago police to use gestapo tactics and an official commission later termed the disorder a police riot, Daley remained popular with his white working-class supporters.

Richard Daley died in 1976, during his sixth consecutive term as mayor, but his two sons would continue to keep the family name politically prominent in the Democratic party of the 1990s, one as mayor of Chicago and the other as President Clinton's secretary of commerce.

SEE ALSO

Democratic National Convention (Chicago, 1968)

FURTHER READING

Sullivan, Frank. *Legend: The Only Inside Story of Mayor Richard J. Daley.* Chicago: Bonus Books, 1989.

Democratic National Convention (Chicago, 1968)

The chaos and violence of the tumultuous year of 1968 climaxed in Chicago during the Democratic National Convention, when bloody battles between protestors and police fractured the Democratic party and helped pave the way for Republican Richard M. Nixon's Presidential victory. As the Democrats prepared for their national convention, leaders of the Mobe (National Mobilization Committee to End the War in Vietnam) and the Yippies (Youth International party) outlined plans to protest against the party of President Lyndon B. Johnson and prospective nominee Hubert Humphrey. Democratic mayor Richard Daley responded to the demonstrators by denying them permits for rallies and marches until the last minute and by stating publicly that the Chicago police would deal harshly with protestors. As

Antiwar protesters file warily past lines of armed troops during the convention in Chicago. Protesters called for an end to U.S. involvement in Vietnam, and when the Democrats rejected an antiwar plank in their platform, rioting erupted in the streets.

a result, fewer than 10,000 of the 100,000 hoped-for demonstrators went to Chicago for the first big Yippie event, the "Festival of Life" (organized to offset the "Convention of Death").

Nevertheless, the mayor and his police force did not take lightly the antics of Yippies Abbie Hoffman and Jerry Rubin, who threatened to dump the hallucinogen LSD in the city's water supply and to run a pig for President as the Yippies' candidate. On August 25, police roughly dispersed more than 1,000 peaceful demonstrators from Lincoln Park using nightsticks and tear gas. On August 28, as convention delegates rejected an antiwar platform plank, the police again clubbed protestors until they were unconscious and shoved some through plate-glass windows. While participants chanted "the whole world is watching," television cameras broadcast these bloody images into the homes of 89 million Americans. When Senator Abraham Ribicoff of Connecticut protested the "gestapo tactics" of the police from the podium of the convention hall, television cameras recorded Mayor Daley shouting expletives at him. Humphrey won the party's nomination, but the violence in the streets hurt his campaign and contributed to his defeat by Richard Nixon in November.

SEE ALSO

Chicago Seven; Daley, Richard J.; National Mobilization Committee to End the War in Vietnam; Youth International party (Yippies)

FURTHER READING

Farber, David. *Chicago '68*. Chicago: University of Chicago Press, 1988.
Mailer, Norman. *Miami and the Siege of Chicago*. New York: World, 1968.
Miller, James. *Democracy Is in the Streets: From Port Huron to the Siege of Chicago*. New York: Simon & Schuster, 1987.
Unger, Irwin, and Debi Unger. *Turning Point: 1968*. New York: Scribners, 1988.

Détente

Détente refers to periods of relaxed tensions between the Soviet Union and the United States during the cold war. Although such a period followed the Cuban missile crisis of 1962, the term *détente* is most commonly applied to the period beginning in 1972 when President Richard M. Nixon visited the secretary-general of the Soviet Communist party, Leonid Brezhnev, in Moscow on May 22 and proclaimed, "There must be room in this world for two great nations with different systems to live together and work together." Nixon was the first U.S. President to visit Moscow. He and Brezhnev signed several agreements leading to arms limits and cooperation in commerce and space exploration.

Late in 1974, President Gerald Ford met with Brezhnev at Vladivostok in Siberia and accepted the framework for another arms-control accord that was to serve as the basis for the second Strategic Arms Limitation Treaty (SALT II). Although President Jimmy Carter signed the agreement, he shelved it in 1979 following the Soviet invasion of Afghanistan; he also suspended grain shipments to the Soviet Union and campaigned for an international boycott of the 1980 Olympics, scheduled for Moscow.

President Gerald Ford meets with Soviet General Secretary Leonid Brezhnev in Vladivostok in 1974 to work out an arms control agreement.

After six years of no face-to-face talks between the leaders of the United States and the Soviet Union, President Ronald Reagan and newly elected Soviet President Mikhail Gorbachev met in Geneva on November 19, 1985, for a series of meetings that led to various agreements on cultural and scientific exchanges. Nearly a year later they met again in Reykjavik, Iceland, and again in Washington on December 9, 1987. There Gorbachev and Reagan signed a historic agreement to destroy their intermediate-range (300 to 3,000 miles) nuclear missiles and allow on-site inspections by each side to verify compliance. It was a major step toward the end of the four-decade arms race between the Soviet Union and the United States.

SEE ALSO

Camp David peace talks; Carter, James Earl, Jr. ("Jimmy"); Ford, Gerald Rudolph; Nixon, Richard Milhous; Reagan, Ronald Wilson;

FURTHER READING

Cahn, Anne Hessing. *Killing Détente: The Right Attacks the CIA.* University Park: Pennsylvania State University Press, 1998.

Young, John W. *The Longman Companion to Cold War and Détente 1941–91.* White Plains, N.Y.: Longman, 1993.

Detroit race riot (1967)

In 1967, Detroit became the site of the bloodiest race riot in the five-year wave of violence and upheaval known as the long, hot summers of 1964–68. Triggered by a series of clashes between black residents and white police, the Detroit riots left 43 dead, more than 1,000 wounded, $500 million in property destroyed, and 14 square miles gutted by fire. Although the Kerner Commission, which President Johnson assigned to study this and the other riots, blamed racism, poverty, and police brutality and called for increased social spending, the municipal governments in Detroit and elsewhere responded primarily by strengthening police enforcement.

SEE ALSO

Kerner Commission (National Advisory Commission on Civil Disorders); Race riots

FURTHER READING

Fine, Sidney. *Violence in the Model City: Race Relations, the Cavanagh Administration, and the Detroit Race Riot of 1967.* Ann Arbor: University of Michigan Press, 1989.

Hersey, John. *The Algiers Motel Incident.* New York: Knopf, 1968.

Locke, Hubert. *The Detroit Riot of 1967.* Detroit: Wayne State University Press, 1969.

Dewey, Thomas E.

- *Born: Mar. 24, 1902, Owosso, Mich.*
- *Accomplishments: Manhattan, N.Y., district attorney, 1937–38; Governor of New York, 1942–54; Republican candidate for President, 1944, 1948*
- *Died: Mar. 16, 1971, Bal Harbour, Fla.*

Thomas E. Dewey twice ran unsuccessfully for President, once against Franklin Delano Roosevelt in 1944 and again in 1948 against Harry S. Truman. The 1948 campaign is best

This cartoon shows a confident Thomas Dewey reviewing poll results with Harry Truman. Although pollsters were convinced Dewey would win the 1948 Presidential election, in fact Truman pulled ahead.

Thomas Dewey faces a phalanx of radio microphones as he tries to explain his loss.

known for the incorrect newspaper headlines proclaiming "Dewey Beats Truman"—the result of pollsters missing the last-minute surge of the Truman campaign. Dewey was so certain he would beat Truman that he ran an uninspired campaign consisting of bland appeals for national unity. But his strategy backfired, and he came off as smug and aloof.

In 1952 Dewey played a major role in securing the Republican Presidential nomination for Dwight D. Eisenhower; after that he retired from politics and practiced law in New York City.

SEE ALSO

Truman, Harry S.

FURTHER READING

Smith, Richard Norton. *Thomas E. Dewey and His Times.* New York: Simon & Schuster, 1982.

Dirksen, Everett McKinley

- *Born: Jan. 4, 1896, Pekin, Ill.*
- *Accomplishments: U.S. representative (Republican–Ill.), 1933–49; U.S. senator (Republican–Ill.), 1951–69*
- *Died: Sept. 7, 1969, Washington, D.C.*

Known as the "Wizard of Ooze," Everett Dirksen employed his eloquent, deep, baritone voice, as well as his skill at legislative maneuvering, to great effect as the Republican minority leader in the Senate.

For much of his congressional career, Dirksen was a mainstay of the conservative coalition of Republicans and southern Democrats who supported high levels of defense spending and a firm anticommunist foreign policy; he sided with business interests on most domestic issues. He enjoyed a particularly close working relationship with Democratic majority leader Lyndon Johnson. After the assassination of President John F. Kennedy on November 22, 1963, President Johnson persuaded Dirksen to get the Republicans to join with northern Democrats and break the southern filibuster that was preventing a vote on the 1964 civil rights bill. "Nothing," Dirksen said, quoting Victor Hugo, "is so powerful as an idea whose time has come."

Everett McKinley Dirksen in 1967, two years before his death.

Dirksen then cooperated with Johnson in 1965 to provide bipartisan support for the Voting Rights Act. However, the race riots and "white backlash" (the 1960s term applied to white resentment against civil rights gains for African Americans) that followed changed Dirksen's mind, and he took no action to prevent a filibuster that killed the administration's next civil rights bill.

SEE ALSO

Johnson, Lyndon Baines; Voting Rights Act (1965)

FURTHER READING

MacNeil, Neil. *Portrait of a Public Man.* New York: World, 1970.

Schapsmeier, Edward L., and Frederick H. Schapsmeier. *Dirksen of Illinois: Senatorial Statesman.* Champaign: University of Illinois Press, 1985.

Dole, Robert J. ("Bob")

- *Born: July 22, 1923, Russell, Kans.*
- *Accomplishments: U.S. representative (Republican–Kans.), 1961–69; U.S. senator (Republican–Kans.), 1969–96; Republican candidate for President, 1996*

An infantryman in World War II, Bob Dole was so severely wounded that he lost the use of an arm and took more than a year to recuperate. He made his mark in Congress as a partisan opponent of Lyndon Johnson's Great Society. A conservative Republican in the House, he voted against the antipoverty program, the creation of Medicare and Medicaid, federal aid to education, and virtually everything else proposed by the Democrats except the civil rights bills of 1964 and 1965.

After winning election to the Senate in 1968, Dole became an outspoken supporter of President Richard Nixon's legislative proposals. The President rewarded him with the chairmanship of the Republican National Committee in 1970 but replaced him with George Bush in 1972. Nevertheless, Dole stood by Nixon throughout the Watergate scandal.

In 1976, when Dole ran with Gerald Ford as the Republican party's Vice Presidential candidate, his excessively bitter, divisive attacks on the opposition provoked much media criticism. He sought the Republican Presidential nomination in 1980 but lost to Ronald Reagan and again in 1988, losing to George Bush.

Dole finally captured the nomination in 1996. He resigned as majority leader of the Senate to campaign against Democrat Bill Clinton but lost in the November election (Dole received 40.71 percent of the vote to Clinton's 49.24 percent). After the election he retired from politics.

FURTHER READING

Dole, Robert J. *Great Political Wit: Laughing (Almost) All the Way.* New York: Doubleday, 1998.
Dole, Robert J. *Unlimited Partners.* New York: Simon & Schuster, 1996.
Thompson, Jake H. *Bob Dole: The Republicans' Man for All Seasons.* New York: Donald I. Fine, 1996.

Drugs

Drugs became a serious problem in U.S. culture in the 1960s and remain a major concern 30 years later. By the end of the 1960s, more than half of U.S. college students reported smoking marijuana. A smaller number also reported using LSD and mescaline, both mind-altering drugs. Drug use was celebrated by the counterculture in literature, music, and movies. Drug use has affected U.S. culture, economy, and even foreign policy. The 1989 U.S. invasion of Panama was undertaken to stop President Manuel Noriega's drug trafficking and deals with Colombia's cocaine producers.

By the 1980s, drug use was prevalent in mainstream U.S. culture as well, with some yuppies (young, urban professionals), celebrities, and athletes moving from marijuana to stronger drugs, such as cocaine. Drug dealing became a risky way to make fast money, and was punished by harsh sentencing; nonetheless, a relatively large number of teenagers, especially from inner cities, began dealing drugs as an escape from minimum-wage jobs. Even

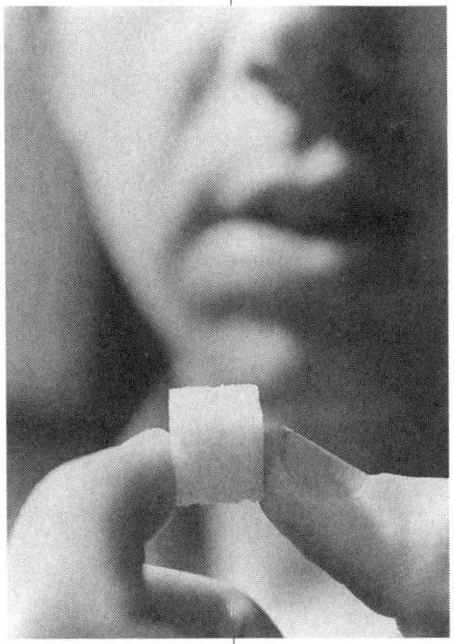

LSD, a popular counterculture drug in the 1960s, was a liquid that was often dripped onto sugar cubes; to "trip" (as the experience of taking LSD was called) the user would eat the sugar.

children as young as eight and nine years old were paid $100 a day to be lookouts for neighborhood dealers.

In the 1980s the first "drug czar" was appointed by President Ronald Reagan to help fight the "war on drugs," and many school districts initiated "Just say no" programs. However, the use of heroin, cocaine, and crack, a cocaine derivative, continued. Fights over drug-dealing turf spurred gang shoot-outs, and there were 387 drug-related deaths in Los Angeles in 1987 alone. The sharing of intravenous needles for drugs spread AIDS. Following in Reagan's footsteps, President George Bush also called for action against drugs, which he called our gravest domestic threat. His program emphasized trying to stop drugs at the nation's borders and handing down severe, long-term prison sentences for both drug sellers and drug dealers. While drug use declined significantly among the white, middle class in the 1990s, its widespread use in poor urban neighborhoods, where it was doing the most severe damage, showed little sign of abating.

SEE ALSO

Bush, George Herbert Walker; Counterculture; Reagan, Ronald Wilson; Yuppies

FURTHER READING

Kronenwetter, Michael. *Drugs in America: The Users, the Suppliers, the War on Drugs*. Issues for the 90s Series. Parsippany, N.J.: Silver Burdett Press, 1990.

Lee, Martin, and Bruce Shlain. *Acid Dreams*. New York: Grove, 1985.

Scarpitti, Frank, and Susan Datesman, eds. *Drugs and the Youth Culture*. Beverly Hills: Sage, 1980.

Wolfe, Tom. *The Electric Kool-Aid Acid Test*. New York: Bantam, 1969.

Dulles, Allen

- *Born: Apr. 7, 1893, Watertown, N.Y.*
- *Accomplishments: Deputy director, CIA, 1951–53; director, CIA, 1953–61*
- *Died: Jan. 29, 1969, Washington, D.C.*

Under President Dwight D. Eisenhower, Allen Dulles, the genial yet equally anticommunist brother of the zealous secretary of state, John Foster Dulles, rose from second in command to chief of the Central Intelligence Agency. A veteran of the wartime Office of Strategic Services (OSS), Allen Dulles had had extensive experience running covert operations during World War II, and he enhanced the CIA's capacity for cloak-and-dagger operations, involving it in the overthrow of governments in Iran (1953) and Guatemala (1954), both of which were considered hostile to U.S. interests.

These coups convinced the White House that the CIA was an inexpensive, clandestine, decisive weapon to deploy in the cold war. A congressional committee agreed, concluding in 1955 that "there are no rules" in the cold

John Foster Dulles (right) greets his brother, Allen, upon returning to the United States from a UN meeting in Paris.

war game and "acceptable norms of conduct do not apply." The CIA expanded rapidly in the 1950s and conducted major operations in Indonesia, Japan, Vietnam, and the Belgian Congo (now Zaire). President John F. Kennedy reappointed Dulles director of the CIA to affirm his own anticommunist credentials, then fired him after the failure of the CIA-trained army of Cuban exiles at the Bay of Pigs on April 17, 1961.

SEE ALSO

Bay of Pigs; Central Intelligence Agency (CIA)

FURTHER READING

Bissell, Richard M., Jr. *Reflections of a Cold Warrior: From Yalta to the Bay of Pigs.* New Haven, Conn.: Yale University Press, 1996.

Grose, Peter. *Gentleman Spy: The Life of Allen Dulles.* Boston: Houghton Mifflin, 1994.

Jeffreys-Jones, Rhodri. *The CIA and American Democracy.* New Haven, Conn.: Yale University Press, 1989.

Dulles, John Foster

- *Born: Feb. 25, 1888, Washington, D.C.*
- *Accomplishments: Secretary of State, 1953–59*
- *Died: May 24, 1959, Washington, D.C.*

The grandson of one secretary of state (John W. Foster, in Benjamin Harrison's administration) and the nephew of another (Robert Lansing, in Woodrow Wilson's), John Foster Dulles served in that position from the inauguration of President Dwight Eisenhower until his death from cancer in 1959. An international attorney who helped establish the United Nations in 1945 and authored the Japanese peace treaty of 1952, Dulles was the chief Republican spokesman on foreign affairs.

Critical of the reactive and defensive containment policy of Harry Truman's administration, Dulles believed that the United States should take the initiative in "rolling back" Soviet gains in Eastern Europe, in "liberating" their captive peoples, and in "unleashing" Chiang Kai-shek, the former leader of China who had fled to Taiwan (Formosa) against the Chinese communists.

A stern Presbyterian moralist whose humorlessness led some to picture him as "Dull, Duller, Dulles," the secretary of state publicly emphasized the necessity of "brinkmanship"—the need to risk war rather than back down. He threatened the Soviet Union with "massive retaliation" and condemned neutralism in the cold war as "immoral." When the Egyptian nationalist Gamal Abdel Nasser declared neutrality in the cold war, Dulles canceled a loan the United States had offered to build the Aswan Dam.

Following the Suez Canal crisis in 1956, Dulles and Dwight Eisenhower's administration outlined the Eisenhower Doctrine, promising to send aid to any Middle East nation threatened by international communism. Privately, however, Dulles recognized the lessening of Soviet bellicosity after the death of Joseph Stalin. He advocated negotiations with the Russians, adopted a cautious approach to the use of nuclear weapons, and essentially accepted and maintained the containment policy of Truman.

Dulles helped keep the United States out of war for six years, yet his aggressive anticommunism in the Third World (that is, the developing nations not allied with either the United States or the Soviet Union) prepared the ground for U.S. crises in Cuba and Vietnam.

SEE ALSO

Cold war; Containment doctrine; Eisenhower, Dwight David; Eisenhower Doctrine; Korean War; Suez crisis (1956); Vietnam War

FURTHER READING

Divine, Robert. "John Foster Dulles: What You See Is What You Get." *Diplomatic History* 15 (Spring 1991): 277-285.
Immerman, Richard, ed. *John Foster Dulles and the Diplomacy of the Cold War.* Princeton, N.J.: Princeton University Press, 1990.
Marks, Frederick. *Power and Peace: The Diplomacy of John Foster Dulles.* Westport, Conn.: Praeger, 1993.

Dylan, Bob (Robert Zimmerman)

- *Born: May 24, 1941, Hibbing, Minn.*
- *Accomplishments: Songwriter and musician*

Often cited as the musical voice of his generation, Bob Dylan spanned the genres of folk and rock music to express the idealism and rebelliousness of 1960s youth. At first, Dylan modeled himself after the radical folk singer Woody Guthrie, denouncing war, racism, and injustice in his early music. His "Blowin' in the Wind" became an anthem of the civil rights movement.

In the mid-1960s, however, Dylan shifted away from folk music and political protest, composing rock songs about personal feelings and drugs, and capturing the mood of the youthful drug culture. Dylan never again made music that spoke to as many people as the music he produced during his 1960s peak, but he has continued to write music, produce albums, and perform in concert; his works are studied in university classes and dissected in doctoral dissertations, and he has become a legend.

In 1966, at the beginning of his long career, Bob Dylan performs at the Olympia Theatre in Paris.

SEE ALSO

Counterculture

FURTHER READING

Benson, Carl, ed. *The Bob Dylan Companion.* New York: Schirmer, 1998.
Dylan, Bob. *Lyrics, 1962–1996.* New York: Villard, 1997.
Shelton, Robert. *No Direction Home: The Life and Music of Bob Dylan.* New York: Morrow, 1986.

Earth Day

Earth Day, a day set aside to emphasize the dangers to the planet from environmental problems, began in 1970 as the brainchild of Senator Gaylord Nelson (Democrat–Wis.) and Representative Paul N. McCloskey, Jr. (Republican–Calif.). On April 22, 1970, some 20 million Americans gathered in parks, planted trees, and staged demonstrations to highlight their concern for the

Marchers celebrate the first Earth Day in Washington, D.C., in 1970.

damage being done to the environment. Their goal was to teach Americans the importance of "living lightly on the earth." President Richard Nixon acknowledged the environmental movement's growing strength by agreeing to the establishment of the Environmental Protection Act in 1970 and by signing into law the Clean Air Act (1970), Clean Water Act (1972), Pesticide Control Act (1972), and Endangered Species Act (1973). Earth Day has continued, and each year on April 22 millions of people from more than 140 countries participate in activities to heighten public awareness of such environmental matters as pollution, toxic wastes, and dwindling resources.

SEE ALSO

Environmental movement

FURTHER READING

Oelschlaeger, Max, ed. *After Earth Day: Continuing the Conservation Effort.* Denton: University of North Texas Press, 1992.

O'Riordan, Timothy, et al. "The Legacy of Earth Day: Reflections at a Turning Point." *Environment* (April 1995): 6–21.

Stefoff, Rebecca. *The American Environmental Movement.* New York: Facts on File, 1995.

Eastland, James O.

- *Born: Nov. 18, 1904, Doddsville, Miss.*
- *Accomplishments: U.S. senator (Democrat–Miss.), 1942–78*
- *Died: Feb. 19, 1986, Forest, Miss.*

Mississippi Senator James O. Eastland defended white supremacy, attacked communists and liberals, and attempted to block civil rights legislation during his 36 years in office. As chairman of the powerful Senate Judiciary Committee during the 1960s, Eastland tried to block major civil rights bills, which made it through Congress only by bypassing his committee.

Eastland spoke of African Americans as "an inferior race" and pledged to keep them separate from whites in public accommodations. Following the *Brown* decision of the Supreme Court in 1954, which declared segregated schooling unconstitutional, he counseled white southerners to resist desegregation measures. He opposed President John Kennedy's New Frontier and President Lyndon Johnson's Great Society programs and symbolized the diehard southern political opposition to civil rights for African Americans.

FURTHER READING

Hunter, Marjorie. Obituary. *New York Times,* February 20, 1986, p. D-23.

Economic Opportunity Act (1964)

The major salvo in Lyndon B. Johnson's War on Poverty, the Economic Opportunity Act of 1964 appropriated $1 billion to fight poverty in America and established the Office of Economic Opportunity. This office coordinated such antipoverty programs as the Job Corps, to teach marketable skills and provide work experience for young people; Project Head Start, to prepare preschoolers from low-income families for grade school; Volunteers in Service to America (VISTA), to place volunteer social workers in economically depressed areas; Upward Bound, to help low-income high school students prepare for college; the Model Cities program, to channel federal funds to upgrade housing and health in targeted neighborhoods; and the Community Action Program, to encourage the maximum feasible participation by the poor themselves on antipoverty governing boards.

The War on Poverty, along with a rising gross national product, helped reduce the number of Americans living in poverty from 25 percent of the population in 1962 to 11 percent in 1973. It did little, however, to reduce poverty in rural areas or among women and children in female-headed families, and it did not discourage the south-to-north migration of the poor that was already overwhelming northern urban areas.

SEE ALSO

Great Society; Johnson, Lyndon Baines; War on Poverty

Eisenhower Doctrine

Following the Suez crisis of 1956—when President Dwight D. Eisenhower forced the British, French, and Israelis to end their invasion of Egypt, and Egypt took possession of the Suez Canal and invited the Soviet Union to build the Aswan Dam—the President proclaimed the Eisenhower Doctrine in March 1957 to protect American interests. The United States would intervene in the Middle East, he declared, if any government threatened by a communist takeover asked for help.

The next month, Eisenhower ordered the U.S. Sixth Fleet to the eastern Mediterranean following rioting in Jordan, and in 1958 he ordered U.S. troops to Lebanon to quell an internal political dispute that the United States feared might be exploited by the communists. The U.S. forces withdrew after the situation stabilized later that year.

SEE ALSO

Eisenhower, Dwight David; Suez crisis (1956)

Eisenhower, Dwight David

- *Born: Oct. 14, 1890, Denison, Tex.*
- *Accomplishments: Commander, Allied forces in Europe, 1942–45; 34th President of the United States, 1953–61*
- *Died: Mar. 28, 1969, Washington, D.C.*

Immensely popular during and after his two Presidential terms, Dwight D. Eisenhower epitomized the hopes and concerns of 1950s America. A 1915 graduate of the U.S. Military Academy at West Point, "Ike," as he was called, went on to lead the U.S. invasions of North Africa (1942) and Western Europe (1944) and to emerge from World War II as an inspirational figure of heroic stature.

A moderate courted by both Democrats and Republicans, Eisenhower easily won the Presidency in 1952 on the Republican ticket with Richard Nixon as his running mate. Ike provided the sense of security and unity that Americans yearned for. With his unbeatable combination of warmth and authority, Eisenhower trounced Democrat Adlai Stevenson for a second time in 1956. Eisenhower's smile, wrote one commentator, "was also a philosophical statement. It was a smile of infinite reassurance," promising benevolence and stability.

In domestic matters, Eisenhower sought a middle-of-the-road course, reducing government spending and taxes yet utilizing the powers of the federal government to stimulate the economy while containing inflation. He described himself as "conservative when it comes to money and liberal when it comes to human beings." More pragmatic than ideological, he labeled his credo "dynamic conservatism" and "modern Republicanism," and he altered his economic program as circumstances warranted.

In both 1953 and 1957, Eisenhower abandoned his commitment to a balanced budget and increased spending on public works projects to end recessions. Working with a Democratic-controlled Congress, he extended Social Security benefits, increased the minimum wage and funding for public housing for low-income families, approved the construction of the St. Lawrence Seaway and the interstate highway system, and established the Department of Health, Education, and Welfare.

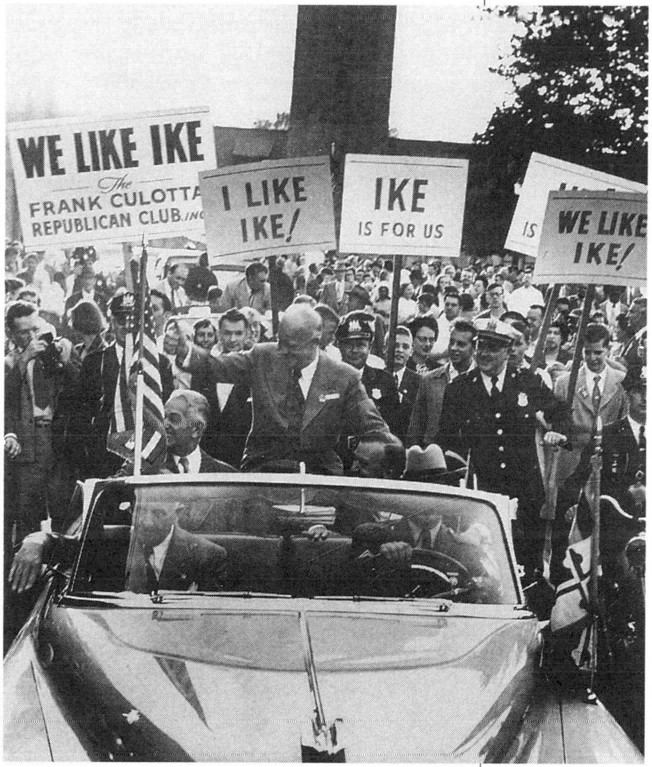

Dwight Eisenhower campaigns for the Presidency from an open car in Baltimore, Maryland, in 1952. The public loved Eisenhower and he won two terms.

Eisenhower proved more cautious in dealing with McCarthyism—the "witch hunt" spearheaded by Senator Joseph McCarthy to root out communists in government and purge the nation of communist influences—and the civil rights movement. Instead of challenging the accusations of McCarthy, Eisenhower waited for McCarthy to destroy himself. This happened during the televised Senate army hearings in 1954, which turned public opinion against the Wisconsin senator. McCarthyism, Ike then gloated, had become "McCarthywasism."

Although not a racist, Eisenhower refused to endorse the Supreme Court's 1954 *Brown* decision, which declared segregated education unconstitutional, or to force white southerners to accept the Court's ruling. Ike claimed, "I don't believe you can change the hearts of men with laws or decisions." In 1957,

Eisenhower visits Korea in December 1952. The conflict ended the next year.

however, Arkansas governor Orval Faubus forced Eisenhower's hand when he used the state's National Guard to defy a federal court order allowing nine black students to attend Little Rock's previously segregated Central High School. In response to Faubus's challenge to federal authority, Eisenhower denounced this "disgraceful occurrence" and placed the Arkansas National Guard under federal control. He also ordered a thousand paratroopers into Little Rock to protect the African-American students for the rest of the school year.

Despite personal reservations, Eisenhower signed the civil rights acts of 1957 and 1960. These measures established the Civil Rights Commission, created a new Civil Rights Division in the Justice Department that could seek injunctions to prevent interference with the right to vote, and provided for federal court referees to register African Americans where a court found a pattern and practice of racial discrimination.

In foreign affairs, Eisenhower maintained the containment policy of the Truman years while seeking a thaw in the cold war. As his first priority, he went to Korea in December 1952 to try to settle the war that had begun there in 1950. Ike later hinted that he might use nuclear weapons in Korea if negotiations remained stalled. The armistice signed on July 23, 1953, ended the fighting but left Korea divided and its political future unresolved. Eisenhower's strategy of threatening nuclear war in Korea, called "brinkmanship" by his secretary of state, John Foster Dulles, offered the budget-minded Eisenhower administration "more bang for the buck" and became an important part of U.S. defense strategy in the 1950s.

This tactic led to vast increases in the U.S. nuclear arsenal and a reduction of conventional forces. But fearing an actual nuclear war, Eisenhower and Dulles did nothing to deter the Soviet Union from brutally crushing insurrections in both East Germany (1953) and Hungary (1956).

Despite Dulles's public talk of "massive retaliation," the Eisenhower administration preferred to use the Central Intelligence Agency (CIA) to protect U.S. interests abroad. In 1953 the CIA overthrew a popularly elected Iranian government sympathetic to the Soviet Union and installed a pro-Western shah in its place. A second CIA operation in 1953 helped the Ferdinand Marcos regime come to power in the Philippines. The following year CIA agents led a force of Guatemalans in staging a military coup against a leftist government that had nationalized 225,000 acres of land owned by the United Fruit Company, a U.S.–owned enterprise.

Fearful of losing Vietnam to communism, and believing that doing so would have a "domino effect," causing all of Asia to fall to communism, Eisenhower increased the flow of U.S. assistance to the French in their fight to keep control of their colony in Indochina. After the French were defeated by the communists, the United States refused to accept the 1954 Geneva peace accords calling for a unified Vietnam after national elections, to be held in 1956. Certain that this would mean a communist victory, Eisenhower instead installed the fiercely anticommunist Ngo Dinh Diem as president of an independent South Vietnam. The CIA trained Diem's armed forces and secret police, helped eliminate his political opposition, and assisted him in blocking the election to reunify Vietnam that the Geneva agreements had specified.

The Eisenhower administration's commitment to "sink or swim with Ngo Dinh Diem" would have fateful consequences in the 1960s as the United States became more deeply involved in the effort to keep South Vietnam independent and non-communist and eventually became embroiled in the war there. The shooting down of a CIA U-2 spy plane on a reconnaissance mission over the Soviet Union in May 1960, moreover, ended a period of improving Soviet-American relations.

In Eisenhower's farewell address, he warned against the disastrous consequences of an unchecked nuclear arms race and against the "acquisition of unwarranted influence . . . by the military-industrial complex." He did not want to see the military and the arms industry gain too much power over civilian life in America.

Most scholars now give Eisenhower's Presidency high marks. He restored a dignity to the White House that had been lost in Truman's acrimonious relations with the Congress and the Republican party, and harmony to the nation by presiding over an economic boom while keeping the United States out of a major war.

SEE ALSO

Brown v. *Board of Education of Topeka, Kansas* (1954); Civil rights movement; Cold war; Containment doctrine; Dulles, Allen; Dulles, John Foster; Korean War; Little Rock, Arkansas, desegregation crisis (1957); McCarthyism; Military-industrial complex; Suez crisis (1956); Truman, Harry S.; U-2 crisis; Vietnam War

FURTHER READING

Ambrose, Stephen. *Eisenhower: Soldier and President.* New York: Simon & Schuster, 1990.

Bischof, Gunter, and Stephen E. Ambrose, eds. *Eisenhower: A Centenary Assessment.* Baton Rouge: Louisiana State University Press, 1995.

Broadwater, Jeff. *Eisenhower and the Anti-Communist Crusade.* Chapel Hill: University of North Carolina Press, 1992.

Greenstein, Fred. *The Hidden Hand Presidency.* New York: Basic Books, 1982.

Halberstam, David. *The Fifties.* New York: Villard Books, 1993.

Pickett, William. *Dwight David Eisenhower, An American Power.* Wheeling, Ill.: Harlan Davidson, 1995.

Warshaw, Shirley Anne, ed. *Reexamining the Eisenhower Presidency.* Westport, Conn.: Greenwood, 1993.

Elementary and Secondary Education Act of 1965

The Elementary and Secondary Education Act of 1965, part of President Lyndon B. Johnson's Great Society legislation, provided the first large-scale federal aid to education in U.S. history. The law earmarked more than $1 billion to assist public and parochial schools in buying textbooks and other educational materials and in establishing special education programs. With his first-grade teacher looking on, Johnson signed the measure in the dilapidated one-room schoolhouse he had once attended.

SEE ALSO

Great Society; Johnson, Lyndon Baines; War on Poverty

Ellison, Ralph

- *Born: Mar. 1, 1914, Oklahoma City, Okla.*
- *Accomplishments: Writer*
- *Major Works:* Invisible Man *(1952),* Shadow and Act *(1964),* Going to the Territory *(1986);* Juneteenth *(1999)*
- *Died: Apr. 16, 1994, New York, N.Y.*

Ralph Ellison's *Invisible Man* (1952), an allegorical novel of an African-American man's education in the South and eye-opening misadventures in a northern city, was judged by *Book Week* to be "the most distinguished single work" published in the United States between 1945 and 1965. With wit and bitter irony, Ellison captures important aspects of the black experience in his portrayal of the president of a black college, patterned after Booker T. Washington's Tuskegee Institute, and of black northern radicals, resembling the black nationalists and communists of New York City in the 1930s and 1940s. The novel illustrates both the efforts of African Americans to define themselves and the Anglo-American refusal to confront racial injustice. "I am invisible, understand," the narrator laments, "simply because people refuse to see me."

Ralph Ellison was not only a superb writer, he was also a teacher, lecturer, sculptor, photographer, and electrician. This formal portrait was used to publicize an appearance he made on public television.

Ellison wrote many essays and short stories both before and after *Invisible Man*, but he never published another novel. He had begun a second novel in the late 1950s but lost most of the manuscript in a house fire in 1967; he reconstructed some of it but it remained unfinished at his death. In 1999 some of the book was put together as a novel and published as *Juneteenth*.

Ellison was not only a writer but a scholar and a mentor to other African-American writers as well. He was one of the most important writers of his generation, and his *Invisible Man* made the African-American experience a bit more visible.

FURTHER READING

Ellison, Ralph. *Going to the Territory.* New York: Vintage Books, 1995.
Ellison, Ralph. *Invisible Man.* New York: Modern Library, 1952.
Ellison, Ralph. *Shadow and Act.* New York: Random House, 1964.
Watts, Jerry Gafio. *Heroism and the Black Intellectual: Ralph Ellison, Politics, and Afro-American Intellectual Life.* Chapel Hill, N.C.: University of North Carolina Press, 1994.

Employment Act of 1946

President Harry S. Truman proposed full-employment legislation in his 21-point message to Congress on September 6, 1945, in order to combat the expected postwar economic downturn. Although it was significantly modified by Congress before being signed into law by Truman on February 20, 1946, as the Employment Act of 1946, the bill made it the responsibility of the federal government to utilize its powers and resources to achieve maximum employment, production, and purchasing power.

Implied in the measure was acceptance of the principle that the federal government would spend more than it collected in taxes (called deficit spending) to spur a sluggish economy—an idea that was borrowed from the influential British economist John Maynard Keynes. The act also authorized the establishment of a Council of Economic Advisors to assist the President in formulating economic policy and a joint congressional committee to report on Presidential recommendations regarding maximum employment.

SEE ALSO

Council of Economic Advisors (CEA); Fair Deal; Keynesian economics; Truman, Harry S.

FURTHER READING

Bailey, Stephen K. *Congress Makes a Law: The Story Behind the Employment Act of 1946.* New York: Columbia University Press, 1950.

Endangered Species Act of 1973

Enthusiastically passed by Congress amid heightened environmental concern in 1973, this act to protect threatened wildlife species has produced mixed results. Most Americans support environmental protection, but not at the cost of a lower standard of living or restricted income growth. Environmental concern has thus surged and ebbed with the state of the economy. Strict enforcement of the act saved the bald eagle, the national symbol, from extinction, but the fate of other species, such as the northern spotted owl and the gnatcatcher, remain in doubt, because protecting their habitats means taking away land from the western timber and construction industries. Each year, the federal government continues to add another 50 or so species to its endangered list.

SEE ALSO

Environmental movement

FURTHER READING

Carpenter, Betsy. "Is He Worth Saving?" *U.S. News & World Report,* July 10, 1995, 43–46.
Galan, Mark, and A. Bruce Babbit. *There's Still Time: The Success of the Endangered Species Act.* Washington, D.C.: National Geographic Society, 1997.
Kohm, Kathryn, ed. *Balancing on the Brink of Extinction: The Endangered Species Act and Lessons for the Future.* Washington, D.C.: Island Press, 1991.

Energy crisis

The 1970s introduced Americans to the idea that there was a limit to the earth's energy resources. After World War II oil and gasoline were plentiful and cheap; Americans became used to the freedom to turn their thermostats up as far as they wanted to, and to take long drives without having to worry about being able to afford the gas. The Organization of Petroleum Exporting Countries (OPEC), a group of mostly Arab nations that controlled most of the oil exported to the West, had been founded in 1960, but it was not until 1973 that it made its power felt.

In 1973, in response to the United States's support of Israel during the Yom Kippur War, OPEC nations worked together to limit the amount of oil they exported. The oil embargo produced an immediate global shortage and a sharp rise in the cost of oil, and it accelerated the inflation already under way in the early 1970s. This led to several measures taken to help Americans conserve resources, including the passage of fuel-efficiency standards for cars, a national speed limit of 55 miles per hour set in 1975, the creation of the Department of Energy, and taxes on oil and gasoline consumption in 1977.

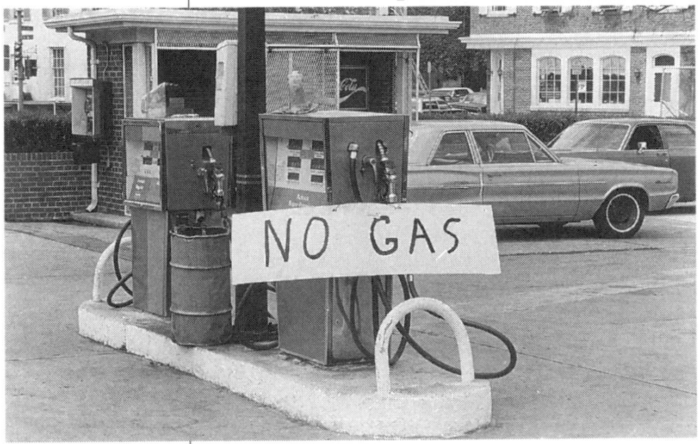

This sign is typical of the welcome that motorists faced as they attempted to buy gas at the height of the OPEC oil embargo.

These measures, as well as the efforts by Americans to lower their thermostats and reinsulate their homes, helped ease U.S. dependence on foreign oil. Nevertheless, renewed violence in the Middle East in 1979 produced a second major fuel shortage in the United States and another sharp price hike by OPEC, causing the cost of crude oil to nearly double and inflation to jump from 7.6 percent to 11.3 percent by year's end. When OPEC increased crude oil prices to more than $30 a barrel in 1979, gas prices rose from 30 cents to almost $1 a gallon.

SEE ALSO
Arab oil embargo

FURTHER READING

Feldman, David, ed. *The Energy Crisis: Unresolved Issues and Enduring Legacies.* Baltimore: Johns Hopkins University Press, 1996.

Kelley, Donald R., ed. *The Energy Crisis and the Environment.* New York: Praeger, 1997.

Parmet, Herbert S. *Richard Nixon and His America.* Boston: Little, Brown, 1990.

Engel v. *Vitale* (1962)

In the 1962 ruling *Engel* v. *Vitale,* the Supreme Court under Earl Warren declared prayer in public schools to be "a practice wholly inconsistent" with the First Amendment of the Constitution. In a 6-to-1 decision, the Court ruled in favor of the New York Civil Liberties Union and the parents of 10 students from Hyde Park, New York, who said that a nondenominational prayer recited each morning in their public schools contradicted their per-

In 1962, the year after Engel v. Vitale, *Madalyn Murray and her sons celebrate their Supreme Court victory as the reading of the Lord's Prayer is found to be unconstitutional.*

sonal religious beliefs. Even though participation in the prayer was voluntary, the Court ruled that the practice violated a clause of the First Amendment prohibiting Congress from making any law "respecting an establishment of religion."

SEE ALSO

Supreme Court; Warren Court

FURTHER READING

Dudley, Mark E. *Engel vs. Vitale (1962): Religion & the Schools.* New York: Twenty First Century Books, 1995.

Haas, Carol. *Engel vs. Vitale: Separation of Church and State.* Springfield, N.J.: Enslow, 1994.

Environmental movement

The upsurge of the modern environmental movement followed the publication of Rachel Carson's *Silent Spring* in 1962. That powerful book awakened Americans to the dangers that human activity posed to the natural environment, and other popular works by scientists Paul R. Erhlich and Barry Commoner alerted them to the ecological hazards of soaring world population growth and nuclear radiation. The establishment of new organizations, such as the Environmental Defense Fund (1967) and Greenpeace (1969), and environmental tragedies like the 1969 oil spill that fouled the beaches and killed wildlife in Santa Barbara, California, further heightened interest in environmental issues. Celebration of the first Earth Day, on April 22, 1970, made environmentalism a truly mass movement.

In its wake, Congress passed the Clean Air Act (1970) and Clean Water Act (1972), and created the Environmental Protection Agency (EPA) in 1970 to set and force pollution standards. In 1973 it enacted the Endangered Species Act to protect threatened wildlife. But as the economy worsened, environmentalism faded, only to be reawakened periodically by news of gross environmental degradation. In 1978, for example, reports that dangerous chemicals had been buried beneath the Love Canal in upper New York State led to numerous protests and the creation by Congress of a "superfund" to finance the cleanup of dangerous toxic waste sites. The need to evacuate 100,000 people the following year in the area surrounding a malfunctioning nuclear reactor on Three Mile Island, Pennsylvania, refueled concerns over nuclear power, causing the Nuclear Regulatory Commission to improve its inspection procedures and strengthen safety standards. Publicity about the dangers of ozone depletion in 1989 brought a cut in the production of chlorofluorocarbons, chemicals that destroy the atmosphere's ozone shield, which protects the earth from the sun's most dangerous rays. Also that year, intense public concern erupted after the U.S. tanker the Exxon *Valdez* spilled nearly 11 million gallons of crude oil into Alaska's Prince William Sound. This spill fouled nearly 1,800 miles of coastline and killed at least 10 percent of the

Members of the environmentalist organization Greenpeace demonstrate against Japanese whaling. They are in a small inflatable boat behind a huge factory ship that is hauling up a harpooned whale calf.

area's birds, fish, sea otters, and other wildlife.

Overall, the environmental movement can take pride in blocking numerous construction projects that would have imperiled the local ecology. It helped make the water supply in the United States the cleanest of any industrial nation. Federal regulations have also significantly reduced smog, smoke, and soot and have curbed automobile and industrial emissions while increasing fuel and appliance efficiency.

Although the U.S. economy grew by 50 percent between 1970 and 1995, energy usage increased by only 10 percent. At the same time, with just 2 percent of the world's population, the United States uses 24 percent of the world's energy, twice as much as western Europe. It also produces twice as much garbage as Europe, continuing to be a throwaway society that cannot be bothered to recycle, as well as a growth-oriented society that prizes economic prosperity over environmental protection. Neither President Ronald Reagan nor George Bush suffered politically when he gutted environmental regulations, nor has President Bill Clinton, despite his foot-dragging on the matter. Thus, half of all U.S. citizens live in counties that violate clean air standards, and some 4,000 lakes and rivers remain threatened by acid rain and toxic chemicals. A fundamental change in America's relationship to nature has not yet occurred.

SEE ALSO

Bush, George Herbert Walker; Carson, Rachel; Clean Air Act of 1963; Earth Day; Endangered Species Act of 1973; Water Quality Act of 1965; Water Quality Improvement Act of 1970

FURTHER READING

Archer, Jules. *To Save the Earth: The American Environmental Movement.* New York: Viking, 1998.

Dunlap, Riley E. *American Environmentalism: The U.S. Environmental Movement, 1970–1990.* Bristol, Pa.: Taylor & Francis, 1992.

Easterbrook, Gregg. *A Moment on the Earth: The Coming Age of Environmental Optimism.* New York: Penguin, 1995.

Hays, Samuel P. *Beauty, Health, and Permanence; Environmental Politics in the United States, 1955–1985.* New York: Cambridge University Press, 1985.

Keene, Ann T. *Earthkeepers: Observers and Protectors of Nature.* New York: Oxford University Press, 1994.

Equal Employment Opportunity Commission (EEOC)

The Equal Employment Opportunity Commission (EEOC) is a federal agency established by the Civil Rights Act of 1964 to eliminate discrimination in hiring based on race, religion, sex, age, or national origin. Since its creation, the duties of the commission have been expanded to ensure equal pay to men and women and to fight discrimination related to pregnancy. The EEOC also enforces the Americans with Disabilities Act, passed by Congress and signed by President George Bush in 1990. In companies with 25 or more employees this act bans job discrimination against the blind, deaf, mentally retarded, and physically impaired, as well as against those who are HIV positive or have cancer. It also requires that reasonable accommodations, such as wheelchair ramps, be made available to workers with disabilities.

SEE ALSO

Civil Rights Act of 1964; Civil rights movement; Great Society

Equal Rights Amendment (ERA)

First proposed in the 1920s, the Equal Rights Amendment (ERA) remained controversial throughout the 20th century. In 1972 Congress passed the ERA and sent it to the state legislatures for ratification, a requirement for any amendment to the Constitution. Twenty-eight states quickly ratified the amendment, which guaranteed that "equality of rights under the law shall not be denied or abridged by the United States or by any State on account of sex."

Following the Supreme Court's 1973 decision in *Roe* v. *Wade* striking down laws that made abortion a crime, the ratification process stalled as many anti-abortion or pro-life women joined Phyllis Schlafly's Stop the ERA campaign. She claimed that the ERA would abolish alimony, legalize homosexual marriages, and lead to unisex toilets. Her efforts helped keep the women's movement three states short of the necessary 38 needed for ratification. In October 1978 Congress granted a 39-month extension to proponents of ratification, but no more states ratified the amendment. The 10-year struggle for its adoption came to an end in 1982.

SEE ALSO

Abortion issue; Feminism; *Roe* v. *Wade* (1973)

FURTHER READING

Chafe, William H. *The Road to Equality.* New York: Oxford University Press, 1994.

Demonstrators in Washington, D.C., in 1977 hold a banner with the full text of the Equal Rights Amendment.

Leo, John. "Return of the ERA." *U.S. News & World Report,* December 18, 1995, 28.

Mansbridge, Jane J. *Why We Lost the ERA.* Chicago: University of Chicago Press, 1986.

Ervin, Sam J.

- *Born: Sept. 27, 1896, Morgantown, N.C.*
- *Accomplishments: U.S. representative (Democrat–N.C.), 1946–47; U.S. senator (Democrat–N.C.), 1954–74*
- *Died: Apr. 23, 1985, Winston-Salem, N.C.*

In February 1973, by a vote of 77 to 0, the Senate established the Select Committee on Campaign Activities to investigate abuses in the 1972 Presidential campaign. Among the incidents under investigation was the break-in at the offices of the Democratic National Committee in the Watergate complex, which had been done by men connected to President Richard Nixon's reelection effort. Folksy 76-year-old Democratic senator Sam Ervin ("I'm just a plain country lawyer") of North Carolina, an expert on constitutional law and a dogged investigator, chaired the committee.

During the televised hearings, Ervin's probing of witnesses exposed the "dirty tricks" of Nixon's operatives. The bombshell came when President Nixon's counsel, John Dean, accused Nixon of ordering and directing the Watergate cover-up and when another White House aide, Alexander Butterfield, disclosed that Nixon had installed a secret taping system in the White House.

Both the Ervin committee and Archibald Cox, who had been appointed Watergate special prosecutor on May 18, 1973, demanded that the tapes be turned over to them (through the legal process of subpoena). This set in motion a train of events that led to the release of the tapes and President Nixon's ultimate resignation from office.

SEE ALSO

Cox, Archibald; Nixon, Richard Milhous; Watergate

FURTHER READING

Dabney, Dick. *A Good Man: The Life of Sam J. Ervin.* Boston: Houghton Mifflin, 1976.

European Recovery Plan

SEE Marshall Plan

Fair Deal

Although President Harry S. Truman would later claim that the 21-point domestic program he sent to Congress in September 1945 marked the beginning of the Fair Deal, he did not actually use that phrase until his 1949 State of the Union address, when he said, "Every segment of our population and every individual has a right to expect from his government a fair deal." He saw it as a means of promoting greater economic opportunity for the mass of the people.

The President won extensions or enlargements of Democratic programs that had been enacted in the 1930s to counter the effects of the Great Depression, such as a higher minimum wage and increased price supports for farmers, more funds for public housing and slum clearance, and coverage for more people under Social Security. Few of his own proposals came to fruition, however. Despite Democratic majorities in

Congress, the conservative coalition that ruled the legislature turned down Truman's requests for national health insurance, federal aid to education, civil rights legislation, and repeal of the Taft-Hartley Act, which made unionizing new industries more difficult.

SEE ALSO

Employment Act of 1946; Truman, Harry S.

FURTHER READING

Donovan, Robert J. *Conflict and Crisis: The Presidency of Harry S. Truman, 1945–1948*. New York: Norton, 1977.

Donovan, Robert J. *Tumultuous Years: The Presidency of Harry S. Truman.* New York: Norton, 1982.

Hamby, Alonzo L. *Beyond the New Deal: Harry S. Truman and American Liberalism.* New York: Columbia University Press, 1973.

Federal Bureau of Investigation (FBI)

The Bureau of Investigation (renamed the Federal Bureau of Investigation in 1935) was created in 1908 but first came to prominence with its investigation of draft resisters and radical foreign-born activists during and after World War I. The FBI steadily grew under J. Edgar Hoover, who became its director in December 1924. Hoover significantly expanded the bureau's jurisdiction and powers following World War II, when it targeted suspected communists and their sympathizers. The bureau played a major role in the prosecutions of Alger Hiss—accused of being a secret communist in the 1930s and of having passed classified documents to the Soviet Union—and of Ethel and Julius Rosenberg, who were convicted of espionage and executed in 1953.

In the 1960s, under the guise of national security, the FBI engaged in the political surveillance of civil rights and antiwar protestors, amassing a total of more than 30,000 linear feet of files on individual citizens, which Hoover used to further the bureau's and his own power. After Watergate, Congress and the attorney general issued guidelines to prevent further illegal investigations and the intrusion into the private lives of U.S. citizens by the FBI. The bureau then shifted its focus to combating organized and white-collar crime, including a sting operation in 1980 that led to the indictment of several members of Congress on charges of accepting bribes in exchange for political favors. In the mid-1980s bureau efforts led to the arrests of more than a hundred top Mafia members.

The FBI played a crucial role in the 1990s in investigating the World Trade Center bombing in New York City and the crash of TWA flight 800.

SEE ALSO

Anticommunism; Hoover, J. Edgar; McCarthyism; Rosenberg case

FURTHER READING

Kovel, Joel. *Red Hunting in the Promised Land.* New York: Basic Books, 1994.

Kronenwetter, Michael. *The FBI and Law Enforcement Agencies of the United States.* Springfield, N.J.: Enslow, 1997.

Theoharis, Athan, and John Stuart Cox. *The Boss: J. Edgar Hoover and the Great American Inquisition.* Philadelphia: Temple University Press, 1988.

Turner, William W. *Hoover's F.B.I.* New York: Thunder's Mouth, 1993.

Federal Employee Loyalty program

In March 1947, President Harry S. Truman signed Executive Order 9835, thus establishing the Federal Employee Loyalty program, which aimed to find communists working for the federal government and remove them from their positions. Under the program, all government employees were subject to a loyalty check. Certain measures built into the program to protect the civil rights of individuals were rarely observed, and government employees were routinely accused of disloyalty without being given the right to face their accusers or be informed of the source of the information.

Between 1947 and 1951 local review boards forced nearly 3,000 government employees to resign and fired an additional 300 for alleged disloyalty. Meanwhile, no evidence of subversion or espionage was ever found.

SEE ALSO

McCarthyism

FURTHER READING

Freeland, Richard M. *The Truman Doctrine and the Origins of McCarthyism: Foreign Policy, Domestic Politics, and Internal Security, 1946–1948.* New York: Knopf, 1972.

Harper, Alan D. *The Politics of Loyalty: The White House and the Communist Issue, 1946–1952.* Westport, Conn.: Greenwood, 1969.

Theoharis, Athan. *Seeds of Repression: Harry S. Truman and the Origins of McCarthyism.* Chicago: Quadrangle, 1971.

Feminism

The postwar phase of the modern feminist movement is often considered to have begun with the publication of Betty Friedan's *The Feminine Mystique* in 1962, which detailed the unhappiness felt by many women trapped in roles that were too tightly defined. The spirit of revolution that characterized the 1960s in general created a new sense of self-awareness and activism among women.

In 1961 John F. Kennedy established the President's Commission on the Status of Women. Its first report, in 1963, showed that women suffered occupational discrimination similar to that of minorities. In 1963 women accounted for 51 percent of the population but constituted only 7 percent of its doctors and 4 percent of its lawyers.

Frustrated with the lack of advocacy from government agencies such as the Equal Employment Opportunity Commission (EEOC), Betty Friedan helped start the National Organization for Women (NOW). NOW is a civil rights advocacy group that has fought for gender equality and helped raise awareness of women's issues.

Ms. magazine, started by Gloria Steinem in 1972, has also helped bring feminist issues to mainstream U.S. culture.

"Women's libbers," as feminists were derisively called, worked to improve the conditions of women's lives by creating health-care clinics, day-care centers, and abortion counseling services. In August 1970, thousands of women across the country commemorated the 50th anniversary of the Nineteenth Amendment, which gave women the vote. Out of those meetings also came large groups of women dedicated to continuing the fight for equal employment opportunities and safe, legal abortions.

In 1973 the Supreme Court upheld a woman's right to abortion in *Roe* v. *Wade*. Other improvements in the lives of women followed: Women were issued credit in their own names, newspapers stopped listing jobs under "male" and "female" headings, and by 1970 some 40 percent of women had full-time jobs outside the home.

This book, first published in 1970, was designed to empower women with knowledge of their bodies, health, and sexuality. The Boston Women's Health Book Collective is still a leading women's advocacy group, and the book is still published; the 1998 edition is called *Our Bodies, Ourselves for the New Century.*

In the 1980s the feminist movement splintered across the spectrum from moderate to radical. The more radical wing saw the failure of the Equal Rights Amendment (ERA) in 1982 and the restriction of the availability of abortion throughout the 1980s as representative of women's status as second-class citizens. Some of them advocated measures to improve women's status, such as the legalization of prostitution or the abolition of marriage, that mainstream U.S. culture found disturbing. Others took a strong stand against pornography. Moderate feminists, represented by Betty Friedan's second book, *Second Stage* (1981), urged feminists to incorporate family issues and men's input into their agenda.

African-American women, too, spoke out in the 1980s. Some argued that because the feminist movement was mainly white and middle class it had failed to include their voices. In her 1981 book, *Ain't I a Woman: Black Women and Feminism,* bell hooks addressed black women's rights.

By the early 1990s, journalist Susan Faludi noted that feminism, in general, had become less and less popular with mainstream American media. In her best-selling 1991 book *Backlash: The Undeclared War Against American Women,* she described this reaction as "an attempt to retract the handful of small and hard-won victories that the feminist movement did manage to win for women." The same year, another feminist writer, Naomi Wolf, criticized the cultural standards of beauty imposed on American women in *The Beauty Myth.*

Divisions within the greater feminist movement continued throughout the 1990s. A new generation of "post-feminists" declared that the feminist movement had created a victimization attitude among women, and that most of the women's rights battles had already been fought. Others argued that while many gains had been won there were other areas, especially having to do with equal pay, sexual harassment, and political power, where there was much progress still to be made.

The fist symbol was used by groups such as the black power and feminist movements to represent power, unity, and militancy.

SEE ALSO

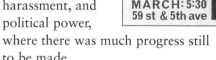

Abortion issue; Equal Rights Amendment (ERA); Friedan, Betty; *Ms.* magazine; Steinem, Gloria

FURTHER READING

Faludi, Susan. *Backlash: The Undeclared War Against American Women.* New York: Crown, 1991.

Friedan, Betty. *The Second Stage.* Cambridge, Mass.: Harvard University Press, 1998.

Friedan, Betty. *The Feminine Mystique.* New York: Dell, 1997.

Hole, Judith, and Ellen Levine. *The Rebirth of Feminism.* New York: Quadrangle, 1971.
hooks, bell. *Ain't I a Woman: Black Women and Feminism.* Boston: South End, 1981.
Morgan, Robin. *Going Too Far: The Personal Chronicle of a Feminist.* New York: Vintage, 1978.
Wolf, Naomi. *The Beauty Myth: How Images of Beauty Are Used Against Women.* New York: Morrow, 1991.

Ferraro, Geraldine

- *Born: Aug. 26, 1935, Newburgh, N.Y.*
- *Accomplishments: U.S. representative (Democrat–N.Y.), 1978–84; first female candidate for Vice President on a major party (Democratic) ticket, 1984*

"Tonight, the daughter of an immigrant from Italy has been chosen to run for vice president in the new land my father came to love," Geraldine Ferraro—former schoolteacher, attorney, and member of Congress from New York's 9th District—told the delegates to the Democratic party convention in 1984. This convention made history by nominating the first woman Vice Presidential candidate on a national party ticket. Her candidacy increased the attention the nation paid to the candidates for Vice President; for the first time, a Vice Presidential debate was covered on national television.

In the end, the Walter Mondale-Geraldine Ferraro ticket could not dent the personal popularity and landslide reelection of Ronald Reagan and George Bush. Also, although she was an articulate and energetic campaigner, Ferraro was hurt by charges that her husband, John Zaccaro, had engaged in illegal financial practices in New York. Still, Ferraro's candidacy helped to reshape the American political and social landscape. Her historic nomination opened the door for increased participation of

Geraldine Ferraro debates George Bush in 1984 as they run against each other for Vice President.

women in national politics, leading to the subsequent selection and election of women at all levels of government.

A graduate of Marymount College and the Fordham University School of Law, Ferraro remained active in New York politics and co-hosted the TV show *Crossfire,* where, in front of an audience of millions, she nightly attacked the economic and social policies of the Reagan and Bush administrations and advocated the causes of the elderly, the needy, and women. Appointed by President Bill Clinton in 1993 to be the United States Ambassador to the United Nations Human Rights Commission, Ferraro represented the United States at various conferences on hunger and the treatment of women. She then unsuccessfully sought the 1998 Democratic nomination for the U.S. Senate.

SEE ALSO

Feminism; Mondale, Walter F.

FURTHER READING

LeVeness, Frank, and Jane Sweeney, eds. *Women Leaders in Contemporary U.S. Politics.* Boulder, Colo.: L. Rienner, 1987.

Ford, Gerald Rudolph

- *Born: July 14, 1913, Omaha, Neb.*
- *Accomplishments: U.S. representative (Republican–Mich.), 1949–73; Vice President, 1973–74; 38th President of the United States, 1974–77*

The first U.S. President who was never elected to that office, Gerald Ford was selected as Vice President by President Richard Nixon following the resignation on October 10, 1973, of Vice President Spiro Agnew, who was accused of receiving bribes and of income tax evasion. Ford was appointed Vice President under the provisions of the 25th Amendment. Then, following the resignation of Richard Nixon, on August 9, 1974, Ford was sworn in as the 38th President.

A Michigan congressman since 1949 who was chosen Republican minority leader in 1965, Ford conveyed decency rather than brilliance. (Lyndon Johnson had once cruelly quipped, "The trouble with Jerry Ford is that he used to play football without a helmet.") Promising to deliver Americans from the "long national nightmare" of Watergate, Ford invoked a storm of protest a month after taking office when he unconditionally pardoned Richard Nixon for any and all crimes committed while in office.

Gerald Ford chose to keep Henry Kissinger as secretary of state and supported détente with China and the Soviet Union. Ford and Kissinger met with Soviet premier Leonid Brezhnev in 1974 to begin negotiating the second phase of the Strategic Arms Limitations Treaty (called SALT II). Richard Nixon had established the Strategic Arms Limitation Treaty (SALT I) with Brezhnev in 1972, which resulted in the reduction of some missiles as well as the limitation of antiballistic missiles by both nations. Ford and Brezhnev agreed to reduce the number of missiles further, but discussions of the treatment of Jews in the Soviet Union froze the talks; SALT II was not signed until the Jimmy Carter administration.

After more than a decade of U.S. efforts in Vietnam, the end of the war there came with the spring 1975 North Vietnamese offensive against the South. Although Ford requested emergency aid for South Vietnam, Congress refused. On April 30, Americans watched on television as North Vietnamese tanks rolled into Saigon and helicopters hastily airlifted desperate officials in the U.S. embassy to ships waiting offshore.

Perhaps the most impressive foreign policy act of Ford's Presidency came with the Helsinki accords, signed in 1975. In them, all the participants, including the Soviet Union, agreed to respect and protect the human rights of their own citizens. President Ford pushed hard for these accords, but they were largely ineffective, because there was no way they could be enforced. However, the accords also renounced the Soviet Union's right to keep its satellite states in line through military intervention. This provision pos-

Gerald Ford attempts to heal the wounds of Watergate as he announces his pardon of his predecessor, Richard M. Nixon, to the nation.

sibly restrained Soviet intervention in Eastern Europe in 1989, when communist party rulers fell from power in Poland, Hungary, Czechoslovakia, Bulgaria, and Romania.

On domestic matters, Ford governed more conservatively than had Nixon, vetoing most of the environmental, social welfare, and public interest measures adopted by the heavily Democratic Congress. Plagued by a series of stiff OPEC (Organization of Petroleum Exporting Countries) price hikes, Ford could do little to control rising consumer prices or jump start a stalled economy. With double-digit unemployment *and* inflation in 1976, Ford barely beat back a challenge for the Republican Presidential nomination by Ronald Reagan. In an inept, lackluster campaign he lost the Presidency to Jimmy Carter. Less than 54 percent of those eligible bothered to vote for either candidate. Ford retired to California in 1977, and he helped his wife Betty recover from cancer and alcohol and drug dependency.

SEE ALSO

Arab oil embargo; Nixon, Richard Milhous; Nuclear arms control; Watergate

FURTHER READING

Cannon, James. *Time and Chance: Gerald Ford's Appointment with History.* Ann Arbor: University of Michigan Press, 1993.

Firestone, Bernard, and Alexej Ugrinsky, eds. *Gerald R. Ford and the Politics of Post-Watergate America.* Westport, Conn.: Greenwood, 1993.

Garthoff, Raymond. *Détente and Confrontation: American–Soviet Relations from Nixon to Reagan.* Washington, D.C.: Brookings Institution, 1987.

Greene, John Robert. *The Presidency of Gerald R. Ford.* Lawrence: University Press of Kansas, 1995.

Randolph, Sallie G. *Gerald R. Ford, President.* New York: Walker, 1987.

Schapsmeier, Edward L., and Frederick H. Schapsmeier. *Gerald R. Ford's Date with Destiny: A Political Biography.* New York: P. Lang, 1989.

Freedom rides

The Congress of Racial Equality (CORE) dispatched black protestors to ride on interstate buses in the spring of 1961 as a way of publicizing the South's defiance of a year-old Supreme Court ruling desegregating interstate

Freedom riders look on as their bombed bus burns in Anniston, Alabama, in 1961.

transportation. Members of the Ku Klux Klan beat the freedom riders and burned their bus in Anniston, Alabama, and a white mob attacked the protestors in Birmingham.

When the freedom riders suffered even more brutal attacks in Montgomery, President John F. Kennedy ordered federal marshals to defend them. Only in the face of continued protests and attacks on the freedom riders, however, did Kennedy finally order the Interstate Commerce Commission to enforce the Supreme Court's ruling.

SEE ALSO

Civil rights movement; Congress of Racial Equality (CORE); Kennedy, John Fitzgerald

FURTHER READING

Haskins, James. *Freedom Rides: Journey for Justice*. New York: Hyperion, 1995.
McAdam, Doug. *Freedom Summer*. New York: Oxford University Press, 1998.

Free speech movement

When administration officials at the University of California, Berkeley, suddenly outlawed setting up fund-raising and recruiting tables on campus for political causes in September 1964, students immediately protested, forming the Berkeley free speech movement. It was the first of many mass protests that would sweep campuses across the country during the 1960s.

Junior philosophy major Mario Savio framed the movement as a natural reaction to a higher education system that, he felt, in serving the interests of corporate America repressed the individuality of the students. He urged students to throw themselves "upon the gears and upon the wheels" of this education "machine" and stop it.

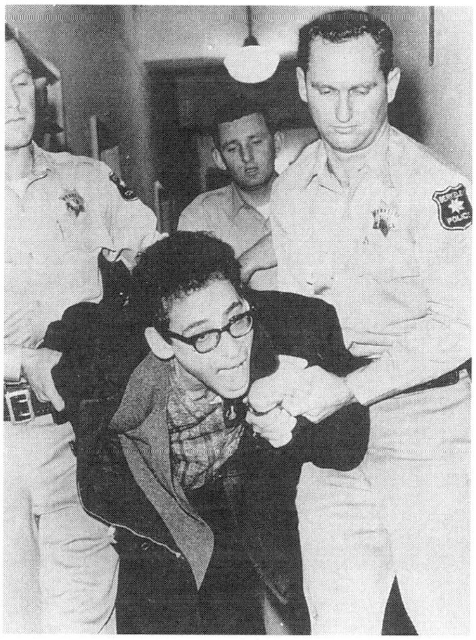

Police officers carry off a student from the University of California, Berkeley, after he participated in a sit-in to protest campus regulations against political fund-raising and recruiting. He is chanting "Freedom now!"

When the university tried to take disciplinary action against leaders of an earlier protest demonstration, hundreds of students responded by occupying Sproul Hall, the campus administration building. Some 800 were eventually arrested. Overwhelming support for the protest by the faculty and student body, however, ultimately forced Berkeley officials to rescind their restrictions on fund-raising and recruitment. This student victory would, in turn, spark numerous other campus protests, including another at Berkeley five years later when hundreds of demonstrators battled police and National Guardsmen to keep the university from building student housing on a vacant lot they claimed as People's Park.

SEE ALSO

New Left; People's Park battle

FURTHER READING

Goines, David Lance. *The Free Speech Movement: Coming of Age in the 1960s*. Berkeley, Calif.: Ten Speed Press, 1993.
Heirich, Max. *The Beginning: Berkeley 1964*. New York: Columbia University Press, 1970.

Friedan, Betty

- *Born: Feb. 4, 1921, Peoria, Ill.*
- *Accomplishments: Feminist leader; author,* The Feminine Mystique

Betty Friedan's book *The Feminine Mystique* (1962) opened a dialogue about women's place in society and earned her the title of "mother of the modern feminist movement." Her investigations in this book revealed what she called "housewives' syndrome," a dissatisfaction felt by middle-class women confined to the roles of mother and housewife. The book invited women to call for increased opportunity in business and education. In 1966 Friedan helped create the National Organization for Women (NOW), a still-active group dedicated to helping improve the status of women in the United States.

As president of the National Organization for Women, Betty Friedan talks to reporters in 1967 about improving the status of women. She had been demonstrating in the lobby of the Assembly building in Albany, New York.

Friedan has been accused of ignoring the problems of women of color and lower-class women, as well as sex segregation. The publication of *Second Stage* in 1981 marked a shift in her thinking toward a broader theory of the family that included male participation in the feminist movement. Her most recent book, *The Fountain of Age* (1991), explores how the aging process of men and women is perceived differently by different segments of society.

SEE ALSO

Feminism

FURTHER READING

Blau, Justine. *Betty Friedan: Feminist.* New York: Chelsea House, 1990.

Friedan, Betty. *The Feminine Mystique.* New York: Norton, 1962.

Friedan, Betty. *Second Stage.* New York: Summit Books, 1981.

Friedan, Betty. *The Fountain of Age.* New York: Simon & Schuster, 1993.

Horowitz, Daniel. *Betty Friedan and the Making of "The Feminine Mystique": The American Left, the Cold War and Modern Feminism.* Amherst: University of Massachusetts Press, 1998.

Fulbright, J. William

- *Born: Apr. 9, 1905, Sumner, Mo.*
- *Accomplishments: U.S. representative, 1942–45; U.S. senator (Democrat–Ark.), 1945–75*
- *Died: Feb. 22, 1995, Washington, D.C.*

The articulate chairman of the Senate Foreign Relations Committee from 1964 to 1974, Democratic senator J. William Fulbright of Arkansas became a leading critic of U.S. involvement in Vietnam.

A Rhodes scholar, Fulbright served as president of the University of Arkansas before being elected to Con-

The hearing into the Vietnam War that J. William Fulbright began in 1966 continued into 1976. Fulbright is in the front row on the left.

gress in 1942. He was elected to the Senate in 1944 and in 1946 sponsored the bill to fund what became known as the Fulbright Scholarship program, which continues to administer grants for foreign exchange among scholars.

In 1964, Fulbright led the effort to pass the Gulf of Tonkin Resolution, which gave President Lyndon Johnson the authority to repel attacks against U.S. forces in Vietnam. Fulbright agreed to work to give Johnson this power after Johnson assured him that the resolution was not a declaration of war and that he would consult with Congress before escalating the Vietnam conflict. Convinced that Johnson had lied to him, in 1966 Fulbright began a series of televised hearings on the Vietnam War. They featured George Kennan explaining why the containment doctrine was not appropriate for Southeast Asia, the respected army general Matthew Ridgway testifying that U.S. military strategy in Vietnam had no chance of achieving victory, and other critics of the escalation of the Vietnam War.

Fulbright (called "half-bright" by Johnson) then became a prominent opponent of the war and conducted hearings of the Senate Foreign Relations Committee, which convinced millions that the Gulf of Tonkin affair had been a hoax to allow Johnson unlimited Presidential power to wage an undeclared war in Vietnam. In 1967 Fulbright wrote *The Arrogance of Power,* an influential book among those opposed to the war, and led the successful fight to repeal the Gulf of Tonkin Resolution in 1970.

SEE ALSO

Containment doctrine; Gulf of Tonkin Resolution (1964); Johnson, Lyndon Baines; Vietnam War

FURTHER READING

Berman, William C. *William Fulbright and the Vietnam War: The Dissent of a Political Realist.* Kent, Ohio: Kent State University Press, 1988.

Woods, Randall Bennett. *J. William Fulbright.* New York: Cambridge University Press, 1998.

Woods, Randall Bennett. *Fulbright: A Biography.* New York: Cambridge University Press, 1995.

Gates, Bill

- *Born: Oct. 28, 1955, Seattle, Wash.*
- *Accomplishments: Co-founder and CEO of Microsoft, Inc.*

America's richest man of the 1990s, inventor and entrepreneur Bill Gates built his vast fortune on the world's insatiable appetite for computer technology. The son of a well-to-do Seattle family, Gates first began experimenting with and profiting from computers in 1967 by preparing class schedules for his school; he was 12 years old. Two years later he was president of his own company, Traf-o-Data, earning $20,000 from the sale of traffic systems to municipalities. In 1973, Gates entered Harvard University, intent on becoming a lawyer. He dropped out as a sophomore, however, moved to Albuquerque, founded Microsoft, and secured a contract with the Tandy Corporation to develop software for Radio Shack computers. Microsoft soon moved to Seattle and produced the MS-DOS operating system for IBM's new product, the personal computer (PC), the success of which made Gates a millionaire. The Windows operating system introduced by Gates in the late 1980s quickly dominated the market, and by the age of 32 Gates was worth a billion dollars. He had more to do with bringing the computer revolution into American homes and offices than any other individual; however, Gates and Microsoft came under investigation by the federal government in the 1990s for business practices that purportedly squelched competition unfairly.

SEE ALSO

Computers

FURTHER READING

Ichbiah, Daniel. *The Making of Microsoft.* Rocklin, Calif.: Prima, 1991.

Wallace, James, Jim Erickson, and James Erickson. *Hard Drive: Bill Gates and the Making of the Microsoft Empire.* Harper Business, 1993.

Gay liberation movement

In the post–World War II period, homosexual men and women have emerged from years of oppression and secrecy to demand their civil rights and proclaim their identities openly. The first stirrings of what would come to be called the gay liberation movement took place in the 1950s, a period of severe repression of homosexuals.

Two Los Angeles men started the Mattachine Society in Los Angeles in 1950, and a group of lesbians started the Daughters of Bilitis in San Francisco in 1955. The Mattachine Society took their name from the Italian *mattachino,* a court jester who dared to tell the truth to the king. The name *Bilitis* came from a French publication that offered translations from the Greek about lesbians in the ancient world. These groups established chapters in other cities and published magazines that dealt with issues concerning homosexuals, but took a nonconfrontational approach to civil rights.

In the 1960s, influenced by African-American civil rights and student antiwar protestors, the gay liberation movement became more militant. Some activists began picketing government agencies, demanding civil rights and opposing police brutality in what became known as the homophile movement.

The major turning point, however, took place after New York City police raided a gay bar in Greenwich Village

This 1979 march took place 10 years after the Stonewall riots in New York City. Demonstrations for gay rights, and to show gay pride, still occur in cities around the country every year.

in 1969 and the patrons fought back. The three ensuing nights of skirmishes between police and homosexuals became known as the Stonewall riot, after the name of the bar. The riot inspired more homosexuals to stand up for their rights and to "come out of the closet," publicly proclaiming their sexual orientation.

On the first anniversary of the riot, 5,000 gay men and lesbians commemorated the event with a protest march through New York City. Over the years, the movement has gained strength and expanded its concerns. In October 1987, some 600,000 marched on Washington. The onset of the deadly AIDS epidemic in the 1980s further mobilized activists and led to militant demands for greater spending on research for a cure of the disease, which has devastated the gay male population. President George Bush significantly increased funding for AIDS research. By the mid-1990s most states had ended criminal penalties for sexual relationships between consenting adults, and hundreds of communities had outlawed discrimination against homosexuals.

SEE ALSO

Acquired immune deficiency syndrome (AIDS); Stonewall riot (1969)

FURTHER READING

Adam, Barry. *The Rise of a Gay and Lesbian Movement.* Boston: Twayne, 1987.

D'Emilio, John. *Sexual Politics, Sexual Communities: The Making of a Homosexual Minority in the United States, 1940–1970.* Chicago: University of Chicago Press, 1983.

Katz, Jonathan. *Gay American History: Lesbians and Gay Men in the U.S.A.* New York: Harper & Row, 1985.

McGarry, Molly, and Fred Wasserman. *Becoming Visible.* New York: Penguin, 1998.

Shilts, Randy. *Conduct Unbecoming: Lesbians and Gays in the U.S. Military.* New York: St. Martin's, 1993.

Generation X

First coined in 1988 by Douglas Coupland in a *Vancouver* magazine article, the term *Generation X* (or, more breezily, *Gen X*) refers to the generation of children born to baby boomers and coming of age in the 1990s. Generation X's members typically have become disillusioned with the materialism of their parents, the yuppies of the 1980s. The poor job market and recession of the early 1990s forced college-educated members of Generation X into low-skilled, low-paying jobs—called "McJobs" in Generation X lingo (for the McDonald's fast-food chain)—and made them the first generation in U.S. history to expect to live at a lower economic level than their parents.

SEE ALSO

Baby boom; Yuppies

FURTHER READING

Coupland, Douglas. *Generation X: Tales for an Accelerated Culture*. New York: St. Martin's, 1991.

Janoff, Joshua B. "A Gen-X Rip Van Winkle: Looking the Part Doesn't Mean I'm a Stereotypical Twentysomething." *Newsweek*, April 24, 1995, 10.

Schoemer, Karen. "Talking About Our Generation." *Newsweek*, December 26, 1994, 32–33.

Geneva Conference (1954)

After the French surrender in Vietnam on May 7, 1954, at the battle of Dien Bien Phu, an international conference in Geneva, Switzerland, in July arranged a cease-fire between France and the Vietminh, a nationalist guerrilla force led by Vietnamese communist Ho Chi Minh. The conference also decided to partition Vietnam at the 17th parallel until unifying elections could be held in 1956.

Fearing the spread of communism in the region and certain that Ho would win a national election, President Dwight Eisenhower's administration helped to establish an independent government in Saigon with the hope of maintaining a noncommunist South Vietnam. CIA agents helped block the reunification election and began training South Vietnamese armed forces,

British prime minister Anthony Eden (right) arrives in Geneva for peace talks between France and the communist Vietnamese. Beside him is Max Petitpierre, president of Switzerland.

thus beginning America's gradual entry into the Vietnam War.

SEE ALSO
Vietnam War

FURTHER READING

Cable, James. *The Geneva Conference of 1954 on Indochina.* New York: St. Martin's, 1986.
Gurtov, Melvin. *The First Vietnam Crisis.* New York: Columbia University Press, 1967.
Halberstam, David. *The Best and the Brightest.* New York: Random House, 1972.
Kahin, George McT. *Intervention: How America Became Involved in Vietnam.* New York: Knopf, 1986.

Gingrich, Newton L. ("Newt")

- *Born: June 17, 1943, Harrisburg, Pa.*
- *Accomplishments: U.S. representative (Republican–Ga.), 1979–99; Speaker of the House of Representatives, 1995–98*

The holder of a doctorate in American history, Newt Gingrich was elected to Congress in 1978 and quickly established himself as a leader of the young conservatives who were attacking 60 years of what they considered welfare-state liberalism. Gingrich initially gained prominence by assailing the ethics of Democratic Speaker of the House James Wright and by opposing President George Bush's 1990 tax-raising budget compromise that was supposed to reduce a mushrooming national deficit.

Capitalizing on the disgruntled mood of the electorate in 1994, Gingrich convinced Republican candidates nationwide to campaign on a "Contract with America" that promised tax cuts, congressional term limits, tougher anticrime laws, and a balanced-budget amendment. The resulting landslide election gave the Republicans control of both houses of Congress for the first time since 1954. The 303 Republican representatives, 73 of them newly elected, proclaimed Gingrich Speaker of the House by acclamation and immediately set out to transform their "contract" into legislation.

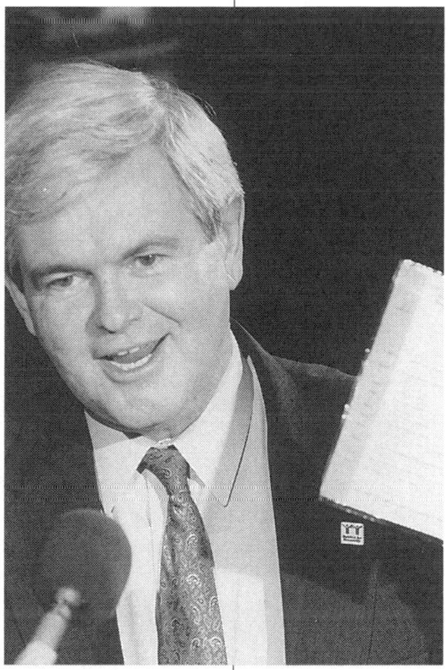

During a 1995 press conference on Congressional term limits, Newt Gingrich displays a copy of the Republicans' "Contract with America." Term limits was one of several hotly-debated topics addressed by the contract.

On such major matters as tax cuts, a balanced budget, and welfare reform, however, Gingrich would be stymied by more moderate Republicans in the Senate. Further, his popularity plummeted when President Bill Clinton adopted a strategy of vetoing unpopular Republican proposals, painting Gingrich as an extremist who would destroy programs dear to the middle class, particularly Social Security and Medicare. His decline continued in 1997 when he was reprimanded by the full House and fined $300,000 after dozens of ethics charges were filed against him. Gingrich resigned from Congress in January 1999 after his party fared poorly in the 1998 midterm elections.

SEE ALSO
Conservatism

FURTHER READING

Gingrich, Newt. *Contract with America: The Bold Plan by Rep. Newt Gingrich, Rep. Dick Armey and the House Republicans to Change the Nation.* New York: Times Books, 1994.
Gingrich, Newt. *Lessons Learned the Hard Way: A Personal Report.* New York: HarperCollins, 1998.
Gingrich, Newt. *To Renew America.* New York: HarperCollins, 1996.

Ginsberg, Allen

- *Born: June 3, 1926, Newark, N.J.*
- *Accomplishments: Poet; an originator of the Beat movement*
- *Major Works:* Howl and Other Poems *(1956),* Kaddish and Other Poems *(1961),* Reality Sandwiches *(1963),* Indian Journals *(1970),* The Fall of America *(1973),* Cosmopolitan Greetings *(1994)*
- *Died: Apr. 5, 1997, New York, N.Y.*

One of the most noteworthy Beat poets, Ginsberg is best known for his first published work, *Howl and Other Poems* (1956). Like other writers of the Beat generation, such as Jack Kerouac, Gregory Corso, and William S. Burroughs, Ginsberg's poetry railed against the materialism of American culture, "whose blood is running money," whose "soul is electricity and banks!" In the 1960s, Ginsberg pursued Buddhist enlightenment, helped raise ecological consciousness, and actively protested the Vietnam War.

SEE ALSO

Beat movement; Kerouac, Jack

FURTHER READING

Ginsberg, Allen. *Howl and Other Poems.* San Francisco: City Lights, 1956.

Kramer, Jane. *Allen Ginsberg in America.* New York: Random House, 1969.

Ginsburg, Ruth Bader

- *Born: Mar. 15, 1933, Brooklyn, N.Y.*
- *Accomplishments: United States Court of Appeals for the District of Columbia circuit judge, 1980–93; Supreme Court justice, 1993–*

Appointed to the Supreme Court in August 1993 by President Bill Clinton, Ruth Bader Ginsburg became the first Jewish Supreme Court justice since Abe Fortas in 1969 and the second woman ever to sit on the court, after Sandra Day O'Connor. She was also the first member appointed by a Democratic President in 26 years.

Ruth Bader Ginsburg is often part of a centrist coalition on the Supreme Court that has made it difficult for onlookers to predict which way the Court will go.

Ginsburg served as counsel to the American Civil Liberties Union in the 1970s and as a judge on a U.S. court of appeals for the District of Columbia during the 1980s. Her political views are generally considered centrist, with strong support for women's rights and conservative views on judicial activism. The Senate confirmed her nomination by a comfortable 96-to-3 vote on August 3, 1993. In 1998, Ginsburg distinguished herself by urging the Court to hear the appeal regarding Independent Counsel Kenneth Starr's investigation of President Bill Clinton. Swayed by conservative Chief Justice William Rehnquist, the court declined to hear the case.

SEE ALSO

Supreme Court

FURTHER READING

Ayer, Eleanor H. *Ruth Bader Ginsburg.* Parsippany, N.J.: Silver Burdett, 1994.

Goldwater, Barry

- *Born: Jan. 1, 1909, Phoenix, Ariz.*
- *Accomplishments: U.S. senator (Republican–Ariz.), 1953–65, 1969–87; Republican candidate for President, 1964*
- *Died: May 30, 1998, Phoenix, Ariz.*

A millionaire department store magnate and ultraconservative senator from Arizona, Barry Goldwater was chosen by the Republican convention to run against

Lyndon B. Johnson in the 1964 Presidential election. The author of *The Conscience of a Conservative* (1960), Goldwater passionately believed in American uniqueness and individual liberty and staunchly opposed what he called "me too" Republicanism, the centrist, middle-of-the-road course advocated by President Dwight Eisenhower. Because of these strongly held convictions, he especially appealed to those who wanted an end to big government, the graduated federal income tax, social welfare programs, and the regulation of business.

Goldwater's vote against the Civil Rights Act of 1964 made him the favored candidate of southern segregationists. Because he was considered an extremist at the time and was seen as trigger happy for advocating the wholesale bombing of North Vietnam, Goldwater's candidacy enabled President Lyndon Johnson to run as a moderate and a proponent of peace. Goldwater carried only six states (Arizona and the Deep South), losing to Johnson in a landslide.

Goldwater's followers remained powerful within the Republican party, however, steadily steering it in a rightward direction, and the conservative views espoused by Goldwater would reap rich rewards for his party throughout the South and West in future elections.

After he lost the Presidential election in 1964, Barry Goldwater's public image gradually transformed from fire-breathing extremist to curmudgeonly libertarian.

SEE ALSO

Conservatism

FURTHER READING

Goldwater, Barry. *Conscience of a Conservative.* Shepherdsville, Ky.: Victor Publishing, 1960.

Goldwater, Barry. *With No Apologies.* New York: Morrow, 1979.

Iverson, Peter. *Barry Goldwater: Native Arizonan.* Norman: University of Oklahoma Press, 1997.

Gore, Albert ("Al"), Jr.

- *Born: Mar. 31, 1948, Carthage, Tenn.*
- *Accomplishments: U.S. representative (Democrat–Tenn.), 1977–84; U.S. senator (Democrat–Tenn.), 1985–93; Vice President, 1993–*

The son of a liberal U.S. senator from Tennessee, Al Gore studied at Vanderbilt and Harvard universities and served in Vietnam before he was elected to Congress in 1976. An outspoken environmentalist and the author of *Earth in the Balance: Healing the Global Environment* (1992), Gore was elected to the Senate in 1984 and ran for the Democratic Presidential nomination in 1988, losing to Michael Dukakis of Massachusetts. In 1992 Bill Clinton rejected the practice of balancing the ticket geographically and demographically by selecting Gore, a fellow border-state moderate, Baptist, and baby boomer, as his running mate.

Albert Gore, Jr., has broken out of the mold of the invisible Vice President to become the most visible and influential second in command of the modern era.

In office, Gore became an influential voice in the policy planning of the Clinton administration. His reputation as a solid family man and moral conservative helped offset Clinton's perceived lack of these attributes.

SEE ALSO

Clinton, William Jefferson ("Bill")

FURTHER READING

Gore, Albert, Jr. *Earth in the Balance.* Boston: Houghton Mifflin, 1992.

Hillin, Hank. *Al Gore Jr.: His Life and Career.* Secaucus, N.J.: Carol Publishing Group, 1992.

Graham, William ("Billy") Franklin

- *Born: Nov. 7, 1918, Charlotte, N.C.*
- *Accomplishments: Popular evangelist and author*

The best-known and most revered American religious figure from the 1950s through the 1980s, Billy Graham mixed an emphasis on the Bible with a clear-cut moral code and opposition to communism ("a great sinister anti-Christian movement masterminded by Satan") to stimulate a huge upsurge of evangelical Protestantism.

In a characteristic pose, Billy Graham exhorts the crowd to join him in his evangelical Protestant beliefs.

Graham's revival meetings became ever more theatrical and attracted larger and larger crowds. His Evangelistic Association, which he started in 1950 in a one-room office with a single secretary, also grew quickly. A master of modern public relations, he soon had a syndicated newspaper column and radio and television shows and was a frequent visitor to the White House; riding the rising wave of evangelism he became America's favorite preacher.

Although Graham generally avoided political partisanship, he endorsed Richard Nixon in 1972. Since then, Graham has concentrated on spreading his message of rediscovering Christ and reaffirming traditional evangelical Protestant beliefs. In the 1980s, when other evangelical media preachers became embroiled in scandals or emerged as key players in the cultural and political conflicts of the day, Graham stayed above the fray as the elder statesman of evangelicalism.

SEE ALSO

Religious fundamentalism

FURTHER READING

Oakley, J. Ronald. *God's Country: America in the Fifties.* New York: Dembner Books, 1986.

Whitfield, Stephen. *The Culture of the Cold War.* Baltimore: Johns Hopkins University Press, 1991.

Grateful Dead

The Grateful Dead became the most enduring rock group to emerge from the drug-influenced "psychedelic" rock scene in San Francisco in the late 1960s. During the next decade the band successfully blended bluegrass, blues, and country music with rock, producing such major hits as "Uncle

John's Band" (1970), "Truckin'" (1971), and "Sugar Magnolia" (1973). For 30 years, until the group broke up in 1995 after the death of its leader, guitarist Jerry Garcia, the Dead attracted the most devoted audience in rock music, with many fans ("Dead Heads") following the band from concert to concert across the country. In a tribute to Garcia, Ben & Jerry's ice cream created a flavor called Cherry Garcia.

SEE ALSO

Counterculture

FURTHER READING

Scully, Rock. *Living with the Dead: Twenty Years on the Bus with Garcia and the Grateful Dead.* Boston: Little, Brown, 1997.

Jackson, Blair. *Garcia: An American Life.* New York: Viking, 1999.

Great Society

President Lyndon B. Johnson's Great Society stands alongside Franklin Roosevelt's New Deal of the 1930s as one of the two major national reform programs of the 20th century. Johnson, a former majority leader in the Senate, managed to push scores of measures through Congress in the mid-1960s, thanks to his massive landslide victory over Barry Goldwater in the 1964 election, huge Democratic majorities in the House and Senate, and his own considerable skills as an arm-twisting legislative leader. These laws, collectively known as the Great Society program, embodied Johnson's dream of an American society with equal rights and opportunities for all.

In his first two years in office, the new President signed into law a massive array of social legislation. Aimed at bringing "an end to poverty and racial injustice," the Great Society was per-

In a poor area of Appalachia in 1964, President Lyndon Johnson talks to a woman in an unemployment office. His Great Society legislation included programs to end poverty in America.

haps the most powerful social reform agenda in U.S. history. The Civil Rights Act of 1964 outlawed segregation in public places; gave new powers to the federal government to enforce voting rights and integrate schools; and established the Equal Employment Opportunity Commission (EEOC) to combat job discrimination against blacks, women, and ethnic and religious minorities. The Voting Rights Act of the following year tripled the number of black voters in the South and significantly changed the nature of U.S. politics.

Johnson also sought to expand economic opportunity with his War on Poverty program. The Economic Opportunity Act of 1964 spent $1 billion to fund job training, volunteer work in poor areas, and early childhood education through such programs as the Job Corps, Volunteers in Service to America (VISTA), Project Head Start, and the Community Action Program. Like most of the Great Society, these programs emphasized empowerment rather than relief, adopting the slogan "a hand up, not a handout." Johnson defined the

Great Society as "a place where every child can find knowledge to enrich his mind and to enlarge his talents."

Other Great Society legislation included the Elementary and Secondary Education Act, which funded textbooks, library material, and special education in grade schools; the Medical Care Act, which provided health insurance (Medicaid and Medicare) for welfare recipients and the elderly; the Omnibus Housing Act, which provided $8 billion in aid for housing for low- and middle-income families; and the Immigration Act, which ended immigration quotas that favored European migrants and led to a major influx of immigrants from Asia and Latin America.

Johnson also proposed, and Congress passed, the Appalachian Regional Development Act, which funded highway construction, health centers, and resource development in depressed areas; the 1965 Higher Education Act, which allocated $650 million to provide low-interest loans and scholarships for needy students and subsidized college libraries and research facilities; an act to establish the National Endowments for the Arts and Humanities, which promoted cultural and artistic programs, especially in remote areas; the Demonstration Cities and Metropolitan Development Act, which helped to clean up slum areas; the Motor Vehicle Safety Act, which set safety standards for automobiles; and the Truth in Packaging Act, which extended government control over the labeling of certain consumer products.

Early in his administration, Johnson recognized the fleeting nature of public support for his programs and implored legislators to pass his social legislation quickly. Johnson saw the escalating war in South Vietnam as a potential threat to his domestic agenda. Spending on the war in Vietnam widely outstripped spending on the War on Poverty, and popular opposition to Johnson's domestic agenda paralleled opposition to the war and the outbreak of race riots that began in 1965. Many white voters in the 1968 election resented the Great Society's extension of benefits to blacks and voted in surprising numbers for the third-party candidate, Alabama governor George Wallace, who was an avowed segregationist.

Although they were frequently a target of conservative criticism, many of the major Great Society measures proved successful and popular and have remained law for more than three decades. They have provided effective protection for civil rights, expanded the U.S. welfare and social insurance system, and given the federal government new responsibilities in such realms as education, the arts, and the environment.

SEE ALSO

Johnson, Lyndon Baines; War on Poverty

FURTHER READING

Kearns, Doris. *Lyndon Johnson and the American Dream.* New York: Harper & Row, 1976.

Matusow, Allen. *The Unraveling of America: A History of Liberalism in the 1960s.* New York: Harper & Row, 1984.

Patterson, James. *America's Struggle Against Poverty, 1900–1980.* Cambridge, Mass.: Harvard University Press, 1981.

Zarefsky, David. *President Johnson's War on Poverty: Rhetoric and History.* Tuscaloosa: University of Alabama Press, 1986.

Greening of America, The

In this best-selling book of 1971, Charles A. Reich analyzed American society in the spirit of 19th-century writer Henry David Thoreau. Reich saw a new consciousness growing among Americans who exhibited a commitment to camaraderie, honesty, and simplicity. This consciousness would help "green" present-day institutions. (To green meant to raise the public's awareness of such issues as ecology, recycling, and the dwindling of natural resources.) Reich believed this showed that Americans had "rediscovered a childlike quality that [they] supremely treasure."

FURTHER READING

Reich, Charles. *The Greening of America.* New York: Cambridge University Press, 1998.

Grenada, U.S. invasion of

A tiny island in the Caribbean, Grenada became independent from Britain in 1974 and was ruled by a corrupt anticommunist government until 1979. Then a leftist government that cooperated with Fidel Castro of Cuba came to power, and in 1983 a coup resulted in an even more radical regime.

On October 25, 1983, some 2,000 U.S. marines invaded the island, supposedly to protect 595 endangered U.S. medical students attending school there. The U.S. forces overthrew the leftist government and installed one friendly to the United States. President Ronald Reagan claimed that U.S. strategic interests in the region justified the action, and other West Indian governments applauded the U.S. intervention. Although the UN General Assembly voted to condemn the invasion and Congress approved resolutions applying the War Powers Act, requiring all U.S. troops to be withdrawn by the end of December, Reagan's decisive action caused his popularity in the United States to soar.

SEE ALSO

Reagan, Ronald Wilson; War Powers Act of 1973

FURTHER READING

Burrowes, Reynold. *Revolution and Rescue in Grenada.* New York: Greenwood, 1988.
O'Shaughnessy, Hugh. *Grenada: An Eyewitness Account of the U.S. Invasion and the Caribbean History That Provoked It.* New York: Dodd, Mead, 1984.

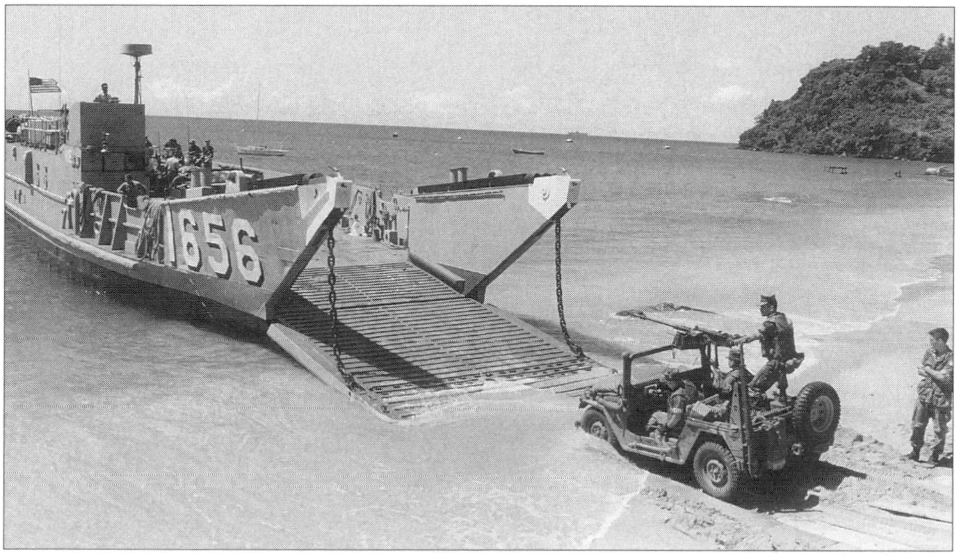

U.S. Marines drive a jeep onto a landing craft as they prepare to leave Grenada.

Gulf of Tonkin Resolution (1964)

In early August 1964, North Vietnamese patrol boats in the Gulf of Tonkin, off the coast of Vietnam, allegedly twice attacked the U.S. destroyer *Maddox*. Evidence of the second attack in particular was dubious. Nevertheless, President Lyndon B. Johnson used the occasion to order retaliatory air strikes against North Vietnam and called for a congressional resolution giving him the authority to "take all necessary measures to repel any armed attack against the forces of the United States and to prevent further aggression."

Johnson compared this resolution, which passed both houses overwhelmingly, to "Grandma's nightshirt—it covered everything," and he accepted it as a blank check to use U.S. military might in Vietnam as he deemed necessary. Ultimately, the authority accorded Johnson by the Gulf of Tonkin Resolution led to a major commitment of U.S. forces in Vietnam. In 1973 Congress passed the War Powers Act, which sought to prevent the granting of such unconditional authority to the President without a formal declaration of war.

SEE ALSO

Johnson, Lyndon Baines; Vietnam War; War Powers Act of 1973

FURTHER READING

Goulden, Joseph C. *Truth Is the First Casualty: The Gulf of Tonkin Affair—Illusion and Reality.* Chicago: Rand McNally, 1969.

Kahin, George. *Intervention: How America Became Involved in Vietnam.* New York: Knopf, 1986.

Gun control

Arguments about whether there should be any restrictions on gun ownership have been going on in the United States for more than 50 years. Since World War II weapons have become increasingly sophisticated and accurate, and so the debate has become increasingly heated. Those who favor strict controls on gun ownership argue that limiting weapons limits the amount of damage they can do. Those who favor looser controls claim that guns actually serve to protect law-abiding citizens and reduce violent crime.

The larger issue at stake in the gun control debate is to what extent the federal government may regulate the activities of its citizens. State and local governments have had regulations dealing with the sale, licensing, and use of firearms since the nineteenth century, when towns in the Wild West required cowboys to check their pistols before entering a saloon. But since World War II, the gun control debate has been carried out on the federal level as states and cities argue that the movement of guns from one part of the country to another makes effective local regulation difficult.

In the years after World War II, there was a shift in the country's demographics as people moved in large numbers from the country to the cities and suburbs. In a more rural society guns were a part of everyday life, used both for protection and to hunt for food. In urban areas guns were used for sport (target shooting, sport hunting) and for protection, but less law-abiding people used them to commit crimes.

Citizens and lawmakers sought to control the kinds of guns that people could buy, who could sell them, and who could own them. Since the 1970s they have also sought to limit the types of ammunition that can be sold and demanded that manufacturers include safety devices and buyers attend mandatory safety training courses. Their position is simple—fewer guns would mean fewer crimes committed with guns and fewer accidental shootings. Many gun control advocates argue that the federal government has the right—even the obligation—to oversee gun use throughout the country.

On the other side of this issue, other citizens and lawmakers believe that guns are often used for self-defense. "Take guns away from honest people, and only criminals will have guns," the argument goes. Many people welcome improved safety and training initiatives but balk at the idea of limiting gun ownership.

Many gun supporters have been appalled at the federal government's entry into the gun control debate. They point to the Second Amendment to the U.S. Constitution, which says that "a well-regulated militia being necessary to the security of a free state, the right of the people to keep and bear arms shall not be infringed." To many people this seems straightforward—people have the right to keep and bear arms. Others believe that the right is limited to state militias, or that regulation is not necessarily infringement.

Because of the tension between advocates and opponents of gun control, there has been an ebb and flow in gun regulation. Generally, gun control advocates gain ground in the aftermath of notoriously violent events and opponents regain ground in the lull between such events. For example, the violence of the early and mid-1960s included the assassinations of President John Kennedy, Robert Kennedy, Martin Luther King, Jr., and Malcolm X. Following these events, Congress enacted the Gun Control Act of 1968, which established stricter licensing and regulation of the firearms industry, and banned the sale of guns through the mail. A few years later, the sale of cheap handguns, the so-called Saturday Night Specials, was banned. In the somewhat calmer 1970s, gun advocates regained some ground. In 1977, in *Moore* v. *East Cleveland,* the U.S. Supreme Court ruled that the "right to bear arms" is specifically guaranteed by the Constitution.

In 1981, President Ronald Reagan and an aide, James Brady, were wounded in an assassination attempt. This led to renewed efforts to institute gun control. Despite intensive lobbying and advertising campaigns, the Brady Bill, which requires background checks on everyone who tries to buy a gun and a waiting period before the sale can be completed, was not passed for 13 years; it was enacted by Congress in 1994. Congress and several states also banned the manufacture and importing of assault rifles following a schoolyard shooting in 1989 in Stockton, California. But gun advocates successfully mobilized supporters and lobbied Congress to block any stronger controls, and many states passed laws that allowed people to carry concealed weapons, something that had been illegal since the 1900s.

In the late 1990s, in the aftermath of a series of shootings at high schools, particularly the massacre at Columbine High School in Littleton, Colorado, in 1999, Congress considered legislation that would require safety locks on all handguns and more in-depth background checks on would-be buyers before sales of handguns could be completed.

FURTHER READING

Diaz, Tom. *Making a Killing: The Business of Guns in America.* New York: New Press, 1999.

Spitzer, Robert J. *The Politics of Gun Control.* 2nd ed. New York: Chatham House, 1998.

Haig, Alexander

- *Born: Dec. 2, 1924, Philadelphia, Pa.*
- *Accomplishments: Military assistant to President for national security affairs, 1969–70; vice chief of staff, U.S. Army, 1973; White House chief of staff, 1973–74; commander in chief, NATO U.S.–European Command, 1974–75; Secretary of State, 1981–82*

A veteran of the Vietnam War, Alexander Haig rose quickly in the ranks to become a key aide of National Security Advisor Henry Kissinger, the successor to H. R. Haldeman as President Nixon's White House chief of staff, and supreme commander of the North Atlantic Treaty Organization (NATO) in 1974.

While serving as President Ronald Reagan's first secretary of state, Haig audaciously suggested that he be the vicar of foreign policy, but the President declined this offer and never gave him full responsibility. Haig's egotistical and flamboyant style alienated many in the Reagan administration, including Jeane Kirkpatrick, the U.S. representative to the United Nations, and Vice President George Bush.

Haig resigned as secretary of state in 1982 and was replaced by George Shultz. In 1988 he sought the Republican presidential nomination but fell by the wayside as George Bush won a string of primaries.

SEE ALSO

Reagan, Ronald Wilson

FURTHER READING

Haig, Alexander. *Caveat.* New York: Macmillan, 1984.

Haight-Ashbury

The neighborhood in downtown San Francisco that centered around the intersection of two streets, Haight and Ashbury, became the center of the counterculture of the 1960s. Drawn there by their predecessors, the Beats, hippies and young radicals made Haight-Ashbury their mecca. Rock groups such as the Grateful Dead played in Haight-Ashbury in 1967 as part of the area's summer of love.

By the early 1970s Haight-Ashbury's free love and experimental drug environment had given way, first to tourism and then to crime and poverty. Those with the will and money left Haight-Ashbury, some to communes but many to more conventional lives back home. Haight-Ashbury underwent another transformation in the 1990s, becoming a neighborhood of upscale cafes and boutiques.

SEE ALSO

Beat movement; Counterculture; Grateful Dead, the; Hippies; Rock and roll; Sexual revolution

FURTHER READING

Davey, Kevin. "Where Have All the Flowers Gone?" *New Statesman and Society.* April 22, 1994, 20–21.

Perry, Charles. *The Haight-Ashbury: A History.* New York: Rolling Stone Press, 1984.

Hamer, Fannie Lou Townsend

- *Born: Oct. 6, 1917, Montgomery County, Miss.*
- *Accomplishments: 1964 Mississippi Freedom Democratic party delegate*
- *Died: Mar. 14, 1977, Mound Bayou, Miss.*

The daughter of dirt-poor Mississippi sharecroppers, Fannie Lou Hamer

At the Democratic National Convention in 1964, Fannie Lou Hamer tells a national television audience about her experiences with segregation and racially motivated violence.

became a leading voice in the civil rights movement of the 1960s. In 1962 she was denied the chance to vote because she failed a literacy test, a device frequently and fraudulently used to exclude African Americans. She responded by attending a civil rights rally in her hometown and joining the Student Nonviolent Coordinating Committee's drive to register black voters.

During the next few years Hamer participated in campaigns of nonviolent protest and helped found the Mississippi Freedom Democratic party (MFDP), which tried unsuccessfully to replace the all-white regular Mississippi delegation at the 1964 national Democratic party convention. Hamer spoke to the Credentials Committee during nationally televised hearings, telling how she had been shot at and beaten for attempting to register to vote. Although the MFDP did not succeed in replacing the white delegates at the 1968 convention, Hamer continued as an active leader in the local civil rights movement until her death in 1977 from breast cancer.

SEE ALSO

Civil rights movement; Mississippi Freedom Democratic party (MFDP); Mississippi Freedom Summer (1964)

FURTHER READING

Mills, Kay. *This Little Light of Mine: The Life of Fannie Lou Hamer.* New York: Dutton, 1993.

Harriman, W. Averell

- *Born: Nov. 15, 1891, New York, N.Y.*
- *Accomplishments: U.S. Ambassador to U.S.S.R., 1943–46; Secretary of Commerce, 1946–48; governor of New York (Democrat), 1955–59; ambassador at-large to Presidents Kennedy and Johnson, 1961–69*
- *Died: July 26, 1986, Washington, D.C.*

The son of wealthy railroad magnate and financier Edward H. Harriman and a successful businessman himself, Averell Harriman held many posts for Democratic Presidents from Franklin Roosevelt to Lyndon Johnson and unsuccessfully sought the party's Presidential nomination in the 1950s.

Appointed ambassador to the Soviet Union in 1943, Harriman became convinced that Stalin could not be trusted and urged the United States to

Averell Harriman, at left, discusses his upcoming testimony before the House Foreign Affairs Committee in 1952. He was offering information about Great Britain, where he had served as ambassador in 1946.

confront the Soviet dictator. As ambassador to Britain and secretary of commerce under Harry Truman, Harriman repeated his warnings and helped to formulate the Marshall Plan and later foreign aid programs. A Democrat and liberal in domestic matters, he was elected governor of New York in 1954 but lost his reelection bid in 1958 to Nelson Rockefeller. During the Presidency of John Kennedy, Harriman played a key role in negotiating the 1963 Nuclear Test Ban Treaty with the Soviet Union and the end of civil war in Laos in 1962.

Less successfully, Harriman sought to convince President Kennedy to work for a cease-fire and a negotiated settlement in Vietnam and to convince President Johnson not to escalate U.S. involvement in that conflict. In 1968 Johnson selected Harriman to head the U.S. delegation at the Paris peace talks with North Vietnam.

FURTHER READING

Abramson, Rudy. *Spanning the Century: The Life of Averell Harriman, 1891–1986*. New York: Morrow, 1992.

Thomas, Evan. *The Wise Men: Six Friends and the World They Made*. New York: Simon & Schuster, 1986.

Hawks and doves

During the era of the Vietnam War, two prominent positions critical of U.S. policy emerged. Although the terms lacked precise definition, "hawks" generally referred to those who believed that the war could be won militarily and consequently favored expanding the air war and advocated sending more U.S. ground troops to South Vietnam. "Doves," on the other hand, opposed U.S. involvement in the war. They protested against sending U.S. combat forces to Vietnam, called for an end to the air war, and urged a negotiated settlement.

These counter-demonstrators —hawks— protest a peace march at the United Nations in New York in 1967. Instead of demanding an end to the war in Vietnam, their signs call for the bombing of Hanoi.

SEE ALSO

Vietnam War

FURTHER READING

Wells, Tom. *The War Within: America's Battle Over Vietnam*. Berkeley: University of California Press, 1994.

Hayden, Thomas ("Tom")

- *Born: Dec. 11, 1939, Detroit, Mich.*
- *Accomplishments: California state assemblyman (Democratic), 1982–90; California state senator, 1992–*

A prominent leader of Students for a Democratic Society (SDS), Tom Hayden personified the New Left. He was the primary author of the Port Huron Statement, the 1962 manifesto calling for disarmament, social justice, and complete racial quality that launched the SDS, and he led an economic research and action project in Newark, New Jersey, in

In 1966 Tom Hayden (second from left) and Staughton Lynd (far right), along with Herbert Aptheker, a left-wing political theoretician (far left) discuss their recent trip to Hanoi with A. J. Muste, chair of the Committee for Nonviolent Action.

the early 1960s. Later he traveled to North Vietnam on fact-finding missions in hopes of determining North Vietnam's negotiating positions and published a book about it, *The Other Side,* with historian Staughton Lynd.

Hayden participated in every major protest of the late 1960s, including the 1968 Columbia University student strike, protests at the 1968 Democratic National Convention in Chicago, and the battles over People's Park in Berkeley, California. Tried and convicted as a member of the Chicago Seven, his conviction was later reversed on appeal. Hayden married actress Jane Fonda in the 1970s but divorced in 1990 and went on to become a reform-minded California state assemblyman.

SEE ALSO

Antiwar movement; Chicago Seven; New Left; Students for a Democratic Society (SDS)

FURTHER READING

Gitlin, Todd. *The Sixties: Years of Hope, Days of Rage.* New York: Bantam, 1987.

Hayden, Tom. *Reunion: A Memoir.* New York: Random House, 1988.

Hayden, Tom, and Staughton Lynd. *The Other Side.* New York: New American Library, 1967.

Miller, James. *Democracy Is in the Streets: From Port Huron to the Siege of Chicago.* New York: Simon & Schuster, 1987.

Helsinki accords

SEE Ford, Gerald Rudolph

Higher Education Act (1965)

SEE Great Society

Hippies

The counterculture of the 1960s saw the emergence of the generation of baby boomers, many of whom rejected what they saw as the materialism and artificiality of their parents and the conformity demanded in the 1950s in favor of a simpler, more "natural" existence and the pursuit of personal pleasure and fulfillment. Often referred to as hippies, they challenged American society, promoting freedom of expression, questioning authority, and communal living, while often indulging in sex, drugs, and rock and roll. The disillusionment of the hippies at the close of the 1960s, caused by the devastation of drug abuse and what many felt were too few significant social changes, brought an end to the era of "flower power." The hippie way of life, however, would be revived in the 1980s and 90s through the com-

Wearing long hair and beads, hippies rejected the materialism of the middle class and embraced personal freedom, peace, and love. These hippies met at a spring celebration in northern California.

mercialization of the counterculture's music and fashions.

SEE ALSO

Baby boom; Counterculture; Haight-Ashbury; Yuppies

FURTHER READING

Dickstein, Morris. *Gates of Eden: American Culture in the Sixties.* Cambridge, Mass.: Harvard University Press, 1997.

Gitlin, Todd. *The Sixties: Years of Hope, Days of Rage.* New York: Bantam, 1987.

Hoffman, Nicholas von. *We Are the People Our Parents Warned Us Against: A Close-up of the Whole Hippie Scene.* Greenwich, Conn.: Fawcett, 1968.

Hiroshima and Nagasaki

SEE Atomic bomb

Hispanic Americans

Since the end of World War II, Hispanic Americans—people from Mexico, Central and South America, and the Caribbean—have become one of the largest minority groups in the United States. In the postwar period, Puerto Ricans, who are U.S. citizens, became the nation's newest minority group, numbering almost a million by 1960. They migrated in large numbers to New York City in search of work, forming an enclave in East, or "Spanish," Harlem. There they were denied access to good jobs and suffered from discrimination and inadequate housing, sanitation, schools, and other amenities. Like other immigrants, Puerto Ricans struggled with the dilemma of trying to fit into a new culture while preserving their ethnic customs and identity.

Mexicans began flooding into the southwestern states in large numbers after World War II to take agricultural jobs created by technological advances in irrigation. Most of these migrants were illegal aliens whom the U.S. government periodically rounded up and sent back to Mexico. But more continued to cross the border for the low-wage jobs that American farm owners were eager to fill. Hostility toward illegal aliens, who were called *mojados,* or "wetbacks," because they swam across the Rio Grande to reach Texas, led to persecution of all Mexican Americans, many of whom could trace their U.S. citizenship back for generations.

By the 1960s, many of the new arrivals had moved off the farm and into U.S. cities. The largest concentration of Mexican Americans is in the Los Angeles area. As discrimination and poverty continued to dominate their lives, these immigrants formed new grass-roots political organizations to demand their rights. Cesar Chavez formed the United Farm Workers of America, which used nonviolent resistance to wrest wage increases and improved working conditions from agricultural employers. The group organized successful nationwide boycotts of grapes and lettuce.

More radical groups, such as the Alianza in New Mexico, the Crusade for Justice in Colorado, the Brown Berets in California, and La Raza Unida (the United People party) in Texas, rejected American mainstream values and embraced the Mexican ethnic heritage and identity. Some began to call themselves Chicanos, demand bilingual education in public schools, and form racially exclusive organizations. Much of the new activism took its cue from the African-American civil

Cuban refugees land at Key West, Florida, in 1965. Between 1960 and 1995, more than 1 million Cubans escaped from Castro's leftist government and arrived in the United States.

rights movement. The Brown Berets, for example, echoed the demand among blacks for black power with their call for Chicano power.

The problem of illegal immigration has continued to generate conflict. In 1986 the Immigration Reform Act imposed penalties on employers who hired illegal immigrants. But the influx continued, and by the early 1990s an estimated 3.2 million illegal immigrants, mostly from Mexico but also from El Salvador, Guatemala, and other countries, had made their way into the United States.

Hostility toward illegal immigration peaked in California and Florida, two states with high percentages of immigrants. And many Americans in the 1990s favored cutting back on legal immigration as well, arguing that immigrants take jobs from other needy Americans or keep wages low because of their competition for jobs.

In his 1992 and 1996 campaigns for the Republican Presidential nomination, conservative TV commentator Patrick Buchanan won considerable support for his proposal to crack down on illegal immigration by building a security fence along the entire length of the Mexican border. Meanwhile, in 1994 California voters approved Proposition 187, which denied education, welfare, and other state-funded social programs to illegal immigrants. The highly controversial measure led to a resurgence of activism in the Mexican-American community.

An ongoing controversy within the Hispanic community itself examines what it should be called. The terms Latino (for men) and Latina (for women) are often used in place of the older Hispanic because Hispanic seems to many people to stress European origins over the indigenous cultures that underlie so much of Latino culture and life.

Today, Hispanics are the fastest-growing minority in the United States and will soon outnumber African Americans as the largest minority group. Symbolic of their increasing political power, President Ronald Reagan appointed Lauro Cavazos as Secretary of Education, President George Bush named Dr. Antonia Coello Nov-

Henry Cisneros, secretary of housing and urban development, meets with residents of a public housing project in Washington, D.C., in 1994. A Mexican American, Cisneros was the first Hispanic to be elected mayor of a major city when he won the post in San Antonio in 1980.

ello to the post of surgeon general, and President Bill Clinton selected both Henry Cisneros and Federico Peña for his cabinet.

In addition, Tony Anaya and Robert Martinez were elected governors of New Mexico and Florida respectively, and cities such as Denver, San Antonio, and Miami have elected Hispanic mayors. At the same time, Latino music and dancing gained widespread popularity; Sandra Cisneros and Oscar Hijuelos have won literary acclaim for their writing; and tacos, fajitas, and salsa have become staples of the U.S. diet.

SEE ALSO

Chavez, Cesar; Chicanos

FURTHER READING

Cockcroft, James D. *The Hispanic Struggle for Social Justice.* The Hispanic Experience in the Americas Series. Danbury, Conn.: Franklin Watts, 1994.

Cockcroft, James D. *Latinos in the Struggle for Equal Education.* The Hispanic Experience in the Americas Series. Danbury, Conn.: Franklin Watts, 1995.

Dunne, John Gregory. *Delano.* New York: Farrar, Straus & Giroux, 1971.

Garcia, Mario. *Mexican-Americans: Leadership, Ideology, and Identity.* New Haven, Conn.: Yale University Press, 1989.

Gutierrez, David. *Walls and Mirrors: Mexican Americans, Mexican Immigrants, and the Politics of Ethnicity.* Berkeley: University of California Press, 1995.

Hoobler, Dorothy and Thomas. *The Cuban American Family Album.* New York: Oxford University Press, 1996.

Hoobler, Dorothy and Thomas. *The Mexican American Family Album.* New York: Oxford University Press, 1994.

Padilla, Elena. *Up from Puerto Rico.* New York: Columbia University Press, 1958.

Suro, Roberto. *Strangers Among Us: How Latino Immigration is Transforming America.* New York: Knopf, 1998.

Homelessness

Homelessness became a prominent national issue in the 1980s. Although it is impossible to know exactly how many people are without shelter for one or more nights, it is estimated that between 1.3 and 2 million people were homeless in the United States at the end of the 1980s.

The causes of homelessness range from underemployment, natural disasters, and farm foreclosures to the release of mental patients from institutions because of funding cutbacks. The process of gentrification—in which middle-class people move into poor neighborhoods and restore old buildings, driving up property values—has reduced the amount of low-income housing available to the poor. Cities have responded by creating temporary shelters, which are

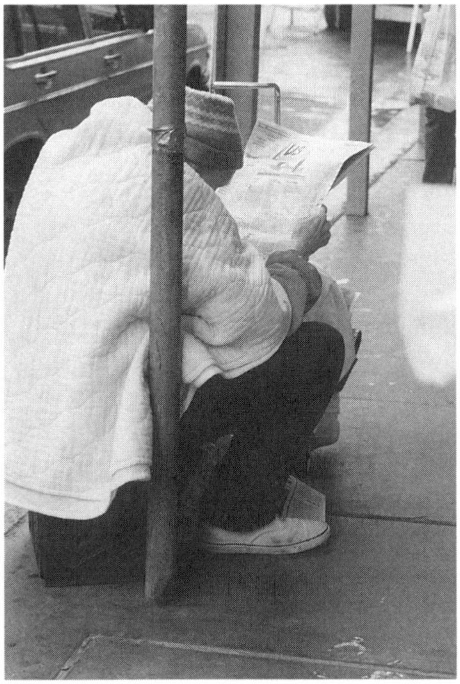

There are many homeless people on the streets of America's big cities. Here, a homeless woman hunkers down against a parking sign near San Francisco's chic Union Square, resting on a milk carton and swathed in what seems to be a mattress cover.

often noisy and dangerous, and by funding the construction of low-income housing through a wide range of public and private agencies.

FURTHER READING

Hopper, K., and J. Hamberg. *The Making of America's Homeless: From Skid Row to New Poor, 1945–84*. New York: Community Service Society of New York, 1984.

"If Autumn Comes . . . ," *America*, October 15, 1994, 3.

Hoover, J. Edgar

- *Born: Jan. 1, 1895, Washington, D.C.*
- *Accomplishments: Director of the FBI, 1924–72*
- *Died: May 2, 1972, Washington, D.C.*

Beginning in World War I, J. Edgar Hoover launched a career-long antiradical crusade when he monitored alien radicals for the Department of Justice. Appointed director of what was then called the Bureau of Investigation in 1924, Hoover skillfully courted favorable publicity. He made himself a popular hero as the FBI battled bank robbers in the 1930s and suspected communists after World War II.

FBI reports and frequent speeches by Hoover emphasizing the dangers posed by communists in the United States added to the hysteria of the second Red Scare and McCarthyism. In the 1960s and early 1970s Hoover shifted his attention from the Old Left to the New Left, aiming to expose, disrupt, misdirect, discredit, or otherwise neutralize the activities of African-American militants and young radicals opposed to the war in Vietnam.

A lifelong bachelor with few interests outside his job, Hoover headed the FBI for 48 years and made both the bureau and himself powers to be feared by those who opposed him. Since his death, interest has centered on Hoover's underhanded spying against politicians and ordinary Americans, his secret vendettas against civil rights leaders and political radicals, and his personal life, spent in the company of his lifelong male partner Clyde Tolson.

SEE ALSO

Federal Bureau of Investigation (FBI); House Un-American Activities Committee (HUAC); McCarthyism

FURTHER READING

Gentry, Curt. *J. Edgar Hoover: The Man and the Secrets*. New York: Norton, 1991.

Powers, Richard Gid. *Secrecy and Power: The Life of J. Edgar Hoover*. New York: Free Press, 1988.

House Un-American Activities Committee (HUAC)

The House Un-American Activities Committee first made a name for itself in 1947 when it announced its intention to assist FBI director J. Edgar Hoover in exposing and eliminating communism in the United States. Originally established in 1938 as the House Committee on Un-American Activities, it had received little notice until after World War II, when it held a series of highly publicized hearings targeting government officials, labor leaders, Hollywood entertainers, and others with perceived liberal leanings. The committee did not distinguish between dissent and disloyalty, or radicalism and subversion, and it was notorious for threatening witnesses with the loss of their livelihood.

HUAC's most famous probes were the two investigations that targeted Hollywood and former government official Alger Hiss. HUAC cited a group of prominent filmmakers with contempt when they refused to cooperate with the committee; many eventually were sent to federal prison. As a result, Hollywood created an unofficial blacklist to prevent the hiring of anyone who might be vulnerable to accusations of disloyalty and started making dozens of propaganda films such as *The Red Menace.* And although Alger Hiss was never convicted of espionage or treason, he was sent to jail for perjury; this sufficiently fueled the fires of anticommunism to set the stage for other zealots like Joseph McCarthy, who followed.

SEE ALSO

Anticommunism; Hoover, J. Edgar; McCarthy, Joseph

FURTHER READING

Goodman, Walter. *The Committee: The Extraordinary Career of the House Committee on Un-American Activities.* New York: Farrar, Straus & Giroux, 1968.
Latham, Earl. *The Communist Controversy in Washington.* Cambridge, Mass.: Harvard University Press, 1966.
O'Reilly, Kenneth. *Hoover and the Un-Americans: The FBI, HUAC, and the Red Menace.* Philadelphia: Temple University Press, 1983.

Humphrey, Hubert Horatio

- *Born: May 27, 1911, Wallace, S.D.*
- *Accomplishments: Mayor of Minneapolis, Minn. (Democrat), 1945–48; U.S. senator (Democrat–Minn.), 1949–65, 1971–78; Vice President, 1965–69*
- *Died: Jan. 13, 1978, Waverly, Minn.*

Born in South Dakota and trained as a pharmacist, Hubert Humphrey came

Hubert Humphrey looks happy to be back in his high school as he campaigns for the Vice Presidency in 1964.

from far behind in the polls in his 1968 campaign for President, only to lose to Richard Nixon on election day by less than one percentage point.

Humphrey, one of the leading champions of liberal causes in the Senate after World War II, was mayor of Minneapolis in 1948 when he burst on the national scene, delivering a rousing speech on behalf of black civil rights at the Democratic National Convention. Humphrey won a U.S. Senate seat in Minnesota that year, embarking on a distinguished legislative career marked by his alliance with Senate majority leader Lyndon B. Johnson. He served as majority whip from 1961 to 1965. In 1964 Johnson chose him as his running mate and the two campaigned on a platform of peace, painting opponent Barry Goldwater as a dangerous warmonger.

Johnson's dogged pursuit of the war in Vietnam turned out to be his own undoing, however. When opposition to the war forced him out of the Presidential contest in 1968, he endorsed Humphrey. In a year marked by two political assassinations and massive protests outside the Democratic convention in Chicago, Humphrey won his party's nomination but also took on the liability of having publicly supported the President's war policies.

Ironically, Humphrey had been one of a few advisors to voice doubts about the administration's war policy. In an exuberant campaign in which he eventually called for a halt to the bombing of Vietnam, Humphrey battled his way back from a seemingly insurmountable deficit in the polls, but he finally lost to Richard Nixon in one of the closest Presidential elections ever.

Humphrey returned to the Senate in 1971, where he continued to champion liberal causes, including the Humphrey-Hawkins Act (1977), which sought to establish the right to employment for all Americans. He launched one last unsuccessful bid for the Democratic Presidential nomination in 1972.

SEE ALSO

Democratic National Convention (Chicago, 1968); Johnson, Lyndon Baines

FURTHER READING

Garretson, Charles Lloyd. *Hubert H. Humphrey: The Politics of Joy.* New Brunswick, N.J.: Transaction Publishers, 1993.

Humphrey, Hubert H. *The Education of a Public Man.* Garden City, N.Y.: Doubleday, 1977.

Solberg, Carl. *Hubert Humphrey.* New York: Norton, 1984.

Thurber, Timothy N. *Politics of Equality: Hubert Humphrey and the African American Freedom Struggle, 1945–1975.* New York: Columbia University Press, 1999.

Hydrogen bomb

After the United States lost its monopoly on atomic weapons when the Soviets successfully tested an atom bomb in 1949, President Harry Truman ordered the Atomic Energy Commission to develop a hydrogen bomb—one with its power measured in millions of tons of TNT rather than in the atom bomb's thousands of tons. A hydrogen bomb is a thousand times more destructive than

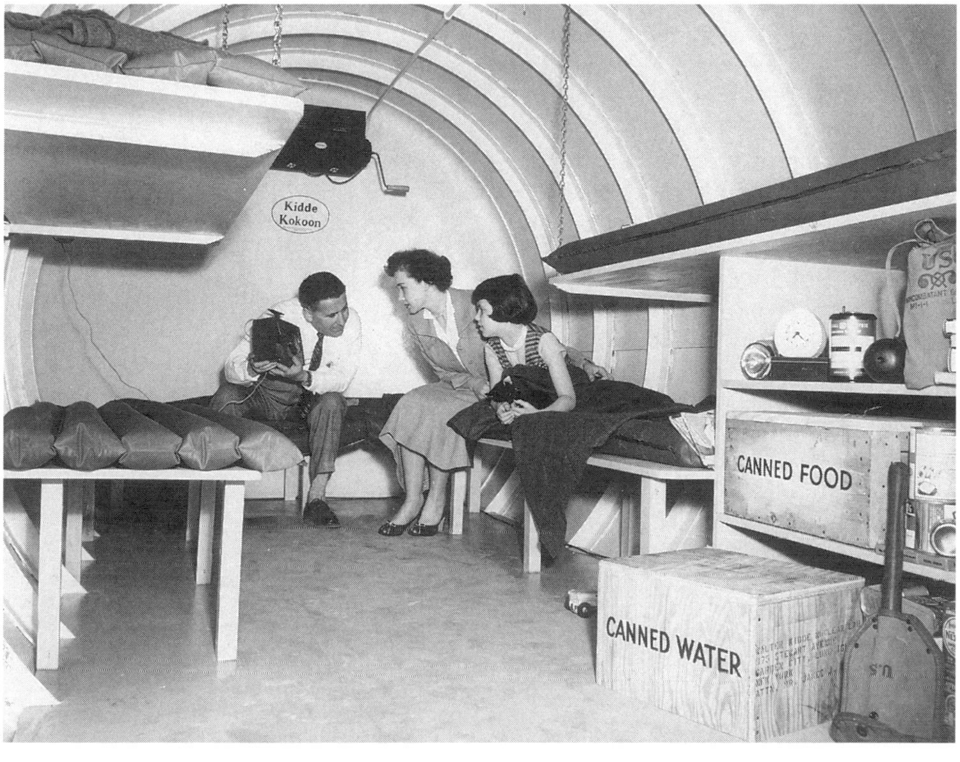

After the United States and the Soviet Union tested hydrogen bombs in the early 1950s, many Americans built bomb shelters. This one was stocked with canned goods, flashlights, and battery-powered radios, among other necessities.

one atomic bomb and is produced through nuclear fusion.

Many scientists believed such a bomb was too complex to construct or opposed the work on moral grounds. Robert Oppenheimer, the scientific director of the Manhattan Project, which built the World War II atom bombs, was against building the hydrogen bomb for moral reasons. Truman, however, insisted on a crash thermonuclear program. Accordingly, on November 1, 1952, a test hydrogen bomb was exploded in the Marshall Islands, sending a radioactive cloud 25 miles into the stratosphere and blasting a canyon in the Pacific Ocean floor a mile wide and 175 feet deep. The Soviets tested a hydrogen bomb in August 1953; the British in May 1957.

SEE ALSO

Arms race; Atomic bomb; Nuclear arms control

FURTHER READING

Rhodes, Richard. *Dark Sun: The Making of the Hydrogen Bomb.* New York: Simon & Schuster, 1995.

York, Herbert. *The Advisors: Oppenheimer, Teller, and the Superbomb.* San Francisco: Freeman, 1976.

Immigration Reform Act of 1965

The Immigration Reform Act of 1965, one of the landmark bills that President Lyndon Johnson proposed as part of his Great Society program, fundamentally changed U.S. immigration laws and the ethnic makeup of the American people. Signed by Johnson in a ceremony on Liberty Island in New York Harbor with Ellis Island showing in the background, the law abolished the discriminatory quotas that dated back to the 1920s, which favored immigrants from northwestern Europe, and set broad annual quotas of 170,000 people from the Eastern Hemisphere and 120,000 from the Western Hemisphere.

Congress enacted the legislation with little opposition, largely because no one expected that it would bring major change. But Asians and Latin Americans flocked to U.S. consulates in search of visas; because the act exempted family members of U.S. citizens from the quotas, each new immigrant soon meant many more. This so-called chain immigration resulted in 3 million of the 4 million immigrants admitted to the United States in the 1970s coming from Asia and Latin America. Likewise, Hispanics and Asians were the largest contingent of new Americans in the 1980s and 1990s.

As a result of the Immigration Reform Act, which abolished all but the most general immigration quotas, many Asians and Latin Americans came to the United States. Here, Korean students in Silver Spring, Maryland, put on a Christmas pageant.

SEE ALSO

Asian Americans; Great Society

FURTHER READING

Daniels, Roger. *Coming to America.* New York: HarperCollins, 1990.

Glazer, Nathan, ed. *Clamor at the Gates: The New American Immigration.* San Francisco: ICS, 1985.

Reimers, David M., ed. *Still the Golden Door: The Third World Comes to America.* New York: Columbia University Press, 1985.

Ungar, Sanford. *Fresh Blood: The New American Immigrants.* New York: Simon & Schuster, 1995.

Imperial Presidency

The increasing centralization of governmental powers in the White House and the Presidential usurpation of legislative prerogatives—what historian Arthur M. Schlesinger, Jr., called the imperial Presidency—is often associated with the Presidencies of Lyndon Baines Johnson and Richard Milhous Nixon. But the major increases in the powers of the Presidency and its dominance over Congress began in earlier administrations and continued in later ones.

Franklin D. Roosevelt signed executive agreements that were in effect treaties, but he never sent them to the Senate for its advice and consent. Harry S. Truman took the nation into the Korean War without securing a congressional declaration of war as required by the Constitution, much as Johnson did in the Vietnam War. Both the invasion of Grenada under Ronald Reagan and of Panama under George Bush were undertaken without congressional consent or declarations of war.

Still, no President went further than Richard Nixon in concentrating powers in the Presidency. He impounded—that is, refused to spend—federal funds that Congress had specifically appropriated for health programs, the environment, and other programs. He claimed executive privilege as a means of withholding evidence from the legislative and judicial branches. He expanded the authority of new cabinet positions without congressional approval. And he widened U.S. involvement in the Vietnam War into Cambodia and Laos without consulting Congress.

To curb such abuses and regain its constitutional prerogatives, in 1973 Congress overrode Nixon's veto and enacted the War Powers Act. This act required future Presidents to consult with Congress before sending U.S. troops into combat abroad and to withdraw those troops within 60 days unless Congress specifically approved their stay. The next year, Congress passed the Congressional Budget and Impoundment Control Act, prohibiting the President from impounding federal funds. To make it easier to uncover crimes by the executive branch, Congress gave the attorney general power to appoint a special prosecutor to investigate accusations of illegal behavior. And to open government to greater public scrutiny, in 1974 Congress strengthened the 1966 Freedom of Information Act, allowing increased access to government documents by private citizens and the press and producing penalties if the government arbitrarily or capriciously withheld such documents.

SEE ALSO

Bush, George Herbert Walker; Johnson, Lyndon Baines; Kennedy, John Fitzgerald; Nixon, Richard Milhous; War Powers Act of 1973

FURTHER READING

Koening, Louis. "Reassessing the 'Imperial Presidency.'" In *The Power to Govern.* Richard M. Pious, ed. New York: Academy of Political Science, 1982.
Pious, Richard M. *The Young Oxford Companion to the Presidency of the United States.* New York: Oxford University Press, 1993.
Schlesinger, Arthur M., Jr. *The Imperial Presidency.* Boston: Houghton Mifflin, 1973.
Theoharis, Athan. *The Truman Presidency: The Origins of the Imperial Presidency and the National Security State.* Stanfordville, N.Y.: Earl M. Coleman, 1979.

Internal Security Act of 1950

Indicative of the anticommunist hysteria of the early 1950s and of the support for strong measures against communism in the United States, Congress passed the McCarran Internal Security Act in 1950. The new law required any organization judged to be communist by the attorney general to register with the Department of Justice and to provide financial documentation and membership lists.

The law also barred communists from employment in defense plants and empowered the government to deny passports to communists. Most ominously, it authorized the government during a national emergency to arrest and detain any person it had reason to believe might engage in acts of espionage or sabotage. In his veto message President Harry Truman claimed that the McCarran Act would put the government into the business of thought control. But Congress easily overrode the veto.

SEE ALSO
Anticommunism; McCarthyism

FURTHER READING

Kovel, Joel. *Red Hunting in the Promised Land: Anticommunism and the Making of America.* New York: Basic Books, 1994.

Powers, Richard G. *Not Without Honor: The History of American Anticommunism.* New York: Free Press, 1995.

The Internet

A global web of computer circuitry, the Internet links computers worldwide into a single network of information. It began in 1969 as the Defense Department's Advanced Research Project Agency; it was a way for military scientists and engineers to share information on a network of computers able to withstand a nuclear attack. In 1986 the National Science Foundation expanded the network to include all researchers at American universities and called it the National Research and Education Network, which eventually became the Internet. By the late 1980s the Internet was widely used by both businesses and individual computer owners as more and more people went online. Today the Internet is most often used as a source for news, investment advice, and information, and many people have come to depend on electronic mail, or E-mail, which allows users to send messages through networked terminals to computer addresses anywhere in the world. The increasing popularity of the World Wide Web, which operates over the Internet and appeared in the early 1990s, made the Internet even more easily accessible to more people. By the end of the 20th century, increasing numbers of Americans were virtually meeting and talking to each other electronically in chat rooms, purchasing books and clothes on the Web, and surfing the Web to do research in digitalized archives. The responses to the new technology have been wide ranging. While many people have praised the new possibilities for individual enterprise, freedom of expression, and decentralization for those able to afford the technology, others warned of the widening gap it accelerated between the haves and have-nots, of the unchecked spread of pornography, of the proliferation of hate sites, and of the alienation resulting from the substitution of technology for genuine human contact.

SEE ALSO

Computers; World Wide Web

FURTHER READING

Hafner, Katie, and Matthew Lyon. *Where Wizards Stay Up Late: The Origins of the Internet*. New York: Touchstone, 1998.

Interstate Highway Act of 1956

The Interstate Highway Act provided federal funding for the construction of a 41,000-mile system of expressways and four-lane superhighways. As the most expensive public works program in the history of the United States, the Interstate Highway Act had far-reaching consequences. It accelerated the growth of suburbs as well as Americans' reliance on cars and trucks, and increased consumption of gasoline. The negative consequences have included urban decay and air pollution, which would become such a problem that the Clean Air Act of 1963 would be passed to regulate automobile emissions.

SEE ALSO

Clean Air Act of 1963; Energy crisis; Suburbs

FURTHER READING

Rose, Mark H. *Interstate: Express Highway Politics, 1939–1989*. Knoxville: University of Tennessee Press, 1990.

Iran-Contra affair

In 1985 the United States secretly shipped 508 antitank missiles to the anti-American government of Iran via Israel in order to secure the release of U.S. hostages held in Lebanon by pro-Iranian radical terrorists. After reports of arms deals between the United States and Iran appeared in the press in 1986, President Ronald Reagan initially maintained that their purpose had only been to encourage "moderate elements" in Iran, not to pay ransom for U.S. hostages.

An investigative panel appointed by the President placed the blame for the matter primarily on Donald Regan, President Reagan's chief of staff, who promptly resigned. But various congressional, prosecutorial, and journalistic investigations into the affair continued between 1987 and 1989, unearthing a covert operation by marine lieutenant colonel Oliver North, who was a National Security Council aide, to divert profits from the Iran arms sales to the U.S.-backed Contra movement in Nicaragua (which was trying to overthrow the Marxist Sandinista government of Nicaragua), despite a specific ban by Congress on sending arms to the Contras. North destroyed all

Lieutenant Colonel Oliver North helped mastermind the scheme to divert profits from Iran arms sales to the Contras in Nicaragua. He testified before Congress that President Ronald Reagan was not involved in the plan.

the incriminating documents and attributed the plan to CIA director William Casey, but Casey's death from a brain tumor in May 1987 ended this line of investigation.

During a House–Senate investigation in 1987, North portrayed himself as a true patriot. He and other members of the Reagan administration claimed that they had concealed the fund-diversion scheme from the President. The congressional committee criticized the lax management style of the President but found no evidence that Reagan had personal knowledge of the illegalities. In 1988 a court-appointed prosecutor issued criminal indictments against North and John Poindexter, the President's national security advisor. The following year a federal jury convicted North of obstructing a congressional inquiry, destroying and falsifying Security Council documents, and accepting a bribe.

Later a federal judge overturned this conviction on technical grounds. Others involved were saved from trial by Presidential pardons issued by George Bush. After launching a successful public-speaking career, North narrowly lost a U.S. Senate race in Virginia in 1994.

SEE ALSO

Middle East–U.S. relations; Reagan, Ronald Wilson

FURTHER READING

Cohen, William S., and George J. Mitchell. *Men of Zeal: A Candid Inside Story of the Iran-Contra Hearings.* New York: Viking, 1988.

Kagan, Robert. *A Twilight Struggle: American Power and Nicaragua, 1977–1990.* New York: Free Press, 1996.

Prados, John. *Presidents' Secret Wars: CIA and Pentagon Covert Operations from World War II Through Iranscam.* New York: Morrow, 1986.

Iranian hostage crisis (1979)

Restored to power with CIA assistance in 1953, Shah Mohammad Reza Pahlavi ruthlessly ruled Iran and kept that country closely allied to the United States. In January 1979, opponents of the shah, led by the spiritual head of Iran's Shiite Islamic majority, the Ayatollah Ruhollah Khomeini, took control of the country, forcing the shah to flee. In November of that year President Jimmy Carter, not fully gauging the depth of the hatred toward the United States felt by Iran's militants, admitted the shah to the United States for treatment of cancer.

Shortly after, Khomeini's followers stormed the U.S. embassy in Teheran and seized 53 U.S. hostages. Television images from Teheran of U.S. flags being burned, anti-American demonstrations, and blindfolded U.S. hostages rubbed American nerves raw. President Carter failed to gain the hostages' release through negotiations and in frustration ordered a helicopter rescue in April 1980. This attempt failed miserably: two helicopters had mechanical problems and one crashed into a U.S. C-130 plane, killing eight Americans.

Secretary of State Cyrus Vance, upset at Carter's decision to intervene militarily, resigned. After holding the hostages for 444 days, Khomeini finally released them on January 20, 1981, just minutes after Ronald Reagan was sworn into office as President.

SEE ALSO

Carter, James Earl, Jr. ("Jimmy"); Middle East–U.S.relations

Iranian demonstrators burn the U.S. flag on top of the U.S. embassy building in Teheran. Militant Iranians had seized the embassy and taken hostages on November 4, 1979.

FURTHER READING

Bill, James. *The Eagle and the Lion: The Tragedy of American-Iranian Relations.* New Haven, Conn.: Yale University Press, 1988.

Cottam, Richard. *Iran and the United States: A Cold War Case Study.* Pittsburgh: University of Pittsburgh Press, 1988.

Jackson, Jesse Louis

- *Born: Oct. 8, 1941, Greenville, S.C.*
- *Accomplishments: Founded Operation PUSH, 1972; founded Rainbow Coalition, 1984; candidate for Democratic Presidential nomination, 1984, 1988; shadow senator for Washington, D.C., 1990–*

The Reverend Jesse Jackson, an aide to Martin Luther King, Jr., gained national fame in the 1980s with two strong campaigns for the Presidency. Born and raised in South Carolina in a very poor family, Jackson attended the University of Illinois and then North Carolina Agricultural and Technical College, majoring in sociology. He studied at the Chicago Theological Seminary and was ordained a Baptist minister in 1968. During that time he joined Martin Luther King and the Southern Christian Leadership Conference (SCLC) in 1965. From 1966 to 1971 he served as director of the organization's Operation Breadbasket, a food program for African Americans living in poverty. Jackson was standing next to King on a motel balcony in Memphis when an assassin's bullet killed the civil rights leader in 1968.

Jackson left the SCLC in 1972 to form Operation PUSH (People United to Save Humanity), a civil rights organization that pressured corporations to provide jobs and economic opportunities to African Americans. He then started PUSH-Excel, often including in his speeches the refrain "I am somebody!" to motivate black students to stay in school and grad-

Jesse Jackson, who is a very powerful and effective public speaker, was the first African American to be a serious contender for the Presidency.

uate. In 1984 Jackson formed the Rainbow Coalition, made up of poor blacks, Hispanics, and antiwar activists, as part of his bid for the Democratic party's nomination for President. He received more than 3 million votes in the primaries and won a substantial number of convention delegates. In 1988 Jackson ran again, this time more than doubling his vote total and improving his leverage at the convention. In both years, Jackson's impassioned speeches electrified the Democratic nominating conventions.

Jackson has been dogged by charges of anti-Semitism, stemming from a 1984 reference to New York City as "Hymietown," his association with Minister Louis Farrakhan of the Nation of Islam, and his meetings with the leader of the anti-Israeli Palestinian Liberation Organization.

During the 1992 election Jackson declined to run for President, although he made another rousing convention speech. In 1996, Jackson's Rainbow Coalition and Operation PUSH merged into the Rainbow/PUSH Coalition in an effort to maximize the resources of both groups.

SEE ALSO

Civil rights movement

FURTHER READING

Colton, Elizabeth O. *The Jackson Phenomenon: The Man, the Power, the Message.* New York: Doubleday, 1989.

Frady, Marshall. *Jesse: The Life and Pilgrimage of Jesse Jackson.* New York: Random House, 1996.

Reed, Adolph, Jr. *The Jesse Jackson Phenomenon: The Crisis of Purpose in Afro-American Politics.* New Haven, Conn.: Yale University Press, 1986.

John Birch Society

Founded by retired candy manufacturer Robert Welch in 1958 to combat what he perceived to be the infiltration of communism into American life, the John Birch Society was named for a Baptist missionary killed by Chinese communists in 1945. Beginning with 11 members, the radical right organization grew rapidly with the support of wealthy reactionaries. Within five years, the so-called Birchers had an estimated annual income of $5 million and a membership of 50,000. Frustrated by the stalemated cold war, the failure to roll back the New Deal, and the downfall of Senator Joseph McCarthy, their adherents believed that Presidents Dwight Eisenhower and John Kennedy were both "dedicated, conscious agents of the Communist conspiracy," as were CIA director Allen Dulles, Chief Justice Earl Warren, and many others. Support for the John Birch Society peaked during the early 1960s; it came from conservatives who were disturbed by the growth of the welfare state and the success of the civil rights movement and were intent on escalating the crusade against communism.

SEE ALSO

Conservatism

FURTHER READING

Whitfield, Stephen. *The Culture of the Cold War.* Baltimore: Johns Hopkins University Press, 1991.

Johnson, Claudia Alta ("Lady Bird") Taylor

- *Born: Dec. 22, 1912, Karnack, Tex.*
- *Accomplishments: First Lady of the United States, 1963–69*

As First Lady, Lady Bird Johnson spearheaded a drive to "beautify" the landscape. The wife of President Lyndon Baines Johnson traveled more than 200,000 miles promoting the project and helped gain passage of the Highway Beautification Act of 1965, popularly known as "the Lady Bird Bill." It eliminated or limited billboards and junkyards alongside major highways. A grove in Redwood National Park in California was named for her in 1969. After her husband's death in 1973, Johnson served as a board member of the LBJ Library, the National Geographic Society, and the National Parks Advisory Board, as well as a regent of the University of Texas.

SEE ALSO

Johnson, Lyndon Baines

FURTHER READING

Gould, Lewis L. *Lady Bird Johnson and the Environment.* Lawrence: University Press of Kansas, 1988.

Johnson, Lyndon Baines

- *Born: Aug. 27, 1908, Stonewall, Tex.*
- *Accomplishments: U.S. representative (Democrat–Tex.), 1937–48; U.S. senator (Democrat–Tex.), 1948–61; Senate majority leader, 1955–60; Vice President, 1961–63; 36th President of the United States, 1963–69*
- *Died: Jan. 22, 1973, Johnson City, Tex.*

Although he signed more major social legislation than almost any other U.S. President, Lyndon B. Johnson (also known by his initials, LBJ) was hounded from office by those who opposed his conduct of the war in Vietnam. One of the most skillful politicians ever to occupy the White House, LBJ had served in Washington continuously since 1932—as congressional aide, federal administrator, representative and senator from Texas, and Senate majority leader—when he ran for the Democratic Presidential nomination in 1960. After losing to John Kennedy, he accepted the Vice Presidential nomination and ascended to the Presidency after Kennedy's assassination on November 22, 1963, in Dallas, Texas.

Johnson then set out to calm and unify the nation and to win a landslide victory in the 1964 Presidential election. He secured congressional approval in 1964 of the War on Poverty program and the first significant civil rights legislation since Reconstruction; and his campaign effort received a major boost when the Republicans nominated as their candidate the very conservative Barry Goldwater. Goldwater campaigned on his opposition to civil rights legislation and most of the New Deal programs for poor and middle-class

Lyndon Johnson cared deeply about the Great Society programs, and used his formidable political skills to get them through Congress. Here he meets with Martin Luther King, Jr., (second from right) and other civil rights leaders and Bobby Kennedy (center) as they prepare to discuss proposed legislation.

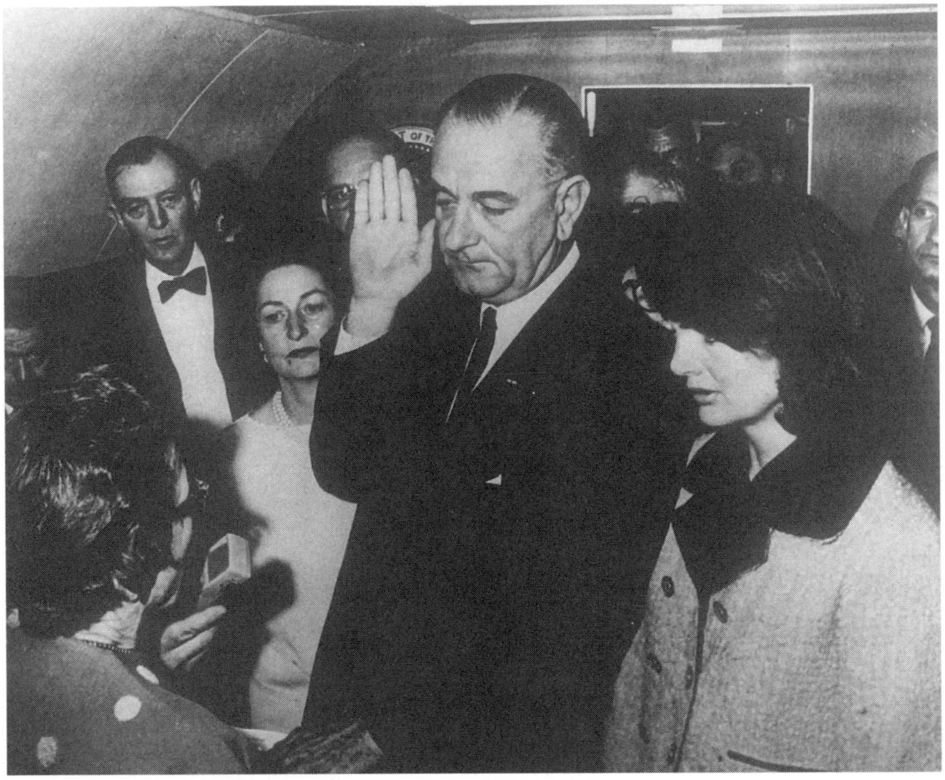

Lyndon Johnson takes the Presidential oath of office on board Air Force One, only a few hours after John Kennedy was assassinated in Dallas on November 22, 1963. He is flanked by Kennedy's widow, Jacqueline (right), and his wife, Lady Bird.

Americans established by President Franklin Roosevelt in the 1930s. After Goldwater implied that he might use nuclear weapons against Vietnam and Cuba, Johnson and his running mate, Hubert H. Humphrey, painted him as a fanatical militarist who could not be trusted with his finger on the atomic button. On Vietnam, Johnson also posed as the voice of moderation, promising that "we are not going to send American boys nine or ten thousand miles from home to do what Asian boys ought to be doing for themselves." With 61 percent of the popular vote, Johnson swept a host of liberal legislators with him into Congress.

Johnson was a far more experienced legislator and political tactician than Kennedy, but he often suffered in comparisons to his more eloquent predecessor. In contrast to Kennedy's sophistication and charm, Johnson seemed crude and unattractive, displaying his surgical scars to reporters and picking his dog up by the ears. Nonetheless, his ability to build consensus and twist legislators' arms enabled Johnson to guide through Congress legislation that had been stalled before the assassination as well as many new proposals. He recognized the fleeting nature of popular support and implored legislators to quickly pass his Great Society legislation (to create "a place where every child can find knowledge to enrich his mind and to enlarge his talents"), a program of domestic reforms matched in U.S. history only by the New Deal. Congress responded positively, passing health insurance for welfare recipients and the elderly (Medicaid and Medicare), voting rights for African Americans, a more liberal immigration law, the creation of the National Endowments for the Arts and Humanities, and legislation to improve education, housing, and transportation.

But Johnson also saw another threat to his domestic policies: the escalating war in South Vietnam. Knowing that his Republican opponents would attack him for being "soft on communism" if the small Southeast Asian country fell to communist rebels, he escalated U.S. military involvement in hopes of staving off defeat. But he also hoped to avoid full-scale U.S. involvement, worrying that the war would undermine support for his most important program, the Great Society.

Johnson's worst fears came true. The United States had slowly increased its involvement in the tiny Southeast Asian country under Dwight Eisenhower and Kennedy, but it was Johnson who first sent U.S. troops in massive numbers. In August 1964, he condemned the North Vietnamese for allegedly attacking U.S. destroyers in the Gulf of Tonkin off the coast of Vietnam. This act of "aggression on the high seas," Johnson told Congress, proved that the President needed authority to "repel any armed attack against the forces of the United States and to prevent further aggression." The Senate (by an 88-to-2 vote) and the House (416 to 0) promptly passed the Gulf of Tonkin Resolution, which served as "the functional equivalent of war" and allowed LBJ to commit U.S. forces at his discretion. Johnson lost little time in using this power, ordering the bombing of North Vietnam the following winter and increasing the number of U.S. troops to 100,000 by the fall of 1965. Congress never officially declared war.

As U.S. casualties mounted, and vivid pictures of a war whose purpose never seemed clear were broadcast on the nightly TV news, antiwar sentiment emerged in the form of protests on college campuses and defeats for the Democrats at the polls in the 1966 midterm elections. Meanwhile, Johnson and his aides continued to promise victory and to send more troops to Vietnam. By 1968 they had stationed more than 500,000 U.S. servicemen in the small Asian nation. Johnson did not want to admit defeat, but no amount of bombing and no level of troop engagement seemed to make a difference in forcing North Vietnam and the Vietcong to relent. In January 1968, just as the generals were again predicting a "light at the end of the tunnel," communist forces launched the Tet offensive against the Saigon government. Television images of the U.S. embassy under siege in the South Vietnamese capital starkly contradicted the official optimistic line on the war and hurt Johnson's credibility with the public. After the President barely defeated an antiwar challenger, Eugene McCarthy, in the New Hampshire primary in March, he announced that he would not run for reelection and would begin to reduce U.S. engagement in the war while entering peace talks with the North Vietnamese.

Voters repudiated Johnson's policies—both foreign and domestic—in the 1968 election, delivering less than 43 percent of the popular vote to his handpicked successor, Vice President Hubert Humphrey. A surprising 13 percent of the vote went to southern segregationist George Wallace, who played to white resentment of Great Society programs that benefited blacks, while the winner, Richard Nixon, campaigned on a promise to promote law and order and pursue a "secret plan to end the war." An unpopular, despondent Johnson left office in January 1969, retiring to his ranch near Johnson City, Texas, where he died of a heart attack in January 1973. His administration marked both the peak of liberal reform and the beginning of its decline.

SEE ALSO

Goldwater, Barry; Great Society; Gulf of Tonkin Resolution; Johnson, Claudia Alta ("Lady Bird") Taylor; Kennedy, John Fitzgerald; Tet offensive; Vietnam War; War on Poverty

FURTHER READING

Bornet, Vaughn. *The Presidency of Lyndon B. Johnson*. Lawrence: =, 1990.

Dallek, Robert. *Flawed Giant: Lyndon B. Johnson, 1960–73*. New York: Oxford University Press, 1998.

Dallek, Robert. *Lone Star Rising: Lyndon Johnson and His Times, 1908–60*. New York: Oxford University Press, 1991.

Gardner, Lloyd C. *Pay Any Price: Lyndon Johnson and the Wars for Vietnam*. Chicago: Ivan R. Dee, 1995.

Herring, George C. *LBJ and Vietnam: A Different Kind of War*. Austin: University of Texas Press, 1994.

Johnson, Lyndon B. *The Vantage Point: Perspectives of the Presidency, 1963–69*. New York: Holt, Rinehart & Winston, 1971.

Kaye, Tony, and Anthony Kaye. *Lyndon B. Johnson*. New York: Chelsea House, 1988.

Kearns, Doris. *Lyndon Johnson and the American Dream*. New York: Harper & Row, 1976.

Kennan, George F.

- *Born: Feb. 16, 1904, Milwaukee, Wis.*
- *Accomplishments: member of the Foreign Service, 1926–53; director of the State Department's Policy Planning Staff, 1946–50; expert on Soviet affairs*

The foremost interpreter of the Soviet Union and U.S. foreign policy in his time, George Kennan was largely responsible for the idea of communist "containment," the cornerstone of U.S. policy for four decades. An 8,000-word telegram he sent from Moscow in 1946, refined in a 1947 article for *Foreign Affairs* and published under the pseudonym "X," concluded that the Soviet Union was waging "a patient but deadly struggle" to expand its influence worldwide and that U.S. policy should be "a long-term, patient, but firm and vigilant containment of Russian expansive tendencies."

Frustrated by the later U.S. emphasis on military force and aggressive confrontation in place of patience and restraint, Kennan retired as head of the State Department's Policy Planning Staff in 1950 and warned in 1957 that "until we stop pushing the Kremlin against a closed door, we shall never learn whether it would be prepared to go through an open one."

In the 1960s Kennan became a critic of America's educational system and lack of national purpose, decrying the overwhelming stress on "personal comfort and amusement." He also attacked the New Left for its assaults on freedom of speech for ideas it did not like.

Kennan emerged as one of the chief opponents of President Lyndon Johnson's escalation of the war in Vietnam. He argued that the United States's preoccupation with a region that was not important to our national security weakened our ability to stand firm in places where the national security could be at risk, such as Japan, Europe, and the oil-producing regions of the Middle East. Kennan described the war as "a massive miscalculation and error of policy, an error for which it is hard to find any parallel in our own history."

SEE ALSO

Cold war; Containment doctrine

FURTHER READING

Gaddis, John Lewis. *Strategies of Containment*. New York: Oxford University Press, 1982.

Hixson, Walter. *George F. Kennan: Cold War Iconoclast*. New York: Columbia University Press, 1989.

Kennan, George F. *The Decision to Intervene: Soviet-American Relations, 1917–1920*. Princeton, N.J.: Princeton University Press, 1989.

Jackie Kennedy, between Robert Kennedy (left) and Edward Kennedy, walks to her husband's funeral mass in Washington, D.C. Her dignity during this national tragedy helped to calm a distraught nation.

Kennedy, Jacqueline Bouvier

- *Born: July 28, 1929, Southampton, N.Y.*
- *Accomplishments: First Lady of the United States, 1961–63*
- *Died: May 19, 1994, New York, N.Y.*

The wife of President John F. Kennedy, Jackie Kennedy was a glamorous First Lady who charmed both American voters and foreign heads of state during her husband's brief term in office. In that time she became a fashion trendsetter and worked to restore the interior of the White House to its original historical décor. She accompanied her husband on trips abroad, where she received adoring attention from foreign crowds and media.

Jackie Kennedy, however, is most widely remembered by the American public for her role as the national chief mourner during her husband's funeral in November 1963. She had accompanied the President on a trip to Dallas on November 22 and was seated next to him when an assassin's bullet ripped through his head. Her dignity and stoic bearing during the funeral procession helped to calm a nation shocked by the traumatic event. From the assassination until her death in 1994, tabloid journalists tracked her around the world, but she maintained a dignified distance from the public eye after her marriage in 1968 to Greek shipping magnate Aristotle Onassis and, following his death in 1975, during her career as a book editor in New York City.

SEE ALSO

Kennedy, John Fitzgerald

FURTHER READING

Birmingham, Stephen. *Jacqueline Bouvier Kennedy Onassis.* New York: Grosset & Dunlap, 1978.

Kennedy, John Fitzgerald

- *Born: May 29, 1917, Brookline, Mass.*
- *Accomplishments: U.S. representative (Democrat–Mass.), 1947–53; U.S. senator (Democrat–Mass.), 1953–61; 35th President of the United States, 1961–63*
- *Died: Nov. 22, 1963, Dallas, Tex.*

John Fitzgerald Kennedy and his glamorous wife, Jacqueline Bouvier Kennedy, infused the Presidency with a feeling of magic and culture for three years. The youngest man and the only Roman Catholic ever elected to the Presidency, Kennedy's term in office was cut short by an assassin's bullet. Although his tenure was too short to allow him to build much of a record in office, Kennedy's idealism, eloquence, and youthful vigor inspired many throughout the world.

Kennedy was the second son of a politically active Massachusetts financier, Joseph P. Kennedy, and Rose Fitzgerald Kennedy, the daughter of a mayor of Boston; all four of the couple's sons were groomed for politics from the time they were small boys. John Kennedy returned from World War II a hero; medals in hand, he was elected to the House of Representatives. After winning reelection twice, in 1952 Kennedy beat incumbent Republican Henry Cabot Lodge, Jr., for a seat in the U.S. Senate.

Four years later, Kennedy campaigned for the Democratic party's nomination for Vice President, losing to Senator Estes Kefauver. Undaunted, he easily won reelection to the Senate and began organizing for a Presidential run. In 1960 he beat Hubert Humphrey in the Democratic primaries and bested Lyndon Johnson, the Senate majority leader, on the first ballot at the convention. Party leaders had feared that the Catholic Kennedy could not win election to the highest office in a predominantly Protestant country, but Kennedy put their fears to rest by winning Protestant votes in the primaries and addressing the issue head on at a meeting of Protestant ministers. At the Democratic convention, Kennedy chose Johnson as his running mate and called on the nation to brave a "new frontier" of "unknown opportunities and perils" in both foreign and domestic policy.

John Kennedy, the first Catholic President of the United States, meets Pope Paul VI at the Vatican in 1963.

Facing a formidable challenger in the election, Vice President Richard M. Nixon, Kennedy, who came off well on camera, used television to propel himself to the Presidency. The turning point in the election came during four televised debates, the first of their kind in U.S. history. Although radio listeners tended to think the debate a draw, the 70 million Americans watching on TV clearly thought the handsome, poised Kennedy a victor over his pale, perspiring, haggard rival.

Kennedy's standing in the polls shot up, and he never lost the lead. Still, the election was the closest since 1888, with Kennedy garnering 49.7 percent of the popular vote to Nixon's 49.5 percent. Lingering prejudice and fears about a Catholic as President had cost Kennedy votes in the South, but his religion had gained him votes in the populous urban centers of the Midwest and Northeast.

The Kennedy administration made economic growth its top priority and helped stimulate the economy by spending billions on defense and space programs. The race to the moon that Kennedy initiated would cost more than $25 billion, and he vastly expanded the United States's arsenal of intercontinental ballistic missiles, medium-range missiles, and nuclear-missile-carrying submarines. Kennedy also increased the country's conventional forces and created the Green Berets to fight guerrilla wars in poorer countries (called, before the collapse of the Soviet Union, Third World countries, because they were not part of alliances with either the United States or the Soviet Union).

By engaging in deficit spending and cutting business taxes, Kennedy's administration doubled the rate of economic growth, decreased unemployment, and held the annual inflation rate below 2 percent, initiating the second-longest period of economic expansion in U.S. history. (This record has been topped only during Bill Clinton's administration in the 1990s.) Much of the rest of Kennedy's domestic agenda languished, however, as a coalition of Republicans and conservative southern Democrats prevented two-thirds of his proposals from becoming law.

To the dismay of the African Americans and liberals who had helped elect him, John F. Kennedy did little to help the civil rights movement during his first two years in office. Fearful of alienating southern white voters and dividing the nation and the Democrats in Congress, Kennedy straddled the civil rights issue. He appointed a record number of African Americans to high positions in government and simultaneously nominated white racists to federal judgeships in the South. He distanced himself from congressional attempts to enact civil rights legislation and dragged his feet for two years before issuing a rather weak executive order banning race discrimination in federally financed housing.

Pushed by events and the courageous acts of black protestors, however, Kennedy sent federal troops south to enforce court-ordered integration at the University of Mississippi in 1962 and prevented Governor George Wallace from blocking the integration of the University of Alabama the following year. Following the 1963 Birmingham demonstrations, he introduced federal civil rights legislation in June of that year, calling black rights a "moral issue" and declaring that "race has no place in American life or law." After the March on Washington, in which 225,000 peaceful demonstrators converged on the capital, Kennedy stepped up his efforts to get the measure through Congress, arguing that "this nation . . . will not be fully free until all its citizens are free." Opponents in Congress continued to block the measure, however, and it passed only after Kennedy's death, thanks in part to the adroit political maneuvering of his successor, Lyndon B. Johnson.

In foreign policy Kennedy proved a formidable cold warrior, promising to "pay any price, bear any burden, meet any hardship, support any friend, oppose any foe to assure the survival and the success of liberty." He tripled the nation's nuclear capability; escalated the war in Vietnam; and established the Agency for International Development, the Peace Corps, the Alliance for Progress, and the Food for Peace programs to give aid to poorer countries that seemed in danger of turning communist. Kennedy inspired Europeans with his support of Berlin after the communists erected a wall there to seal the communist eastern section off from the capitalist West. He traveled there in 1961, proclaiming in German "Ich bin ein Berliner" ("I am a Berliner") to the delight of an adoring crowd.

Kennedy's worst failure and greatest triumph in foreign affairs both involved Cuba. With Kennedy's approval, in 1961 the Central Intelligence Agency trained and sponsored an invasion of the island by 1,500 Cuban exiles in the hope of overthrowing Fidel Castro's new communist regime. Wanting to hide U.S. involvement, Kennedy refused to provide air cover for the insurgents, who were easily overwhelmed by Cuban military forces. Kennedy accepted full responsibility for the failed Bay of Pigs invasion, which had been planned earlier by Dwight Eisenhower's administration, but neither apologized for it nor stopped other attempts to depose Castro.

In October 1962 aerial photographs taken over Cuba revealed that the Soviet Union was constructing nuclear missile bases there. Demanding their immediate and total removal, the President ordered a naval blockade of Cuba, initiating a potentially catastrophic showdown with Soviet leader Nikita Khrushchev. "We were eyeball to eyeball," Secretary of State Dean Rusk said, and for three days the world stood on the brink of nuclear war. Then Khrushchev sent a message to Kennedy agreeing to remove the missiles if the United States agreed not to invade Cuba. On October 27, 1962, Kennedy did so, and the world stepped back from the edge of annihilation.

Understanding how close they had come to war, the United States and the Soviet Union agreed to install a telephone hot line to ensure direct communication between the superpowers in the future. Both sides made efforts to relax the tensions between them, including the signing of the Limited Nuclear Test Ban Treaty, which permitted them to test nuclear weapons only underground.

President Kennedy works at his desk during the tense days of late October 1962, as he and the country teetered on the edge of war with Cuba.

In other foreign affairs, Kennedy involved the United States further in the conflict in Vietnam. U.S. "advisors" to the South Vietnamese government were increased from 700 in 1961 to 16,000 in 1963. Kennedy pushed President Ngo Dinh Diem to pass economic and political reform in order to increase his popularity and support. Instead, Diem brutally crushed student demonstrations. The CIA then gave the green light to South Vietnamese generals to overthrow his government (Diem was assassinated during this coup) and install a new government that the Kennedy administration hoped would conduct the war against the Vietnamese communists more effectively.

A month later, on November 22, 1963, Kennedy was shot and killed while riding in an open car with his wife on a political visit to Dallas, Texas. A stunned nation mourned and watched on television as incredible events unfolded: the assassination of the President; the arrest of his suspected killer, Lee Harvey Oswald; the murder of Oswald by Dallas nightclub owner Jack Ruby; and the state funeral. Although the Warren Commission, a fact-finding body set up to inquire into the circumstances of the assassination, concluded that Oswald had indeed killed the President and had acted alone, public skepticism about that finding remains strong. The Warren Commission had worked hastily, eager to still rumors of a conspiracy. That did not happen. Critics charged the Commission with slipshod research, and a host of books, television programs, films, and a 1979 congressional investigation rebutted some of the Warren Commission's findings and portrayed a conspiracy to assassinate the President involving the CIA, the Mafia, Fidel Castro, extreme conservatives, the Vietnamese, and even Lyndon Johnson. Although no credible evidence of such a conspiracy surfaced, belief in it persisted because of the later assassination of other American leaders, revelations of actual high-level conspiracies—such as the Watergate cover-up and the Iran-Contra affair—and the desire of many Americans to make sense out of a shocking, meaningless act.

Kennedy's assassination marked the beginning of the divisive, tragic, tumultuous period of the 1960s. Considering what happened later, many Americans looked back longingly on the Kennedy years as a brief shining moment of promise, a lost era of "Camelot." (References to the mythical city of King Arthur were frequent, fueled by the hit Broadway musical by Lerner and Loewe that began its run during the Kennedy years.) People remembered the Kennedy administration's style more than its substance, its spirit of adventure and its cultured tone; more than anything else they remembered its bloody end. Even though revelations of John and Robert Kennedy's compulsive womanizing and other personal failings in recent years have significantly tarnished the Kennedy image, the American public remains fascinated with this period of history.

SEE ALSO

Alliance for Progress; Arms race; Bay of Pigs; Berlin Wall; Birmingham civil rights demonstrations (1963); Civil rights movement; Cold war; Cuban missile crisis (1962); Johnson, Lyndon Baines; Kennedy, Jacqueline Bouvier; New Frontier; Oswald, Lee Harvey; Peace Corps; Vietnam War; Warren Commission

FURTHER READING

Brown, Thomas. *JFK: History of an Image.* Bloomington: Indiana University Press, 1988.

Giglio, James. *The Presidency of John F. Kennedy.* Lawrence: University Press of Kansas, 1991.

Parmet, Herbert. *J.F.K.: The Presidency of John F. Kennedy.* New York: Dial, 1983.

Reeves, Richard. *President Kennedy: Profile of Power.* New York: Simon & Schuster, 1993.

Kennedy, Robert F. ("Bobby")

- *Born: Nov. 20, 1925, Brookline, Mass.*
- *Accomplishments: U.S. attorney general, 1961–64; U.S. senator (Democrat–N.Y.), 1965–68*
- *Died: June 6, 1968, Los Angeles, Calif.*

A younger brother of John F. Kennedy, Bobby Kennedy had a career that was integrally linked to his brother's. After John was elected to the U.S. Senate,

Attorney General Robert Kennedy testifies before Congress in support of civil rights legislation. He said that racial problems should be handled in the courts, "not in the streets."

Bobby served as chief counsel to its Permanent Committee on Investigations. There Bobby gained fame for his aggressive investigation of corruption within Jimmy Hoffa's International Brotherhood of Teamsters union and organized labor.

After winning the Presidency in 1960, John Kennedy appointed Bobby attorney general, joking that he saw nothing wrong with giving Robert some legal expertise before he went out to practice law. As attorney general, Bobby shared his brother's initial reluctance to further the cause of civil rights, fearing to alienate white southern Democratic voters and their powerful representatives in Congress. But, repeatedly prodded by the violence against civil rights protestors, the brothers changed their position in 1963 and began to act forthrightly against racial segregation.

Following John Kennedy's assassination, Bobby resigned as attorney general and successfully ran for the U.S. Senate from New York in 1964. As a senator, Bobby Kennedy fought for civil rights and for the poorest Americans, and he became a vocal critic of Lyndon Johnson's policies in Vietnam. He was, wrote one columnist, our first politician for the pariahs, our great national outsider. In March 1968 he entered the contest for the Democratic Presidential nomination. He won several primaries, but after celebrating victory in California on June 5, 1968, Bobby Kennedy was shot by Sirhan Sirhan, a Palestinian immigrant who opposed Kennedy's pro-Israel sympathies. His assassination, following those of John Kennedy, Malcolm X, and Martin Luther King, Jr., disillusioned many Americans, especially the young, with the political process. One young person remarked, "I won't vote. Every good man we get they kill."

SEE ALSO

Johnson, Lyndon Baines; Kennedy, John Fitzgerald; Vietnam War

FURTHER READING

Burner, David, and Thomas R. West. *The Torch Is Passed: The Kennedy Brothers and American Liberalism.* Boston: Athenaeum, 1984.

Mathews, Tom. "The Lessons of Bobby." *Newsweek,* May 31, 1993, 26–28.
Newfield, Jack. *Robert Kennedy: A Memoir.* New York: Dutton, 1969.
Schlesinger, Arthur M., Jr. *Robert Kennedy and His Times.* Boston: Houghton Mifflin, 1978.

Kent State University (1970)

Reacting to President Richard Nixon's April 30, 1970, announcement that U.S. troops were going to invade neutral Cambodia as part of the war effort in Vietnam, students at scores of campuses across the country spontaneously took to the streets in protest. At Kent State University in Ohio, most students engaged in peaceful protest, but a small group of radicals attempted to firebomb the ROTC building and threw rocks and bottles at police. Ohio governor James Rhodes established martial law at Kent State and ordered 3,000 National Guard troops to the campus.

The next day, May 4, 1970, the guardsmen advanced on a student rally and fired canisters of tear gas. As hundreds of demonstrators ran from the advancing guard, the soldiers from Troop G suddenly opened fire. Four students were killed and 13 others wounded. The White House coldly commented, "This should remind us all once again that when dissent turns to violence, it invites tragedy." Within days, approximately 1.5 million students went on strike, closing one-fifth of the nation's colleges and universities, some for the rest of the school year.

At first the Justice Department refused to conduct an inquiry into the guard's actions; eventually a grand jury indicted eight of the guardsmen but the charges were dismissed for lack of evidence. A report issued by the President's Commission on Campus Unrest found that the guardsmen's actions had been "unnecessary, unwarranted, and inexcusable."

SEE ALSO
Cambodia, bombing and invasion of

FURTHER READING

Michener, James. *Kent State: What Happened and Why.* New York: Random House, 1971.

Armed National Guard troops face off against crowds of students at Kent State University on May 4, 1970. The National Guard is preparing to throw tear gas at the students.

Kerner Commission (National Advisory Commission on Civil Disorders)

The federal advisory board formally known as the National Advisory Commission on Civil Disorders but commonly called the Kerner Commission reported in 1968 that rioting among blacks in urban ghettos sprang inevitably from the oppression of blacks in U.S. society. Rioting in hundreds of cities during the so-called long, hot summers from 1964 to 1968 left 200 people dead, 7,000 injured, and $200 million worth of property destroyed. The board, which was chaired by Senator Otto Kerner of Illinois, blamed the rioting on the effects of "white racism," including the confinement of blacks to ghettos characterized by poverty, poor housing, inadequate education, and police brutality. The nation, Kerner warned, "is moving toward two societies, one black, one white—separate and unequal." The commission recommended the creation of 2 million new jobs and 6 million units of public housing, the end of school segregation based on segregated neighborhoods, and a "federal system of cash payments to increase the income of the nation's poorest families." Conservatives denounced the commission's recommendations and called for more policing instead. Worried about white backlash, President Lyndon B. Johnson declined to act on the findings. Twenty years later, with conditions basically unchanged, blacks in Los Angeles again erupted in violence in response to the acquittal by an all-white jury of the policemen who had been caught on film beating a black suspect, Rodney King.

SEE ALSO

Detroit Race Riot (1967); King, Rodney; Race riots

FURTHER READING

Button, James. *Black Violence: Political Impact of the 1960s Riots.* Princeton, N.J.: Princeton University Press, 1978.

United States. Kerner Commission. *Report of the National Advisory Commission on Civil Disorders.* Washington, D.C.: United States Government Printing Office, 1968.

Kerouac, Jack

- *Born: Mar. 12, 1922, Lowell, Mass.*
- *Accomplishments: Writer*
- *Major Works:* On the Road *(1957),* The Dharma Bums *(1958),* Book of Dreams *(1961),* Big Sur *(1963),* Desolate Angels *(1965)*
- *Died: Oct. 21, 1969, Saint Petersburg, Fla.*

The leading writer of the Beat movement, Jack Kerouac shot to fame after a glowing review of his novel *On the Road* (1957) appeared in the *New*

Jack Kerouac, talented, charismatic, and restless as a young man, became increasingly embittered and reclusive, dying as an alcoholic at the age of 47.

York Times. Feeling cramped by the empty "togetherness" of 1950s America, Kerouac used his writing and lifestyle to symbolize the open road as the path to excitement and enlightenment. Kerouac, as well as such fellow Beats as Allen Ginsberg, Neal Cassady, and William F. Burroughs, rebelled against a U.S. culture that Kerouac described as "rows of well-to-do houses with lawns and television sets in each living room with everybody looking at the same thing at the same time." His rejection of the materialism and conformity of the 1950s, indeed of all the established values of U.S. society, provided the inspiration for his work.

SEE ALSO

Beat movement; Ginsberg, Allen

FURTHER READING

Coolidge, Clark. "Kerouac." *The American Poetry Review* (Jan.–Feb. 1995): 43–50.
Kerouac, Jack. *On the Road*. New York: Viking, 1957.
McNally, Dennis. *Desolate Angel: Jack Kerouac, the Beat Generation, and America*. New York: Random House, 1979.
Nicosia, Gerald. *Memory Babe: A Critical Biography of Jack Kerouac*. New York: Grove, 1983.

Keynesian economics

First proposed by British economist John Maynard Keynes (pronounced "Canes") in his *Treatise on Money* (1930) and *The General Theory of Employment, Interest, and Money* (1936), Keynesian economics has been very influential in U.S. politics and economic policy. The guiding principle behind Keynes's theory is that the government has a responsibility to control the economy for the good of the people.

There are several ways a government can do this, he argued. The first is deficit spending to compensate for the uncertainties of private industry. The government can accomplish this by borrowing money (thereby spending more money than it receives in taxes) to pump money into the economy during a time of weak economic growth.

Another way a government can affect the economy is to influence the amount of money available, through increases and decreases in the tax rate. The third strategy is to institute a progressive tax rate (in which those who earn more pay a higher percentage of their income in taxes). The last option is to lower interest rates, thereby stimulating business investment.

U.S. economic policymakers have used Keynesian economics on several occasions. President Franklin Delano Roosevelt employed Keynesian economic theory as the basis for his New Deal policies, although he never really accepted the idea of deficit spending as a solid theory of economics. President Richard Nixon declared in 1971, "I am now a Keynesian," when he began deficit spending to help relieve the recession of that year. And President Ronald Reagan's supply-side economic policy of lowering taxes to stimulate business growth was yet another variant of Keynesian theory.

SEE ALSO

Reagan, Ronald Wilson

FURTHER READING

Fanning, Connell et al., *The General Theory of Profit Equilibrium: Keynes and the Entrepreneur Economy.* New York: St. Martin's, 1997.
Keynes, John Maynard. *The General Theory of Employment, Interest, and Money.* 1936. Reprint, New York: Prometheus, 1997.
Stein, Herbert. *The Fiscal Revolution in America*. Chicago: University of Chicago Press, 1969.

Khmer Rouge

After being deposed by a pro-Western military leader in March 1970, Cambodian prince Norodom Sihanouk joined forces with communist rebels known as the Khmer Rouge, led by Pol Pot, in order to take back his country. (The French word for "red"—*rouge*—refers to the group's communism; the Khmers are a native people of Cambodia.) North Vietnam sent additional troops into Cambodia to support the Khmer Rouge, which led President Richard Nixon to order U.S. and South Vietnamese ground forces into Cambodia. This initiative widened the war in Southeast Asia.

After the U.S. withdrawal from Indochina, the Khmer Rouge seized power in 1975 and killed 3 million Cambodians in mass exterminations and "relocations" from Phnom Penh to the countryside. The Khmer Rouge was defeated by the Vietnamese Army in 1979 and driven from power.

SEE ALSO

Cambodia, bombing and invasion of; Vietnam War

FURTHER READING

Kiernan, Ben. *The Pol Pot Regime.* New Haven, Conn.: Yale University Press, 1996.

King, Martin Luther, Jr.

- *Born: Jan. 15, 1929, Atlanta, Ga.*
- *Accomplishments: President, Southern Christian Leadership Conference, 1957–68; Nobel Peace Prize, 1964*
- *Died: Apr. 4, 1968, Memphis, Tenn.*

The best-known figure of the civil rights movement of the 1950s and 1960s, the Reverend Dr. Martin Luther King, Jr., advocated a nonviolent approach to protest. During his graduate education at Crozer Theological Seminary and Boston University, King was influenced by the Indian pacifist Mohandas Gandhi, who led his country's successful independence movement in the 1940s, and by the American transcendentalist writer and philosopher Henry David Thoreau, who practiced civil disobedience in the 19th century.

After receiving his doctorate in philosophy from Boston University, King returned to the South to take a position as pastor of the Dexter Avenue Baptist Church in Montgomery, Alabama. Seven months later, in December 1955, he was thrust into the leadership of a successful year-long boycott of the segregated Montgomery bus system. The boycott and a bombing of his home pushed King into the national spotlight, and he became the major spokesman of the civil rights movement.

In 1957 King joined with 60 other African-American ministers to form the Southern Christian Leadership Conference (SCLC), which he served as president until his death. In the next few years he led peaceful demonstrations across the South and to the nation's capital, enduring death threats, an assassination attempt, and a jailing for practicing civil disobedience against local segregation laws.

After Presidential candidate John F. Kennedy helped win King's release from an Atlanta jail in 1960, King and other civil rights leaders endorsed the senator's campaign. Kennedy's administration, however, did little to advance civil rights, and in 1963 King and his staff initiated a major confrontation in Birmingham, Alabama, where police violence against unarmed black demonstrators generated newspaper headlines around the world and an upsurge of

The Reverend Martin Luther King, Jr. (right), and the Reverend Ralph Abernathy change their socks during the civil rights march from Selma to Montgomery, Alabama, in 1965.

support in the United States for an end to racial segregation in the South. King's "Letter from a Birmingham Jail," written during his imprisonment there, defended the civil rights movement as a justifiable disobedience of unjust laws.

Civil rights leaders then organized the August 28, 1963, March on Washington, where King delivered one of the most eloquent speeches in American history. "And when we allow freedom to ring," King said, "when we let it ring from every village and hamlet, from every state and city, we will be able to speed up that day when all of God's children—black men and white men, Jews and Gentiles, Catholics and Protestants—will be able to join hands and to sing in the words of the old Negro spiritual, 'Free at last, free at least; thank God Almighty, we are free at last.'" King received the Nobel Peace Prize in 1964 and continued to agitate nonviolently for civil rights, despite increasing criticism of his tactics by angrier, more impatient blacks.

In March 1965 King's attempts to lead a march from Selma, Alabama, to Montgomery led to clashes between protestors and local police. In an address to Congress on March 15 President Lyndon Johnson responded by denouncing racial violence, urging passage of a voting rights bill, and quoting the civil rights anthem "We Shall Overcome." King was present in the White House when Johnson signed the Voting Rights Act later that year.

In 1966 King turned his attention northward, organizing and unsuccessfully leading a campaign against segregated housing in Chicago. Moved by the depth of racial problems and the desperation of poverty in northern ghettos, King grew steadily more radical, shifting his attack from legal discrimination to the less obvious forms of segregation and discrimination in housing and the workplace. He denounced the Vietnam War, which was taking resources away from Johnson's War on Poverty, and in early 1968 worked on plans for a poor people's march on Washington.

In April 1968, while organizing the march, he traveled to Memphis to protest in support of the city's striking sanitation workers. There, on April 4, while standing on the balcony of a motel, King was shot in the head and killed by a white assassin, James Earl Ray.

Although he was condemned by some, King was revered by many for his martyrdom on behalf of nonviolence. In 1986 Congress approved, and President Ronald Reagan signed, a bill making the third Monday of January a federal holiday: Martin Luther King Day.

SEE ALSO

African Americans; Civil rights movement; "Letter from a Birmingham Jail" (April 1963); March on Washington (1963); Montgomery bus boycott (1955–56); Southern Christian Leadership Conference (SCLC)

FURTHER READING

Archer, Jules. *They Had a Dream: The Civil Rights Struggle from Frederick Douglass to Marcus Garvey to Martin Luther King and Malcolm X*. New York: Puffin, 1996.
Branch, Taylor. *Parting the Waters: America in the King Years, 1954–1963*. New York: Simon & Schuster, 1988.
Clayton, Ed. *Martin Luther King: Peaceful Warrior*. New York: Pocket Books, 1996.
Fairclough, Adam. *Martin Luther King, Jr.* Athens: University of Georgia Press, 1990.
Garrow, David J. *Bearing the Cross: Martin Luther King, Jr., and the Southern Christian Leadership Conference*. New York: Morrow, 1986.
Jakoubek, Robert. *Martin Luther King, Jr.* New York: Chelsea House, 1989.
Lewis, David L. *King: A Biography*. Urbana: University of Illinois Press, 1978.
Ralph, James R., Jr. *Northern Protest: Martin Luther King, Jr., Chicago, and the Civil Rights Movement*. Cambridge, Mass.: Harvard University Press, 1993.

King, Rodney

• *Born: April 2, 1965; Sacramento, Calif.*

An unemployed African American on parole for robbery, Rodney King achieved national fame in 1992 as the victim of one of the most celebrated cases of police brutality in U.S. history. TV newscasts repeatedly played the 80-second videotape, filmed by a bystander, of a group of Los Angeles police officers standing around the prone King, taking turns kicking him and beating him with their nightsticks. Audio tapes also caught racist comments by police officers on their way to the scene of King's arrest for disorderly conduct.

When four of the officers charged with assault were acquitted by a jury that included no African Americans in February 1993, the predominantly black south-central part of Los Angeles erupted in a destructive riot of arson and looting, primarily by gangs of young blacks, Hispanics, and whites. King went on TV to make a poignant plea for an end to the destruction ("Can we all get along?" he asked). But by then, the riot had resulted in more than 50 deaths and $1 billion in property damage.

SEE ALSO

Race riots

FURTHER READING

Cannon, Lou. *Official Negligence: How Rodney King and the Riots Changed Los Angeles and the L.A.P.D.* New York: Times Books, 1998.
Gooding-Williams, Robert, ed. *Reading Rodney King, Reading Urban Uprising*. New York: Routledge, 1993.

Kinsey Report

The first of the pioneering reports on American sexuality that shocked the postwar public was published in 1948 by Dr. Alfred Kinsey, director of the Institute for Sex Research at Indiana University. Based on interviews with some 12,000 men, Kinsey claimed in *Sexual Behavior in the Human Male* that 95 percent of all American men had engaged in masturbation, premarital or extramarital intercourse, or homosexual behavior, and that most had become sexually active by the age of 15. Still more shocking, Kinsey's *Sexual Behavior in the Human Female* five years later revealed that 62 percent of women masturbated and 50 percent had intercourse before marriage. A far cry from much of the research on sex previously published, the objective, nonjudgmental tone of Kinsey's reports—despite being widely condemned at the time for their "statistical filth"—helped make possible over time a significant shift in what was considered to be normal and to a liberalization of sexual beliefs and standards.

FURTHER READING

Jones, James Howard. *Alfred C. Kinsey: A Public/Private Life*. New York: Norton, 1997.

Kinsey, Alfred C., and the Institute for Sex Research, Indiana University. *Sexual Behavior in the Human Female*. Philadelphia: Saunders, 1983.

Kinsey, Alfred C, Wardell B. Pomeroy, and Clyde E. Martin. *Sexual Behavior in the Human Male*. Philadelphia: Saunders, 1948.

Kissinger, Henry

- *Born: May 27, 1923, Fürth, Germany*
- *Accomplishments: Secretary of State, 1973–77; Nobel Peace Prize, 1973*

Born in Germany of Jewish parents, Henry Kissinger came to the United States in 1938, served in the U.S. Army during World War II, then taught international relations at Harvard University. He wrote *Nuclear Weapons and Foreign Policy*, a widely heralded study which insisted that the limited use of nuclear weapons should be a U.S. policy option.

As President Richard Nixon's national security advisor, Henry Kissinger maintained a heavy travel schedule and did much of his work between appointments.

Chosen by President Richard Nixon to be his special advisor on national security, then later to be the head of the National Security Council, and finally secretary of state, Kissinger saw his primary duty as one of stopping Soviet opportunities for expansion. To that end, he wooed the shah of Iran, dictatorial regimes in South Korea and the Philippines, and military governments in Latin America, and he supported a right-wing coup that overthrew the duly elected government of Chile. Kissinger also engineered President Nixon's trip to China, which led to the end of the 20-year ostracism of Beijing by Washington. The Soviet fear of Chinese-American détente, in turn, led to Nixon's summit meeting with Soviet premier Leonid Brezhnev in Moscow in May 1972 and to the signing of the Strategic Arms Limitation Treaty (SALT I). At the same time, Kissinger and Nixon pursued a face-saving end to the war in Vietnam by holding secret negotiations in Paris with the Vietnamese while also conducting invasions of Cambodia and Laos and a sustained bombing of North Vietnam.

After the cease-fire agreement was signed on January 23, 1973, Kissinger focused on checkmating the Soviet Union in the Middle East. His dramatic "shuttle diplomacy" between Cairo and Jerusalem helped to end the Arab-Israeli Yom Kippur War, restore good relations between Egypt and the United States, and secure the Nobel Peace Prize for himself. As secretary of state under President Gerald Ford, Kissinger furthered the peace process between Israel and Egypt, and negotiated another strategic arms agreement with the Soviet Union. But his reputation faded with the victory of the communists in Cambodia and Vietnam and the gradual crumbling of détente.

After leaving office, Kissinger continued to exert influence on U.S. foreign policy as head of an international consulting agency, author, and frequent commentator on television.

SEE ALSO

Arab oil embargo; China–U.S. relations; Cold war; Middle East–U.S. relations; Nixon, Richard Milhous; Nuclear arms control

FURTHER READING

Isaacson, Walter. *Kissinger: A Biography.* New York: Simon & Schuster, 1992.

Kissinger, Henry. *White House Years.* Boston: Little, Brown, 1979.

Kissinger, Henry. *Years of Renewal.* New York: Simon & Schuster, 1999.

Schulzinger, Robert D. *Henry Kissinger: Doctor of Diplomacy.* New York: Columbia University Press, 1989.

Thornton, Richard C. *The Nixon-Kissinger Years: Reshaping America's Foreign Policy.* New York: Paragon, 1989.

Korean War

After World War II, Korea was temporarily divided along the 38th Parallel. The U.S. Army held the south, and a communist army backed by the Soviet Union controlled the north. With the emerging cold war, however, the two sectors became the Soviet-backed People's Democratic Republic in North Korea and the U.S.-supported Republic of Korea in South Korea, with both sectors vowing to unify the nation under their own rule.

On June 25, 1950, North Korean troops swept into South Korea. Although the offensive took Moscow by surprise and the North Koreans

The 38th parallel divided communist-controlled North Korea from U.S.-backed South Korea after World War II. At the end of the Korean War, the nation remained divided along the same line.

received little aid from the Soviets throughout the war, President Harry Truman viewed the attack as Soviet-directed aggression and a test of the U.S. containment policy to hold the line against Soviet expansionism. He was determined to end the communist threat by pushing the North Koreans back to the 38th Parallel. Without consulting Congress or requesting a declaration of war, Truman quickly secured United Nations approval for a "police action" against the North Korean aggressor, ordered U.S. forces to the aid of the South Koreans, and appointed General Douglas MacArthur to head the U.N. forces.

After the North Koreans rapidly pushed the U.N. forces back to the southeastern tip of the peninsula, MacArthur executed a brilliant amphibious assault on September 15 at Inchon, north of Seoul, forcing a massive North Korean retreat across the 38th Parallel. Now opting to liberate North Korea and create a single, unified nation of Korea, Truman gave MacArthur permission to push north of the 38th Parallel.

As U.N. troops neared the Yalu River, the boundary between China and North Korea, Mao Zedong warned that China would not stand by if its border were threatened. Ignoring the Chinese warnings, MacArthur deployed his troops in a thin line below the river. The result was a startling blow for the U.N. forces when 33 Chinese divisions counterattacked on November 25 and soon rolled the U.N. troops back below the 38th Parallel. The U.N. forces were able to regain their position early in 1951, and less than a year from the initial North Korean offensive the fighting had settled at the 38th Parallel.

Then Truman once again reversed course and in the spring of 1951 sought a negotiated peace, based on the original objective of securing the protection of South Korea from communist aggression rather than of liberating North Korea. But talks dragged on for more than two years as both sides continued fighting a restricted yet deadly war.

General Douglas MacArthur watches the shelling of Inchon from the USS Mt. McKinley *on September 15, 1950.*

Unable to stomach a stalemate, General MacArthur wanted to expand the war by bombing and blockading China and by unleashing Chiang Kai-shek's Nationalist Chinese troops against Mao's communist regime. Truman rejected this course of action, arguing that "we are trying to prevent a world war—not to start one." MacArthur responded by publicly criticizing Truman's policy, maintaining that in "war there is no substitute for victory." Truman then relieved MacArthur of his command, replacing him with General Matthew Ridgway on April 10, 1951.

After the death of more than 54,000 Americans, and with more than 100,000 wounded or missing and the expenditure of some $54 billion, a cease-fire ended the war on July 26, 1953, leaving the Korean Peninsula divided, just as it had been at the war's start, at the 38th Parallel. The U.S.

intervention had preserved a precarious balance of power in Asia. The war also intensified anticommunism campaigns at home, helped Dwight Eisenhower and the Republicans win the White House in 1952, accelerated the desegregation of the U.S. armed services, speeded up a massive U.S. military buildup, transformed the containment doctrine into a general global policy, and escalated U.S. assistance to the French fighting against an independence movement in Vietnam—a step that would soon result in Americans fighting another war in Asia.

SEE ALSO

Cold war; Containment doctrine; Eisenhower, Dwight David; Southeast Asia Treaty Organization (SEATO); Truman, Harry S.

FURTHER READING

Blair, Clay. *The Forgotten War: America in Korea, 1950–1953.* New York: Times Books, 1987.
Dolan, Edward F. *America in the Korean War.* Brookfield, Conn.: Millbrook Press, 1998.
Foot, Rosemary. *A Substitute for Victory: The Politics of Peacemaking at the Korean Armistice Talks.* Ithaca, N.Y.: Cornell University Press, 1990.
Halliday, Jon, and Bruce Cumings. *Korea: The Unknown War.* New York: Pantheon, 1988.
Kaufman, Burton. *The Korean War: Challenges in Crisis, Credibility, and Command.* New York: Knopf, 1986.
Stein, R. Conrad. *The Korean War: "The Forgotten War."* Springfield, N.J.: Enslow, 1994.

Ku Klux Klan

An ultra-racist terrorist organization first formed during Reconstruction following the Civil War and later revived in the 1920s, the Ku Klux Klan had its third incarnation in the 1950s and 1960s. Rising up in response to the Supreme Court's *Brown* v. *Board of Education* decision, which ordered desegregation of all public schools, the new Klan sought to halt the civil rights movement by intimidating its leaders with threats, murders, bombings, and other terrorist acts.

After a black family moved into a white neighborhood in Chicago in 1963, racists began burning crosses to scare them away. The Ku Klux Klan gained strength in the 1960s as some whites tried to threaten and intimidate African Americans committed to fighting for their civil rights.

Klansmen beat "freedom riders," activists seeking to integrate interstate bus transportation, and burned the bus in which they were riding in Anniston, Alabama, in 1961. The first Mississippi Klan of the 20th century sprang up in 1964 to oppose the Mississippi Freedom Summer project and harassed civil rights activists seeking to register black voters in the state. The Klan was responsible for burning several black churches and killing three civil rights workers there. According to a paid informant, Klan members had pulled the workers out of their car, chanting in unison, "Ashes to ashes, dust to dust, if you'd stayed where you belonged, you wouldn't be here with us," and shot them.

Klan violence, however, helped mobilize public support for the passage of civil rights legislation. In 1965 President Lyndon B. Johnson promised to use the law to control this "hooded society of bigots," a reference to the white sheets with hoods that Klan members wore.

A combination of public disapproval and federal prosecution has kept the modern Klan weak, although it periodically makes newspaper headlines, as when North Carolina Klansmen formed a United Racist Front in 1979 with the state's Nazi party. Other Klan groups have allied themselves with the Aryan Nation, a white supremacist group, and with various groups of skinheads, bigots who harbor fantasies of starting a race war in the United States and who can be identified by their shaved heads. Klanwatch, a project of the Southern Poverty Law Center in Alabama, monitors Klan activity.

SEE ALSO

Civil rights movement; Massive resistance

FURTHER READING

Carnes, Jim. *Us and Them: A History of Intolerance in America.* New York: Oxford University Press, 1996.

Chalmers, David Mark. *Hooded Americanism: The History of the Ku Klux Klan.* Durham, N.C.: Duke University Press, 1987.

Cook, Fred J. *The Ku Klux Klan: America's Recurring Nightmare.* Parsippany, N.J.: Silver Burdett, 1989.

Wade, Wyn Craig. *The Fiery Cross: The Ku Klux Klan in America.* New York: Simon & Schuster, 1987.

Labor movement

As the nation emerged from World War II, 35 percent of the U.S. workers who did not work on farms counted themselves as members of labor unions. The labor movement was at the peak of its strength. During the next 50 years, however, this strength declined sharply; by the mid-1990s organized labor was as weak as it had been in the 1920s, before it had first begun to gather strength.

In 1946 more strikes were held than in any other single year in U.S. history. As soldiers returned home and the labor pool swelled, workers protested the resulting layoffs and reduced hours. In the first sign of things to come, in 1947 the Republican-controlled Congress responded by passing the Taft-Hartley Act over the veto of President Harry Truman. It was specifically designed to alter the National Labor Relations Act of 1935, commonly called the Wagner Act, which supported the right of workers to join unions and to engage in collective bargaining with employers. The Taft-Hartley Act also established the National Labor Relations Board to settle disputes between employers and employees and allowed states to pass right-to-work laws that would prohibit union-only shops. It banned certain labor practices, such as forced contributions to political campaigns, and allowed the President to call a 60-day postponement of any strike that might affect national security or health.

During the 1950s and 1960s, general economic prosperity undermined labor's militancy. The improvement of the standard of living among all classes of Americans and the rise of a consumer-oriented society soon caused a blending of the working class and the middle class. More Americans could now afford their own homes and were receiving expanded benefits packages from employers that included pension plans as well as health and life insurance.

Moreover, with the rise of the New Left, the militancy of the civil rights and antiwar movements replaced that of labor. The young activists of the New Left saw unions as part of the establishment (in part because of their

During a coffee break, telephone workers in 1969 listen to a union representative for the Communications Workers of America.

support for U.S. policy in Vietnam and because of the underrepresentation of minorities in leadership positions in unions). Consequently they never considered joining forces with labor, as student revolutionaries had done in France in 1968. One of the few highlights for organized labor in the 1960s came when Cesar Chavez led the United Farm Workers (UFW) in successful boycotts of grape and lettuce growers in California, winning formal recognition of the UFW as well as higher wages and improved working conditions for farm laborers.

From the 1970s to the 1990s, the surviving labor movement was devastated by a momentous shift in the United States from a work force based in manufacturing industries to one grounded in the service industries. Rather than investing in the basic industries in the United States (for instance, steel, automotive, and rubber), corporations began investing outside the country. Business leaders claimed that the high wages won by organized U.S. labor kept manufacturers from being competitive with companies in other countries. As a result, many moved large segments of their operations outside the United States to find a cheaper labor force.

In the 1980s, the atmosphere of deregulation promoted by Ronald Reagan's administration—as seen, for example, in his breaking the air-traffic controllers' union—led to a rolling back of health and safety regulations for workers, reduced unemployment benefits, and a stagnating minimum wage. Reagan's firing of 12,000 striking air traffic controllers in August 1981 and the subsequent prosecution of their union leaders proved to be a powerful symbol of the American attitude toward organized labor. Between 1980 and 1995, the percentage of the nation's workers who were union members declined from nearly 25 percent to less than 15 percent.

SEE ALSO

Chavez, Cesar; United Automobile Workers (UAW); United Farm Workers of America (UFW)

FURTHER READING

Buhle, Paul, and Alan Dawley, eds. *Working for Democracy: American Workers from the Revolution to the Present.* Urbana: University of Illinois Press, 1985.

Geoghegan, Thomas. *Which Side Are You On?* New York: Farrar, Straus & Giroux, 1991.

Greene, James R. *The World of the Worker: Labor in Twentieth-Century America.* New York: Hill & Wang, 1980.

Laos, bombing of

During the Vietnam War, North Vietnamese forces took advantage of routes through the neutral nations of Laos and Cambodia in their efforts to supply guerrillas in South Vietnam. The main route was the Ho Chi Minh Trail. Beginning in 1965, President Lyndon B. Johnson ordered a bombing campaign of the Ho Chi Minh Trail that lasted through 1967 and gradually evolved into an operation of 3,000 sorties, or raids, each month. Bad weather and rugged mountain jungle terrain made most of the small roads of the trail difficult to detect, however. The bombing increased under President Richard Nixon but still had little impact on the traffic of enemy supplies or the existence of Vietcong sanctuaries.

SEE ALSO

Vietnam War

FURTHER READING

Castle, Timothy. *At War in the Shadow of Vietnam.* New York: Columbia University Press, 1993.

Dommen, Arthur. *Conflict in Laos.* New York: Praeger, 1971.

Leary, Timothy

- *Born: Oct. 22, 1920, Springfield, Mass.*
- *Accomplishments: Psychologist; writer*
- *Died: May 31, 1996, Beverly Hills, Calif.*

Timothy Leary, a professor of psychology at Harvard, ran a project that studied the effects of psychedelic drugs on people in the early 1960s. He became an advocate of drug use—particularly of LSD—as a way to enhance spiritual awareness, and as a result in 1963 he and a colleague, Richard Alpert (later known as Ram Dass) were fired. Leary continued his work at a privately funded institute as he wrote and spoke on what he presented as the virtues of mind-altering substances. In his most widely disseminated phrase, he urged the young to "turn on, tune in, and drop out." Leary's advocacy of marijuana and LSD as liberating drugs and as ingredients in the search for greater self-awareness and inner peace made him a major figure in the counterculture, but his frequent arrests for carrying the drugs led to several jail sentences and to some dashing escapes. As the counterculture weakened so did Leary's influence, but he resurfaced in the news when he was diagnosed with incurable cancer in the early 1990s. Leary's response to his impending death was to use the Internet as a way to spread the details of his experiences, enabling many people to follow the course of his physical decline and spiritual reaction to it.

In 1967, Timothy Leary tells college students that tripping on LSD could help in their spiritual growth.

SEE ALSO

Counterculture; Drugs

FURTHER READING

Leary, Timothy. *Flashbacks: An Autobiography.* Los Angeles: Tarcher, 1983.

Moseley, Bill. "Still Crazy After All These Years." *Psychology Today,* Jan.–Feb. 1995, 30–34.

Lebanon, invasion of (1982)

Following the shooting of the Israeli ambassador to Britain by extremists within the Palestine Liberation Organization (PLO) in June 1982, Prime Minister Menachem Begin ordered an invasion of Lebanon to destroy the PLO infrastructure based there.

President Ronald Reagan then sent 2,000 U.S. troops to Lebanon to help enforce a cease-fire, but the Muslim militias viewed them as favoring Israel. In April 1983 a bomb exploded in the U.S. embassy in Beirut, killing 63 people. In October, a Shiite Muslim extremist crashed an explosive-laden truck into a poorly guarded barracks, killing 240 U.S. Marines. Reagan withdrew the troops in early 1984, leaving Lebanon a chaotic battlefield of warring Muslim factions, Christians, and troops from the Syrian army who were supporting Lebanese Muslims.

SEE ALSO

Middle East–U.S. relations; Reagan, Ronald Wilson

FURTHER READING

Friedman, Thomas. *From Beruit to Jerusalem*. New York: Anchor, 1990.

Weinberger, Caspar W. *Fighting for Peace: Seven Critical Years in the Pentagon*. New York: Warner, 1990.

"Letter from a Birmingham Jail" (April 1963)

After his arrest during a civil rights protest in Birmingham, Alabama, Martin Luther King, Jr., composed his most eloquent justification of nonviolent civil disobedience. Addressing those who shared his goals but urged patience and more moderate tactics, King explained that only pressure could induce privileged groups to act justly.

Martin Luther King, Jr., gazes pensively through the bars of the cell where he composed his "Letter from a Birmingham Jail" in 1963. King revisited the jail late in 1967, just months before he was assassinated.

King then spelled out the grief, humiliation, and frustration of living under the cloud of racial oppression that made patience impossible. "When you are harried by day and haunted by night by the fact that you are a Negro," he wrote, "plagued with inner fears and outer resentments . . . then you will understand why we find it difficult to wait."

This "Letter" has been published widely in a variety of texts and articles on racism and civil rights and has become one of the most widely read and frequently quoted documents of the civil rights movement.

SEE ALSO

Birmingham civil rights demonstrations (1963); Civil rights movement; King, Martin Luther, Jr.

FURTHER READING

Hanigan, James P. *Martin Luther King, Jr., and the Foundations of Militant Nonviolence*. Lanham, Md.: University Press of America, 1984.

Levittown

SEE Suburbs

Lewis, John Robert

- *Born: Feb. 21, 1940, Troy, Ala.*
- *Accomplishment: Civil rights activist*
- *Government service: U.S. representative (Democrat–Ga.), 1986–*

A leading member of the Student Nonviolent Coordinating Committee (SNCC) in the early 1960s, John Lewis has served in the U.S. House of Representatives since 1986. Born the son of a sharecropper, Lewis began agitating for civil rights as a college student at the American Baptist Theological Seminary and served as chairman of SNCC from 1963 to 1966. Replaced by more radical leaders at SNCC, Lewis continued to work on registering black voters with the Southern Regional Council and the Voter Education Project.

In the 1970s, Lewis became an officeholder, first as a federal appointee in Jimmy Carter's administration in 1977, then as an Atlanta city councilor, and finally as a congressman from Georgia. Lewis has been a member of the Congressional Black Caucus and has consistently supported liberal legislation.

SEE ALSO

Civil rights movement; Student Nonviolent Coordinating Committee (SNCC)

FURTHER READING

Lewis, John, and Michael D'Orso. *Walking with the Wind: A Memoir of the Movement*. New York: Simon & Schuster, 1998.

Liberalism

A 19th-century term meaning a belief in limited government and laissez-faire economics (in which government is supposed to take no part), "liberalism" was a little-used term until Franklin Roosevelt chose to use it to describe his New Deal. In the 20th century, liberalism has come to mean a system in which the government serves as guardian of the individual against the influence of big business. As Roosevelt put it, liberalism is "plain English for a changed concept of the duty and responsibility of government toward economic life." That meant, among many other things, government protection for the right of labor to organize, government-insured protection for bank deposits, and a government-administered Social Security system to guard against the ravages of old age and unemployment.

After World War II, liberalism during Harry Truman's Presidency became less associated with schemes that favored the have-nots, and increasingly committed to protecting civil liberties and managing the economy to maintain full employment and economic growth. The returning veterans and their families benefited from such liberal programs as the G.I. bill, which established hospitals for veterans, set up vocational rehabilitation programs for them, gave them favorable home mortgages, and paid their college tuition and living expenses.

The tradition of New Deal liberalism was continued by President Lyndon B. Johnson and his Great Society programs, which provided a cornucopia of direct benefits to the poor and elderly as well as civil rights for African Americans. Johnson's Presidency was destroyed by the war in Vietnam, though, and by the late 1960s liberalism was in retreat. It was attacked by the New Left for fighting an immoral war in Vietnam instead of battling racial bigotry, and it was hounded by those on the right for what they called tax-and-spend policies that brought neither victory abroad nor order and stability in the United States.

The height of postwar liberalism was in the 1960s, when John Kennedy and Lyndon Johnson worked to pass progressive legislation that would guarantee civil rights, reduce poverty, and decrease unemployment.

As political labels grew more complicated in the 1970s with the lingering bitterness left by the war in Vietnam, and with the direct effects of the G. I. bill and other benefits no longer new or as deeply felt, liberalism became primarily a series of unconnected legal challenges by African Americans, environmentalists, gays, Hispanics, Native Americans, feminists, and other groups seeking their own specific entitlements and reforms. By the 1980s, popular resentment of school busing, affirmative action, crime, welfare dependency, and the spectacular popularity of President Ronald Reagan and his brand of conservatism had made the term *liberal* the "L word," an epithet shunned by many politicians. In the 1990s, however, the close identification of conservatism with right-wing ideologies and militant evangelical Christians led to a revival of the liberal tradition of strong governmental engagement with social issues and the economic concerns of the vast American middle class.

SEE ALSO

Conservatism; Johnson, Lyndon Baines; New Left; Reagan, Ronald Wilson; Truman, Harry S.

FURTHER READING

Hamby, Alonzo L. *Beyond the New Deal: Harry S. Truman and American Liberalism.* New York: Columbia University Press, 1973.

Leuchtenburg, William E. *In the Shadow of FDR: From Harry Truman to Ronald Reagan.* Ithaca, N.Y.: Cornell University Press, 1983.

Matusow, Allen J. *The Unraveling of America: A History of Liberalism in the 1960s.* New York: Harper & Row, 1984.

Little Rock, Ark., desegregation crisis (1957)

In September 1957, despite the Supreme Court's 1954 decision in *Brown* v. *Board of Education*, which found school segregation to be illegal, Arkansas governor Orval E. Faubus defied a federal court order by deploying the state's National Guard to prevent nine black students from enrolling at Little Rock's Central High School. When another court order prevented Faubus from using the guard units, a menacing white mob blocked the school entrance.

Finally, President Dwight D. Eisenhower called in federal troops to carry out the court order. The troops patrolled the school halls for the rest of the year. Rather than submit, Governor Faubus shut down the city's schools the follow-

Brave in their new school dresses, four of the nine black students who desegregated Central High School prepare to enter the school. From left to right: Carlotta Walls, Melba Patillo, Elizabeth Eckford, and Minnie Jean Brown.

ing year. Court proceedings dragged on into 1959 before the Little Rock schools reopened. The news reports on national television out of Little Rock helped make school desegregation a national issue.

SEE ALSO

Brown v. *Board of Education of Topeka, Kansas* (1954); Civil rights movement; Eisenhower, Dwight David; Massive resistance

FURTHER READING

Beals, Melba. *Warriors Don't Cry: A Searing Memoir of the Battle to Integrate Little Rock's Central High.* New York: Pocket Books, 1994.

Branch, Taylor. *Parting the Waters: America in the King Years, 1954–63.* New York: Simon & Schuster, 1988.

LSD (lysergic acid diethylamide)

SEE Counterculture; Drugs; Leary, Timothy

MacArthur, Douglas

- *Born: Jan. 26, 1880, Little Rock, Ark.*
- *Accomplishments: U.S. Army chief of staff, 1930–35; supreme commander, Allied forces in the Pacific, 1942–45; supreme Allied commander, U.S., U.N., South Korean forces in Korea, 1950–51*
- *Died: Apr. 5, 1964, Washington, D.C.*

The son of a general and first in his class at West Point, Douglas MacArthur served as a division commander in World War I, army chief of staff from 1930 to 1935, and military advisor to the Philippine government before President Franklin D. Roosevelt appointed him commander of U.S. army forces in the World War II campaign against Japan.

After accepting Japan's surrender aboard the USS *Missouri* in Tokyo Bay on September 2, 1945, MacArthur took charge of the U.S. occupation of Japan from 1945 to 1950, drafting a new Japanese constitution and instituting many successful reforms. Following the invasion of South Korea by North Korean forces in late June 1950, President Harry S. Truman named him supreme Allied commander of all U.S., U.N., and South Korean troops.

The North Koreans initially pushed the U.S. forces to the southeastern tip of the peninsula. Then a dashing amphibious landing at Inchon by MacArthur's troops in mid-September turned the tides of war, forcing the North Koreans to retreat across the 38th Parallel. A triumphant MacArthur ordered his armies to pursue, disregarding Chinese warnings that they would not stand idly by as U.N. troops approached the Yalu River, which marked the border between North Korea and China. On November 25, 33 Chinese divisions (about 300,000 men) counterattacked, driving MacArthur's stunned troops back into South Korea.

MacArthur's public calls for a larger war against China clashed with the policies of the Truman administration, which feared full-scale atomic war. MacArthur's continued insistence that there was no substitute for victory in a military conflict led the President to remove him from command in 1951 and order him home. MacArthur returned to a hero's welcome, briefly sought the Republican nomination for the Presidential election of 1952, then faded from public prominence.

SEE ALSO

Korean War; Truman, Harry S.

FURTHER READING

MacArthur, Douglas. *Reminiscences.* New York: Time, 1964.

Perret, Geoffrey. *Old Soldiers Never Die: The Life of Douglas MacArthur.* New York: Random House, 1996.

Schaller, Michael. *Douglas MacArthur: The Far Eastern General.* New York: Oxford University Press, 1989.

Mad magazine

Mad Magazine was created by Harvey Kurtzman, a comic book illustrator, writer, and editor, in 1952, and its gap-toothed cultural cartoon icon Alfred E. Neuman appeared in 1956, asking "What? Me Worry?" The magazine's satire mocked all aspects of society, ranging from spoofs of television commercials to biting social commentary on suburbia, politics, and the smugness of the "American way of life." In *Mad*'s world, everything was silly and worthy of scorn. *Mad*'s first publisher was William Gaines, who was the son of M. C. Gaines, considered to be the father of the comic book form; *Mad* itself was originally published as a comic book before it was reshaped into a magazine to avoid the strictures of the Comic Book Code. The magazine, published eight times a year, had a circulation of more than 800,000 in 1992.

FURTHER READING

Feldstein, Albert E., ed. *William M. Gaines' The Mad Frontier.* New York: Signet, 1962.

Madonna (Madonna Louise Ciccone)

- *Born: August 16, 1958; Bay City, Mich.*
- *Accomplishments: Singer and actress; entertainment mogul*

Madonna is notorious for her erotic music videos, songs, and tours, as well as for her ability to constantly reinvent herself. Her music career took off in 1984 with the release of *Madonna.* Her distinctive early style—underwear worn as outerwear, large crucifixes, lace gloves, all shown to good advantage in the 1985 movie "Desperately Seeking Susan"—was imitated by many teenagers who the media called "wannabes." Soon after becoming famous, Madonna dramatically changed her style. In the 1985 video "Material Girl," she wore elaborate dresses and jewelry as a Marilyn Monroe-esque starlet, embracing the materialistic values of the Reagan 80s by refusing to accept any suitor who could not finance her luxurious lifestyle. Over time, Madonna has accumulated the wealth she desired. She is a shrewd businesswoman who took control of her career early and by 1989 became the highest-grossing woman in the entertainment field, with a net worth of about $70 million. Maverick, her record company, has been very successful, featuring popular recording artists such as Alanis Morissette. Her success has often resulted from her ability to attract media attention through controversy and scandal.

Madonna performs in the mid-1980s, showing off one of her earliest styles. This was a look that many of her young listeners coveted and imitated.

Among Madonna's most controversial projects were the film *Truth or Dare,* a documentary of her life while on tour, and her 1993 book *Sex,* in which she poses in various provocative positions with other stars. Also, in 1996, she realized a long-term dream of starring in a film version of the Andrew Lloyd Webber musical *Evita.* The birth of her daughter Lourdes in

1996 attracted a great deal of media attention. On her 1998 album *Ray of Light* Madonna changed her image once again, singing not about sex but spirituality. The album featured a song, "Little Star," about the role her daughter plays in her life.

FURTHER READING

Allen, Steve. "Madonna." *Journal of Popular Culture* 27 (1993): 1–11.
Ferguson, Andrew. "Bad Girls Don't Cry." *National Review,* May 30, 1994, 72.

Mailer, Norman

- *Born: Jan. 31, 1923, Long Branch, N.J.*
- *Accomplishments: Writer; journalist; cultural critic*
- *Major Works:* The Naked and the Dead *(1948),* The White Negro *(1959),* The Armies of the Night *(1968)*

Novelist and journalist Norman Mailer is regarded as one of the most talented American writers of the 20th century. His writing, like his personality, is brash and controversial. Following his first novel, *The Naked and the Dead* (1948), based on his experiences in World War II, Mailer's work focused on sexual conflict, radical politics, and the violence in American life. The hipster revolting against middle-class morality and conventions that he described in his influential essay *The White Negro* became a model for the hippies of the 1960s counterculture, and Mailer himself became one of the chief critics of all that was stultifying in American culture.

Long an opponent of rigid U.S. cold war policies, Mailer also became prominent in the anti–Vietnam War movement, participating in teach-ins and marches against the war. His involvement in the October 1967 march on the Pentagon led to a much-publicized arrest and his brilliant account of the antiwar demonstration, *The Armies of the Night.* The book, which won Mailer a Pulitzer Prize in 1969, exemplified the so-called new journalism of the 1960s, using novelistic techniques to portray the essential rather than the literal truth about a person or an event.

FURTHER READING

Mailer, Norman. *The Armies of the Night.* New York: New American Library, 1968.
Mailer, Norman. *The Naked and the Dead.* New York: Rinehart, 1948.
Mailer, Norman. *The White Negro.* San Francisco: City Light Books, 1959.
Manso, Peter. *Mailer: His Life and Times.* New York: Simon & Schuster, 1985.

Malcolm X (Malcolm Little)

- *Born: May 19, 1925, Omaha, Neb.*
- *Accomplishments: Militant black leader*
- *Died: Feb. 21, 1965, New York, N.Y.*

Malcolm X became the leading symbol of urban black rage during the civil rights movement of the 1960s. While serving a term in prison for burglary, Malcolm was attracted to the ideas of the Nation of Islam. Upon his release in 1952, he dropped his surname Little, what he called his "slave name," and substituted the "X" to symbolize his stolen African identity.

Through the teachings of Elijah Muhammad, who founded the Nation of Islam in 1931, Malcolm reformed his ways, gave up drugs and crime, and dedicated himself to religious study and self-discipline. He became a minister in the church, Muhammad's No. 1

Malcolm X speaks at a news conference held at a New York hotel in early 1964. He discusses his move away from the Black Muslims and his plans for a new mosque; he also warns that there will be "more violence on the racial scene in 1954 than Americans have ever witnessed."

spokesman, and was a favorite of the mainstream media.

Calling on blacks to separate themselves from the "white devils," to be proud of their blackness, and to renounce nonviolence in favor of self-defense "by any means necessary," Malcolm became a popular speaker among blacks and a fearful figure to whites. He gained national attention in a television documentary about Black Muslims and was featured on talk shows and in newspaper articles.

In 1964 Malcolm broke with Elijah Muhammad to form his own, more orthodox, Islamic sect, traveled to Africa and Mecca, and softened his antiwhite rhetoric. Returning to the United States as El-Hajj Malik El-Shabazz, he founded the Organization of Afro-American Unity. He was assassinated in February 1965, probably by members of the Nation of Islam in retaliation for statements he had made against Elijah Muhammad.

More influential in death than in life, Malcolm gained attention with *The Autobiography of Malcolm X* (1965), an account of his journey from degradation to devotion to his people. It became a best-seller and played a significant role in the black power movement and later campaigns for human rights.

SEE ALSO

Black Muslims; Black nationalism; Black power; Civil rights movement

FURTHER READING

Dyson, Michael Eric. *Making Malcolm: The Myth and Meaning of Malcolm X.* New York: Oxford University Press, 1994.

Goldman, Peter. *The Death and Life of Malcolm X.* Urbana: University of Illinois Press, 1979.

Malcolm X, as told to Alex Haley. *The Autobiography of Malcolm X.* New York: Grove Press, 1965.

Perry, Bruce. *Malcolm: The Life of a Man Who Changed Black America.* Barrytown, N.Y.: Station Hill, 1991.

Rummel, Jack. *Malcolm X.* New York: Chelsea House, 1989.

Manson, Charles

- *Born: Nov. 12, 1934, Cincinnati, Ohio*

One of the most infamous criminals in U.S. history, Charles Manson began his reign of terror by starting a cult dedicated to worshiping both God and the Devil. The cult members, known as the Manson Family, were completely under his control. On August 10, 1969, acting on Manson's orders, members of the Manson Family hacked pregnant actress Sharon Tate and six of her friends to death in Tate's house in Beverly Hills and then sat down to eat dinner amid the murdered and mutilated bodies. Manson was convicted of the murders, even though he was not present at the crime, and sentenced to death. His sentence was later reduced to life in prison, where he remains today.

FURTHER READING

Bugliosi, Vincent. *Helter Skelter: The True Story of the Manson Murders.* New York: Bantam, 1974.

March on Washington (1963)

On August 28, 1963, an estimated 150,000 black and 75,000 white protestors from every part of the country gathered on the Washington Mall in front of the Lincoln Monument to demonstrate their support for federal action in favor of civil rights. A. Philip Randolph, an organizer of the protest, had first proposed a march on Washington in 1941 to protest racial discrimination in the armed services and defense employment. Twenty-two years later, he led this March for Jobs and Freedom.

In the most memorable event of the day, Martin Luther King, Jr., delivered his rousing "I Have a Dream" speech, expressing the highest aspiration of the civil rights movement: that "all God's children, black men and white men . . . will be able to join hands and sing in the words of that old Negro spiritual, 'Free at last! Free at last! Thank God almighty, we are free at last!' "

SEE ALSO

African Americans; Civil rights movement; King, Martin Luther, Jr.

FURTHER READING

Branch, Taylor. *Parting the Waters: America in the King Years, 1954–63.* New York: Simon & Schuster, 1988.

Marshall, George Catlett

- *Born: Dec. 31, 1880, Uniontown, Pa.*
- *Accomplishments: Army Chief of Staff, 1939–45; Secretary of State, 1947–49; Secretary of Defense, 1950–51; Nobel Peace Prize, 1953*
- *Died: Oct. 16, 1959, Bethesda, Md.*

Widely recognized for his planning, strategic, and organizational skills during World War I, General George Marshall was appointed army chief of staff by President Franklin D. Roosevelt on September 1, 1939, the day World War II began in Europe. Marshall held that position throughout the war.

Secretary of State George Marshall (stepping off plane, center) visits Italy in 1948, a year after he devised an economic recovery plan to help rebuild war-torn Western Europe.

Shortly after Marshall retired as chief of staff, President Harry Truman sent him to China to mediate the civil war between the communists and the nationalists. Although Marshall failed in that mission, Truman appointed him secretary of state in 1947, and in that capacity Marshall played a key role in formulating the Truman Doctrine—the policy that the United States would aid all free peoples resisting communist takeovers. As secretary of state, Marshall secured passage of the U.S. economic assistance plan for European postwar recovery—called the Marshall Plan—and won congressional approval for the creation of the North Atlantic Treaty Organization (NATO). After a brief second retirement for Marshall, Truman recalled him to duty as secretary of defense at the start of the Korean War. Marshall retired for the last time in September 1951 and became the only U.S. general ever to be awarded the Nobel Peace Prize.

SEE ALSO

Korean War; Marshall Plan; North Atlantic Treaty Organization (NATO); Truman, Harry S.; Truman Doctrine

FURTHER READING

Cray, Ed. *General of the Army: George C. Marshall, Soldier and Statesman.* New York: Norton, 1990.
Pogue, Forrest. *George C. Marshall: Statesman, 1945–1949.* New York: Viking, 1987.

Marshall Plan

A month after the announcement of the Truman Doctrine, which declared that the United States would aid all free peoples in resisting communist takeovers, Secretary of State George C. Marshall, former army chief of staff, proposed a massive U.S. assistance program for European recovery in 1947. The European Recovery Plan, popularly called the Marshall Plan, sought to end the postwar economic devastation that communism could easily exploit.

Marshall characterized the plan as directed not against any country or doctrine but against hunger, poverty, desperation, and chaos. Nevertheless, in keeping with U.S. economic goals and cold war policies, nations requesting aid had to agree to U.S. conditions and controls, including the removal of trade barriers and greater economic cooperation. Not unexpectedly, the Soviet Union and its allies rejected participation.

Many in Congress initially balked at President Harry Truman's request for $17 billion in aid to Europe. Critics on the right saw it as a burden on U.S. taxpayers (a "share the American wealth" plan) while those on the left saw it as an attack on socialism (the "Martial" Plan). But the Soviet takeover of Czechoslovakia in February 1948 effectively ended debate over the Marshall Plan, and Congress approved the first installment of $5.3 billion that April.

Aid workers distribute orange juice concentrate in Great Britain as part of the Marshall Plan.

The plan proved an enormous economic and political success. It rebuilt the economic infrastructure of Western Europe and fostered its economic integration. By 1952 Western Europe was flourishing, and communism there had lost much of its appeal. The plan also created stable markets for U.S. goods and enhanced the prestige of the United States abroad.

SEE ALSO

Marshall, George Catlett; Truman Doctrine

FURTHER READING

Gimbel, John. *The Origins of the Marshall Plan.* Stanford, Calif.: Stanford University Press, 1976.
Hogan, Michael J. *The Marshall Plan: America, Britain, and the Reconstruction of Western Europe, 1947–1952.* New York: Cambridge University Press, 1987.

Marshall, Thurgood

- *Born: July 2, 1908, Baltimore, Md.*
- *Accomplishments: Judge, Second District Court of Appeals, 1962–65; U.S. solicitor general, 1965–67; U.S. Supreme Court justice, 1967–91*
- *Died: Jan. 24, 1993, Bethesda, Md.*

Thurgood Marshall was a leader of America's legal struggle for civil rights and the first black member of the Supreme Court. As special counsel of the National Association for the Advancement of Colored People (NAACP) from 1938 to 1962, Marshall became the nation's primary civil rights attorney, seeking to break down legal barriers to black equality and winning 29 of 32 cases.

In 1954 Marshall argued the most significant civil rights case of the 20th century: *Brown* v. *Board of Education of Topeka, Kansas,* in which the Supreme Court ordered the desegregation of public schools. After a brief tenure as Second District Court of Appeals judge from 1962 to 1965, Marshall was appointed solicitor general by President Lyndon B. Johnson to argue the administration's cases before the Supreme Court. In 1967 Johnson nominated Marshall to the Supreme Court.

In his 24 years of service on the high court, Marshall took consistently liberal stands, supporting affirmative action and school busing for racial balance and opposing the death penalty and all efforts to restrict the right of women to obtain abortions. After his retirement in 1991, President George Bush replaced Marshall with another African American, Clarence Thomas, one of the most conservative justices on the Supreme Court in the 1990s.

SEE ALSO

Affirmative action; *Brown* v. *Board of Education of Topeka, Kansas* (1954); National Association for the Advancement of Colored People (NAACP); Supreme Court

FURTHER READING

Aldred, Lisa. *Thurgood Marshall.* New York: Chelsea House, 1990.
Greenberg, Jack. *Crusaders in the Courts.* New York: Basic Books, 1994.
Rowan, Carl T. *Dream Makers, Dream Breakers: The World of Justice Thurgood Marshall.* Boston: Little, Brown, 1993.
Tushnet, Mark. *The NAACP's Legal Strategy Against Segregated Education, 1925–1950.* Chapel Hill: University of North Carolina Press, 1987.
Williams, Juan. *Thurgood Marshall: American Revolutionary.* New York: Times Books, 1988.

Massive resistance

Southern segregationists pledged that they would meet the federal authorities who were ordering desegregation of schools and other public facilities in the South during the 1950s with "massive resistance." Across the South, politicians vowed to ignore the Supreme Court's 1954 *Brown* v. *Board of Education* decision, which called for the desegregation of public schools, and in 1956 more than 100 members of Congress signed the Southern Manifesto, denouncing the *Brown* decision as a clear abuse of judicial power.

Southern vigilantes mobilized the Ku Klux Klan to harass and terrorize black schoolchildren who tried to integrate all-white schools, while reactionary groups like the White Citizens' Councils used their economic strength and political influence to thwart desegregation. Southern resistance reached a climax in September 1957 when Arkansas governor Orval E. Faubus and jeering white mobs sought to defy a federal court order to allow nine African-American students to attend Little Rock's Central High School.

SEE ALSO

African Americans; Civil rights movement; *Brown* v. *Board of Education of Topeka, Kansas* (1954); Ku Klux Klan; Little Rock, Arkansas, desegregation crisis (1957)

FURTHER READING

Bartley, Numan V. *The Rise of Massive Resistance.* Baton Rouge: Louisiana State University Press, 1970.

McMillen, Neil R. *The Citizens' Councils: Organized Resistance to the Second Reconstruction, 1954–1964.* Urbana: University of Illinois Press, 1971.

Massive retaliation

SEE Cold war

McCarran Act (1950)

SEE Internal Security Act of 1950; McCarthyism

McCarthy, Eugene Joseph

- *Born: Mar. 29, 1916, Watkins, Minn.*
- *Accomplishments: U.S. representative (Democrat–Minn.), 1949–59; U.S. senator (Democrat–Minn.), 1959–70; Democratic candidate in the 1968 primary election; Liberal Independent Presidential candidate, 1976*

Eugene McCarthy served in the House of Representatives for five terms and was elected to represent Minnesota in the Senate in 1959. A Democrat, the professorial McCarthy became an early critic of U.S. policy in Vietnam; in 1967 he announced his candidacy as he challenged his party's incumbent, Lyndon Johnson, for the Presidency.

McCarthy's stance against the war attracted a wide following among college students, thousands of whom, neatly attired with fresh haircuts, went "Clean for Gene" and volunteered for his campaign. McCarthy shocked the nation by winning 42 percent of the vote in the New Hampshire Democratic primary. Lyndon Johnson soon withdrew from the race, but McCarthy lost key primaries to Robert F. Kennedy, and after Kennedy was assassinated he proved unable to wrest the nomination from Johnson's Vice President, Hubert Humphrey. McCarthy chose not to run for reelection to the Senate in 1970, deciding instead to devote himself to writing poetry and commentaries on current events.

SEE ALSO

Johnson, Lyndon Baines; Vietnam War

FURTHER READING

Chester, Lewis, et al. *An American Melodrama: The Presidential Campaign of 1968.* New York: Viking, 1969.

McCarthy, Eugene J. *The Year of the People.* Garden City, N.Y.: Doubleday, 1969.

McCarthy, Joseph

- *Born: Nov. 14, 1908, Grand Chute, Wis.*
- *Accomplishments: Wisconsin circuit judge, 1939–42; U.S. Marines, 1942–46; U.S. senator (Republican–Wis.), 1946–57*
- *Died: May 2, 1957, Bethesda, Md.*

A former circuit judge and a marine lieutenant in World War II, Joseph

Senator Joseph McCarthy accuses the U.S. Army of harboring communists. During the 1954 Senate hearing, army counsel Joseph Welch (left) is dismayed as he listens to the accusations.

McCarthy won election to the Senate in 1946. Although he had served as an intelligence officer and spent most days at his desk, his campaign brochures stated that he had been known in the South Pacific as "Tail-gunner Joe." Such hyperbole would later mark his Senate career.

In 1950 McCarthy claimed to have evidence of communists in the State Department, but he never produced it. Nevertheless, he attracted a devoted following and created a new Red scare (the first was right after World War I) almost single-handedly. He was reelected in 1952 and assumed the chairmanship of the Senate Permanent Investigations Committee, which gave him the ideal forum for hunting communists.

In 1954, however, McCarthy's charges grew more irresponsible and resulted in nationally televised hearings investigating the army. McCarthy's bullying during the hearings provoked public outrage. The army was cleared of the charges, and in December the Senate voted to censure McCarthy. A heavy drinker, McCarthy died in 1957 from effects associated with deterioration of his liver.

SEE ALSO

Anticommunism; Army–McCarthy hearings (1954); McCarthyism

FURTHER READING

Oshinsky, David. *A Conspiracy So Immense: The World of Joe McCarthy.* New York: Free Press, 1983.
Reeves, Thomas C. *The Life and Times of Joe McCarthy: A Biography.* New York: Stein & Day, 1982.
Rovere, Richard H. *Senator Joseph McCarthy.* New York: Harper & Row, 1959.

McCarthyism

On February 9, 1950, Senator Joseph R. McCarthy of Wisconsin announced to a Republican party women's meeting in Wheeling, West Virginia, that he had in his hand "a list of 205 . . . names known to the secretary of state as being members of the Communist party and who nevertheless are still working and shaping policy" in the State Department.

Although he produced no evidence to prove his claim, McCarthy quickly gained national attention as an aggressive fighter of domestic communism and as an immensely controversial figure. In the years since McCarthy's brief fame, *McCarthyism* generally has been defined as unsubstantiated public accusations of disloyalty without concern for fundamental civil liberties.

McCarthyism generated significant support at first and became a potent political and social force. In part, developments abroad were responsible for this. The "loss" of China to communism in 1949, the successful test of an atomic bomb in the Soviet Union that same year, and the war against communist forces in Korea created a profound anxiety among many Americans about the spreading influence of the "Red menace."

In addition, McCarthyism built on earlier anticommunist ventures, including the Federal Employee Loyalty Program (1947), which aimed at rooting out subversives in the government, and the efforts of the House Un-American Activities Committee, which sought to expose the influence of communism in everyday American life. Americans, shocked by the accusations of espionage against Alger Hiss and Ethel and Julius Rosenberg, sensed a new vulnerability of the U.S. government to espionage. As a result, McCarthy's strident attacks on domestic communism seemed reasonable. The second Red scare (the first occurred just after World War I) was under way.

Although McCarthy's original charges regarding the State Department were called "a fraud and a hoax" by a Senate investigative committee, McCarthy continued to capitalize on the fear of communism in the United States. Before the end of 1951, he had attacked Secretary of State Dean Acheson as the "Red Dean," Secretary of Defense George C. Marshall as someone who had "aided and abetted a communist conspiracy so immense as to dwarf" any others, and President Harry S. Truman for dismissing General Douglas MacArthur.

McCarthy's anticommunism won support among several groups. Catholic ethnic groups often saw anticommunism as an ideal vehicle for demonstrating loyalty and becoming accepted as "100 percent Americans." Others appreciated McCarthy's criticism of the Eastern establishment, the "striped-pants boys in the State Department." Still others were Republicans who were happy to use anticommunism for political means as they tried to supplant the Democrats in the White House. Democrats who attacked McCarthy were easily made to appear "soft" on communism.

McCarthy conducted a highly publicized campaigned against Communists in Hollywood; here some Hollywood stars—including Humphrey Bogart and Lauren Bacall in the front row—fight back, flying to Hollywood to protest McCarthy's actions.

In the end, however, McCarthy's own party turned on him. After the elections of 1952, the Republicans controlled both the White House and Congress, and they hoped that McCarthy would fade away. He did not. In 1953, he stepped up his campaign against the State Department, causing the firing of many but resulting in no indictments for espionage or subversive activity.

In addition, McCarthy forced the U.S. Information Agency to remove books by "communists, fellow travelers, etc." from the shelves of their overseas libraries. This resulted in the clearing of books by such great American writers as Ralph Waldo Emerson, Henry David Thoreau, and Mark Twain. When the army drafted one of his aides, David Schine, McCarthy went on the offensive again, accusing the army of favoritism toward communists.

The Senate responded with an investigation of McCarthy's charges in the nationally broadcast Army–McCarthy hearings in 1954. More than 20 million viewers tuned in to see McCarthy in action. What they saw shocked them. McCarthy bullied the army lawyers and repeatedly interrupted the proceedings, shouting "Point of order, Mr. Chairman, point of order!" The mood of the nation shifted against him, and Senate Republicans, with the blessing of President Dwight Eisenhower, organized a vote to censure McCarthy for his "unbecoming behavior."

Politically, McCarthy was finished. But the fears he had exploited significantly affected both government actions and the everyday behavior of ordinary Americans, many of whom were subjected to security investigations and required to sign loyalty oaths. McCarthyism destroyed the political left, discredited liberalism, and sapped labor militancy. It spawned a silent generation of students and widespread political apathy. And the purge of controversial government employees ensured foreign policy rigidity and the postponement of domestic reforms.

SEE ALSO

Anticommunism; Army–McCarthy hearings (1954); Chambers, Whittaker; McCarthy, Joseph; Rosenberg case

FURTHER READING

Caute, David. *The Great Fear.* New York: Simon & Schuster, 1978.

Fried, Albert. *McCarthyism: The Great American Red Scare: A Documentary History.* New York: Oxford University Press, 1996.

Fried, Richard M. *Nightmare in Red: The McCarthy Era in Perspective.* New York: Oxford University Press, 1990.

Griffith, Robert. *The Politics of Fear: Joseph R. McCarthy and the Senate.* Amherst: University of Massachusetts Press, 1970.

McLuhan, Marshall

- *Born: July 21, 1911, Edmonton, Alberta, Canada*
- *Accomplishments: Writer; cultural critic*
- *Died: Dec. 31, 1980, Toronto, Canada*

Marshall McLuhan, a writer and media theorist who had earned a doctorate from Cambridge University, studied the overriding effects of mass media on society and their extensions on the senses of the individual viewer. He argued that the development of new mass media significantly changes aesthetic and intellectual standards and that it is the form of the medium, rather than the content, that determines what is communicated. In short, in his famous phrase, the medium is the message. Although many critics derided McLuhan's ideas, they were popular with college students in the 1960s and caused many of them to think about how different media—television, photography, movies, books, or speech—influence the meaning of the message.

SEE ALSO

Television

FURTHER READING

Benedetti, Paul, and Nancy DeHart, eds. *Forward Through the Rearview Mirror: Reflections on and by Marshall McLuhan.* Cambridge, Mass.: M.I.T. Press, 1997.

Gordon, Terrence. *Marshall McLuhan.* New York: Basic Books, 1997.

McLuhan, Marshall. *Understanding Media: The Extensions of Man.* New York: McGraw-Hill, 1964.

McLuhan, Marshall, and Quentin Fiore. *The Medium Is the Message: An Inventory of Effects.* New York: Bantam, 1967.

McNamara, Robert Strange

- *Born: June 9, 1916, San Francisco, Calif.*
- *Accomplishments: U.S. Secretary of Defense (1961–68)*

As part of his plan to fill his cabinet with academics and intellectuals, President John F. Kennedy appointed Robert S. McNamara, the president of Ford Motor Company, as secretary of defense. McNamara applied his widely heralded management expertise to the administration of the Pentagon and became an early proponent of escalating the war in Vietnam.

By 1967, however, McNamara acknowledged that "the picture of the world's greatest superpower killing or seriously injuring a thousand noncombatants a week, while trying to pound a tiny backward country into submission on an issue whose merits are hotly disputed, is not a pretty one." By 1968 McNamara's switch from pro-war "hawk" to antiwar "dove" caused him to leave Lyndon Johnson's administration and become president of the World Bank, a position he held until 1981. Clark Clifford replaced McNamara as secretary of defense.

In 1995 McNamara published his memoirs, in which he stated that "we were wrong, terribly wrong" to have escalated the war in Vietnam. Many of McNamara's critics, noting that this was the former secretary of defense's first public criticism of the war, remained unimpressed with this belated courage and honesty.

SEE ALSO

Clifford, Clark; Hawks and doves; Vietnam War

FURTHER READING

Kinnard, Douglas. *The War Managers.* Hanover, N.H.: University Press of New England, 1977.

McNamara, Robert Strange. *In Retrospect: The Tragedy and Lessons of Vietnam.* New York: Times Books, 1995.

Medicare and Medicaid

President Lyndon B. Johnson signed legislation creating the Medicare and Medicaid medical insurance programs for the elderly, the disabled, and the poor on July 30, 1965. The legislation, in the form of an amendment to the 1935 Social Security Act, has proved to be the most costly yet the most enduring aspect of Johnson's sweeping Great Society agenda.

Medicare—Title XVIII of the Social Security Act—provides health insurance for people aged 65 and over and those seriously disabled. The insurance covers short-term hospital and nursing home expenses, physician and

Retired workers picket in favor of Medicare at the American Medical Association convention in 1965. The AMA was trying to decide whether to fight the federal Medicare program.

outpatient services, and home health care. It does not cover long-term nursing home care, dental and eye care, or prescription drugs. Beneficiaries pay a portion of the insured services.

Medicaid, or Title XIX, provides insurance for certain needy individuals. The federal government provides partial funding and allows states to run the program within broad guidelines. Therefore, Medicaid programs vary significantly from state to state. The states must cover hospital, physician, diagnostic, and home health services; nursing home care; and family planning for beneficiaries. Coverage of prescription drugs, eyeglasses, and intermediate care is optional. Medicaid helps many families pay for nursing home or state hospital care for their elderly relatives. It also provides money for the treatment of patients with acquired immune deficiency syndrome (AIDS).

The costs associated with both Medicare and Medicaid have been far more expensive than Congress expected, primarily because of the growing number of elderly people in the population, the increasing use of expensive medical technology, and the expanding access to medical care. As costs escalated, lawmakers enacted cost-containment measures—including caps on reimbursements—in the 1970s and 1980s. However, coverage was also extended, and the programs continue to face financial problems in the 1990s. When a Republican-led Congress attempted to reduce the size of projected increases in funding to the programs in 1995, President Bill Clinton refused to approve the budget.

Medicare and Medicaid represent a historic step forward in the United States's provision of services to those in need, but cost control remains an unsolved problem and is likely to be a political issue for years to come.

SEE ALSO

Great Society; Johnson, Lyndon Baines

FURTHER READING

Berkowitz, Edward D. *America's Welfare State: From Roosevelt to Reagan.* Baltimore, Md.: Johns Hopkins University Press, 1991.
David, Sheri I. *With Dignity: The Search for Medicare and Medicaid.* Westport, Conn.: Greenwood, 1985.
Stevens, Rosemary. *American Medicine and the Public Interest.* Berkeley: University of California Press, 1998.

Meredith, James Howard

- *Born: June 25, 1933, Kosciusko, Miss.*
- *Accomplishments: First black student admitted to University of Mississippi; lawyer; politician*

In October 1962, James Meredith became the first African American to attend the University of Mississippi. Earlier that year the Fifth Circuit Court of Appeals held that Meredith had been rejected by the university solely because of his race and therefore ordered his admission.

James Meredith registers at the University of Mississippi in 1962 while U.S. marshals stand guard on the campus.

When Meredith, who had been studying at the all-black Jackson State College, sought entry to the all-white University of Mississippi, Governor Ross Barnett blocked his attempt, invoking the right of state sovereignty against the federal government. "We must either submit to the awful dictate of the federal government or stand up like men and tell them, 'Never,'" Barnett announced on television, and he vowed to defy the court order.

President John F. Kennedy responded by mobilizing the National Guard to enforce the court order and allow Meredith to enroll. Meredith graduated in 1963 with a degree in political science and went on to study law at Columbia Law School. He took a break from his legal studies in 1966 to join in civil rights demonstrations in the South and was shot by an unknown gunman. He recovered and later went on to graduate from law school. In 1972, he ran unsuccessfully in Mississippi for the U.S. Senate as a Republican. Growing increasingly conservative in 1990, Meredith supported former Ku Klux Klan leader David Duke's campaign for governor of Louisiana.

SEE ALSO

Civil rights movement; Kennedy, John Fitzgerald

FURTHER READING

Meredith, James. *Three Years in Mississippi.* Bloomington: Indiana University Press, 1966.

Middle East–U.S. relations

The United States did not develop an interest in the Middle East until after World War II. Britain had been the main opponent of communism and the Soviet Union in the region, and it was not until 1947 that Britain, itself under economic strain, bailed out of Greece and Turkey, and the United States become a dominant force in the area. The U.S. then became the major Western patron of the conservative, oil-rich Arab regimes and in 1948 became the primary ally of the new state of Israel as well. The need to balance these dual and often conflicting interests would prove a major problem in U.S. foreign policy for the next half-century.

During the Suez Canal crisis in 1956, Israeli, British, and French forces attacked Egypt. The United States sided with Egypt and against its major allies, because it was primarily concerned with preventing the Soviets from exploiting the crisis. Israel, however, continued to be the chief recipient of U.S. financial, military, and diplomatic support, and the Israeli–Arab war of June 1967 again created problems for the United States. The Arab countries resented U.S. aid to the Jewish state and later denounced Israel for the flood of homeless Palestinian refugees created in that war and for not evacuating the territory it had conquered from Egypt, Jordan, and Syria. United States policymakers continued to try to walk a thin line in the Middle East, supporting Israel while not alienating the sources of oil for its allies and not allowing Moscow to gain undue influence in the region.

Tensions grew when the Palestine Liberation Organization (PLO) was established in 1968 with Yasir Arafat as its leader. The PLO wanted an Arab state in Palestine and vowed to eradicate Israel. The crisis erupted again in 1973 when Egypt and Syria launched a surprise attack on Israel in an attempt to regain the territory lost during the 1967 war. The Israelis weathered the assault, which began on the Jewish religious holiday of Yom Kippur, then counterattacked deeply into its foes' territory.

Americans felt the effect of the Yom Kippur War in 1973 with the Arab oil embargo and its resulting huge increases in oil and gasoline prices. The Organization of Petroleum Exporting Countries (OPEC) successfully enforced the embargo from 1973 to 1974, forcing the United States to turn increasingly to the shah of Iran, who secretly shipped oil to the United States in return for higher prices and massive arms shipments.

Secretary of State Henry Kissinger's rounds of negotiations in 1973–74—dubbed "shuttle diplomacy" by the press—produced a cease-fire in the Yom Kippur War and led Israel to withdraw from some of the territory it had taken from Egypt and Syria. Although it did not bring permanent peace on either of Israel's fronts, Kissinger's efforts prepared the way for the Camp David peace accords. Signed by Sadat and Israeli prime minister Menachem Begin in 1978, the agreement brought Egyptian recognition of Israel's sovereignty in return for Israel's return of the Sinai to Egypt.

But failure to resolve the Palestinian refugee dilemma led to yet another crisis in the Middle East when Israel invaded Lebanon in 1982 in order to prevent PLO attacks coming from that country. Israeli forces pushed the PLO out of southern Lebanon, and President Ronald Reagan, neither supporting nor opposing the invasion, sent U.S. forces as peacekeepers to enforce a negotiated settlement. In April 1983 a bomb exploded in the U.S. embassy in Beirut, killing 46 people, and on October 23, 1983, an Islamic terrorist drove a vehicle packed with explosives into a Marine barracks, killing 241 Americans. Reagan pulled the U.S. troops out in early 1984, leaving Lebanon a battlefield of warring Muslim and Arab Christian groups.

Despite the end of the cold war, the United States has maintained a strong presence in the Middle East, primarily to protect the flow of Arab oil to the West. It tilted toward Iraq when Saddam Hussein's army attacked Iran in 1980, viewing the Islamic fundamentalism of Iran's Ayatollah Khomeini as its chief threat, but changed course when the Iraqi army occupied Kuwait in August 1990, now fearing Saddam Hussein's quest for greater control over the Middle East's oil reserves.

President George Bush quickly gained the backing of the Soviet Union and the UN for his condemnation of Iraq's "naked aggression" and for his threat to use force if Iraq did not withdraw from Kuwait by January 15, 1991. The Iraqis did not withdraw, and the first planes and missiles of Operation Desert Storm began to hit Iraq on January 17. Within six weeks the U.S. forces, combined with those of 27 other nations, had triumphed. The

Iraqi soldiers set this Kuwaiti oil well on fire before Allied troops drove them from the country. In the foreground is a lake of oil created by uncapped oil wells. In 1991, the United Nations dispatched a special mission to Kuwait to assess the damage done to the country by the Iraqi invasion.

United States maintained its military presence in the Persian Gulf and its strong support of Israel. Nonetheless, the problems of the Middle East remain, and peaceful solutions seem nowhere near.

SEE ALSO

Arab oil embargo; Camp David peace talks; Iran-Contra affair; Iranian hostage crisis (1979); Lebanon, invasion of (1982); Persian Gulf War; Suez crisis (1956)

FURTHER READING

Dudley, William. *The Middle East: Opposing Viewpoints.* San Diego, Calif.: Greenhaven, 1992.

Friedlander, Melvin A. *Conviction and Credence: U.S. Policymaking in the Middle East.* Boulder, Colo.: Lynne Rienner, 1991.

Lenczowski, George. *American Presidents and the Middle East.* Durham, N.C.: Duke University Press, 1990.

Morris, Benny. *The Birth of the Palestinian Refugee Problem, 1947–1949.* New York: Cambridge University Press, 1989.

Quandt, William B. *Peace Process: American Diplomacy and the Arab-Israeli Conflict Since 1967.* Berkeley: University of California Press, 1993.

Rossi, Lorenza. *Who Shall Guard the Guardians Themselves: An Analysis of U.S. Strategy in the Middle East Since 1945.* European University Studies: History & Allied Studies Series, vol. 3. New York: Peter Lang, 1998.

Military-industrial complex

President Dwight D. Eisenhower warned against the emergence of a "military-industrial complex" in his farewell address to the nation on January 17, 1961. Referring to the "conjunction of an immense military establishment and a large arms industry that is new in the American experience," and whose influence was felt in "every city, every State house, every office of the Federal government," Eisenhower said that the continuing cold war threatened to make the military too powerful in U.S. life, and that freedom of education and scientific research might be in danger as well. He urged Americans not to succumb to the unwarranted leverage of the "military-industrial complex" and to guard against its immense power.

FURTHER READING

Leslie, Stuart. *The Military-Industrial-Academic Complex at M.I.T. and Stanford.* New York: Columbia University Press, 1993.

Milliken v. *Bradley* (1974)

In *Milliken* v. *Bradley,* the Supreme Court established the limits of judicial remedies to end school segregation. By a narrow 5-to-4 majority, the Court overturned a lower-court ruling that Detroit schools should be integrated by busing students between the city and surrounding suburbs.

Because of the recent flight of white families to nearby suburbs, a majority of students in Detroit public schools were black, while white students made up 81 percent of those attending suburban schools. Writing for the majority, Chief Justice Warren Burger ruled that the desegregation plan in Detroit requiring the transfer of students from the city to the suburbs was unconstitutional, because the suburbs had not caused the segregated schooling in Detroit. Dissenting Justice Thurgood Marshall, who had argued the landmark case *Brown* v. *Board of Education of Topeka, Kansas* in 1954, which ended legal segregation in public schools, said the Court was reacting "to a perceived public mood that we have gone far enough in enforcing the Constitution's guarantee of equal justice."

SEE ALSO

Brown v. *Board of Education of Topeka, Kansas* (1954); Burger, Warren; Marshall, Thurgood; Supreme Court

FURTHER READING

Wilkinson, J. Harvie. *From Brown to Bakke: The Supreme Court and School Integration.* New York: Oxford University Press, 1979.

Mills, C. Wright

- *Born: Aug. 28, 1916, Waco, Tex.*
- *Accomplishments: Sociologist; theorist*
- *Died: Mar. 20, 1962, Nyack, N.Y.*

In the 1950s and 1960s, the work of sociologist C. Wright Mills greatly influenced protest movements developing in association with the New Left. Readers of Mills's *White Collar* (1951) and *The Power Elite* (1956) found a new analysis of class structure in the United States that did not square with the conventional view of this country as a classless society.

Mills criticized the new middle class as "politically impotent" and attacked the power elite (composed of military, political, and corporate leaders) for dominating the rest of society. New Left spokesmen such as Tom Hayden borrowed Mills's belief in "participatory democracy" (the idea that ordinary citizens should have much more say in decisions being made at all levels of government) and used it as the central tenet of student movements in the 1960s. Mills died in 1962, the same year the New Left's Port Huron Statement, which called for just such a participatory democracy, was released.

SEE ALSO

Hayden, Thomas ("Tom"); New Left; Port Huron Statement

FURTHER READING

Mills, C. Wright. *The Power Elite.* New York: Oxford University Press, 1956.
Mills, C. Wright. *White Collar.* New York: Oxford University Press, 1951.

Miranda v. *Arizona* (1966)

In one of the landmark civil liberties cases of the century, in 1966 the Supreme Court ruled 5-to-4 in *Miranda* v. *Arizona* that police must inform defendants of their right to remain silent during interrogation and of their right to consult with a lawyer.

After a two-hour interrogation in Arizona, Ernesto Miranda had confessed to committing rape. The Supreme Court then held that Miranda had not been adequately informed of

WARNING AS TO YOUR RIGHTS

You are under arrest. Before we ask you any questions, you must understand what your rights are.

You have the right to remain silent. You are not required to say anything to us at any time or to answer any questions. Anything you say can be used against you in court.

You have the right to talk to a lawyer for advice before we question you and to have him with you during questioning.

If you cannot afford a lawyer and want one, a lawyer will be provided for you.

If you want to answer questions now without a lawyer present you will still have the right to stop answering at any time. You also have the right to stop answering at any time until you talk to a lawyer. P-4475

As a result of the Miranda *v.* Arizona *case, police officers now must inform an accused person of these rights as soon as an arrest is made.*

his right to counsel and had not been warned that his statements could be held against him in a trial.

Miranda was one of several decisions the Supreme Court headed by Earl Warren made that strengthened the rights of defendants in the criminal justice system. These measures were attacked by conservative opponents of the high court as giving "a green light to criminals." Although several Supreme Court rulings in the 1990s have narrowed the rights of the accused, the *Miranda* ruling essentially remains in force.

SEE ALSO

Supreme Court; Warren Court

FURTHER READING

Baker, Liva. *Miranda: Crime, Law, and Politics*. New York: Athenaeum, 1983.

Leo, Richard A., and George C. Thomas III, eds. *The Miranda Debate: Law, Justice, and Policing*. Boston: Northeastern University Press, 1998.

Mississippi Freedom Democratic Party (MFDP)

In 1964 civil rights activists from the Student Nonviolent Coordinating Committee and the Congress of Racial Equality who had participated in the Mississippi Freedom Summer organized a new political party in Mississippi to challenge the exclusively white state Democratic party. Unable to register blacks in the state Democratic party, the activists—who were harassed, beaten, and sometimes even murdered by white supremacists—registered nearly 60,000 voters for the Mississippi Freedom Democratic Party (MFDP).

The MFDP then sent delegates, including Fannie Lou Hamer, to the 1964 national Democratic convention to challenge the right of the all-white delegation to be seated and to demand that the MFDP delegates be seated in their place. President Lyndon B. Johnson, fearful of alienating southern white voters, declined to bar the Mississippi whites but suggested that the MFDP be granted two at-large seats. Although the Democrats barred delegations from states that discriminated against African-American voters at future conventions, the rejection of the MFDP bid for recognition widened the split between the moderate and radical forces in the civil rights movement.

SEE ALSO

Civil rights movement; Hamer, Fannie Lou Townsend; Mississippi Freedom Summer (1964)

FURTHER READING

Dittmer, John. *Local People: The Struggle for Civil Rights in Mississippi*. Urbana: University of Illinois Press, 1994.

Mississippi Freedom Summer (1964)

In the summer of 1964, civil rights activists from the Student Nonviolent

Coordinating Committee and the Congress of Racial Equality sought to register black voters in Mississippi. A thousand volunteer college students moved into the state to help establish "freedom schools," which taught black history and fostered racial pride; to register black voters; and to organize the Mississippi Freedom Democratic Party (MFDP) to provide an alternative to the existing all-white state Democratic party.

Despite police harassment, arrests, beatings, and the murders of three volunteers—James Chaney, Andrew Goodman, and Michael Schwerner—by the Ku Klux Klan, the movement registered 1,200 black voters and signed up 60,000 people for the MFDP. This new party sent delegates to the national Democratic convention to challenge the right of the all-white official state delegation to be seated. Pressure by prominent Democratic politicians and mainstream African-American leaders was brought to bear on MFDP representatives to compromise; the deal offered them was that they would accept just two MFDP delegates being seated along with the regular slate. Although the deal was sweetened with promises of reform in the delegate selection process, the MFDP rejected the compromise proposal and walked out of the convention in protest. The sense of betrayal felt by SNCC protestors would play a key role in the subsequent conflict within the civil rights movement between militants and moderates, and between blacks and whites.

SEE ALSO

Civil rights movement; Hamer, Fannie Lou Townsend; Mississippi Freedom Democratic party (MFDP); Student Nonviolent Coordinating Committee (SNCC)

FURTHER READING

Dittmer, John. *Local People: The Struggle for Civil Rights in Mississippi.* Urbana: University of Illinois Press, 1994.

McAdam, Doug. *Freedom Summer.* New York: Oxford University Press, 1988.

Moody, Anne. *Coming of Age in Mississippi.* New York: Dell, 1970.

Payne, Charles M. *I've Got the Light of Freedom: The Organizing Tradition and the Mississippi Freedom Struggle.* Berkeley: University of California Press, 1995.

Mitchell, John N.

- *Born: Sept. 15, 1913, Detroit, Mich.*
- *Accomplishments: Attorney general, 1969–72*
- *Died: Nov. 9, 1988, Washington, D.C.*

Having made his fortune as a municipal bond attorney, John Mitchell managed Republican Richard Nixon's 1968 Presidential campaign and served as his attorney general. Mitchell cultivated the "silent majority" of Americans who feared the radical changes promoted by various social movements and the disorder caused by radical protests and demonstrations. He appealed to them by promoting tough anticrime actions, a slowdown of school desegregation, and the appointment of conservatives to the Supreme Court.

Mitchell resigned as attorney general in 1972 to head CREEP (Committee to Re-elect the President). Funding the project with secret corporate contributions to CREEP, Mitchell approved a series of so-called dirty tricks to spread dissension within Democratic ranks as well as a plan by former FBI agent G. Gordon Liddy to wiretap the Democratic National Committee headquarters.

Following the arrest of the five burglars in the Watergate complex, where the Democratic headquarters were located, on June 17, 1972, Mitchell told the press that the intruders "were not operating either in our behalf or with our consent." At Nixon's behest, Mitchell resigned from CREEP with the excuse that his wife was ill, but he continued to work with John Dean, Nixon's special counsel, to cover up the White House involvement in the Watergate affair.

In April 1973, Nixon wanted Mitchell in effect to fall on his sword and be his scapegoat. Mitchell refused and instead implicated the White House "in a design not to have the stories come out." Indicted by the Watergate grand jury, along with other former White House and CREEP officials, for conspiracy to obstruct justice, Mitchell was found guilty and sentenced to jail. The last of the Watergate conspirators to be released from prison, Mitchell was paroled on January 19, 1979.

SEE ALSO
Nixon, Richard Milhous; Watergate

Model Cities Act of 1966

Originally called the Demonstration Cities and Metropolitan Development Act, the Model Cities Act of 1966 was one of dozens of pieces of Great Society legislation signed by President Lyndon B. Johnson aimed at reducing poverty in the United States. The program provided funding for slum clearance, mass transportation, and recreational facilities in urban areas.

Instead of focusing on a few "model cities" as originally intended, the program was applied widely. Consequently, its meager and thinly spread resources had little impact on the depressing progress of urban decay.

SEE ALSO
Great Society

Mondale, Walter F.

- *Born: Jan. 5, 1928, Ceylon, Minn.*
- *Government service: Attorney general of Minnesota, 1960–64; U.S. senator (Democrat–Minn.), 1964–77; Vice President, 1977–81; U.S. ambassador to Japan, 1993–97*

Walter Mondale came out of the Minnesota Democratic Farmer Labor party, within the liberal wing of the national Democratic party. After serving as the state attorney general, he was appointed by President Lyndon B. Johnson to the U.S. Senate in 1964 to fill the vacancy left by Hubert Humphrey when he was elected Vice President in 1964. Voters kept Mondale in the Senate until he joined Jimmy Carter's Presidential ticket in 1976.

Under Carter, Mondale was free to increase the authority and influence of the Vice President's office. He had a White House office, assisted Carter in making cabinet appointments, shared supervisory responsibilities over the White House staff, and was a principal advisor to the President on economic policy.

In 1984 Mondale was nominated for President by the Democrats but failed to raise much enthusiasm for his campaign, despite choosing as his running mate New York congresswoman Geraldine Ferraro, the first woman to run on a major-party Presidential ticket. Incumbents Ronald Reagan and George Bush defeated Mondale and Ferraro in a landslide. In 1993 Walter Mondale was named U.S. ambassador to Japan.

SEE ALSO

Ferraro, Geraldine

FURTHER READING

Gillon, Steven. *The Democrats' Dilemma: Walter F. Mondale and the Liberal Legacy.* New York: Columbia University Press, 1992.

Montgomery bus boycott (1955–56)

The first major success of the modern civil rights movement, the boycott by African Americans of the Montgomery, Alabama, public transportation system forced the city to integrate its bus lines and propelled Dr. Martin Luther King, Jr., to national prominence.

The boycott began December 5, 1955, after Rosa Parks, a black seamstress, was arrested for refusing to move to the back of the bus, which was set aside for blacks. For the next year, black riders refused to travel on the buses and instead walked or carpooled to work. The boycott was organized by groups such as the Women's Political Council, composed of college-educated black women; the council's president was Jo Ann Robinson, an instructor at Montgomery State College. Some whites honored the boycott, but the mayor and local vigilantes sought to break the boycott through intimidation and violence.

King, for example, was indicted for conducting an "illegal" boycott and arrested for driving 30 miles per hour in a 25-mile-an-hour zone. In January 1956 a bomb exploded outside his house. The nonviolent bus boycott continued, however, and on December 21, 1956, in response to a Supreme Court ruling that bus segre-

Martin Luther King, Jr. (left), and Ralph Abernathy ride on the first desegregated bus in Montgomery, Alabama, in 1956.

gation was unconstitutional, Montgomery's bus system was desegregated.

SEE ALSO

African Americans; Civil rights movement; King, Martin Luther, Jr.

FURTHER READING

Dornfeld, Margaret. *The Turning Tide: From the Desegregation of the Armed Forces to the Montgomery Bus Boycott (1948–1956).* Broomall, Pa.: Chelsea House, 1995.

Garrow, David, ed. *The Montgomery Bus Boycott and the Woman Who Started It: The Memoir of Jo Ann Gibson Robinson.* Knoxville: University of Tennessee Press, 1987.

King, Martin Luther, Jr. *Stride Toward Freedom: The Montgomery Boycott.* New York: Harper & Row, 1958.

Moral Majority

Jerry Falwell, a family-oriented fundamentalist Christian whose weekly "Old Time Gospel Hour" show was broadcast on more than 600 radio and TV stations, organized the Moral Majority in 1979 "to bring about a moral and conservative revolution." Within a year the Moral Majority claimed more than 4 million members, particularly among Southern Baptists.

The evangelical minister Jerry Falwell, who had already started a church, a highly successful television program and then a college, organized the Moral Majority in 1979. The organization's goal was to foster a "conservative revolution" in the United States.

Campaigning against "secular humanism," abortion, divorce, homosexuality, pornography, federal involvement in education, and the Equal Rights Amendment, the Moral Majority registered an estimated 2 million new voters in 1980 and 1984. The Moral Majority also hosted political seminars and workshops for its adherents and issued a "morality rating" for members of Congress.

In 1989 television evangelist Pat Robertson's Christian Coalition succeeded the Moral Majority. Effectively directed by Ralph Reed, the Christian Coalition mobilized conservative activists to run for local political offices, building a religious nation at the grass roots, and to work to transform the Republican party into the party of "traditional family values." Largely successful in altering the political agenda of the 1990s, the religious right had become a major force in American life.

SEE ALSO

Conservatism; Religious fundamentalism

FURTHER READING

Frederick, Arthur. *Idol Worshippers in 20th Century America: Phyllis Schafly, Ronald Reagan, Jerry Falwell, and the Moral Majority on Women, Work, and Homosexuality.* Irving, Tex.: Monument, 1985.

Snowball, David. *Continuity and Change in the Rhetoric of the Moral Majority.* Westport, Conn.: Greenwood, 1991.

Morrison, Toni

- *Born: Feb. 18, 1931, Lorain, Ohio*
- *Accomplishments: Writer; Pulitzer Prize for Fiction, 1988; Nobel Prize for Literature, 1993*

• *Major Works:* The Bluest Eye: A Novel *(1972),* Sula *(1974),* Tar Baby *(1981),* Song of Solomon *(1977),* Beloved: A Novel *(1987),* Jazz *(1992),* Paradise *(1998).*

Born Chloe Anthony Wofford, Toni Morrison is the only African-American writer to win the Nobel Prize for Literature. She began her career as a writer in her late 30s with the publication of *The Bluest Eye,* the story of a black girl who is raped by her father.

When Toni Morrison won the Nobel Prize for literature in 1993, the Academy said that she was someone "who, in novels characterized by visionary force and poetic import, gives life to an essential aspect of American reality."

Morrison's career took off in 1977 with the publication of her third novel, *Song of Solomon,* and in 1988 she won the Pulitzer Prize and other prestigious awards for *Beloved,* a novel about slavery. Awarded the Nobel Prize for Literature in 1993, Morrison has also worked as a senior editor at Random House, a major publishing company, and has taught literature at Howard University, Princeton University, and other colleges.

FURTHER READING

Samuels, Wilfred D., and Clenora Hudson-Weems. *Toni Morrison.* Boston: Twayne, 1990.

Moses, Robert Parris

• *Born: Jan. 23, 1935, New York, N.Y.*
• *Accomplishments: civil rights activist*

Robert Moses served as field secretary of the Student Nonviolent Coordinating Committee (SNCC) during its drive to register black voters in Mississippi in 1964. Raised in Harlem, Moses embraced the philosophy of nonviolence and worked for Martin Luther King, Jr.'s' Southern Christian Leadership Conference (SCLC) before joining SNCC.

During the voter registration drive, Moses began to move away from the legal focus of the early civil rights movement and became increasingly concerned with the needs of poor blacks in rural Mississippi. After the elections of 1964, he rejected integrationist politics, became an outspoken opponent of the war in Vietnam, and moved to Canada rather than comply with the military draft. In recent years, Moses founded the Algebra Project in Cambridge, Massachusetts, teaching inner-city minority students math skills in various cities and states.

SEE ALSO

Civil rights movement; Southern Christian Leadership Conference (SCLC); Student Nonviolent Coordinating Committee (SNCC)

FURTHER READING

Burner, Eric R. *And Gently He Shall Lead Them: Robert Parris Moses and Civil Rights in Mississippi.* New York: New York University Press, 1994.

Movies

In the late 1940s and early 1950s, many Americans moved from cities to suburbs. At the time, movie theaters were still primarily located in the cities. This migration resulted in a decrease in movie ticket sales. The introduction of television to the general public in 1946 further decreased ticket sales. Television provided Americans with moving pictures in the comfort of their own living rooms. Movies began to gain popularity in the suburbs only later in the century with the introduction of drive-in theaters and mall multiplexes.

Nevertheless, Hollywood studios continued to make outstanding movies throughout the 1940s and 1950s. These films expressed the hopes and fears of a generation recovering from World War II. In *The Best Years of Our Lives,* released in 1946, young soldiers return to find a deeply changed world. Alienated from former friends, they learn to cope with lost opportunities. One of the stars of the film is Harold Russell, an amateur actor who lost both of his arms in the war. For his performance, he won the Academy Award for Best Supporting Actor. *It's a Wonderful Life,* also released in 1946, provided a more uplifting vision of American life. Jimmy Stewart stars in the film as George Bailey, a man whose financial losses nearly drive him to suicide. When convinced by an angel that he plays a crucial role in his community, he decides to go on living. *It's a Wonderful Life* has become a popular favorite during the Christmas holiday season.

Most films made in Hollywood during the 1950s adhered to a particular genre—a category of movie with a particular style and set of conventions. Popular genres included the musical, the western, and the film noir. Musicals featured singing, dancing, and very elaborate, colorful sets. Many musicals were adaptations of Broadway shows, including the Leonard Bernstein hit *On the Town* and a lavish CinemaScope version of *Oklahoma!* There were also musicals written exclusively for the movies, including *Singin' in the Rain* and *An American in Paris,* both starring the talented actor, choreographer, dancer, and singer Gene Kelly.

Westerns were often set during the period of western expansion in the mid to late 19th century. Although these films are often remembered for the violent, simplistic confrontations between cowboys and Indians, some westerns were highly sophisticated. One of the most well regarded films in the genre is *The Searchers* (1956), starring John Wayne as an ex-Confederate soldier trying to find his kidnapped niece. The character played by Wayne is a violent racist who seeks revenge on the Comanche chief who killed most of his family. As he becomes entirely absorbed in his search for the chief, he alienates both his friends and his family. The complex moral struggle in *The Searchers* takes place in a beautiful western American landscape, captured in lush Technicolor by director John Ford.

The film noir, influenced by prewar German expressionist directors Fritz Lang and F. W. Murnau, featured dark visions of the city and complex detective stories. Orson Welles, the legendary director of *Citizen Kane*, starred in and directed *Touch of Evil* (1958). The mysterious crimes committed by a corrupt American policeman, played by Welles, are revealed by a decent Mexican narcotics officer, played by Charlton Heston. *Touch of Evil* is a typical film noir, featuring complicated plot twists and a great deal of violence.

In the 1960s, many filmmakers began to break with the conventions of earlier Hollywood films. In 1963, a year after the Cuban missile crisis, Stanley Kubrick's film *Dr. Strangelove* was released. The film was a wild farce that dared to mock the United States military and its nuclear capacity. The rebellious baby boom generation went to the theaters to see *Bonnie and Clyde,* starring Warren Beatty and Faye Dunaway as a doomed couple on the run from the law. Directed by Arthur Penn, *Bonnie and Clyde* combined a loose, freewheeling style of direction with unprecedented realism, especially in the depiction of violence. Another popular depiction of the lives of young rebels is the 1969 film *Easy Rider,* starring Peter Fonda and Jack Nicholson. *Easy Rider* features a rock soundtrack and a celebration of the lives of hippies and bikers. The brutal violence at the end of the film keenly reflects the uneasy spirit of the times in the year of the Manson family murders and a disastrous Rolling Stones concert at Altamont. In the late 1960s, "underground" directors such as John Cassavetes and Andy Warhol attracted attention with their experimental films, some of which broke nearly every existing convention of filmmaking.

The freedom and experimentation introduced in American movies of the 1960s inspired many talented young directors in the 1970s. Two of the most acclaimed directors who emerged from this era are Martin Scorsese and Francis Ford Coppola. Coppola's *The Godfather* and *The Godfather: Part Two* tell the epic story of a Sicilian organized crime family. Featuring brutal violence and performances by Marlon Brando, Al Pacino, and Robert DeNiro, both *Godfather* films won critical acclaim. Brando also starred in Coppola's Vietnam film *Apocalypse Now* (1979), an adaptation of the Joseph Conrad novel *Heart of Darkness* that set the standard for war movies in the 1980s and 90s with its unflinching portrayal of bloodshed and expensive fireworklike display of gunfire and explosions. Scorsese presented a bleak vision of New York City, more personal and less epic than Coppola's, in films such as *Mean Streets* and *Taxi Driver.* All of his films combine brutal realism with intricate camera work.

In 1977 another talented young director, George Lucas, came to prominence. His film *Star Wars,* widely expected to be a huge flop, was an enormous success. The film was a throwback to old Hollywood action movies—it featured a romantic soundtrack, swashbuckling battles, and a struggle between forces of good and evil. *Star Wars'* special effects were imitated in many later films. *Raiders of the Lost Ark,* directed by Steven Spielberg, was another success derived from earlier films. Starring Harrison Ford as Indiana Jones, a crusading archaeologist in

Gene Kelly dances up a storm in Singing in the Rain *(1952), one of the first musicals to be written for the movies.*

search of stolen treasure, *Raiders* was influenced heavily by old Hollywood serials—early action movies that were shown in parts before feature films. Throughout the 1980s, Hollywood studios made a number of action movies that tried to match the success of *Star Wars* and *Raiders of the Lost Ark*.

In the late 1980s and early 1990s, there was a resurgence of American films made by independent filmmakers. Independent directors, like the "underground" directors of the 1960s and Coppola and Scorsese in the 1970s, work primarily outside the Hollywood studio system. These filmmakers often have the freedom to pursue more personal or political subjects that larger studios tend to avoid. The first successful independent director of the 1980s, Spike Lee makes films with African-American casts and controversial political messages. His success helped him secure the money to make an epic adaptation of the *Autobiography of Malcolm X,* starring Denzel Washington as the slain religious leader. Quentin Tarantino is another prominent independent director. His ultraviolent comedies have been commercial and critical successes. Weaving together several plots, Tarantino's *Pulp Fiction* features witty dialogue full of pop culture references and a style reminiscent of French art cinema. Tarantino is considered by many critics a postmodern director because of his often jarring combinations of styles and language from different eras and areas.

In 1997, twenty years after the release of *Star Wars,* another unexpected success evoked classic Hollywood movies: *Titanic.* Most observers did not expect the film to be a hit, because it was aimed at a mostly female audience. One of the most expensive films ever made, *Titanic* cost over $200 million dollars. The huge expense required to make *Titanic* reflected the incredibly high costs of special effects and star actors, some of whom were paid more than $20 million per film. Starring teen heartthrob Leonardo DiCaprio, *Titanic* was a typical Hollywood story of the doomed love affair of a beautiful young couple. *Titanic* won eleven Academy Awards, including Best Picture and Best Director.

SEE ALSO
Television

FURTHER READING

Nowell-Smith, Geoffrey. *The Oxford History of World Cinema.* Oxford: Oxford University Press, 1996.
Parkinson, David. *The Young Oxford Book of the Movies.* New York: Oxford University Press, 1995.
Sarris, Andrew. *The American Cinema.* New York: Dutton, 1968.
Smith, Diane G. *Great American Film Directors.* New York: Julian Messner, 1987.

Moynihan, Daniel Patrick

- *Born: Mar. 16, 1927, Tulsa, Okla.*
- *Accomplishments: Assistant secretary of labor, 1963–65; U.S. ambassador to India, 1973–75; chief U.S. delegate to United Nations, 1975–76; U.S. senator (Democrat–N.Y.), 1977–*

A longtime senator from New York, Daniel Patrick Moynihan has been a key figure in the Democratic party since the 1960s. As assistant secretary of labor under President Lyndon B. Johnson, in 1965 Moynihan issued a report entitled "The Negro Family" that focused on the harmful consequences of slavery, which he found responsible for the alarmingly high rates of divorce, separation, desertion, and illegitimacy among African Americans. Although Moynihan's aim had been to draw attention to a problem so that action could be taken to remedy it, the so-called Moynihan Report offended many African Americans, who branded it racist, widening the rift then opening between black militants and white liberals.

In 1969 President Richard M. Nixon appointed Moynihan, then the director of the Joint Center for Urban Studies at Harvard University and the Massachusetts Institute of Technology, executive secretary of his Urban Affairs Council. When a memorandum Moynihan wrote calling for a period of benign neglect on the subject of race was leaked to the press in February 1970, his standing among liberals and African Americans, already low, sank yet lower, and he soon resigned to teach. A scholar as well as a politician, Moynihan taught government at various academic institutions, including Harvard, Syracuse, and Cornell Universities.

But politics beckoned again in 1976, when Moynihan won election to the Senate as a Democrat from New York. Since then, he has played a prominent role in the Senate as a highly independent moderate, often breaking with his party to support a strong military defense system and welfare reform.

FURTHER READING

Glazer, Nathan, and Daniel Patrick Moynihan. *Beyond the Melting Pot: The Negroes, Puerto Ricans, Jews, Italians, and Irish of New York City.* 1963. Reprint, Cambridge, Mass: M.I.T. Press, 1970.

Moynihan, Daniel Patrick. *The Negro Family: The Case for National Action.* Washington, D.C.: U.S. Government Printing Office, 1965.

Ms. magazine

Now considered one of the most important icons of the feminist movement, *Ms.* magazine was founded by Gloria Steinem, Dorothy Pitman Hughes, and the Women's Action Alliance in 1972. Its feminist articles spread the message of the women's movement. After some financial difficulty *Ms.* stopped production in 1989. In 1990, after a battle with advertisers, *Ms.* became the first magazine to survive solely on subscriber contributions, eliminating all advertising, because the editors felt that much of the advertisers' messages undermined the feminist message of the magazine.

This 1972 cover of Ms. *magazine shows a superheroine grabbing warplanes out of the sky as she leaps large streets in a single bound. Her slightly harassed expression seems to ask if a woman's work is* ever *done.*

SEE ALSO

Feminism; Steinem, Gloria

FURTHER READING

Farrell, Amy Erdman. *Yours in Sisterhood: Ms. Magazine and the Promise of Popu-*

lar Feminism, Gender and American Culture. Chapel Hill: University of North Carolina Press, 1998.
Steinem, Gloria. "The Birth of *Ms.*" *New York,* April 19, 1993, 134–35.
Thom, Mary. *Inside Ms.: 25 Years of the Magazine and the Feminist Movement.* New York: Henry Holt, 1998.

Multiculturalism

The idea of multiculturalism rejects the notion that U.S. society is based on one set of coherent cultural traditions. According to the multiculturalists, the United States is a pluralistic society where a variety of cultural traditions have coexisted and thrived.

Advocates of multiculturalism have expanded U.S. history and literature curricula to include the experiences and writings of Americans from many different ethnic and religious traditions. Their more inclusive view, they argue, leads not only to a more accurate picture of reality but also tends to foster greater tolerance.

Opponents argue that multiculturalism creates destructive divisions among the American people and underemphasizes the traditions and beliefs that hold the country together. The concept of multiculturalism became a hotly contested issue, especially in public schools and on college campuses, in the 1990s.

FURTHER READING

Bernstein, Richard. *Dictatorship of Virtue: Multiculturalism and the Battle for America's Future.* New York: Knopf, 1994.
Hollinger, David A. *Postethnic America: Beyond Multiculturalism.* New York: Basic Books, 1995.

My Lai massacre

On the morning of March 16, 1968, U.S. soldiers belonging to the 1st and 2nd Platoons of Charlie Company, 1st Battalion, 11th Infantry Brigade, armed with machine guns and grenade launchers, succumbed to the stress of jungle combat and the hatred generated by the killings of their buddies, and slaughtered between 300 and 400 civilians in the hamlets of My Khe and My Lai in the Quang Ngai province of South Vietnam.

An elaborate cover-up orchestrated by the army prevented the American public from learning of the massacre until November 1969. All of the 13 soldiers (including 4 officers) who were charged with crimes against humanity and war crimes were acquitted or had the charges against them dropped, except for Lieutenant William Calley.

Members of Calley's 1st Platoon were responsible for the deaths of more than 200 of the women, children, and old men killed. On Calley's orders, these people had been marched into a ditch and gunned down. He was convicted of mass murder in 1971 and sentenced to life imprisonment; the sentence was later reduced to ten years.

SEE ALSO

Vietnam War

FURTHER READING

Hammer, Richard. *One Morning in the War: The Tragedy at Son My.* New York: Coward-McCann, 1970.
Hersh, Seymour M. *Cover-Up: The Army's Secret Investigation of the Massacre at My Lai 4.* New York: Random House, 1972.
Peers, William R. *The My Lai Inquiry.* New York: Norton, 1979.

National Advisory Commission on Civil Disorders

SEE Kerner Commission

National Association for the Advancement of Colored People (NAACP)

The oldest existing civil rights organization in the United States, the National Association for the Advancement of Colored People (NAACP) played a central role in the civil rights revolution of the 1950s and 1960s.

The NAACP was founded in 1909 by a group of black civil rights leaders, including the scholar W. E. B. Du Bois, and prominent white progressives. The organization quickly surpassed other racial protest groups, doggedly promoting civil rights by investigating lynchings and other violence against blacks, lobbying lawmakers, publicizing efforts to improve civil rights, and, most important, by challenging racist laws in the courts.

After decades of a few hard-won legal and political battles, the NAACP's legal strategy paid off in 1954 when the Supreme Court ordered the desegregation of public schools in the *Brown* v. *Board of Education of Topeka, Kansas,* decision. Under the leadership of Thurgood Marshall and Roy Wilkins, the organization continued to fight legal battles and successfully lobbied for the Civil Rights Act of 1964 and the Voting Rights Act of 1965.

Four of the leaders of the NAACP (from left): Henry L. Moon, director of public relations; Roy Wilkins, executive secretary; Herbert Hill, labor secretary; and Thurgood Marshall, special counsel.

The group has also been instrumental in defeating Supreme Court nominees it viewed as hostile to civil rights, including Clement F. Haynesworth in 1969, G. Harrold Carswell in 1970, and Robert H. Bork in 1986. In the 1990s, the organization was plagued by controversy under the leadership of Benjamin Chavez, who was accused of financial mismanagement and sexual harassment and who courted the support of radical black nationalists, including the Nation of Islam's leader, Louis Farrakhan. Myrlie Evers Williams, widow of slain NAACP organizer Medgar Evers, replaced Chavez in 1995. In 1996 Kweisi Mfume, who had represented Maryland in the House of Representatives for ten years, gave up his seat there to become president of the organization.

SEE ALSO

Civil rights movement; Marshall, Thurgood; Supreme Court; Wilkins, Roy

FURTHER READING

Finch, Minnie. *The NAACP, Its Fight for Justice.* Metuchen, N.J.: Scarecrow Press, 1981.
McPherson, James M. *The Abolitionist Legacy: From Reconstruction to the NAACP.* Princeton, N.J.: Princeton University Press, 1995.
Reed, Christopher Robert. *The Chicago NAACP and the Rise of Black Professional Leadership, 1910–1966.* Bloomington: Indiana University Press, 1997.

National Endowments for the Arts and Humanities (NEA and NEH)

The National Endowment for the Arts (NEA) and National Endowment for the Humanities (NEH) were established by Congress in 1965 to sponsor artistic and cultural development. The endowments have proven to be one of the more controversial elements of Lyndon B. Johnson's sweeping reform legislation, the Great Society.

The humanities endowment sponsors the work of historians, folklorists, librarians, museum curators, and others seeking to preserve the United States's cultural heritage. The Endowment for the Arts subsidizes painters, photographers, musicians, writers, and other artists. The arts foundation was the subject of particularly bitter criticisms in the 1980s and 1990s after it subsidized works of art that some members of Congress labeled obscene or irreligious. The Republican Congress of 1995–96 moved to cut the budgets of both endowments substantially and appropriations for the agencies have been highly controversial ever since.

These Native American artists are partially supported by a grant from the National Endowment for the Arts.

SEE ALSO

Great Society; Johnson, Lyndon Baines

FURTHER READING

Netzer, Dick. *The Subsidized Muse: Public Support for the Arts in the United States.* New York: Cambridge University Press, 1978.

Zeigler, Joseph Wesley. *Arts in Crisis: The National Endowment for the Arts vs. America.* Chicago: A Cappella Books, 1994.

National Housing Act of 1949

The aim of the National Housing Act of 1949, a part of President Harry S. Truman's Fair Deal domestic program, was to provide "a decent home and a suitable living environment for every American family." Supported by the construction industry, the bill passed Congress. Housing projects did not always prove to be successful, and some large high-rise developments are being torn down, to be replaced by more smaller-scale projects.

SEE ALSO

Fair Deal; Truman, Harry S.

Chicago's Cabrini-Green, a housing project built with high hopes in the late 1950s, was torn down in the later 1990s as it became clear that massive high-rises could not provide residents with a healthy community life. Andrew Cuomo, Secretary of Housing and Urban Development, said in 1997 that "Public housing was and is a good idea, but sometimes when we've implemented that good idea, it's been perverted in the actual construction."

FURTHER READING

Hamby, Alonzo. *Man of the People: A Life of Harry S. Truman.* New York: Oxford University Press, 1995.

O'Davies, Richard. *Housing Reform During the Truman Administration.* Columbia: University of Missouri Press, 1966.

National Liberation Front (NLF)

On December 20, 1960, South Vietnamese communist delegates at a secret meeting in Saigon organized the National Liberation Front (NLF) to direct activities aimed at overthrowing the autocratic rule of Ngo Dinh Diem and ousting his U.S. military advisors. The NLF gradually recruited most of the anti-Diem guerrilla forces, known as the Vietcong (for Vietnamese communists), which had been fighting the South Vietnamese government since 1957, and escalated the conflict throughout the South Vietnamese countryside. The inability of the government in Saigon to put down the NLF rebellion ultimately forced the United States to undertake a full-scale intervention.

SEE ALSO

Vietnam War

FURTHER READING

Henderson, William D. *Why the Vietcong Fought.* Westport, Conn.: Greenwood, 1979.

Pike, Douglas. *Viet Cong: The Organization and Techniques of the National Liberation Front of South Vietnam.* Cambridge, Mass.: M.I.T. Press, 1966.

National Mobilization Committee to End the War in Vietnam

After its success in organizing massive demonstrations against the Vietnam War on April 15, 1967, the Spring Mobilization Committee to End the War in Vietnam converted itself into the National Mobilization Committee to End the War in Vietnam, also known as the Mobe. The Mobe attempted to draw together numerous groups of antiwar activists and organizations to stage large-scale protests against the war.

Participants in the Mobe included members of groups such as Women Strike for Peace, the Chicago Area Draft Resisters, the Resistance, Students for a Democratic Society (SDS), the Socialist Workers party, the National Conference for New Politics, the Congress of Racial Equality (CORE), and the Youth International party (Yippies). Although the organization orchestrated many events, the Mobe's most successful demonstrations include the October 21–22, 1967, march of more than 50,000 antiwar demonstrators on Washington, D.C., and their subsequent clash with police and military troops at the Pentagon, as well as the 1971 March against Death in Washington on Vietnam Moratorium Day.

SEE ALSO

Antiwar movement; Congress of Racial Equality (CORE); New Left; Students for a Democratic Society (SDS); Youth International party (Yippies)

FURTHER READING

Breines, Wini. *Community and Organization in the New Left, 1962–1968.* New York: Praeger, 1982.

Chatfield, Charles. *The American Peace Movement: Ideals and Activism.* New York: Twayne, 1992.

DeBenedetti, Charles. *An American Ordeal: The Antiwar Movement of the Vietnam Era.* Syracuse, N.Y.: Syracuse University Press, 1990.

National Organization for Women (NOW)

SEE Feminism

National Security Act of 1947

The National Security Act of 1947 established the Department of Defense, with subcabinet departments for the army, navy, and air force; the Central Intelligence Agency (CIA), to coordinate intelligence-gathering activities; and a new National Security Council (NSC). The NSC coordinates and analyzes foreign policy information for the President and advises on all matters of national security.

From President John Kennedy on, the national security advisor, who heads the NSC, has become increasingly more important than the State Department in working with the President to formulate U.S. foreign policy.

SEE ALSO

Central Intelligence Agency (CIA); National Security Council report (NSC-68); Truman, Harry S.

FURTHER READING

Leffler, Melvyn. *A Preponderance of Power: National Security, the Truman Administration, and the Cold War.* Stanford, Calif.: Stanford University Press, 1992.

Yergin, Daniel. *Shattered Peace: The Origins of the Cold War and the National Security State.* Boston: Houghton Mifflin, 1977.

National Security Council report (NSC-68)

The assumptions and strategic recommendations of the 1950 report of the National Security Council (called NSC-68) governed U.S. foreign policy through much of the cold war. Following on the heels of the 1949 communist victory in China and the Soviet explosion of a nuclear device in August 1949, NSC-68 stated that the Soviet Union, "unlike previous aspirants to hegemony, is animated by a new fanatic faith, antithetical to our own, and seeks to impose its absolute authority over the rest of the world." The report envisioned "an indefinite period of tension and danger." Therefore, the United States could not, in Secretary of State Dean Acheson's words, "pull down the blinds and sit in the parlor with a loaded shotgun, waiting." Rather, it had to embark on a massive military buildup at home and create "situations of strength" abroad, whatever the cost.

Although the top Soviet expert and author of the containment doctrine, George Kennan, believed that Soviet premier Joseph Stalin had little intention and no ability to conquer the world, President Harry Truman approved NSC-68 as official U.S. policy in mid-1950. This decision solidified the inclinations of U.S. policymakers to view communist gains anywhere in the world as a loss for the vital interests of the United States, and it rapidly escalated the Soviet–U.S. race for nuclear and conventional military superiority.

SEE ALSO

Cold war; Containment doctrine; Kennan, George F.; Truman, Harry S.

FURTHER READING

Gaddis, John Lewis. *Strategies of Containment.* New York: Oxford University Press, 1982.

Sagan, Scott D. *Moving Targets: Nuclear Strategy and National Security.* Princeton, N.J.: Princeton University Press, 1990.

Nation of Islam

SEE Black Muslims; Black nationalism

Native Americans

In the postwar era, Native Americans finally seemed to reverse the processes that had begun in 1492 of the destruction of their culture, the devastation of their population, and the loss of their ancestral lands. Initially, however, the fortunes of Native Americans hit rock bottom.

These young Indians show their solidarity as they demonstrate for Native American civil rights on Alcatraz Island in 1971.

In the 1950s, Congress granted U.S. citizenship to Indians but also liquidated reservations and ended many federal benefits and social services to tribes. The tribes also now had to pay state taxes, and to do so many tribes sold their lands and mineral rights to outside interests. Most tribes were now far worse off than ever, and by the end of the 1960s half the Native American population had abandoned their reservations and relocated to urban areas.

In 1961, activists from 67 tribes met in Chicago to draft a Declaration of Purposes, calling attention to their plight and to the dire poverty of most Indians. Suffering the poorest education, the highest disease and death rates, and the most substandard housing of any ethnic group in the United States, delegations of Indians went to Washington in 1964 to argue for their inclusion in President Lyndon B. Johnson's War on Poverty. Johnson responded by channeling special antipoverty funds into Indian communities.

In 1968 militant protestors began to demand preferential hiring of Indians, Native American studies programs in higher education, and reimbursement for lost lands. Chippewa Indians

Three of the founding members of the American Indian Movement (AIM) stand together in 1989. From left, they are Dennis Banks, Eddie Benton Benia, and Clyde Bellecourt.

in Minnesota founded the American Indian Movement (AIM), emphasizing the right of Native Americans to control their own affairs. Like the Black Panthers, AIM's armed patrols sought to protect Indians from harassment and brutality by the police.

AIM began a confrontational protest campaign in 1969 by occupying Alcatraz Island near San Francisco. The group also occupied the federal Bureau of Indian Affairs in 1972 and a trading post at Wounded Knee, South Dakota, in 1973. These protests drew attention to the dire plight of American Indians and led to a reversal of federal policy. In 1970 President Richard M. Nixon ended the policy of closing reservations and began to give more control of Indian affairs back to the tribes. This approach culminated in the Indian Self-Determination Act of 1974.

Since the 1970s, ethnic pride has flourished among Indians. Although the stereotype of the drunken, impoverished Indian continues, there has also been a growing appreciation among the general population of Native American art, religion, and culture.

The number of people identifying themselves as Indian has more than doubled between 1970 and 1990, reflecting both a natural increase and the growing number of Indians eager to affirm their ethnic roots. There was also a boom in industrial and commercial development on reservations, providing jobs and helping to reduce, thought not eliminate, poverty, alcoholism, and inadequate health care. Many tribes sought to generate income by operating gambling casinos (permitted by a 1961 law). While some grew rich, the casinos also exacerbated intratribal disputes and conflicts with non-Indians who were opposed to commercialized gambling.

Finally, in the past 25 years tribes have won a series of legal battles in which they successfully sued for the return of lands taken over the years in violation of treaties. The Sioux in

South Dakota, the Penobscot in Maine, the Eskimo, or Inuit and Aleuts, in Alaska, and the Puyallups in Washington have all won large monetary or land awards in court decisions since 1970. Various tribes have also been successful in demanding that museums return Indian skeletal remains and sacred items from graves.

SEE ALSO

American Indian Movement (AIM); Wounded Knee (1973)

FURTHER READING

Griffin-Pierce, Trudy. *The Encyclopedia of Native America.* New York: Viking, 1995.

Hoxie, Frederick E., ed. *Encyclopedia of North American Indians.* Boston: Houghton Mifflin, 1996.

Hoxie, Frederick E., ed. *Indians in American History: An Introduction.* Arlington Heights, Ill.: Harland Davidson, 1988.

Matthiessen, Peter. *In the Spirit of Crazy Horse.* New York: Viking, 1983.

New Frontier

In accepting the 1960 Democratic Presidential nomination, John F. Kennedy called on the nation to brave a "new frontier" of "unknown opportunities and perils" in both foreign and domestic policy. The phrase became a catchall for Kennedy's administration policies, including proposals for civil rights legislation, the Clean Air Act of 1963, the space program, a 20 percent increase in the defense budget, and proposed tax cuts for business.

Most of Kennedy's domestic proposals became bottled up in a conservative Congress, and liberals accused the President of failing to expend political capital to push them through. Meanwhile, Kennedy proved a formidable cold warrior. He tripled the nation's nuclear capability; escalated the war in Vietnam; and established the Agency for International Development, the Peace Corps, the Alliance for Progress, and the Food for Peace programs to give aid to poorer countries in danger of turning communist. Although his legislative record was weak, Kennedy's call to action and his rousing speeches inspired many young Americans to enter public service.

SEE ALSO

Kennedy, John Fitzgerald

FURTHER READING

Giglio, James. *The Presidency of John F. Kennedy.* Lawrence: University Press of Kansas, 1991.

Parmet, Herbert. *J.F.K., The Presidency of John F. Kennedy.* New York: Dial, 1983.

Schlesinger, Arthur M., Jr. *A Thousand Days: John F. Kennedy in the White House.* Boston: Houghton Mifflin, 1978.

Sorensen, Theodore C. *Kennedy.* New York: Harper & Row, 1965.

New Left

In the late 1950s, campus activists at some of the United States's largest state universities and elite eastern schools began to formulate critiques of U.S. society that would form the theoretical basis for an emerging New Left. Early New Leftists were generally white, middle- and upper-class college students, often with socialist leanings (many were so-called "red-diaper babies," or children of communists and socialists). Their vision for the United States stressed a blend of participatory democracy (in which citizens would control all decisions on which their well-being depended), human rights, and cultural change.

A member of Students for a Democratic Society displays antiwar buttons championing the New Left.

The postwar rhetoric of U.S. greatness and later calls to service by President John F. Kennedy bred a certain optimism that did not square with what members of the New Left saw as the evils present in racial injustice, the military-industrial complex, and the continuing buildup of U.S. nuclear weapons. Inspired by the success of the early civil rights movement, the New Left sought to make a difference.

The Port Huron Statement—the manifesto of Students for a Democratic Society (SDS), the most important New Left organization—provided the framework for their efforts. It proposed a strategy of "participatory democracy," calling for young activists to work for radical social and political change through grass-roots organizing. Ultimately, thousands of people who considered themselves part of the New Left participated in events such as the Freedom Summer of 1964, the free speech movement at the University of California at Berkeley, and SDS's economic research and action projects; perhaps most important, they became the driving force in the movement to stop the war in Vietnam.

SEE ALSO

Port Huron Statement; Students for a Democratic Society (SDS)

FURTHER READING

Breines, Wini. *Community and Organization in the New Left.* New Brunswick, N.J.: Rutgers University Press, 1983.

Gitlin, Todd. *The Sixties: Years of Hope, Days of Rage.* New York: Bantam, 1987.

Hayden, Tom. *Reunion: A Memoir.* New York: Random House, 1988.

Horowitz, David, and Peter Collier. *Destructive Generation.* New York: Summit, 1989.

Isserman, Maurice. *If I Had a Hammer: The Death of the Old Left and the Birth of the New Left.* New York: Basic Books, 1987.

Unger, Irwin. *The Movement: A History of the American New Left, 1959–1972.* New York: Harper & Row, 1974.

New York Times v. *Sullivan* (1964)

In its unanimous *New York Times* v. *Sullivan* decision, the Supreme Court strengthened the press's 1st Amendment protection against libel. An Alabama jury had ordered the *Times* and four black clergymen to pay $500,000 each in damages to an elected Montgomery city commissioner for allegedly false and defamatory statements that appeared in a full-page advertisement promoting the black civil rights movement; the ad was paid for by the clergymen.

The Supreme Court, however, ruled that public officials cannot recover damages for falsehoods relating to their official conduct unless they prove malicious intent and "reckless disregard" for the truth. The decision strengthened the civil rights movement and the power of the press.

SEE ALSO

Civil rights movement; Massive resistance

FURTHER READING

Fireside, Harvey. *New York Times v. Sullivan: Affirming Freedom of the Press.* Springfield, N.J.: Enslow, 1999.

Smolla, Rodney A. *Suing the Press.* New York: Oxford University Press, 1986.

Nixon, Richard Milhous

- *Born: Jan. 9, 1913, Yorba Linda, Calif.*
- *Accomplishments: U.S. representative (Republican–Calif.), 1947–50; U.S. senator (Republican–Calif.), 1951–53; Vice President, 1953–61; 37th President of the United States, 1969–74*
- *Died: Apr. 22, 1994, New York, N.Y.*

Raised in California, Richard Nixon grew up in difficult circumstances; while he was still an adolescent, two of his brothers died. The family was not wealthy, and the young Nixon worked hard in his family's store. He was a serious student and found success in academics, graduating from Whittier College in 1934 and from Duke University Law School in 1937. He practiced law in California, where he met and married Thelma ("Pat") Ryan.

After serving as a navy supply officer during World War II, Nixon was elected to the House of Representatives in 1946 as a Republican. His political career gained momentum during the post–World War II Red scare. Convinced that Alger Hiss, a respected former diplomat, was actually a communist spy, Nixon led the House Committee on Un-American Activities (HUAC) in one of its most highly publicized hearings. Being associated with the Hiss case and establishing himself as a hard-line anticommunist earned Nixon the undying hatred of liberals, who tagged him "tricky Dicky". But these efforts paid off for Nixon, who won a Senate seat from California in 1950 and then was chosen by Dwight Eisenhower as his Vice Presidential nominee. Eisenhower won the election in 1952 and Nixon faithfully served him for eight years. The highlight of Nixon's term as Vice President came in 1959 in the famous "kitchen debate" with Soviet premier Nikita Khrushchev. As they stood before a mock kitchen at a U.S. trade exhibition show in Moscow, the two men argued about the superiority of Western consumer goods.

Nixon won the Republican nomination for President in 1960 but narrowly

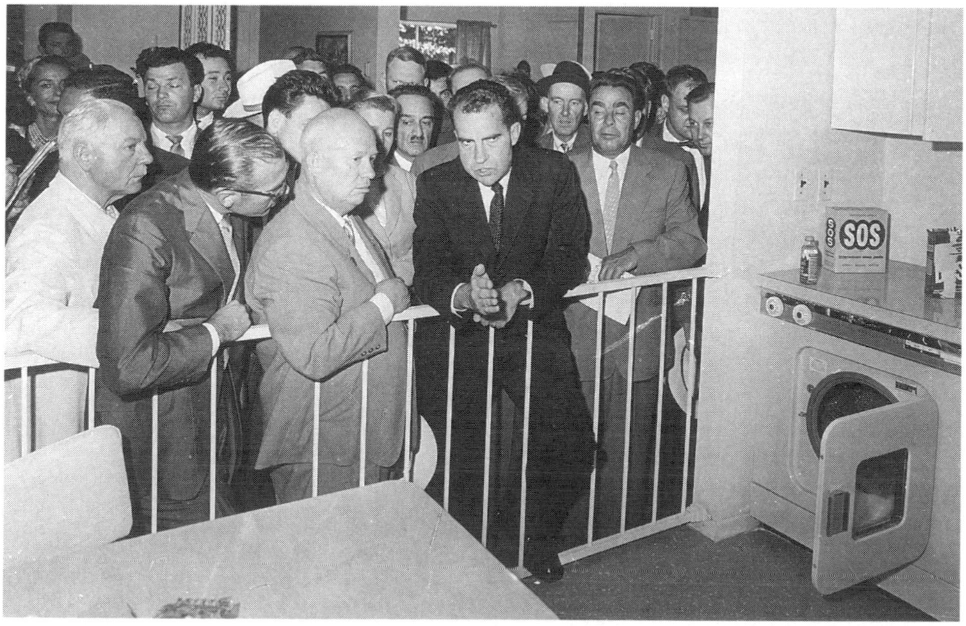

Vice President Richard Nixon and Soviet premier Nikita Khrushchev engage in the "kitchen debate" at an exhibition of U.S. technology in Moscow in 1959. Nixon argued that Western consumer goods were superior to Soviet ones.

lost the race to John F. Kennedy. Two years later he sought the governorship of California but again lost. Depressed and disillusioned, Nixon declared his retirement from politics—he told reporters "you won't have Dick Nixon to kick around anymore"—and moved to New York to practice corporate law. Soon, however, he began traveling the country to campaign for Republican candidates, rebuilding his political base.

In 1968, with the American people tired of Lyndon Johnson's failing Great Society liberalism, race riots, and the Vietnam War, Nixon reentered the political arena, offering himself as a "new Nixon," a candidate for the Presidency who would end the war in Vietnam and restore "law and order" at home. What started as a runaway race in the polls after the disastrous Chicago convention for the Democrats turned out to be almost as close as the Kennedy–Nixon race eight years earlier. Nixon won the Presidential election of 1968 against Hubert Humphrey and third-party candidate George Wallace but captured only 43.4 percent of the popular vote.

Above all, as President, Nixon was determined to make his place in history as an international statesman. His dreams of a new era of détente, or improved international relations, first required getting U.S. fighting forces out of the unpopular war in Vietnam. Nixon's solution came to be known as "Vietnamization"—a gradual replacement of U.S. troops with South Vietnamese troops trained and equipped to fight a ground war.

When that failed to achieve Nixon's "peace with honor," the President intensified the bombing of North Vietnam and expanded the war to neighboring Cambodia and Laos. After four more years of war, hostilities between the United States and North Vietnam ended with the signing of the Paris accords on January 23, 1973, which required the withdrawal of all remaining U.S. troops, provided for the return of prisoners of war, and allowed North Vietnamese troops to remain in South Vietnam—the communists' primary objective.

President Richard Nixon visits U.S. soldiers in Vietnam in 1969. In an attempt to end the unpopular war there, Nixon intensified the bombing campaign and expanded the fighting into neighboring countries.

Meanwhile, in February 1972 Nixon traveled to the People's Republic of China to initiate the normalization of relations with that communist power, and in an equally significant step he visited Moscow in May 1972 to conclude agreements with the Soviets on trade and technological cooperation and to sign the first Strategic Arms Limitation Treaty (SALT I). Historic milestones, the two trips began a new era of détente and enhanced Nixon's stature as a proponent of world peace and stability.

Domestically, Nixon's program mixed a moderate extension of Great Society programs with a "southern strategy" designed to court the angry whites who had voted for Wallace. Nixon cooperated with the Democratic-controlled Congress to enact environmental safeguards, expand the Job Corps, increase Social Security benefits, provide subsidized housing for low- and middle-income families, and grant the vote to 18-year-olds. He also proposed a Family Assistance Plan that would guarantee an annual minimum income to all Americans, but he failed to win Senate approval for the program.

Simultaneously, Nixon and Vice President Spiro Agnew took a tough stand on crime and drug use, combated antiwar activists and militant blacks, sought to hamper the desegregation of schools in the South and to stop court-ordered school busing, and appointed to the Supreme Court nominees who would not "meddle" in social issues or be "soft on criminals."

Constant paranoia led Nixon to try to sabotage his political opposition. He compiled an "enemies list" of Americans to be harassed by the government, approved a scheme known as the Huston Plan that employed the CIA and FBI in an array of illegal operations against his opponents, and created the White House unit nicknamed the "plumbers" to stop leaks to the press and discredit his political opposition.

This pattern of secrecy, duplicity, and illegality would lead to the break-in at the headquarters of the Democratic National Committee in the Watergate apartment and office complex on June 17, 1972. The arrest of the White House operatives who did the job led, in turn, to a host of revelations of "dirty tricks" and illegal acts committed by the President and his underlings, particularly their active involvement in the cover-up of the break-in. This scandal would lead eventually to Nixon's resignation on August 9, 1974.

Despite the disgrace associated with his resignation, Nixon's reputation as a brilliant statesman and manipulator of foreign policy persisted, and even grew, after he left office. Unrepentant about Watergate—describing the scandal in 1991 as "one part wrongdoing, one part blundering, and one part political vendetta" by his enemies—Nixon wrote a series of books combining memoirs and foreign policy advice and became a highly respected consultant and TV pundit.

SEE ALSO

Agnew, Spiro; China–U.S. relations; Middle East–U.S. relations; Nuclear arms control; Vietnam War; Watergate

FURTHER READING

Ambrose, Stephen E. *Nixon: The Triumph of a Politician, 1962–1972.* New York: Simon & Schuster, 1989.

Cahill, Michael. *A Nixon Man.* New York: St. Martin's, 1998.

Hoff, Joan. *Nixon Reconsidered.* New York: Basic Books, 1994.

Nixon, Richard M. *RN: The Memoirs of Richard Nixon.* New York: Grosset & Dunlap, 1978.

Parmet, Herbert S. *Richard Nixon and His America.* Boston: Little, Brown, 1990.

North Atlantic Treaty Organization (NATO)

Established in 1949 as a response to the Soviet threat to Western Europe during the cold war, the North Atlantic Treaty Organization (NATO) was the first peacetime military alliance in the history of the United States. Ten European nations, Canada, and the United States agreed in April 1949 that an attack on any one of the member nations would be considered an attack

President Harry Truman displays the document ratifying NATO, after signing it on July 25, 1949.

on all and would be responded to appropriately. Greece and Turkey joined NATO in 1952, West Germany in 1955.

In 1955 this alliance prompted the Soviets to establish the Warsaw Pact, which was essentially an East European version of NATO. The dissolution of the Soviet Union and the end of the cold war in 1989, the reunification of the two Germanys in 1990, and the end of the Warsaw Pact in 1991 have led to NATO's expansion to include former communist regimes in eastern Europe and to its peacekeeping role in Bosnia and Kosovo, both part of what once was Yugoslavia. At the Madrid Summit in July 1997, the Czech Republic, Hungary, and Poland began negotiations to become members of the Alliance; they formally entered NATO in March 1999.

SEE ALSO

Bosnia, United States and; Cold war; Eisenhower, Dwight David

FURTHER READING

Henderson, Nicholas. *The Birth of NATO.* Boulder, Colo.: Westview, 1983.

Nuclear arms control

Since the start of the arms race, the two superpowers—the United States and the Soviet Union—have attempted various negotiations and treaties to limit and control their nuclear arsenals. President John F. Kennedy and Premier Nikita Khrushchev signed the first arms-control pact, agreeing to ban nuclear tests in the air and underwater, in the Limited Nuclear Test Ban Treaty of 1963. The Nuclear Nonproliferation Treaty (1968) was designed to prevent nations not yet having nuclear weapons from getting them.

In the Strategic Arms Limitations Treaty (SALT) agreements that Richard Nixon negotiated with Leonid Brezhnev, the Soviet Union and the United States agreed to limit the number of their long-range missiles (called intercontinental ballistic missiles, or ICBMs) and antiballistic missile systems (called ABMs). SALT II, negotiated by President Gerald Ford and Brezhnev in 1974, reduced the number of missiles further, but other issues, particularly U.S. dissatisfaction with the treatment of Jews in the Soviet Union, froze the talks, and SALT II was not signed until Jimmy Carter's administration, in 1979.

In 1987 Premier Mikhail Gorbachev traveled to Washington and joined President Ronald Reagan in signing the Intermediate Nuclear Forces (INF) Treaty, which removed 2,500 U.S. and Soviet missiles from Europe and renewed the arms-control process. In 1991 President George Bush went to Moscow to sign the START treaty cutting the two nations' nuclear arsenals by one-quarter. Later that year, the fragmentation of the Soviet Union further advanced the arms-control process, and the new Russian president, Boris Yeltsin, pledged to destroy all of Russia's land-based MIRV missiles and to deactivate all missiles targeted on the United States. However, in the mid1990s, as right-wing nationalists and former communist officials regained influence in Russia, Americans feared the stalling of further efforts to control and limit nuclear arms.

SEE ALSO

Carter, James Earl, Jr. ("Jimmy"); Cold war; Ford, Gerald Rudolph; Kennedy, John Fitzgerald; Nixon, Richard Milhous; Reagan, Ronald Wilson

FURTHER READING

Broad, William J. *Teller's War: The Top-Secret Story Behind the Star Wars Deception.* New York: Simon & Schuster, 1992.

Bundy, McGeorge. *Danger and Survival: Choices About the Bomb in the First Fifty Years.* New York: Random House, 1988.

Roman, Peter J. *Eisenhower and the Missile Gap.* Ithaca, N.Y.: Cornell University Press, 1996.

Nuclear freeze movement

SEE Antinuclear movement

O'Connor, Sandra Day

- *Born: Mar. 26, 1930, El Paso, Tex.*
- *Accomplishments: Arizona state senator (Republican), 1969–74; Arizona Court of Appeals judge (1974–81); U.S. Supreme Court justice, 1981–*

After gaining an undergraduate and a law degree from Stanford University, Sandra Day O'Connor practiced law in Arizona, then served in the Arizona state senate and on the Arizona court of appeals. In 1981, when Supreme Court justice Potter Stewart announced his retirement, President Ronald Reagan nominated her to be the first female justice of the United States Supreme Court.

Since her confirmation, O'Connor has been a force for moderation and often the pivotal center vote on a Court split between liberals and conservatives. She has, for example, generally upheld restrictions on abortion but was the swing vote in refusing to overturn *Roe v. Wade*. She has also voted in favor of affirmative action programs designed to combat specific governmental discrimination while voting against less specific programs. In May 1999 she voted with the majority in favor of states' rights, a move enthusiastically favored by conservatives; in the same week she voted, again with the majority, to uphold the rights of students to be protected by their schools from sexual harassment by other students, a position endorsed by liberals.

SEE ALSO

Supreme Court

President Ronald Reagan, Chief Justice Warren Burger, and Sandra Day O'Connor all beam shortly after she was sworn in as a Supreme Court Justice.

FURTHER READING

Deegan, Paul. *Sandra Day O'Connor.* Supreme Court Justices Series. Minneapolis, Minn.: ABDO, 1992.

Huber, Peter William. *Sandra Day O'Connor.* American Women of Achievement Series. Broomall, Pa.: Chelsea House, 1992.

Office of Economic Opportunity (OEO)

The Office of Economic Opportunity (OEO) was established in 1964 to run President Lyndon B. Johnson's War on Poverty program. Created by the Economic Opportunity Act, a $1 billion antipoverty program, the OEO was charged with funding and coordinating the Jobs Corps to train young people in marketable skills; Project Head Start to provide preschooling for children of needy families; VISTA (Volunteers in Service to America) to place voluntary social workers in economically depressed areas; and the Community Action Program to increase the political participation of the poor. The OEO never received the funding initially promised it, and all of its programs were terminated or transferred to other departments during Richard Nixon's administration.

President Lyndon Johnson visits a printing class at a vocational school in Maryland. Helping young people learn marketable skills was one of Johnson's goals in establishing the Office of Economic Opportunity.

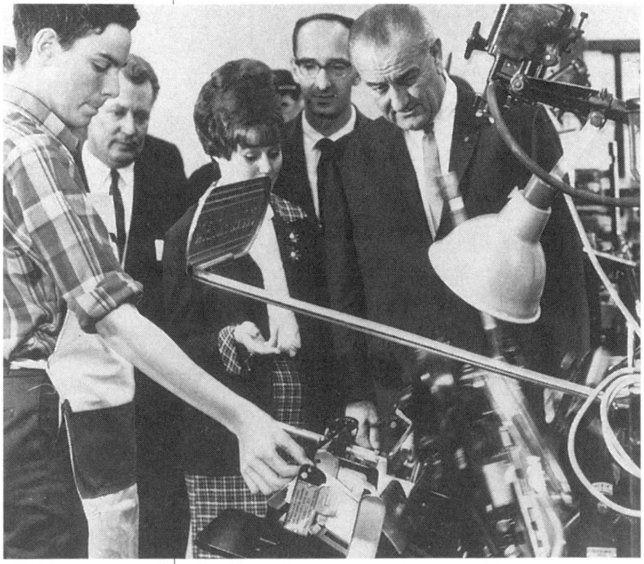

SEE ALSO

War on Poverty

FURTHER READING

Harrington, Michael. *The Other America: Poverty in the United States.* New York: Macmillan, 1962.

Zarefsky, David. *President Johnson's War on Poverty: Rhetoric and History.* Tuscaloosa: University of Alabama Press, 1986.

Oil embargo (1973)

Sparked by the Arab–Israeli War of October 1973, OPEC (the Organization of Petroleum Exporting Countries) ordered an oil embargo against the United States and its allies, which extended to Japan and Western Europe, late that year. Oil prices tripled within a few months and created panic around the world. In the United States, drivers had to wait in long lines at gas stations, their tempers boiling as they sat; the national speed limit was lowered and air conditioner thermostats raised in an attempt to save oil. The subsequent hike in energy costs as people chased after the oil that was available caused the rate of inflation to skyrocket.

A second oil crisis occurred in 1979 with the start of war between Iran and Iraq. The new oil embargo forced nations to look for other resources and by the late 1970s the world demand for oil fell for the first time since the Great Depression of the 1930s. This trend continued until by 1985 only 39 percent of the world's energy needs were dependent on oil, compared to 46 percent in 1979.

Gas ration stamps were prepared in 1974, during the oil embargo. Although the stamps were never used, the long lines and frayed tempers at the gas stations were an unavoidable part of drivers' lives that season.

SEE ALSO

Energy crisis

FURTHER READING

Kalt, Joseph P. *The Economics and Politics of Oil Price Regulation: Federal Policy in the Post-Embargo Era.* Cambridge, Mass.: M.I.T. Press, 1983.

Matusow, Allen J. *Nixon's Economy: Booms, Busts, Dollars, and Votes.* Lawrence: University Press of Kansas, 1998.

Parmet, Herbert S. *Richard Nixon and His America.* Boston: Little, Brown, 1990.

Oswald, Lee Harvey

- *Born: Oct. 18, 1939, New Orleans, La.*
- *Died: Nov. 24, 1963, Dallas, Tex.*

The assassination of President John F. Kennedy has fascinated people since 1963; the role Lee Harvey Oswald played in the assassination has been the subject of much fiery debate. Oswald, who was a drifter, a loner, a Marine Corps veteran, and a one-time defector who had recently returned from the Soviet Union, was arrested by Dallas police shortly after Kennedy's assassination. Oswald was shot dead by Dallas nightclub owner Jack Ruby two days later as Oswald was being transferred to another jail. Later the commission headed by Chief Justice Earl Warren to investigate the assassination concluded that Oswald was the lone gunman; he alone shot Kennedy on November 22, 1963. This conclusion was challenged by many critics who suspected Oswald of having ties to the Left and/or the Right, of being pro- or anti-Castro, of being connected to the CIA or the Mafia, and of being incapable of scarrying out the assassination alone. These critics, often called "conspiracy buffs" or "conspiracy theorists," believe that various groups of people worked together to frame or manipulate Oswald and kill Kennedy. Government investigations, though, have continued to maintain that Oswald alone killed John F. Kennedy.

SEE ALSO

Kennedy, John Fitzgerald; Warren Commission

FURTHER READING

Beck, Melinda. "The Mind of the Assassin." *Newsweek,* November 22, 1993, 71–72.

Mailer, Norman. *Oswald's Tale: An American Mystery.* New York: Ballantine, 1996.

Posner, Gerald. *Case Closed: Lee Harvey Oswald and the Assassination of JFK.* New York: Random House, 1993.

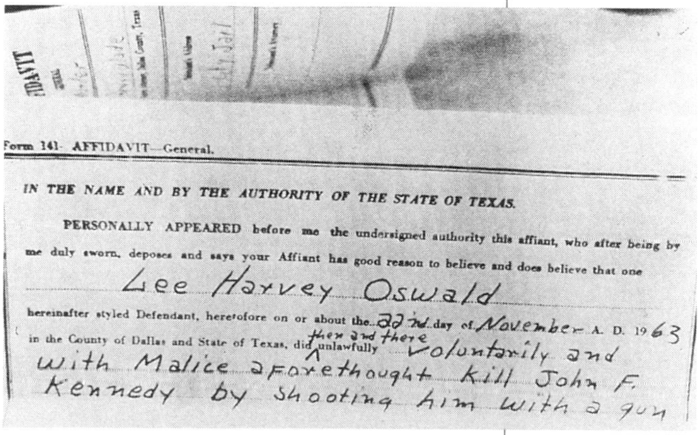

Form 141 AFFIDAVIT—General.

IN THE NAME AND BY THE AUTHORITY OF THE STATE OF TEXAS.

PERSONALLY APPEARED before me the undersigned authority this affiant, who after being by me duly sworn, deposes and says your Affiant has good reason to believe and does believe that one Lee Harvey Oswald hereinafter styled Defendant, heretofore on or about the 22nd day of November A. D. 1963 in the County of Dallas and State of Texas, did then and there unlawfully voluntarily and with Malice aforethought kill John F. Kennedy by shooting him with a gun

This affidavit charges Lee Harvey Oswald with the murder of President John Kennedy. The charge was brought against Oswald the day after the shooting.

Other America, The

Michael Harrington's book *The Other America,* published in 1962, helped to generate public support for Lyndon B. Johnson's Great Society antipoverty programs in the mid-1960s by showing that nearly a quarter of the nation's population lived in poverty. At the peak of postwar affluence, Harrington wrote, a hidden minority lacked adequate nutrition, housing, education, medical care, and employment opportunities. Particularly vulnerable were the elderly, blacks in the inner cities, migrant farm workers, Native Americans on reservations, miners in Appalachia, and single-parent families.

FURTHER READING

Harrington, Michael. *The Other America: Poverty in the United States.* New York: Macmillan, 1962.

Paris peace talks

Representatives of the United States, South Vietnam, and North Vietnam met in Paris in May 1968 to begin peace talks. The talks stalled as the war continued, but finally extensive U.S. bombing raids over Cambodia and North Vietnam broke the stalemate in 1972. Then, after the South Vietnamese rejected a cease-fire agreement in October, discussions once again broke down, and President Richard M. Nixon responded with the so-called Christmas bombings of Hanoi and Haiphong.

The talks between Henry Kissinger, Nixon's special assistant for national security affairs, and Le Duc Tho, the chief North Vietnamese negotiator, began again on January 8, 1973. On January 27, four days after the death of former President Lyndon B. Johnson, under whose administration the war had escalated, the Paris peace accords were signed by all three parties.

The settlement called for an immediate cease-fire, U.S. withdrawal within 60 days, and the return of U.S. prisoners of war within 60 days; it allowed 150,000 North Vietnamese Army troops to stay in South Vietnam and established two commissions to enforce the cease-fire.

SEE ALSO

Kissinger, Henry Alfred; Vietnam War

FURTHER READING

Porter, Gareth. *A Peace Denied: The United States, Vietnam, and the Paris Agreement.* Bloomington: Indiana University Press, 1975.

Peace Corps

Founded in 1961 during John Kennedy's administration, the Peace Corps sends volunteers abroad to aid developing countries in such fields as agriculture, education, and health care. Initially very popular among idealistic college graduates, the Peace Corps represented the best of the Kennedy legacy and the inspirational spirit of the early 1960s. It fell out of favor with youth during the Vietnam War and suffered from meager funding in the 1970s and 1980s.

The opening of Eastern Europe in the 1990s rejuvenated the corps, attracting a new generation of young Americans eager to work at promoting economic development and a higher

A Peace Corps teacher in the Philippines plays with her students on the beach.

standard of living throughout the world.

SEE ALSO

Kennedy, John Fitzgerald; New Frontier

FURTHER READING

Hoffman, Elizabeth Cobbs. *All You Need Is Love: The Peace Corps and the Spirit of the 1960s.* Cambridge, Mass.: Harvard University Press, 1998.

Searles, P. David. *The Peace Corps Experience: Challenge and Change, 1969–1976.* Lexington: University Press of Kentucky, 1997.

Thomsen, Moritz. *Living Poor: A Peace Corps Chronicle.* Seattle: University of Washington Press, 1997.

Peace movement

SEE Antiwar movement

Pentagon Papers

On June 13, 1971, the *New York Times* began publication of the so-called Pentagon Papers, a secret record of U.S. involvement in Vietnam prepared by the Department of Defense (DOD) during Lyndon Johnson's administration. The papers had been leaked by DOD analyst Daniel Ellsberg. Their publication proved to the public that the government had been engaged in a lengthy campaign of systematic deceit.

Not only did the Pentagon Papers reveal that the government had lied about its intentions in Vietnam but they also showed that much of U.S. policy-making had been devised out of a profound concern for maintaining the United States's image rather than aiding South Vietnam. Even though Richard Nixon's administration escaped criticism in the Pentagon Papers—the analysis ended with 1967—Nixon obtained a court injunction to prevent further publication of the documents. The Supreme Court ruled 6-to-3 that the injunction constituted censorship and found it to be unconstitutional under the 1st Amendment.

FURTHER READING

Graham, Katharine. *Personal History.* New York: Knopf, 1997.

Herring, George C., ed. *The Pentagon Papers.* New York: McGraw-Hill, 1993.

New York Times. *The Pentagon Papers.* New York: Quadrangle Books, 1971.

Rudenstine, David. *The Day the Presses Stopped: A History of the Pentagon Papers Case.* Berkeley: University of California Press, 1998.

The press chief checks the first edition of the Washington Post *announcing the Supreme Court's decision about the Pentagon Papers. The Court ruled that prohibiting their publication amounted to censorship.*

People's Park battle

In the spring of 1969, people from all segments of the community of Berkeley, California, came together to build a park—People's Park—on a three-acre lot owned by the University of California. The university had cleared the lot 10 months earlier in order to build an intramural soccer field but had no immediate plans to start construction. For those who participated in the building, the park stood as a landmark to community cooperation.

For the university's administration, however, the park amounted to a land seizure. In a move indicative of the times, on May 15, 1969, the police bulldozed the park and put up a fence. Later in the day, several thousand protestors converged on the park to tear down the fence but were met by a squad of Alameda County sheriff's deputies who fired birdshot and buckshot into the crowd and at others in the area. Some 150 demonstrators were shot; one died four days later. Governor Ronald Reagan sent in 3,000 National Guard troops who, despite numerous skirmishes, maintained martial law for 17 days.

People's Park became a symbol of radical struggle, of a communal alternative to private property. It also heralded the emergence of ecological concerns among students and activists, pitting organic gardeners against bulldozers and tear gas.

SEE ALSO

Free speech movement

FURTHER READING

Gitlin, Todd. *The Sixties: Years of Hope, Days of Rage.* New York: Bantam, 1987.

McGill, William J. *The Year of the Monkey: Revolt on Campus, 1968–69.* New York: McGraw-Hill, 1982.

Persian Gulf War

On August 2, 1990, Iraq invaded and quickly overwhelmed its small, oil-rich neighbor Kuwait. Iraq's ruler, Saddam Hussein, dismissed Kuwait's independent-nation status as a creation of Western imperialists and annexed Kuwait to gain its oil reserves and to intimidate other petroleum-producing nations into setting very high prices on oil.

President George Bush immediately condemned the invasion but was careful not to repeat the mistakes the United States had made in Vietnam. Only after gaining the support of the United Nations, Congress, and the American people did Bush clearly demand Hussein's withdrawal from Kuwait and deploy more than 400,000 U.S. troops to Saudi Arabia to achieve that goal.

Ignoring U.S. threats and U.N. resolutions and sanctions, Hussein refused to withdraw from Kuwait. A massive air attack by U.S. B-52 and F-16 bombers opened the war on January 16, 1991. The air campaign lasted six weeks and culminated in a ground attack by U.S. and allied troops. Commanded by General H. Norman Schwarzkopf, the allied armies liberated Kuwait in less than five days of fighting. United States casualties were light, including 148 dead, compared to more than 100,000 Iraqi deaths. After the debacle in Vietnam, millions of Americans were thrilled that the United States had swiftly won a war with few casualties—although Hussein remained in power and many of the U.S. troops later claimed that they suffered

Television viewers at home were shown a great deal of detail about the Persian Gulf War. CNN and its anchors were familiar presences in many people's lives.

from injuries caused by chemicals used in the war.

SEE ALSO

Bush, George Herbert Walker; Middle East–U.S.relations

FURTHER READING

Graubard, Stephen R. *Mr. Bush's War.* New York: Hill & Wang, 1992.

Sifry, Mica, and Christopher Cerf, eds. *The Gulf War Reader.* New York: Random House, 1991.

Phoenix program

From 1968 to 1972, the CIA directed the Phoenix program, a secret military and intelligence operation aimed at identifying and eliminating Vietcong leaders during the Vietnam War. (The Intelligence Coordination and Exploitation [ICEX], as it was known in its preliminary stages in 1967, was officially renamed "Phoenix" in early 1968. Though the CIA gave a variety of explanations for the name, none were clearly documented.)

Through this program, Vietcong leaders were imprisoned, often tortured, and in some cases killed. Despite CIA denials, for many the Phoenix program amounted to little more than a vicious assassination project operating outside normal legal and ethical standards.

SEE ALSO

Vietnam War

Port Huron Statement

Written primarily by Tom Hayden and adopted by the newly formed Students for a Democratic Society (SDS) at Port Huron, Michigan, in 1962, the Port Huron Statement became the manifesto for the New Left. Influenced by the work of sociologist C. Wright Mills, Hayden criticized the complacency and indifference he and other New Left leaders saw in U.S. society.

The Port Huron Statement portrayed the nation as militaristic, bureaucratic, and above all undemocratic. Yet Hayden implied that change could occur within the system through the use of technological, academic, corporate, and government resources to combat poverty and racism. In addition, the Port Huron Statement called for the building of a "participatory democracy" in which the "decision making of basic social consequences [is] carried on by public groups," and it argued that politics should bring people together as a community.

SEE ALSO

Hayden, Thomas ("Tom"); New Left; Students for a Democratic Society (SDS)

FURTHER READING

Hayden, Tom. *Reunion: A Memoir.* New York: Random House, 1988.

Sale, Kirkpatrick. *SDS.* New York: Random House, 1973.

Potsdam Conference

From July 17 to August 2, 1945, with World War II over in Europe and weeks away from an end in the Pacific, the big three leaders of the Allied forces—British prime minister Winston Churchill (who was replaced by his successor, Clement Attlee, on July 28), Soviet premier Joseph Stalin, and U.S. President Harry Truman (who had just assumed the Presidency after Franklin Roosevelt's death)—met in Potsdam, Germany. They issued a declaration demanding "unconditional surrender" from Japan and established plans for the military administration of Germany, the trial of war criminals, and the payment of reparations by Germany. The thorniest matters, regarding the status of Poland and the dominance of Soviet troops in Eastern Europe, were left to a council of foreign ministers to resolve later.

President Harry Truman (just left of center, with his back to the camera) meets with Soviet premier Joseph Stalin (in the center at right) and British prime minister Winston Churchill (at left, with cigar) at Potsdam, Germany, in 1945 to figure out their postwar plans for Germany and to call for the surrender of Japan.

FURTHER READING

Gormly, James L. *From Potsdam to the Cold War: Big Three Diplomacy 1945–1947*. Wilmington, Del.: Scholarly Resources, 1990.

Mee, Charles L. *Meeting at Potsdam*. New York: Harper's Magazine Foundation, 1995.

Powell, Adam Clayton, Jr.

- *Born: Nov. 29, 1908, New Haven, Conn.*
- *Accomplishments: U.S. representative (Democrat–N.Y.), 1945–67, 1969–71*
- *Died: Apr. 4, 1972, Miami, Fla.*

The Reverend Adam Clayton Powell, Jr., crusaded for civil rights in Congress from his election in 1944 to his controversial departure at the end of the 1960s. The charismatic pastor of the Abyssinian Baptist Church in Harlem rose to prominence during World War II as a member of the New York City Council, where he demanded that blacks receive equal treatment in the armed forces.

Adam Clayton Powell was a glamorous man who aroused strong emotions in his supporters and his opponents.

As Harlem's representative to Congress beginning in 1945, Powell fought to integrate dining facilities on Capitol Hill, sought to outlaw the poll tax that discouraged black voting in many southern states, advocated legislation to make lynching a federal offense, and continued his crusade to end discrimination in the armed forces.

In March 1967, the House of Representatives voted to unseat Powell because of several disputes, including his refusal to pay a settlement in a slander case. Powell nevertheless won a special election held later that year and then the regular election in 1968. In 1970 Powell was denied renomination by the Democratic party and lost his bid as an independent. He died shortly after leaving office in 1971.

FURTHER READING

Hamilton, Charles V. *Adam Clayton Powell, Jr.: The Political Biography of an American Dilemma.* New York: Atheneum, 1991.

Powell, Adam Clayton, Jr. *Adam by Adam.* New York: Dial, 1971.

Powell, Colin Luther

- *Born: Apr. 5, 1937, New York, N.Y.*
- *Accomplishments: Vietnam War veteran; national security advisor, 1987–89; chairman of the Joint Chiefs of Staff, 1989–93*

Born to a Jamaican-American family in New York City, Colin Powell attended the City University of New York and rose through the Reserve Officer Training Corps (ROTC) and service in Vietnam to the top ranks of the U.S. Army in the 1970s. President Ronald Reagan tapped him to be his advisor on national security, and in 1989 Powell became the first African American to head the Joint Chiefs of Staff.

As commander of U.S. forces in the Persian Gulf War of 1991, Powell applied the lessons he learned from the Vietnam War, particularly that the commitment of U.S. forces had to be overwhelming and accompanied by clear political and legal direction. Following his retirement in 1992, Powell led a U.S. delegation to Haiti in 1994 to convince that country's military ruler, General Raoul Cedras, to return power to democratically elected Jean-Bertrand Aristide or face U.S. military action. Cedras quit. In 1996 Powell declined to run for the Republican Presidential nomination, despite many pleas that he do so.

Colin Powell sits next to President George Bush at a meeting of the Joint Chiefs of Staff. Bush strongly encouraged Powell to ally himself with the Republican Party once he had retired.

SEE ALSO

Persian Gulf War

FURTHER READING

Powell, Colin L. *My American Journey: An Autobiography.* New York: Random House, 1995.

Presley, Elvis Aaron

- *Born: Jan. 8, 1935, Tupelo, Miss.*
- *Accomplishments: Singer; early pioneer of rock-and-roll music*
- *Died: Aug. 16, 1977, Memphis, Tenn.*

Emerging from poverty and obscurity in the mid-1950s, Elvis Presley became rock music's first superstar and the undisputed king of rock and roll. In 1954, just one year after his high school graduation, Presley made his first professional recording. Two years later he released a million-selling record, "Heartbreak Hotel," and from 1956 to 1958 he produced 14 more gold records while developing a fanatically devoted teenage audience.

With his long, greased-back hair, surly expression, and suggestively gyrating hips, Presley became a symbol

Elvis Presley and Ann Margret in Viva Las Vegas *in 1964. The movie had an unconvincing plot about a boy, his girl, and his car, but that did not deter Elvis's fans.*

of rebellious youth and an object of parental anxiety. When he appeared on "The Ed Sullivan Show," he was filmed only from the waist up.

Presley's hits included "Hound Dog," "Jailhouse Rock," and "Don't Be Cruel." He appeared in several films in the 1960s, but his career declined as teenagers shifted their attention to rock groups like the Beatles. Presley died in 1977 after a long period of drug addiction. He retained a strong following until and beyond his death.

SEE ALSO

Rock and roll

FURTHER READING

Goldman, Albert. *Elvis.* New York: McGraw-Hill, 1981.

Guralnick, Peter: *Last Train to Memphis: The Rise of Elvis Presley.* Boston: Little, Brown, 1994.

Guralnick, Peter. *Careless Love: The Unmaking of Elvis Presley.* Boston: Little, Brown, 1999.

Quayle, J. Danforth III (Dan)

- *Born: Feb. 4, 1947, Indianapolis, Ind.*
- *Accomplishments: U.S. representative (Republican–Ind.), 1977–81; U.S. senator, 1981–89; Vice President, 1989–93*

In 1988 President George Bush surprised the nation when he chose a little-known young senator from Indiana, J. Danforth Quayle III, as his Presidential running mate. Quayle was the son of a wealthy Indiana newspaper publisher and had served two terms in the House of Representatives and twice been elected to the Senate. He received overwhelmingly negative media coverage both during the campaign (due in part to revelations that he had pulled strings to evade service in Vietnam at a time when his family's newspapers supported the war) and while in office. As Vice President, the conservative Quayle played an important role as chair of the White House Council on Competitiveness, which promoted deregulation of business.

During the 1992 Presidential campaign, Quayle was highly visible in attacking what he called the "cultural elite": academics, journalists, and producers in the film and television industry whom he accused of undermining traditional family values.

After leaving Washington, Quayle moved to Arizona. In the 1990s he chaired a national political action committee (Campaign America), raised funds for Republican candidates, wrote books, and served as a guest professor of international studies.

FURTHER READING

Broder, David S., and Bob Woodward. *The Man Who Would Be President: Dan Quayle.* New York: Simon & Schuster, 1992.

Fenno, Richard. *The Making of a Senator: Dan Quayle.* Washington, D.C.: Congressional Quarterly, 1989.

Race riots

Looters take advantage of the destruction left by a riot in 1964, casually walking across the glass-littered streets with stolen goods.

Race riots have taken place in U.S. cities from time to time since the Civil War, but during the "long, hot summers" of the 1960s they erupted with greater frequency and ferocity than they had before. Unlike most earlier riots, in which blacks had been the victims of white mobs, African Americans started and participated in the riots of the 1960s. Between 1964 and 1968, 200 people were killed, 7,000 injured, and 40,000 arrested; $200 million worth of property was destroyed in ghettos of hundreds of U.S. cities.

The riots were frequently triggered by incidents of police brutality, as was the riot in Detroit in 1967, but the underlying causes, according to the Kerner Commission, a panel chartered to study the riots, were the frustrations of chronic poverty, racism, and unemployment. The rioting peaked in 1968 after the assassination of civil rights leader Martin Luther King, Jr., when disorders took place in 100 cities. Although the ghettos quieted down after the end of the decade, the underlying problems remained, and unrest erupted once again in 1992 when blacks in south-central Los Angeles initiated the most devastating race riot in U.S. history in response to the acquittal of white police officers who had been filmed beating a black suspect, Rodney King.

SEE ALSO

Detroit race riot (1967); Kerner Commission (National Advisory Commission on Civil Disorders); King, Rodney

FURTHER READING

Button, James. *Black Violence: Political Impact of the 1960s Riots.* Princeton, N.J.: Princeton University Press, 1978.

Feagin, Joe, and Harlan Hahn. *Ghetto Revolts.* New York: Macmillan, 1973.

Horne, Gerald. *Fire This Time: The Watts Uprising and the 1960s.* Charlottesville: University Press of Virginia, 1996.

Rayburn, Sam

- *Born: Jan. 6, 1882, Kingston, Tenn.*
- *Accomplishments: U.S. representative (Democrat–Tex.), 1913–61; Speaker of the House of Representatives, 1949–53*
- *Died: Nov. 16, 1961, Bonham, Tex.*

Sam Rayburn set a record for time served in the House of Representatives—he held a seat there for 48 years.

"Mr. Sam" served as Speaker of the House for 17 of those years, also a record; his motto was "to get along, go along," and he based that advice on his own personal experience. Rayburn was enormously skillful at using the committee system through which the House does most of its work; he usually was able to keep open combat on controversial issues from erupting in the House, and most of the time he was able to deliver the votes that they wanted to the Democratic Presidents then in office. One of his protégés, a younger congressman from his home state, Texas, was Lyndon Johnson; Rayburn helped Johnson learn how to handle himself in the House. In 1965 the new House Office Building was named in Rayburn's honor.

SEE ALSO

Johnson, Lyndon Baines

FURTHER READING

Hardeman, D. B., and Donald C. Bacon. *Rayburn: A Biography.* Austin: Texas Monthly Press, 1987.

Ritchie, Donald A. *The Young Oxford Companion to the Congress of the United States.* New York: Oxford University Press, 1993.

Reagan, Ronald Wilson

- *Born: Feb. 6, 1911, Tampico, Ill.*
- *Government service: Governor of California (Republican), 1967–74; 40th President of the United States, 1981–89*

The 1980 Presidential election ushered in a new era in U.S. political history, often referred to as the "Reagan Revolution." That year, Ronald Reagan, a former radio sports announcer, Hollywood movie actor, and two-term governor of California, defeated Jimmy Carter in an electoral college landslide. Although his long-standing conservatism was well known, Reagan's campaign optimism appealed to a wide range of voters when he said, "Let's make America great again." In stump speeches, Reagan's constant query, "Are you better off today than you were four years ago?" was almost always met with a chorus of "No!" When he took office in January 1981, at nearly 70 years of age, he was the oldest man elected President and the first to have been divorced.

Once a liberal, Reagan had been a staunch Democrat and an avid fan of Franklin Delano Roosevelt. He served as president of the Screen Actors' Guild in 1947 and supported Harry Truman in 1948. Although he did not register to vote as a Republican until 1962, Reagan became more conservative in the 1950s. After some well-received campaign speeches on behalf of Republican Presidential candidate Barry Goldwater in 1964, Reagan's popularity helped him garner the support of wealthy California conservatives who helped him defeat then-governor Edmund G. ("Pat") Brown in 1966.

Reagan served in Sacramento for eight years, six with a Democratic legislature. Although verbally assaulting big government, he enlarged the state budget. While increasing funding to California's public colleges and universities by more than 100 percent, he was quick to use force in suppressing student demonstrations against the Vietnam War, once exclaiming, "If it takes a bloodbath, let's get it over with. No more appeasement." Reagan first ran for President in 1968 and again in 1976, each time failing to win the Republican nomination. In 1980 he easily defeated former CIA director George Bush for the nomination and then chose Bush as his running mate.

Much of Reagan's appeal came from his economic proposals, later known as Reaganomics. Reagan promised to cut spending, reduce government regulation of private industry, and lower taxes. Tax cuts were at the heart of his "supply side" economic plan; money saved from lower taxes would be spent by individuals and corporations, thereby fueling growth throughout the economy. The plan proved to be very attractive to most Americans.

Reagan's Presidency began on a positive note when the government of Iran released the Americans whom it had held hostage for 444 days. Two months later, Reagan was shot by John W. Hinckley, Jr., outside a Washington hotel. Although he had lost a substantial amount of blood, Reagan was able to quip to his doctors, "I hope you're all Republicans!" He soon recovered and won his first major legislative victory when Congress voted to cut income taxes by 25 percent.

To balance the loss of revenue, Reagan persuaded Congress to cut more than $40 billion in domestic spending in 1981, much of it in social programs. In addition, Reagan attempted to cut the size and expense of government itself while freeing certain industries from regulations deemed burdensome by the administration.

Because the Federal Reserve increased interest rates to lower inflation, the U.S. economy went into a recession by the end of 1981. The economy began to rebound in 1983, however, helping Reagan win an easy second-term election victory over former Vice President Walter Mondale in 1984. The expansion of the economy in Reagan's second term created millions of new jobs and fueled huge corporate profits. This feel-good economy of the mid-1980s was welcomed as a positive change by many Americans.

Ronald Reagan loved going to his ranch for a temporary respite from the pressures of the Presidency. Here he prepares for one of his favorite activities, riding.

At the same time, however, budget deficits grew to hitherto unknown proportions as the total national debt increased from $1 trillion to $3 trillion and the number of Americans in poverty increased from 12 percent to 15 percent. By the end of the decade, a pattern of the rich getting richer and the poor getting poorer was firmly established. Meanwhile, without the stricter regulatory controls of the past, savings and loan officials took advantage of a wide range of previously unavailable investment and loan options. Many of these officials used poor judgment in making risky loans and then attempted to cover up their losses. Ultimately, Congress passed a $150 billion bailout program to stabilize the industry.

One of the major reasons for the growing budget deficit was a huge increase in defense spending. Between 1981 and 1986, Reagan increased defense spending by 50 percent, to $300 billion per year. In addition, he unveiled a missile defense system that quickly became known as "Star Wars." The objective of this Strategic Defense Initiative (SDI) was to be able to defend territory against a Soviet missile attack by launching intercepting missiles from space. Reagan's success in gaining congressional approval for more defense spending was due in part to heightened tensions between the United States and the Soviet Union, which he denounced as an "evil empire." In his second term, however, Reagan reached a détente with Soviet leader Mikhail Gorbachev and would later take credit for the fall of communist rule in Moscow, claiming that the Soviet economy had crumbled as that nation tried to keep pace with U.S. defense spending.

The resurrection of anticommunism as a rallying cry was central to much of Reagan's foreign policy. Early in his Presidency, he supported the ruling military junta in El Salvador despite its use of "death squads" in suppressing leftist rebels. In Nicaragua, beginning in 1982, the CIA implemented a plan to organize and finance the Contras, an army of 10,000 whose objective was to overthrow the Sandinistas, the ruling leftist government. In October 1983, Reagan ordered 2,000 U.S. Marines onto the tiny West Indian island of Grenada to overthrow a new radical leftist government and help install a regime friendly to the United States.

Meanwhile, as part of a multinational peacekeeping force, U.S. Marines were sent to Beirut, Lebanon. Muslims there considered the marines to be supporters of their Christian rivals. When a Shiite Muslim driving a truck full of explosives crashed into a marine barracks in 1883, killing 239 marines, Reagan withdrew all U.S. forces from Lebanon.

Although Reagan firmly asserted that he would never negotiate with terrorists, he approved the 1985 secret sale of 508 antitank missiles to Iranian moderates in exchange for the release of U.S. hostages in Lebanon. These dealings came to be recognized as one side of the Iran-Contra scandal. The other side slowly came to light when congressional investigators revealed that a National Security Council aide, Lieutenant Colonel Oliver North, had illegally funneled millions of dollars of profits from the Iranian arms deal to support the military operations of the Contras in Nicaragua, an operation specifically prohibited by Congress. Ultimately, it could not be proven that the President had any personal knowledge that his subordinates were illegally diverting funds to the Contras. The congressional inquiry into Iran-Contra led to the resignation of several members of the administration, the attempted suicide of national security advisor Robert McFarlane, and the appointment of an independent counsel who secured criminal indictments against McFarlane's successor, John Poindexter, as well as against North.

Reagan's popularity seemed unaffected by such setbacks, and he left office as the most popular President since Dwight Eisenhower. Dubbed the "Great Communicator," Reagan possessed an uncanny ability to articulate the beliefs, aspirations, and fears of millions of Americans. After leaving office, he retired to his ranch near Santa Barbara, California, and devoted much of his energy to planning his Presidential library and writing his memoirs. In 1994 he was diagnosed with the degenerative neural disorder Alzheimer's disease.

SEE ALSO

Iran-Contra affair

FURTHER READING

Boyer, Paul, ed. *Reagan as President: Contemporary Views of the Man, His Politics, and His Policies.* Chicago: Ivan R. Dee, 1990.

Cannon, Lou. *President Reagan: The Role of a Lifetime.* New York: Simon & Schuster, 1991.

Johnson, Haynes. *Sleepwalking through History: America in the Reagan Years.* New York: Norton, 1991.
Strober, Deborah Hart. *Reagan: The Man and His Presidency.* Boston: Houghton Mifflin, 1998.
Wills, Garry. *Reagan's America.* New York: Doubleday, 1987.

Reconversion

Reconversion was the shift from a wartime economy to a peacetime economy after World War II. The industry that felt the transition most strongly was manufacturing, as production switched from the supplies needed to fight a war to consumer goods. This is often a temporarily painful process. In 1945 more than 1 million defense jobs were eliminated as defense spending plummeted from $76 billion to $20 billion in 1946. The economy began to pick up in 1946, however, starting a 25-year run of unprecedented economic prosperity. The 1944 Serviceman Readjustment Act, or "G.I. Bill of Rights," provided $15 billion in funds for veterans to go to college, receive medical attention, and buy houses. A business tax cut in 1945 combined with wartime profits left companies with enough capital to open new factories to produce consumer goods. Americans who had saved and rationed throughout the war could not wait to buy the products of these factories, ushering in the consumer culture of the 1950s.

SEE ALSO

Consumer culture

FURTHER READING

McCullough, David G. *Truman.* New York: Simon & Schuster, 1992.
Savage, Sean J. *Truman and the Democratic Party.* Lexington: University of Kentucky Press, 1997.

Red scare

SEE McCarthyism

Religious fundamentalism

Church membership in the United States surged after World War II. A public opinion poll in 1948 found that 95 percent of the respondents believed in God and 90 percent prayed to him. Cold war emotions and fears stimulated the rising religiosity, and in 1954 *Time* magazine affirmed that the Christian faith was "back at the center of things." Benefiting from the talents of spellbinding preachers like the young Billy Graham and Oral Roberts, the evangelical Protestant fundamentalists grew more rapidly than any other religious group. The fundamentalists preached against the materialism, hedonism, and secularism of modern American life and linked their beliefs to the political crusade against communism. Using television, mass mailings, and advertising techniques, fundamentalist

Pat Robertson, head of the Christian Coalition, meets with President Ronald Reagan in 1985. The coalition has been a major influence on the Republican party.

preachers appealed particularly to relatively poor, less educated Americans searching for unambiguous truths and the consolation that at least they did not share in the immorality of the affluent middle class.

Indicative of the depth of fundamentalism, Hal Lindsey's *The Late Great Planet Earth*—which described a nuclear apocalypse caused by an anti-Christ and the return to earth of Jesus Christ to save mankind—was one of the best-selling book of the 1970s. In 1977 a survey revealed that more than 70 million Americans described themselves as born-again Christians who had a direct, personal relationship with Jesus. During the 1970s, moreover, Supreme Court rulings in favor of abortion and the right to teach evolution, and against prayer in public schools and the censorship of pornography, incensed religious fundamentalists and many grew increasingly conservative and active in politics.

Jerry Falwell and Pat Robertson led the movement to ally fundamentalism with right-wing Republicanism. By 1980 the Republican platform echoed many of the concerns of such groups as Falwell's Moral Majority, and in the 1990s no single organization held greater sway within the Republican party than Pat Robertson's Christian Coalition.

SEE ALSO

Conservatism; Graham, William ("Billy") Franklin; Moral Majority

FURTHER READING

Balmer, Randall H. *Mine Eyes Have Seen the Glory: A Journey into the Evangelical Subculture in America.* Expanded ed. New York: Oxford University Press, 1993.

Carpenter, Joel A. *Revive Us Again: The Reawakening of American Fundamentalism.* New York: Oxford University Press, 1997.

Ribbuffo, Leo. "God and Contemporary Politics." *Journal of American History* 79 (March 1993): 1,515–33.

Wuthnow, Robert. *The Restructuring of American Religious Society and Faith Since World War II.* Princeton, N.J.: Princeton University Press, 1991.

Richardson, Elliot Lee

- *Born: July 20, 1920, Boston, Mass.*
- *Accomplishments: Lieutenant Governor of Massachusetts, 1965–67; Massachusetts state attorney general, 1967–69; U.S. Secretary of Health, Education, and Welfare, 1970–73; U.S. Secretary of Defense, 1973; U.S. Attorney General, 1973; U.S. Ambassador to Great Britain, 1975–76; U.S. Secretary of Commerce, 1976–77; U.S. Ambassador at Large, 1977*

President Richard Nixon's attorney general after the resignation of Richard Kleindienst, Elliot Richardson appointed Archibald Cox, a Harvard law professor and Democrat, as the special prosecutor to pursue the Watergate investigation. When Cox sought a court order for the release of tapes of White House conversations, Nixon, not willing to release the incriminating evidence, ordered his attorney general to fire Cox. Richardson refused to fire him and resigned in protest, as did the deputy attorney general. Known as the "Saturday Night massacre," the firing and resignations sent Nixon's public-approval ratings plummeting.

SEE ALSO

Cox, Archibald; Nixon, Richard Milhous; Watergate

FURTHER READING

Richardson, Elliot. *Reflections of a Radical Moderate.* New York: Pantheon, 1996.

Robeson, Paul Leroy

- *Born: Apr. 19, 1898, Princeton, N.J.*
- *Accomplishments: Singer; actor; civil rights activist*
- *Died: Jan. 23, 1976, Philadelphia, Pa.*

Perhaps the greatest African-American performer of the first half of the 20th century, Paul Robeson was also well known as a radical political activist who fought for civil rights, campaigned against lynching, and advocated communism. In 1949 he told a Paris audience that it would be "unthinkable" for African Americans to go to war against the Soviet Union. This remark in particular swayed public opinion against Robeson, and he was blacklisted and prevented from performing at most concert halls in the United States. Official action was taken against him—his passport was revoked, and he was blacklisted from theaters and concert halls—and mobs took after him was well; once he was attacked and driven off the stage during a concert. Robeson got his passport back in 1958 and took an extended trip to Europe. He returned to the United States in 1963, but illness forced his retirement from public life.

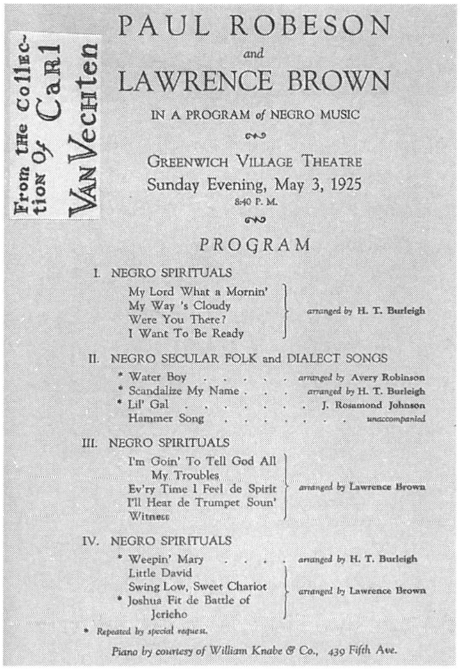

From the Collection of Carl Van Vechten

PAUL ROBESON
and
LAWRENCE BROWN

IN A PROGRAM *of* NEGRO MUSIC

GREENWICH VILLAGE THEATRE
Sunday Evening, May 3, 1925
8:40 P. M.

PROGRAM

I. NEGRO SPIRITUALS
My Lord What a Mornin'
My Way 's Cloudy
Were You There?
I Want To Be Ready
— *arranged by* H. T. Burleigh

II. NEGRO SECULAR FOLK and DIALECT SONGS
* Water Boy . . . . . . *arranged by* Avery Robinson
* Scandalize My Name . . . *arranged by* H. T. Burleigh
* Lil' Gal . . . . J. Rosamond Johnson
Hammer Song . . . . *unaccompanied*

III. NEGRO SPIRITUALS
I'm Goin' To Tell God All My Troubles
Ev'ry Time I Feel de Spirit
I'll Hear de Trumpet Soun'
Witness
— *arranged by* Lawrence Brown

IV. NEGRO SPIRITUALS
* Weepin' Mary . . . . *arranged by* H. T. Burleigh
Little David
Swing Low, Sweet Chariot
* Joshua Fit de Battle of Jericho
— *arranged by* Lawrence Brown

* *Repeated by special request.*

Piano by courtesy of William Knabe & Co., 439 Fifth Ave.

A 1925 program for a performance of spirituals and folk songs by Paul Robeson and pianist Lawrence Brown.

FURTHER READING

Brown, Lloyd L. *The Young Paul Robeson: "On My Journey Now."* Boulder, Colo.: Westview, 1997.

Duberman, Martin B. *Paul Robeson.* New York: Knopf, 1988.

Robeson, Paul. *Here I Stand.* Boston: Beacon, 1958.

Robinson, Jackie

- *Born: Jan. 31, 1919, Cairo, Ga.*
- *Accomplishments: Major league baseball player, 1947–56*
- *Died: Oct. 24, 1972, Stamford, Conn.*

The first African American to join a major league baseball team, Jackie Robinson (born Jack Roosevelt Robinson) also won Rookie of the Year honors in 1947, his first season in the majors. Robinson had played in the Negro Leagues until 1945, when the Brooklyn Dodgers, propelled by their general manager, Branch Rickey, purchased his contract. Robinson was sent to one of the Dodgers' farm teams and carefully groomed, both physically and emotionally, for what would await him once he joined the Dodgers. In 1947, finally in the majors, Robinson endured taunts and jeers from both spectators and other players, yet sportswriters voted him the league's most

After he retired from baseball, Jackie Robinson became active in the struggle for civil rights. In 1963, his son at his side, he makes a statement to the press at the March on Washington.

valuable player in 1949. He was inducted into the Hall of Fame in 1962. After Robinson, other major league teams quickly moved to sign Negro League stars; by 1959, when the Boston Red Sox signed Elijah ("Pumpsie") Green, all the major league teams were integrated. Robinson retired in 1956 with a .311 career batting average.

FURTHER READING

Robinson, Jackie. *Breakthrough to the Big League: The Story of Jackie Robinson.* New York: Harper & Row, 1965.

Tygiel, Jules. *Baseball's Great Experiment: Jackie Robinson and His Legacy.* New York: Oxford University Press, 1983.

Rock and roll

A blend of country, gospel, and the blues, rock and roll came into prominence in the 1950s. African-American musicians developed an early form of rock and roll, first called "race music" and then "rhythm and blues," which was popular among black audiences well before a white disk jockey from Cleveland, Alan Freed, coined the term *rock and roll* in 1951. White performers like Elvis Presley and Bill Haley, imitating the vocal style of such blues masters as Muddy Waters and B. B. King, and adding their own gyrating hips and provocative lyrics, revolutionized the popular music industry and helped create a distinctive youth culture that rebelled against the constraints of the traditional adult white culture.

In the 1960s rock and roll, now termed rock music, became an important part of the anti–Vietnam War movement and the counterculture. Rock and roll subsequently subdivided into numerous categories, including folk rock, acid rock, heavy metal, rap music, raga rock, and hard rock. Throughout its history, rock has been the target of critics for its presumed contributions to juvenile delinquency, drug addiction, and sexual immorality. In the 1980s the Parents' Music Resource Center, founded by Tipper Gore, the wife of then future Vice President Al Gore, led a campaign to label records with graphic lyrics as a warning to the parents of young consumers. The so-called "parental advisory stickers" were put into effect in the 1990s, instigating a bitter debate between anti-censorship activists and child protection advocates.

SEE ALSO

Counterculture; Presley, Elvis Aaron

FURTHER READING

Marcus, Greil. *Mystery Train: Images of America in Rock 'n' Roll Music.* New York: Dutton, 1976.

Shaw, Arnold. *The Rock Revolution.* New York: Crowell-Collier, 1969.

Ward, Ed, et al. *Rock of Ages: The Rolling Stone History of Rock and Roll.* New York: Rolling Stone Press, 1986.

Roe v. *Wade* (1973)

Jane Roe was the pseudonym of an unmarried pregnant woman who lived in Texas and wanted an abortion; Texas law did not allow abortions except to save the mother's life. The case was a class action suit brought to determine not only Jane Roe's rights, but also the rights of all women in the same or similar situations. It challenged the statute on a number of constitutional grounds, including equal protection of the law, due process of law, and the right to privacy.

State laws prohibiting abortions in the first trimester were struck down as unconstitutional by the Supreme Court

Sarah Weddington was the lawyer who presented Jane Roe's case to the Supreme Court and argued that state laws prohibiting abortion were unconstitutional.

in *Roe* v. *Wade* and the companion case *Doe* v. *Bolton* in 1973. The constitutional "right to privacy," proclaimed in *Griswold* v. *Connecticut* (1965), which held that Connecticut's ban on contraception violated a long-established right to privacy, formed the basis of the 7-to-2 ruling written by Justice Harry Blackmun. The Court declared that the right to privacy "includes the right of a woman to decide whether or not to terminate her pregnancy."

The ruling struck down all prohibitions against abortions in the first trimester but allowed states to regulate or restrict abortions later in the pregnancy. A highly controversial decision, *Roe* v. *Wade* provoked a groundswell of political activity by "prolife" groups, who pressed for a reversal of the decision, and by "prochoice" supporters, who defended abortion as an inalienable constitutional right.

Since 1973 the Supreme Court has consistently upheld states' procedural regulations on abortion, but in the case *Planned Parenthood of Southeastern Pennsylvania* v. *Casey* (1992), the high court reaffirmed the constitutionality of *Roe*.

SEE ALSO

Abortion issue

FURTHER READING

Garrow, David G. *Liberty and Sexuality: the Right to Privacy and the Making of Roe vs. Wade*. New York: Macmillan, 1994.

Luker, Kristin. *Abortion and the Politics of Motherhood*. Berkeley: University of California Press, 1984.

Petchesky, Rosalind. *Abortion and Woman's Choice: The State, Sexuality, and Reproductive Freedom*. Rev. ed. Boston: Northeastern University Press, 1990.

Roosevelt, Eleanor

- *Born: Oct. 11, 1884, New York, N.Y.*
- *Accomplishments: First Lady of the United States; reformer; women's rights and civil rights activist*
- *Died: Nov. 7, 1962, New York, N.Y.*

Eleanor Roosevelt was one of the most popular and active First Ladies in U.S. history. Significantly expanding the role of the political wife, she became a powerful voice in the 1930s for civil rights, women's rights, and employment programs for young people as she fought for the powerless and traveled the country serving as her husband President Franklin D. Roosevelt's "eyes and ears." In 1945 President Harry Truman named her a U.S. delegate to the United Nations. She served in that post until 1952, playing a major role in the drafting of the Universal Declaration of Human Rights and as an advocate for world peace and international cooperation. Active in Democratic politics during the 1950s, Roosevelt supported numerous liberal candidates and movements for social change, especially civil rights for African Americans and full equality for women. At her death in

Eleanor Roosevelt was an activist who kept on fighting for issues in which she believed long after she left the White House. In the 1950s, as honorary national chairman of Americans for Democratic Action, she attacked President Eisenhower for not confronting McCarthyism.

1962, most tributes saluted her as the 20th century's most influential woman.

FURTHER READING

Black, Allida M. *Casting Her Own Shadow.* New York: Columbia University Press, 1996.
Roosevelt, Eleanor. *The Autobiography of Eleanor Roosevelt.* 1961. Reprint, New York: Da Capo, 1992.
Roosevelt, Eleanor. *On My Own.* New York: Harper, 1958.

Rosenberg case

In March 1951, in the culmination of the most sensational case of the second Red scare, Julius and Ethel Rosenberg were convicted of conspiracy to commit espionage and sentenced to death. The Rosenbergs had been arrested in 1950 after Ethel's brother, David Greenglass, a machinist who had worked on the Manhattan project, the secret government research program to develop an atomic bomb during World War II, confessed to supplying secret information to the Soviet Union through a spy ring planned and operated by his sister and brother-in-law.

The Rosenbergs denied any part in the conspiracy, insisting that Greenglass's story was a fabrication. Nevertheless, a jury in New York found the Rosenbergs guilty and Judge Irving Kaufman handed down a death sentence, tying the Rosenbergs' espionage to the Korean War, which was raging at the time. Protesting their innocence to the end, and refusing repeated offers to have their sentence changed to life imprisonment if they confessed, Ethel and Julius Rosenberg were electrocuted on June 19, 1953. Even many who considered them guilty regarded the sentence as barbaric.

Ethel and Julius Rosenberg are transported to jail after being found guilty of espionage and conspiracy in 1951.

Arguments about the case have continued since the Rosenbergs' execution. Although some people maintain that they were innocent, documents made public in the 1990s indicate that Soviet records identify the Rosenbergs as espionage agents.

SEE ALSO

House Un-American Activities Committee (HUAC); McCarthyism

FURTHER READING

Coover, Robert. *The Public Burning.* New York: Grove, 1998.
Radosh, Ronald, and Joyce Milton. *The Rosenberg File: A Search for the Truth.* New York: Holt, Rinehart & Winston, 1983.

Rusk, David Dean

- *Born: Feb. 9, 1909, Cherokee County, Ga.*
- *Accomplishments: Secretary of State, 1961–69*
- *Died: Dec. 20, 1994, Athens, Ga.*

A career diplomat and former head of the Rockefeller Foundation, Dean Rusk became President John Kennedy's secretary of state in 1961. Although he argued against an air strike during the Cuban missile crisis, Rusk repeatedly warned that all of Southeast Asia would fall to communism if U.S. forces withdrew from Vietnam.

Following Kennedy's assassination, President Lyndon Johnson kept Rusk on as secretary of state and agreed with his view that appeasement in Vietnam would send a message of weakness to the Soviet Union and lead to a larger war in Vietnam and communist-inspired guerrilla wars in other countries. Despite indications that North Vietnam was willing to negotiate, Rusk urged Johnson to escalate the war to sustain the international credibility of the United States. Not until after the Tet offensive of 1968 did Rusk recommend that the United States call a partial bombing halt in North Vietnam as a signal of U.S. readiness to engage in peace talks. After leaving office, Rusk taught international law at the University of Georgia.

SEE ALSO

Johnson, Lyndon Baines; Kennedy, John Fitzgerald; Vietnam War

FURTHER READING

Cohen, Warren I. *Dean Rusk.* Totowa, N.J.: Cooper Square, 1980.
Schoenbaum, Thomas J. *Waging Peace and War: Dean Rusk in the Truman, Kennedy, and Johnson Years.* New York: Simon & Schuster, 1988.

Salinger, J. D.

- *Born: Jan. 1, 1919, New York, N.Y.*
- *Accomplishments: Writer*
- *Major Works:* The Catcher in the Rye *(1951),* Nine Stories *(1953),* Franny and Zooey *(1961),* Raise High the Roof Beams, Carpenters *(1963)*

Salinger's first novel, *The Catcher in the Rye,* has been a favorite of high school and college students since its publication in 1951. It is the story of Holden Caulfield, a soon-to-be-expelled prep-school student with an honest and idiosyncratic voice, as he wanders throughout New York City trying to figure out himself and the world. His fight against the phoniness of the adults who surround him has continued to ring true to teenagers and young adults since the book was published. *The Catcher in the Rye* was so successful when it was first published that Salinger, who did not want to live the life of a famous writer, moved to rural New Hampshire, where he has been fending off attacks on his privacy ever since.

FURTHER READING

Bloom, Harold, ed. *Holden Caulfield.* Broomall, Pa.: Chelsea House, 1991.
French, Warren. *J. D. Salinger.* Boston: Twayne, 1976.
Salinger, J. D. *The Catcher in the Rye.* New York: Little, Brown, 1951.
Salzman, Jack, ed. *New Essays on "The Catcher in the Rye."* New York: Cambridge University Press, 1991.

Sandinistas

Largely composed of Nicaraguan peasants, the Sandinista movement came to power in 1979 by overthrowing a long-standing pro-American dictatorship headed by the Somoza family. The revolutionaries had at first been accepted by the administration of Jimmy Carter, but relations cooled when they curbed civil liberties and moved closer to Castro's Cuba. President Carter then cut off U.S. aid to the Sandinistas, and his successor, Ronald Reagan, convinced that the Sandinistas were trying to spread communism throughout Central America, sought to assist their opponents.

Under Director William Casey, in 1982 the CIA organized and financed an anti-Sandinista guerrilla army, called the Contras, to fight a civil war in Nicaragua. It failed to oust the Sandinista regime, but in 1990 Nicaraguans voted to replace the Sandinistas with a non-Marxist government. The Iran-Contra affair, the Reagan administration's attempt to funnel money to the Contras, unraveled and for a time embroiled the administration in scandal, although it had few long-term effects on the reputations of the main figures it involved.

SEE ALSO

Iran-Contra affair; Reagan, Ronald Wilson

FURTHER READING

Nolan, David. *Ideology of the Sandinistas and the Nicaraguan Revolution.* Coral Gables, Fla.: University of Miami North/South Center Press, 1984.

Roger, Miranda, and William Ratliff. *The Civil War in Nicaragua: Inside the Sandinistas.* New Brunswick, N.J.: Transaction, 1993.

Saturday Night massacre

SEE Cox, Archibald; Richardson, Elliot Lee; Watergate

Savings and loan scandal

The savings and loan (S&L) industry, which for decades had provided home loans and a secure return on investments, collapsed when nearly 600 S&Ls failed between 1988 and 1990, wiping out the savings of many depositors. Swept up in the get-rich-quick mood of the 1980s, the newly deregulated S&Ls made risky loans on speculative real estate ventures, and when the economy cooled in the late 1980s, depressing the real estate market, many of those investments went bad.

The federal government, which insures savings and loan deposits, spent some $400 billion to bail out the industry and repay depositors.

FURTHER READING

Calavita, Kitty, and Henry N. Pontell. *Big Money Crime: Fraud and Politics in the Savings and Loan Crisis.* Berkeley: University of California Press, 1997.

White, Lawrence J. *The S & L Debacle: Public Policy Lessons for Bank and Thrift Regulation.* New York: Oxford University Press, 1991.

Schwarzkopf, H. Norman

- *Born: Aug. 22, 1934, Trenton, N.J.*
- *Accomplishments: Commander in Chief of the U.S. Army Central Command, 1988–92*

The U.S. commander of Operation Desert Storm in the Persian Gulf War of 1991, General Norman Schwarzkopf led the 28-nation U.N. force against Iraq in what Iraqi leader Saddam Hussein called the "mother of all battles." In less than six weeks, the U.N. allies controlled the air, rained bombs on strategic sites throughout Iraq, and liberated Kuwait City, which Iraq had invaded.

Both a good media presence and a master of press conferences, Schwarzkopf immediately became a public hero. In his address to Congress after the war, the general emphasized the diversity of the allied forces: "Protestants and

Catholics and Jews and Muslims and Buddhists . . . fighting for a common and just cause. . . . We were black and white and yellow and brown and red, and we noticed when our blood was shed in the desert, it didn't separate by race but it flowed together."

SEE ALSO

Persian Gulf War

FURTHER READING

Schwarzkopf, Norman. *It Doesn't Take a Hero*. New York: Bantam, 1992.

Selma civil rights demonstrations (1965)

In March 1965, Martin Luther King, Jr., and his Southern Christian Leadership Conference (SCLC) sought to publicize the need for a federal voting rights act by launching a voter registration drive in Selma, Alabama. Although half of the population in the county was black, only 1 percent of the potential black voters were registered to vote.

When protestors lined up for a peaceful march on the city, the county sheriff, Jim Clark, sent policemen on horseback to attack them with tear gas, clubs, and whips. Film footage of the attack appeared on the evening news and won support for the federal Voting Rights Act, which was signed into law in August 1965.

SEE ALSO

Civil rights movement; King, Martin Luther, Jr.

FURTHER READING

Fager, Charles. *Selma, 1965: The March That Changed the South*. Boston: Beacon, 1985.

Garrow, David J. *Protest at Selma: Martin Luther King, Jr., and the Voting Rights Act of 1965*. New Haven, Conn.: Yale University Press, 1978.

While walking from Selma to Montgomery, Alabama, civil rights marchers encountered a few white protesters with Confederate flags, but it was not enough to stop them. Martin Luther King, Jr. (bottom center), leads the march.

Sexual revolution

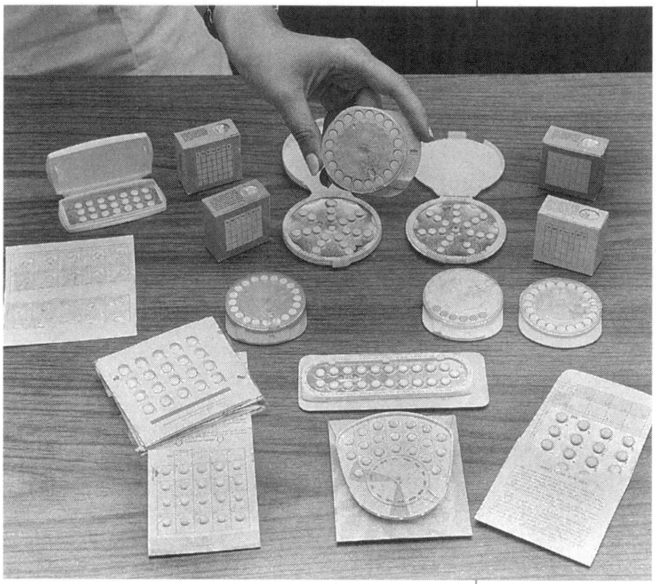

Different forms of the birth control pill in 1968. Women's new ability to control their fertility spurred the sexual revolution.

In the 1960s, the United States experienced a relaxation of sexual taboos and greater permissiveness in sexual activity known as the sexual revolution. It arose in part from the counterculture's emphasis on liberation from restraints, a "do your own thing" sentiment, but also in part from women's new freedom from pregnancy as birth control became more readily available. In 1965 the Supreme Court found in *Griswold* v. *Connecticut* that the state could not ban the sale or use of contraceptives; the decision was based on the right to privacy, but the effect of the decision was far reaching. Women's roles, too, were changing; the newly recharged feminist movement was encouraging women to be more active in seeking fulfillment, sexual and otherwise.

By 1970, 12 million women were taking oral contraceptives ("the pill") and even more used an intrauterine device (IUD). Abortion was legalized throughout the nation in 1973 with the *Roe* v. *Wade* decision by the Supreme Court. In the 1980s and 90s, however, the spread of AIDS changed Americans' focus from "free love" to "safe sex" and fear of infection caused many people to avoid casual sexual relations.

A more tolerant attitude toward sexual matters was also promulgated by Supreme Court decisions in the 1960s that declared unconstitutional nearly all restrictions on the right of an adult to obtain sexually explicit books and magazines. Hollywood movies likewise grew bolder, with the most sexually explicit films being the most successful at the box office. Meanwhile, the growing insistence on the right to sexual pleasure and the more permissive view of sexual behavior led to greater numbers of couples living together without getting married first; homosexuality, too, became more widely accepted in mainstream culture.

By the late 1970s, though, many people had started to moderate their behavior as the risks became more clear. Feminists who had at first thought that liberation meant always being free to say yes soon came to relish the right to say no as the boundaries between wanted and unwanted sex—date rape, for example—began to blur. Another undesirable side effect of sex, disease, became more of a threat. In the late seventies venereal diseases began to appear more frequently and the herpes simplex virus loomed as a danger that could make sex painful and pregnancies more risky. Those medical problems, though, paled by comparison to the AIDS virus, which first began its deadly assault in the early 1980s and affected behavior throughout the 80s and 90s. As a result, the ideals of celibacy and virginity made somewhat of a comeback in the 1990s.

SEE ALSO

Abortion issue; Acquired immune deficiency syndrome (AIDS); Counterculture; Feminism; *Roe* v. *Wade* (1973)

FURTHER READING

D'Emilio, John. *Sexual Politics, Sexual Communities: The Making of a Homosexual Minority in the United States, 1940–1970.* Chicago: University of Chicago Press, 1983.

Halberstam, David. "Discovering Sex." *American Heritage,* May–June 1993, 39–52.

McLaughlin, Loretta. *The Pill, John Rock, and the Church: The Biography of a Revolution.* Boston: Little, Brown, 1982.

Yankelovich, Daniel. *The New Morality.* New York: McGraw-Hill, 1974.

Silent Spring

SEE Carson, Rachel

Sit-ins (1960–61)

On February 1, 1960, four freshmen from a local black college sat down at the lunch counter of Woolworth's in Greensboro, North Carolina. Denied service, they sat at the counter for the rest of the day and promised to return and occupy the seats until they were served. By the end of the week, enough black students had joined the demonstration to fill the lunchroom completely. Six months later, city officials agreed to integrate public restaurants.

African Americans wait to be served at a lunch counter in Jackson, Mississippi, in 1963. The restaurant was closed after they entered.

The Greensboro sit-in inspired similar protests elsewhere in North Carolina and neighboring states. Eventually, about 70,000 students participated in sit-ins across the South. The movement not only won access to public accommodations for blacks but also revitalized the civil rights movement; it was students who took part in the sit-in who also formed the Student Nonviolent Coordinating Committee (SNCC) in April 1960.

SEE ALSO

Civil rights movement; Student Nonviolent Coordinating Committee (SNCC)

FURTHER READING

Chafe, William. *Civilities and Civil Rights: Greensboro, North Carolina, and the Black Struggle for Freedom.* New York: Oxford University Press, 1980.

Wolff, Miles. *Lunch at the Five and Ten: The Greensboro Sit-ins: A Contemporary History.* New York: Stein & Day, 1970.

Southeast Asia Treaty Organization (SEATO)

The Southeast Asia Collective Defense Treaty, patterned after the NATO agreement and establishing the Southeast Asia Treaty Organization (SEATO), was signed in Manila, the Philippines, on September 8, 1954, by Australia, Britain, France, New Zealand, Pakistan, the Philippines, Thailand, and the United States. Designed to check the spread of communism in Asia after the end of French dominance in Indochina, the signatories agreed that any attack against the treaty area, including Indochina, would be considered aggression against all.

In 1972 Pakistan withdrew from SEATO, as did France the following year, and in 1975 Thailand and the Philippines recommended that SEATO, no longer being necessary, be phased out. It formally ended on June 30, 1977.

SEE ALSO

Korean War; North Atlantic Treaty Organization (NATO); Vietnam War

Southern Christian Leadership Conference (SCLC)

The Reverend Martin Luther King, Jr., the Reverend Ralph David Abernathy, and other southern ministers formed the Southern Christian Leadership Conference (SCLC) in 1957 to end segregation and discrimination against blacks in the South through a campaign of nonviolent protest.

The organization grew out of the Montgomery, Alabama, bus boycott of 1955–56, which had forced the city to integrate the local transportation system. Under King's leadership, the group brought its tactics of nonviolent protest and civil disobedience to cities across the South and later in the 1960s to northern cities as well. King served as president of the organization until his assassination in 1968 and was succeeded first by Abernathy, then by the Reverend Joseph E. Lowery.

SEE ALSO

Civil rights movement; King, Martin Luther, Jr.; Montgomery bus boycott (1955–56)

FURTHER READING

Fairclough, Adam. *To Redeem the Soul of America: The Southern Christian Leadership Conference and Martin Luther King, Jr.* Athens: University of Georgia Press, 1978.

Garrow, David. *Bearing the Cross: Martin Luther King, Jr., and the Southern Christian Leadership Conference.* New York: Morrow, 1988.

Soviet Union

SEE Cold war

Space program

One year after the Soviet Union successfully launched the first artificial satellite, *Sputnik,* Congress passed and President Dwight Eisenhower signed the 1958 law creating a civilian agency, the National Aeronautics and Space Administration (NASA), charged with conducting scien-

Apollo 11 *prepares to launch men to the moon in 1969.*

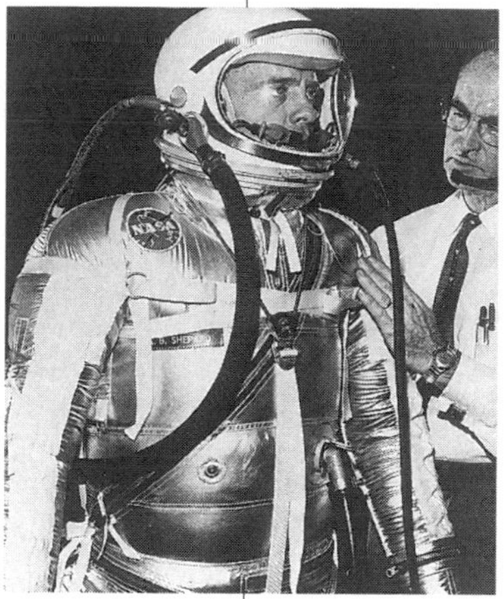

Alan Shepard tests his space suit during preparations for Project Mercury in 1961.

tific space exploration. The space race between the two superpowers had now begun in earnest, and President John Kennedy soon committed the United States to landing a man on the moon before the end of the 1960s.

Although the Russian astronaut Yuri Gagarin became the first man in space in April 1961, the United States quickly passed the Soviet space program with its Mercury missions. On May 5, 1961, Alan Shepard became the first American in space, making a successful suborbital flight aboard the capsule *Freedom Seven;* on February 20, 1962, John Glenn made the first U.S. orbital flight, circling the globe three times.

Project Gemini in 1965 brought the first U.S. walk in space, by Edward White; the successful rendezvous of two Gemini capsules 185 miles above the earth; and the placing in orbit of *Early Bird,* the world's first commercial communication satellite. The following year, NASA began preparations for Project Apollo, which was to set U.S. astronauts on the moon. After a setback in 1967 in which a fire in an Apollo module killed three astronauts, *Apollo 11* orbited the moon on July 20, 1969, and its Lunar Excursion Module *Eagle* descended to a landing site near the Sea of Tranquillity. As Americans watched Neil Armstrong walk on the moon from their televisions, they heard him say, "That's one small step for man, one giant leap for mankind."

The Apollo missions ended in December 1972, and NASA then began a program to develop a manned orbital space station, which led in 1975 to Soviet and U.S. spacecraft linking up and docking in orbit. This achievement was followed by the lift-off of the first space shuttle, *Columbia,* in 1981, and a flight in 1983 that included astronaut Sally Ride, the first U.S. woman in space.

NASA experienced a number of setbacks in the 1980s, including a devastating blow when the space shuttle *Challenger* exploded after lift-off on January 28, 1986, killing all seven crew members, including Christa McAuliffe, a New Hampshire schoolteacher who had been chosen as the first civilian to go into space and had planned to give televised lessons during the flight. Although a special commission investigating the disaster did not hold NASA officials responsible for the design flaws in the shuttle's components, it did recommend a thorough overhaul of the agency, and the space program was put on hold until September 1988, when *Discovery* was launched.

By then, declining public interest and congressional support for space exploration had led to fewer manned space flights. Despite shrinking budgets in the 1990s, NASA launched the unmanned *Mars Observer* in 1992 to prepare for the eventual flight of humans to the so-called "red planet" and continued its plans to develop a permanent lunar base and construct the space station *Freedom.* In 1998 John Glenn, by then a U.S. senator from Ohio, revived public interest by becoming the oldest man to take part in a space mission.

A souvenir medal commemorates the first moon landing.

SEE ALSO

Sputnik

FURTHER READING

Crouch, Tom D. *The National Aeronautics and Space Administration.* New York: Chelsea House, 1990.

Kerrod, Robin. *The Illustrated History of NASA.* New York: Gallery Books, 1988.

Longsdon, John M. *The Decision to Go to the Moon: Project Apollo and the National Interest.* Cambridge, Mass.: M.I.T. Press, 1970.

McDougall, Walter. *The Heavens and the Earth: A Political History of the Space Age.* New York: Basic Books, 1985.

Spock, Benjamin

- *Born: May 2, 1903, New Haven, Conn.*
- *Accomplishments: Physician; writer; child-care specialist*
- *Died: Mar. 15, 1998, San Diego, Calif.*

Dr. Benjamin Spock's immensely popular child-rearing manual, *Baby and Child Care,* first published in 1946, made him a household name and the guru to a generation of parents who reared the children of the baby boom. As the first person in the United States to be trained as both a psychiatrist and a pediatrician, Dr. Spock emphasized the proper techniques needed to raise physically healthy as well as psychologically well-adjusted children.

Spock's focus on the importance of maternal tenderness and a mother's attention to her children fit well with the popularity of domesticity and the preoccupation with family life in the 1950s. His child-centered home became the ideal for baby boomers across the United States. Since the 1960s, feminists have criticized him for stressing the necessity of full-time mothering, while conservatives have blamed the misbehavior of youth on his "permissive" advice.

Later in his career, Spock became a spokesman for the Committee for a Sane Nuclear Policy (SANE) and was very active in the anti–Vietnam War movement. He ran for President in 1972 as a member of the People's party.

Since its initial publication Spock's *Baby and Child Care* has sold over 50 million copies, in six editions and forty-two languages. It was updated using less gender-specific language—in other words, babies were not always called "he"—as its author's ideas about the effects of such language changed; other philosophical changes, such as the proper role for each parent, also were reflected in the book.

While he waits to give testimony to the House Ways and Means Committee about Medicare, Dr. Benjamin Spock listens to advice from a three-year-old.

SEE ALSO

Baby boom

FURTHER READING

Bloom, Lynn. *Doctor Spock: Biography of a Conservative Radical.* Indianapolis: Bobbs-Merrill, 1972.

Spock, Benjamin. *Baby and Child Care: 6th Edition, Fully Revised and Updated for the 90s.* New York: Dutton, 1992.

Spock, Benjamin. *Spock on Spock: A Memoir of Growing Up with the Century.* New York: Pantheon, 1989.

Sputnik

Launched by the Soviet Union in October 1957, *Sputnik* (which means "traveling companion") was the first artificial satellite placed in orbit. Weighing 184 pounds, it orbited the earth every 96 minutes for twenty-one days and transmitted a radio signal back to earth. Concerned that the Soviet science program was superior to that of the United States, President Dwight D. Eisenhower mobilized schools and industry to wage a race in technology and science against the Soviets.

SEE ALSO

Space program

FURTHER READING

Divine, Robert. *The Sputnik Challenge: Eisenhower's Response to the Soviet Satellite.* New York: Oxford University Press, 1993.

Cohodas, Nadine. *Strom Thurmond and the Politics of Southern Change.* New York: Simon & Schuster, 1993.

Star Wars

SEE Nuclear arms control; Reagan, Ronald Wilson

States' Rights Democratic party (Dixiecrats)

The States' Rights Democratic party was formed in July 1948 when a group of disgruntled whites from several southern states, angered at the endorsement of a civil rights plank in the Presidential platform, walked out of the Democratic national convention. Led by Mississippi governor Fielding Lewis Wright, the segregationists met in Jackson, Mississippi, to nominate South Carolina governor Strom Thurmond for President and Wright for Vice President.

The party hoped to win all the southern states and thus deny victory to Democrat Harry S. Truman, who had endorsed the civil rights plank. During the campaign, however, many southerners abandoned the Dixiecrats, who carried only four states in the general election, and Truman won reelection. The States' Rights party soon ceased to exist.

FURTHER READING

Berman, William C. *The Politics of Civil Rights in the Truman Administration.* Columbus: Ohio State University Press, 1970.

Steel mill seizure (1952)

President Harry S. Truman seized control of the nation's steel mills on April 8, 1952, when he feared that a steelworkers' strike would threaten steel production during the Korean War. Issuing Executive Order 10340, Truman seized the mills on his constitutional authority as commander in chief of the armed forces.

In a rare decision (*Youngstown Sheet and Tube* v. *Sawyer,* 1952), the Supreme Court ruled that Truman's executive order was unconstitutional, stating that Congress had legislative steps in place to deal with wartime strikes that should have been used instead. This is one of only a few times that an executive order has been ruled unconstitutional. The strike was resolved seven weeks after the mills were returned to their owners.

SEE ALSO
Korean War; Truman, Harry S.

FURTHER READING

Marcus, Maeva. *Truman and the Steel Seizure Case.* New York: Columbia University Press, 1977.

Steinem, Gloria

- *Born: Mar. 25, 1934, Toledo, Ohio*
- *Accomplishments: Writer; feminist leader*

One of the best-known feminists and advocates of women's rights in the

Gloria Steinem has been one of the most well-known feminists in the United States since the early 1970s.

United States, Steinem has also been a strong political proponent of civil rights, liberal Democratic candidates, and the United Farm Workers.

Steinem cofounded *Ms.* magazine in 1972 to challenge all forms of sexism and gender discrimination and stayed on as editor until the late 1980s. Under her direction, *Ms.* became the chief popular medium advocating equality and self-determination for women. ("God bless Gloria Steinem," exclaimed the mother of Sally Ride, the first U.S. woman astronaut.)

In 1992 Steinem published *The Revolution from Within,* in which she asserted that improvements in women's lives must come from internal searching and individual transformation as well as from political solutions.

SEE ALSO

Feminism; *Ms.* magazine

FURTHER READING

Steinem, Gloria. *Moving Beyond Words.* New York: Simon & Schuster, 1995.

Steinem, Gloria. *Outrageous Acts and Everyday Rebellions.* New York: Henry Holt, 1995.

Steinem, Gloria. "The Birth of *Ms.*" *New York,* April 19, 1993, 134–35.

Winokur, L. A. "Gloria Steinem." *The Progressive,* June 1995, 34–37.

Stevenson, Adlai Ewing

- *Born: Feb. 5, 1900, Los Angeles, Calif.*
- *Accomplishments: Senior Advisor, U.S. delegation, General Assembly of the United Nations, 1946; Governor of Illinois (Democrat), 1949–53*
- *Died: July 14, 1965, London, England*

Adlai Stevenson, the eloquent Democratic governor of Illinois who pledged to carry on President Harry S. Truman's Fair Deal and foreign policies, ran against Dwight D. Eisenhower for the Presidency in 1952 and lost. Renominated by the Democrats in 1956, he again ran and lost to Eisenhower.

Despite his moderate stance on issues such as civil rights and public housing, Stevenson was especially popular with intellectuals and liberal Democrats. In 1960 he sought the Presidential nomination yet again, but he failed to stop the Democrats from choosing John F. Kennedy as their nominee. Following his election, Kennedy appointed Stevenson ambassador to the United Nations. There Stevenson vigorously defended the naval blockade of Cuba by the United States during the 1962 missile crisis and supported U.S. involvement in the Vietnam War.

SEE ALSO

Eisenhower, Dwight David; Kennedy, John Fitzgerald

FURTHER READING

Baker, Jean H. *The Stevensons: A Biography of an American Family.* New York: Norton, 1997.

Broadwater, Jeff. *Adlai Stevenson and American Politics: The Odyssey of a Cold War Liberal.* New York: Twayne, 1994.

Martin, John Bartlow. *Adlai E. Stevenson and the World.* New York: Doubleday, 1976.

Stimson, Henry L.

- *Born: Sept. 21, 1867, New York, N.Y.*
- *Accomplishments: Secretary of War, 1911–13, 1940–45; Secretary of State, 1929–33*
- *Died: Oct. 20, 1950, Huntington, N.Y.*

Appointed secretary of war by President William Howard Taft and then secretary of state by President Herbert

Hoover, lifelong Republican Henry Stimson returned as secretary of war in 1940 as President Franklin D. Roosevelt sought to undercut isolationist Republican criticisms.

During World War II Stimson considered himself the "President's senior advisor on the military employment of atomic energy" and advocated dropping the newly developed atomic bomb on Japan to bring the war to a swift conclusion. Stimson called the atomic bomb a "badly needed equalizer" in the struggle with the Soviet Union and believed it would give President Harry Truman the leverage he needed to make the Soviet Union more accommodating. Soon after the war, however, Stimson grew critical of what he considered Truman's heavy-handed atomic diplomacy.

SEE ALSO

Atomic bomb

FURTHER READING

Herken, Gregg. *The Winning Weapon: The Atomic Bomb in the Cold War, 1945–1950.* New York: Knopf, 1980.
Hodgson, Godfrey. *The Colonel: The Life and Wars of Henry Stimson, 1867–1950.* Boston: Northeastern University Press, 1992.

Stockman, David

- *Born: Nov. 10, 1946, Fort Hood, Tex.*
- *Accomplishments: U.S. representative (Republican–Mich.), 1976–80; Director, Office of Management and Budget, 1981–85*

When Ronald Reagan took over the White House in 1981, he appointed David Stockman, a congressman from Michigan, as director of the Office of Management and Budget. A workaholic who believed that cutting both spending and taxes as well as deregulating business would lead to economic growth, Stockman became one of the primary architects of Reaganomics.

The theory behind Stockman's proposals, known as supply-side economics, was to replace the Democrats' "demand side" emphasis on high taxes and lavish federal spending with big cuts in taxes and domestic expenditures. This supposedly would rejuvenate the economy, because people would be able to keep more of their income to invest and spend, which would increase the government's tax revenues. However, the sweeping tax cuts of 1981 were combined with huge increases in defense spending that Reagan insisted on, and the result was historically high budget deficits. This situation coincided with a period of high interest rates, which caused the deepest recession of the postwar era. "None of us really understands what's going on with all these numbers," Stockman later admitted.

SEE ALSO

Reagan, Ronald Wilson

FURTHER READING

Greider, William. *The Education of David Stockman and Other Americans.* New York: Dutton, 1982.
Reeves, Richard. *The Reagan Detour.* New York: Simon & Schuster, 1985.
Schaller, Michael. *Reckoning with Reagan: America and Its President in the 1980s.* New York: Oxford University Press, 1992.

Stonewall riot (1969)

Rioting between New York City police and the patrons of a gay bar in the Greenwich Village section of New York City in 1969 marked the beginning of a militant grass-roots gay liberation

The Stonewall riots spurred gay men and lesbians to fight against discrimination and to speak out for their rights. Here a protester is out on the street, kneeling on the sidewalk to finish lettering a sign.

movement in the United States. The riot was a spontaneous act of resistance to the police harassment inflicted on the homosexual community since the inception of modern vice squads. These squads would routinely raid gay establishments; the excuse for the raid would be to serve warrants for the unauthorized sale of liquor, but the real reason would be to harass gay men and lesbians. When police raided the Stonewall Inn on June 27, 1969, the patrons of the bar fought back and returned the following two nights to defy police again.

Although a gay rights movement had begun before Stonewall, the riot emboldened more homosexuals to come out of the closet, publicly proclaiming their sexual orientation, and to demand an end to police brutality and other forms of discrimination. On the first anniversary of the Stonewall riot, 5,000 gay men and lesbians commemorated the event with a protest march through New York City. Subsequently, Gay Pride Month has been celebrated each June, with annual parades in New York City and elsewhere.

SEE ALSO

Gay liberation movement

FURTHER READING

D'Emilio, John. *Sexual Politics, Sexual Communities: The Making of a Homosexual Minority in the United States, 1940–1970.* Chicago: University of Chicago Press, 1983.

Katz, Jonathan. *Gay American History: Lesbians and Gay Men in the U.S.A.* New York: Harper & Row, 1976.

Students for a Democratic Society (SDS)

The organization most closely associated with the New Left, Students for a Democratic Society (SDS), began the decade of the 1960s aiming to transform the United States into a more egalitarian, democratic society, but finished it in violent fragments, a victim of internal disputes and external pressures.

The founding members of SDS adopted the Port Huron Statement, written primarily by Tom Hayden, as their manifesto in 1962. Calling for citizens to make the decisions that affect their lives, the statement served as the initial guide for SDS members as they began grass-roots organizing in urban slums and then participated in the Freedom Summer in Mississippi.

In 1965 SDS took the lead in organizing protests against the expanding U.S. military role in Vietnam, and its ranks swelled as it became a major force in the antiwar movement. By 1968 the organization had some 100,000 members and hundreds of chapters on col-

Students for a Democratic Society march in Washington, D.C., to protest the war in Vietnam.

lege campuses across the country. It achieved a level of power and prominence unprecedented for a student organization when it led the strike and occupation of campus buildings at Columbia University in New York City that April.

As the war raged on, however, and U.S. society seemed far less open to change than SDS members had first thought that it would be, the organization moved quickly leftward. In 1969 it splintered into several factions, including the Weathermen, who believed that only violent action would end the war and bring about social transformation.

SEE ALSO

Hayden, Thomas ("Tom"); New Left; Weathermen

FURTHER READING

Gitlin, Todd. *The Sixties: Years of Hope, Days of Rage.* New York: Bantam, 1987.
Harris, David. *Dreams Die Hard.* New York: St. Martin's, 1982.
Isserman, Maurice. *If I Had a Hammer: The Death of the Old Left and the Birth of the New Left.* New York: Basic Books, 1987.
Levitt, Cyril. *Children of Privilege: Student Revolt in the Sixties.* Toronto: University of Toronto Press, 1984.
Miller, James. *"Democracy Is in the Streets": From Port Huron to the Siege of Chicago.* Cambridge, Mass.: Harvard University Press, 1994.
Sale, Kirkpatrick. *SDS.* New York: Random House, 1973.

Student Nonviolent Coordinating Committee (SNCC)

Answering the call of Southern Christian Leadership Conference (SCLC) organizer Ella Baker, student activists involved in the lunch counter sit-in movement met at Raleigh, North Carolina, on April 17, 1960, to form the Student Nonviolent Coordinating Committee (SNCC). It was an idealistic interracial civil rights organization that sought to attack the southern strongholds of racism through nonviolent means.

SNCC (pronounced "snick"), under the leadership of Marion Barry, James Forman, John Lewis, and Bob Moses,

Members of SNCC and the Congress of Racial Equality have chained themselves to a federal courthouse in New York to protest civil rights abuses in Jackson, Mississippi.

became the cutting edge of most of the major civil rights campaigns of the 1960s, playing a key role in the freedom rides aimed at desegregating interstate transportation facilities and in the black voter registration drives. In its best-known campaign, SNCC joined forces with the Congress of Racial Equality (CORE) to organize 1,000 black and white college students for the Mississippi Freedom Summer project of 1964.

After the failure of the Mississippi Freedom Democratic party to unseat the regular all-white state delegation at the 1964 Democratic convention, a disillusioned SNCC reexamined its integration goals and its strategy of nonviolent direct action to gain liberal support and federal intervention. During the summer of 1966, led by Stokely Carmichael, SNCC adopted the "black power" slogan to emphasize the necessity of African-American self-reliance and the building up of black-controlled institutions.

Carmichael's successor, H. Rap Brown, preaching that "violence is as American as cherry pie," advocated violence as a legitimate means of self-defense and in 1969 he changed the organization's name to the Student National Coordinating Committee. Weakened by internal dissension and the lack of outside support, SNCC declined rapidly at the end of the 1960s, the victim of repression by the FBI and of a civil rights movement in disarray.

SEE ALSO

Black power; Carmichael, Stokely; Civil rights movement; Lewis, John Robert; Mississippi Freedom Democratic party (MFDP); Mississippi Freedom Summer (1964); Moses, Robert Parris; Sit-ins (1960–61)

FURTHER READING

Carson, Clayborne. *In Struggle: SNCC and the Black Awakening of the 1960s.* Cambridge, Mass.: Harvard University Press, 1981.

Forman, James. *The Making of Black Revolutionaries.* Washington, D.C.: Open Hand, 1985.

King, Mary. *Freedom Song: A Personal Story of the 1960s Civil Rights Movement.* New York: Morrow, 1987.

Sellers, Cleveland, with Robert Terrell. *The River of No Return: The Autobiography of a Black Militant and the Life and Death of SNCC.* New York: Morrow, 1973.

Student protest movement

SEE New Left; Students for a Democratic Society (SDS)

Suburbs

The United States was the first suburban nation, with 45 percent of the population living in suburbs by 1990. Suburbs are politically and legally independent towns that are outside a big city but economically and socially linked to it.

The growth of suburbs began in the 1890s but exploded in the years following World War II as millions of middle-class white Americans fled the perceived crime and filth of the city, seeking the space and other amenities that the automobile made accessible. In this outmigration, often referred to as "white flight," many white Americans moved to the suburbs also to escape the desegregated school systems ordered by the 1954 *Brown* Supreme Court decision and the mass migration of African Americans from the rural South to the northern cities.

Since the 1960s, a greater percentage of the population has lived in the suburbs than in the cities. Suburbanites are usually wealthier, better educated, and more likely to live in two-parent families than city dwellers.

Levittown, Long Island, a suburb of New York City, is the classic example of a post–World War II suburban community. In 1947 developer William Levitt built 17,000 mass-produced homes along the same design so that average families could afford them and neighboring children would feel comfortable in each other's houses. The town also included schools, shopping centers, and playgrounds. After the success of the Long Island Levittown, Levitt constructed new Levittowns in New Jersey and Pennsylvania, and other builders, too, put up developments in what had been the countryside.

Although the suburbs have often been derided by some observers for what they saw as their tacky sameness, suburbs have continued to be the location of choice for most U.S. families. In no other nation in the world has the suburban pattern of residence been more pronounced than in the United States.

By the 1970s, suburbs heavily influenced the American way of life; this influence increased as the decades passed. Shopping malls, which grew ever larger and began to include more and more besides simple stores—including rides, theme restaurants, and live entertainment—emerged as suburban social and commercial centers. The style born of suburban culture was visible in the California teenagers known as "Valley Girls," whose slang expressions became synonymous with early 80s consumerism. As malls grew they replaced urban downtowns as the American commercial center, making the suburbs much less dependent on the cities they surround.

An aerial view of Levittown, Long Island, in 1950 indicates the sprawling sameness of this postwar suburb.

FURTHER READING

Boulton, Alexander D. "The Buy of the Century." *American Heritage*, July–August 1993, 62–69.

Fishman, Robert. *Bourgeois Utopias: The Rise and Fall of Suburbia*. New York: Basic Books, 1987.

Halberstam, David. *The Fifties*. New York: Villard, 1993.

Jackson, Kenneth. *Crabgrass Frontier: The Suburbanization of the United States*. New York: Oxford University Press, 1985.

Miller, Douglas T., and Marion Nowak. *The Fifties: The Way We Really Were*. Garden City, N.Y.: Doubleday, 1977.

Polenberg, Richard. *One Nation Divisible*. New York: Penguin, 1980.

Suez crisis (1956)

First overthrowing King Farouk of Egypt, in 1952 the nationalist general Gamal Abdel Nasser took power there. President Dwight D. Eisenhower initially supported Nasser's demand for the withdrawal of British troops from the Suez Canal zone as well as his request for financial assistance to build a dam and hydroelectric plant at Aswan on the Nile River. But Nasser's neutrality in the U.S.–Soviet cold war, his recognition of the People's Republic of China, and his purchase of arms from communist Czechoslovakia infuriated Secretary of State John Foster Dulles, and the United States abruptly canceled its loan offer.

Nasser retaliated by nationalizing the Suez Canal Company to finance the dam, directly threatening the British and French with loss of control of the Suez Canal, which connects the Mediterranean Ocean with the Red Sea and was crucially important for shipping goods through the area. Then, on October 29, 1956, Israel attacked Egypt, and two days later Britain and France began bombing Egyptian military installations and landing paratroopers to retake the canal. Furious at the two allies for breaking their promise not to use force to resolve the crisis, Eisenhower approved the U.N.'s condemnation of imperialistic aggression and forced the British, French, and Israeli troops to withdraw.

At the same time, Eisenhower placed U.S. military units on worldwide alert to warn the Soviet Union that its threat to intervene on behalf of Egypt would mean war with the United States. The Soviet Union backed down, the Western alliance (although temporarily strained) survived, and the United States became the major power in the Middle East and the chief guardian of Western oil interests in the region.

SEE ALSO

Eisenhower, Dwight David; Middle East–U.S. relations

FURTHER READING

Divine, Robert. *Eisenhower and the Cold War.* New York: Oxford University Press, 1981.

Kingseed, Cole C. *Eisenhower and the Suez Crisis of 1956.* Political Traditions in Foreign Policy Series. Baton Rouge: Louisiana State University Press, 1995.

Kunz, Diane. *Economic Diplomacy of the Suez Crisis.* Chapel Hill: University of North Carolina Press, 1991.

Sun belt

During and following World War II, and especially from the 1960s to the 1990s, a mass migration of Americans and their jobs from the North and East to the southern and western regions of the country created the so-called sun belt. The tax incentives and laws hampering union organizing in the states stretching from Virginia across Texas to California made them particularly inviting for businesses wishing to relocate both their corporate headquarters and their plants.

At the same time, an attractive quality of life, enhanced by the air conditioner, led to a vast inmigration by retirees. By 1980 the population of the sun belt exceeded that of the northern and eastern regions of the country (the so-called frost belt), and the increasing political power of the sun belt played a major role in the resurgence of conservatism during the 1970s and 1980s.

FURTHER READING

Shulman, Bruce. *From Cotton Belt to Sunbelt.* New York: Oxford University Press, 1991.

Supreme Court

After a markedly liberal trend in the 1950s and 1960s, the Supreme Court has returned to a more moderately conservative stance in recent decades. Under Earl Warren, Chief Justice from 1953 to 1968, the Court outlawed racial segregation, bolstered the rights of the accused in the criminal justice system, prohibited prayer in public schools, and extended the right of free speech.

During the chief justiceship of Warren Burger (1969–86), the Supreme Court narrowed the rights of criminal defendants while ruling against almost all laws that prohibited abortion early in the pregnancy. Since 1986, when William Rehnquist became chief justice, the high court has shifted even further to the right.

The Warren Court's most momentous decision came in 1954 when it ruled unanimously in *Brown* v. *Board of Education of Topeka, Kansas,* that racial segregation in public schools was unconstitutional. This decision led to others that outlawed segregation everywhere else as well and contributed enormously to the massive civil rights movement among blacks in the South.

The Court also protected the voting rights of African Americans and struck down laws that prohibited interracial marriages. It required states to redraw their election districts, making them as equal in population as possible, establishing the principle of one person, one vote. Further, the rights of the accused were strengthened by requiring states to pay for attorneys to represent poor defendants and by requiring police to advise suspects of their constitutional rights upon arrest.

Attorneys E. C. Hayes, Thurgood Marshall, and James M. Nabrit congratulate each other after the Supreme Court ruled in Brown *v.* Board of Education *that school segregation was unconstitutional.*

Finally, the Court broadened the right of free speech. In 1957 it overturned the conviction of communist party officials under the Smith Act, emphasizing in *Yates* v. *United States* the differences between teaching general revolutionary ideology and the specific advocacy of unlawful acts. In the 1960s, moreover, it extended First Amendment protection to sexually explicit material and limited libel suits against the press.

The Warren Court became increasingly liberal as John Kennedy's two appointees, Byron White and Arthur Goldberg, and then Lyndon Johnson's two, Abe Fortas and Thurgood Marshall (the civil rights lawyer who had argued the *Brown* case), joined the Court. Conservative politicians campaigned against the Warren Court in the 1960s, and in 1968 Richard M. Nixon promised that if he were elected he would appoint justices more concerned with law and order than with individual rights.

In 1969 Nixon (who of course did win the election) appointed Warren Burger chief justice. The rest of his appointees—Harry Blackmun, Lewis Powell, and William Rehnquist—were thought not to favor liberal interpretations of the Constitution. It turned out that Nixon was right about Rehnquist, but Powell usually took a centrist position and Blackmun was considered by most to be a liberal, particularly on the issue of abortion.

The Burger Court pleased conservatives by validating increased powers for police and greater latitude for community efforts to control pornography, as well as by agreeing to limits on the right of a defendant to appeal state convictions to the federal judiciary. However, it ruled liberally in favor of the use of forced busing to achieve racial balance in schools, in overturning existing capital punishment statutes, and in striking down laws forbidding abortions. In 1981 President Ronald Reagan nominated Sandra Day O'Connor as the first woman justice on the Supreme Court; in 1986 he elevated Rehnquist to chief justice and replaced the retiring Burger with Antonin Scalia, and in 1988 he named Anthony Kennedy to the Court.

President George H. Bush further blunted the social-activist thrust of the Supreme Court with his appointments of David Souter in 1990 and Clarence Thomas in 1991. Nominated to replace the retiring Marshall, Thomas, a conservative African American, was accused during his confirmation hearings of sexual harassment of a former associate, Anita Hill, and only narrowly won Senate confirmation, by a vote of 52 to 48.

With a new conservative majority, the Rehnquist Court chipped away at the liberal gains made under the leadership of Warren and Burger without wholly repudiating them. Its decisions limited but did not reverse women's rights to abortion, restricted affirmative action remedies, further narrowed the rights of people who have been arrested, and struck down legislative districts whose geographic borders had been drawn to create African-American majority voting districts.

A more moderate, divided court emerged with the appointments by President Bill Clinton of Ruth Bader Ginsburg in 1993 and Stephen Breyer in 1994; neither David Souter nor Sandra Day O'Connor have proven to be entirely reliable votes for the conservatives either.

SEE ALSO

Baker v. *Carr* (1962); *Bakke* v. *Board of Regents of California* (1978); *Brown* v. *Board of Education of Topeka, Kansas* (1954); Burger, Warren; *Engel* v. *Vitale* (1962); Ginsburg, Ruth Bader; Marshall, Thurgood; *Milliken* v. *Bradley* (1974); *Miranda* v. *Arizona* (1966); *New York Times* v. *Sullivan* (1964); O'Connor, Sandra Day; *Roe* v. *Wade* (1973); *Swann* v. *Charlotte–Mecklenburg Board of Education* (1971); *United States* v. *Richard M. Nixon* (1974); Warren, Earl

FURTHER READING

Hall, Kermit L. *The Oxford Companion to the Supreme Court of the United States*. New York: Oxford University Press, 1992.

Lindop, Edmund. *The Changing Supreme Court*. Danbury, Conn.: Franklin Watts, 1995.

Patrick, John J. *Young Oxford Companion to the Supreme Court of the United States*. New York: Oxford University Press, 1998.

Rosenberg, Gerald. *The Hollow Hope: Can Courts Bring About Social Change?* Chicago: University of Chicago Press, 1990.

Schwartz, Bernard. *Super Chief: Earl Warren and His Supreme Court*. New York: New York University Press, 1983.

Simon, James. *The Center Holds: The Power Struggle Inside the Rehnquist Court*. New York: Simon & Schuster, 1995.

Urofsky, Melvin. *A Conflict of Rights: The Supreme Court and Affirmative Action*. New York: Scribners, 1991.

Swann v. *Charlotte–Mecklenburg Board of Education* (1971)

Following its ruling in *Alexander* v. *Holmes County Board of Education* (1969), which ordered an immediate end to segregated dual school systems, the Supreme Court in its 1971 *Swann* decision permitted busing as a remedy for fashioning interracial schools in districts that had practiced segregation by law.

James Swann, a black man, had sued to force the Charlotte–Mecklenburg, North Carolina, school board to bus black students into white schools and vice versa. The district court ruled against the school board, which then appealed the decision all the way to the Supreme Court. The Court sided unanimously with the local court.

President Richard M. Nixon denounced the decision in a televised address and asked Congress to place a moratorium on busing. His proposal failed, and the *Swann* decision led to the widespread use of busing in the South to achieve integration in education. By the mid-1970s, 47 percent of the African-American students in the South were attending schools with a white majority, a higher percentage than in the North.

SEE ALSO

Brown v. *Board of Education of Topeka, Kansas* (1954); Burger, Warren; Supreme Court

FURTHER READING

Gaillard, Frye. *The Dream Long Deferred.* Chapel Hill: University of North Carolina Press, 1988.

Wilkinson, J. Harvie. *From Brown to Bakke: The Supreme Court and School Integration, 1954–1978.* New York: Oxford University Press, 1979.

Taft-Hartley Act (1947)

Referred to as the "slave labor law" by labor union officials, the Taft-Hartley bill was cosponsored by Senator Robert A. Taft of Ohio and Representative Fred Hartley, Jr., of New Jersey, both Republicans. Enacted by Congress in June 1947, then passed over President Harry S. Truman's veto, the Taft-Hartley Act was designed to roll back the gains made by organized labor during the 1930s.

The Taft-Hartley Act outlawed the closed shop (companies that would hire only union members), jurisdictional strikes (in which rival unions contended for organizing rights in a given plant or industry), and the secondary boycott (in which a union striking one company persuades other unions to strike companies doing business with the initial company), and it allowed states to pass right-to-work laws prohibiting union shops (where workers must join a union after being hired).

A tie calling for the repeal of the Taft-Hartley Act shows a worker in chains. The act reversed some of the gains made earlier in the decade by organized labor.

Taft-Hartley also required officers of national unions to file affidavits that they were neither members of nor sympathizers with communist groups. Reviving the use of injunctions to end strikes, Taft-Hartley gave the President the authority in cases of national emergency to seek a court injunction to call off strikes for up to 80 days while labor and management tried to negotiate a settlement.

Although Taft-Hartley did not threaten most existing large unions, it made unionizing new industries much more difficult. This reflected the anti-union sentiment in the country following the labor unrest at the end of World War II (there were more than 5,000 strikes in 1946 alone).

The identification of the Republican party with Taft-Hartley and then Truman's veto of it brought organized labor back into the Democratic fold and helped tilt the balance in the 1948 Presidential election to Truman.

SEE ALSO

Taft, Robert A.; Truman, Harry S.

FURTHER READING

Hartmann, Susan. *Truman and the Eightieth Congress.* Columbia: University of Missouri Press, 1971.

Patterson, James T. *Mr. Republican: A Biography of Robert A. Taft.* Boston: Houghton Mifflin, 1972.

Taft, Robert A.

- *Born: Sept. 8, 1889, Cincinnati, Ohio*
- *Accomplishments: U.S. senator (Republican–Ohio), 1938–53*
- *Died: July 31, 1953, New York, N.Y.*

A voice for isolationism in a period of great interventionism in foreign affairs, Senator Robert A. Taft stood alone in fighting against many of the most popular policies of the cold war. While favoring Soviet containment, Taft believed that many of President Harry S. Truman's policies were too costly and dangerous for U.S. security. Taft opposed the Marshall Plan to appropriate U.S. aid for European economic recovery and believed that the North Atlantic Treaty Organization (NATO) would spark an arms race between the United States and the Soviet Union. He disapproved of most U.S. involvements outside the Western Hemisphere as unnecessary.

On the domestic front, Taft was a principal opponent of most Fair Deal measures of the Truman administration and played a key role in dashing liberal hopes for a postwar expansion of reforms. Best known for cosponsoring the Taft-Hartley Act (1947), which curbed the power of labor unions, Taft sought the Republican Presidential nomination three times—in 1940, 1948, and 1952—but lost each time.

SEE ALSO

Taft-Hartley Act (1947); Truman, Harry S.

FURTHER READING

Kirk, Russell, and James McClellan. *The Political Principles of Robert A. Taft.* New York: Fleet Press, 1967.

Patterson, James T. *Mr. Republican: A Biography of Robert A. Taft.* Boston: Houghton Mifflin, 1972.

Television

Experiments with television technology began in the 1920s, but television was not introduced to the public until 1946, when the Federal Communications Commission licensed 26 television stations to serve the public. It was an almost instant success. The number of American households with a television set increased from 940,000 in 1949 to more than 20 million in 1953 and more than 40 million by 1959. (By the early 1960s, 90 percent of all homes had at least one TV.) Comedy was king in TV's early days as America tuned in to Uncle Miltie Berle, Sid Caesar, and Red Skelton.

Mimicking the infrastructure already set up for radio, television programming quickly became sponsored and influenced by advertising. Television was a part of the consumer culture of the 1950s and corporations took advantage of this new medium to convince Americans that they needed all sorts of products.

In the main, television provided entertainment, not intellectual enlightenment. Soap operas dominated the daytime airwaves, and while children watched *Howdy Doody Time* or dreamed of becoming a Mouseketeer, their parents focused on *Dragnet* and *I Love Lucy*. In the 1950s, family-oriented sitcoms prevailed. Programs such as *Leave It to Beaver* idealized white middle-class culture. There was little diversity in television programming until the 1970s, when programs about black families, such as *The Jeffersons,* began to appear. At the same time, television made sports an increasingly important part of popular culture. As it did so, it elevated African-American and Hispanic players to unprecedented fame. TV also turned sports into big business; the negotiations between professional sports leagues and the networks, and the signing of multimillion-dollar contracts by star athletes, became major events. Indeed, wealth and escapism were the hallmarks of the most popular TV shows in the 1980s, such as the prime-time soap opera *Dallas* and *Lifestyles of the Rich and Famous.*

Television also brought world events much closer to the average American. Events such as the assassination of John F. Kennedy and the Vietnam War were brought into the living rooms of Americans, intensifying the impact of such events. In 1991, however, the all-news CNN (Cable News Network) broadcast of Operation Desert Storm against Iraq made the war appear less destructive and harrowing. To the millions of Americans watching, the scenes of U.S. Patriot missiles destroying Scud missiles launched by Iraq resembled video games in countless shopping-mall arcades.

During the 1960 Presidential election, Richard Nixon and John Kennedy debated on TV. Nixon lost the election, in part, because he seemed less comfortable on television and was less photogenic; therefore viewers considered him to have lost the debate.

Television allowed the airing of political wrongdoings, such as the McCarthy hearings in the 1950s and the Iran-Contra hearings in the 1980s, but tended to shortchange reasoned discussions of the issues. Used primarily as a simplifying and sensationalizing medium, television seemed to "keep it simple, stupid." Visceral, uncomplicated images, rather than more serious or abstract ideas, have dominated the television screen. Accordingly, the media consultants of politicians devised brief "sound bites" that played well on the evening news, and television reporters emphasized the "game" of politics rather than substantive issues.

In the 1990s television once again came under scrutiny for its supposed encouragement of violence and its obsessions with self-gratification, consumerism, and vicarious sex. Although research on the effects of violence and sex on television remained controversial, it became a popular political issue, and the major networks—ABC, CBS, Fox, and NBC—agreed to implement a voluntary rating system to prevent federal regulation. At the same time, the rise of cable TV in the 1990s halved the networks' share of the audience. Increasing numbers of viewers watched channels specializing in just religion, or business, or black interests, and so on, further isolating and segmenting Americans from each other and diminishing the possibility of a common public discourse or sense of community.

FURTHER READING

Allen, Robert C. *Channels of Discourse: Television and Contemporary Criticism.* Chapel Hill: University of North Carolina Press, 1987.
Arlen, Michael. *Living Room War.* New York: Penguin, 1982.
Barnouw, Eric. *Tube of Plenty.* New York: Oxford University Press, 1990.
Ewen, Stuart, and Elizabeth Ewen. *Channels of Desire: Mass Images and the Shaping of American Consciousness.* 2d ed., Minneapolis: University of Minnesota Press, 1992.
Postman, Neil. *Amusing Ourselves to Death.* New York: Viking, 1985.
Spigel, Lynn. *Make Room for TV: Television and the Family Ideal in Postwar America.* Chicago: University of Chicago Press, 1992.

Teller, Edward

- *Born: Jan. 15, 1908, Budapest, Austria-Hungary*
- *Accomplishments: Scientist*

Born in Hungary, Edward Teller was a precocious young boy who often requested that his family not talk at the dinner table because he was working on a mathematical formula in his head. He came to the United States in 1935 at the age of 26.

One of the world's greatest physicists, Teller worked with Robert Oppenheimer on the Manhattan Project's secret development of atomic bombs for the U.S. government. Teller, however, was more interested in developing a hydrogen, or fusion, bomb, despite the opposition of Oppenheimer and other scientists who feared the strength of such a weapon. However, when the Soviet Union successfully exploded an atomic bomb in 1949, President Harry S. Truman launched a race for a hydrogen bomb, with Teller leading the project.

The so-called father of the H-bomb, Teller would later propose a space-based defensive shield to destroy incoming missiles. President Ronald Reagan championed this idea in his Strategic Defense Initiative, nicknamed "Star Wars" by the media.

SEE ALSO

Atomic bomb; Hydrogen bomb

FURTHER READING

Teller, Edward, Wendy Teller, and Wilson Talley. *Conversations on the Dark Secrets of Physics.* New York: Plenum, 1991.

Terrorism

Despite the easing of cold war tensions in the mid-1980s, danger still threatened, primarily in the form of terrorism—acts committed by relatively weak groups who could not compel the more powerful to heed their demands by using political power or more conventional military methods. The 1983 bombing of the U.S. Marine barracks in Beirut, Lebanon, by Islamic terrorists ignited a firestorm of killings and hijackings by shadowy groups linked to the Palestine Liberation Organization (PLO), to Iran's Hezbollah (Party of God), and to Libyan ruler Mummar el-Qaddafi, primarily directed against Israel and its allies. In 1985, Palestinian terrorists hijacked a TWA flight over Greece and held 135 passengers captive for 17 days. Later that year, Palestinians seized an Italian cruise ship and murdered an elderly, wheelchair-bound Jewish-American man. In 1986, a

Berlin discotheque frequented mainly by American servicemen was blown up, and in 1988 a Pan Am jet exploded over Scotland, killing all 259 aboard, including many American students. Both events were attributed to Libyans. At the same time, dozens of Americans and Europeans were kidnapped and held hostage in the Middle East, particularly in Lebanon, then a hotbed of Palestinian militancy.

In February 1993 horror struck in the United States when terrorists planted a massive bomb in a parking garage under the twin towers of New York's World Trade Center. The explosion killed six people and injured scores of others. Ultimately, followers of a militantly anti-Israeli sheik were arrested by the FBI, tried, and convicted. Still, terrorism continued, and the fears it engendered persisted. Fanatical opponents of abortion murdered doctors who performed abortions and firebombed the clinics in which abortions were performed. Citizens' militias sprouted, especially in the Rocky Mountain states. Primarily composed of working-class whites, the militias felt threatened by social movements that promoted such causes as feminism, minority rights, gay rights, and environmentalism, and were disenchanted with a federal government that seemed hostile to their interests. They used violence to defend their generally authoritarian and racist way of life from a sinister global conspiracy that supposedly controlled the U.S. government, sometimes engaging in gun fights with federal officials. Terrorists who held similar beliefs bombed the Oklahoma City federal building in 1995, killing 169 people. Their vague motive and formless anger was best expressed by a character in the popular 1976 film *Network,* who yelled, "We're mad as hell and we're not going to take it anymore."

FURTHER READING

Cormier, Robert. *After the First Death.* New York: Bantam Doubleday, 1991.

Gaines, Ann. *Terrorism.* Broomall, Pa.: Chelsea House, 1998.

Tanter, Raymond. *Rogue Regimes: Terrorism and Proliferation.* New York: St. Martin's, 1999.

Tet offensive

SEE Vietnam War

Three Mile Island nuclear accident

The first major U.S. nuclear scare occurred when a valve malfunctioned and led to a leak of radioactive steam in the Unit 2 reactor at the Three Mile Island nuclear plant, near Harrisburg, Pennsylvania, on March 28, 1979. By

One of the reactors at the Three Mile Island nuclear plant malfunctioned in 1979, sparking fears of a major nuclear catastrophe.

March 30, some 133,000 people had fled the surrounding towns and Governor Richard Thornburgh recommended that all pregnant women and preschool children within a five-mile radius be evacuated.

The reactor was deemed stabilized by April 1, but the incident, coming at the same time that a Hollywood film, *The China Syndrome,* portrayed the possibility of a "meltdown" at a nuclear plant, furthered fears of nuclear energy and strengthened support for the antinuclear movement. An even greater awareness of the potential dangers of nuclear power followed the much more serious disaster at the Soviet plant in Chernobyl in April 1986.

SEE ALSO

Antinuclear movement

FURTHER READING

Bolch, Ben, and Harold Lyon. *Apocalypse Not: Science, Economics, and Environmentalism.* Washington, D.C.: Cato Institute, 1993.

Bramwell, Anna. *Ecology in the Twentieth Century: A History.* New Haven, Conn.: Yale University Press, 1989.

Warshal, Peter. "Three Mile Island Revisited." *Whole Earth Review* (Winter 1995): 46.

Thurmond, J. Strom

- *Born: Dec. 5, 1902, Edgeville, S.C.*
- *Accomplishments: Governor of South Carolina (Democrat), 1947–51; U.S. senator (Democrat–S.C.), 1954–*

Governor Strom Thurmond of South Carolina ran for President in 1948 for the States' Rights, or Dixiecrat, party. The Dixiecrats hoped to win 100 electoral votes in the election to reassert their control of the Democratic party, fight the civil rights movement, and protect "the southern way of life." It failed to do so, garnering just 39 electoral votes, but even that made Democrats fear sponsoring civil rights legislation for another decade.

Thurmond served as the chair of the powerful Senate Judiciary Committee from 1981 to 1987. Reelected to the Senate in 1996, when he was 94 years old, Thurmond was the oldest member of Congress.

SEE ALSO

States' Rights Democratic party (Dixiecrats)

FURTHER READING

Cohodas, Nadine. *Strom Thurmond and the Politics of Southern Change.* New York: Simon & Schuster, 1993.

Lachiotte, Alberta. *Rebel Senator: Strom Thurmond from South Carolina.* New York: Devin-Adair, 1967.

Truman Doctrine

In 1946, the Soviets pressured Turkey to ally itself with the Soviet Union in that nation's struggle for power with the United States. At the same time, the Soviets were aiding guerrillas who were waging a war against the government in Greece.

President Harry S. Truman believed that the United States had to act to stop this expansion of Soviet power. To do so, he stated on March 12, 1947, that it would be up to the United States to support free peoples everywhere who were "resisting attempted subjugation by armed minorities or by outside pressures." Truman later wrote that this "served notice that the march of Communism would not be allowed to succeed by default." Known as the Truman Doctrine, this statement essentially committed the United States to the role of global policeman and was the cornerstone of U.S. cold war foreign policy for the next four decades.

SEE ALSO

Cold war; Containment doctrine; Korean War; Middle East–U.S. relations

FURTHER READING

Gardner, Lloyd C. *Architects of Illusion: Men and Ideas in American Foreign Policy, 1941–1949*. Chicago: Quadrangle, 1970.

Jones, Howard. *"A New Kind of War": America's Global Strategy and the Truman Doctrine in Greece*. New York: Oxford University Press, 1989.

Maddox, Robert J. *From War to Cold War: The Education of Harry S. Truman*. Boulder, Colo.: Westview, 1988.

Truman, Harry S.

- *Born: May 8, 1884, Lamar, Mo.*
- *Accomplishments: U.S. senator (Democrat–Mo.), 1935–45; 33rd President of the United States, 1945–53*
- *Died: Dec. 26, 1972, Kansas City, Mo.*

The first President to enter office while the country was at war, Harry S. Truman became President when Franklin Delano Roosevelt died on April 12, 1945, one month before Germany's surrender to the Allies and just 82 days after Truman began his Vice Presidency.

With little experience in foreign affairs, Truman immediately faced major issues. In July 1945, he met with Soviet leader Joseph Stalin at the Potsdam Conference to discuss the status of Germany at the end of the war. Neither man trusted the other and little progress was made.

While in Potsdam, Truman authorized the use of atomic bombs against Japan, in order, he claimed, to save the lives of tens of thousands of U.S. troops who would have died in an invasion of that empire. The first bomb fell on Hiroshima on August 6, 1945, and the second on Nagasaki three days later. World War II ended with Japan's unconditional surrender on August 14, 1945.

President Harry Truman explains his 1954 budget to reporters at a press conference.

The end of World War II did not end Truman's problems with foreign policy, however. In September 1945 he abruptly terminated the wartime shipment of arms and supplies to the Soviet Union, straining already poor East–West relations. In early 1947, facing a communist uprising in strategically important Greece and Soviet threats against Turkey, Truman responded by assuring the world that the United States would support any free nation "resisting attempted subjugation by armed minorities or by outside pressures."

This statement, called the Truman Doctrine, placed the United States in the role of global policeman. The Marshall Plan, which was also enacted in 1947, assisted Western European nations in their economic recovery from the devastation of the war. The United States hoped that economically strong nations would be less likely to fall to communist uprisings. In 1949 the North Atlantic Treaty Organization (NATO), the nation's first peacetime military pact, was signed by the United States, Canada, and Western European nations to strengthen militarily the alliance of European and American democracies against the communist nations aligned with the Soviet Union.

Truman's domestic program, the Fair Deal, was, he said, a continuation of Franklin Roosevelt's New Deal with "differences, not of principle but of pace and personnel." It called for a rise in the minimum wage, farm aid, broader unemployment insurance, and federal housing assistance. But facing strong opposition from conservative southern Democrats allied with Republicans, the Employment Act of 1946 became the only major item of the Fair Deal to be enacted by Congress in Truman's first term.

Truman was more successful on the civil rights front. In 1948 he ordered the desegregation of the armed forces and schools financed by the federal government, and he urged the Justice Department to pursue and support civil rights cases more vigorously. Truman's civil rights proposals to Congress, the first since Reconstruction, lost him much support in the South and divided the Democratic party.

Truman's popularity wavered throughout the rest of the nation as well. He had the impossible task of filling the shoes of one of the most charismatic and popular Presidents ever, Franklin D. Roosevelt, and Truman's more folksy style, emphasizing his common-man roots, made him appear a less forceful leader than Roosevelt. The postwar economic troubles facing the nation also caused problems. By trying to end the massive waves of strikes across the country, involving more than 4.5 million workers in 1946, Truman lost the support of labor, and by trying to control prices he angered businesses as well. Truman was able to regain labor support only by vetoing the Taft-Hartley Act, which sought to restrict labor union activity, in 1947. Congress, however, overrode his veto and the bill became law.

By the end of Truman's first term, it seemed unlikely that he would be reelected. There were four major candidates in the 1948 election: Truman ran as the Democratic candidate, Thomas E. Dewey as the Republican one, Henry Wallace as the Progressive party nominee, and Strom Thurmond ran as the States' Rights party, or Dixiecrat, candidate. Truman's "give 'em hell" attitude appealed to Americans as he campaigned across the nation. The race was so close that some newspapers erroneously reported Dewey's victory, but with 49.5 percent of the popular vote Truman was elected to a second term.

Truman's domestic program was only slightly more successful in his second term than in his first. He was able to push both increases to Social Security and the National Housing Act of 1949, which provided low-cost housing, through Congress. The rest of his Fair Deal program died in Congress.

International affairs were not much better for Truman in his second term than in his first. In 1949, China's Nationalist party gave up the fight against the communist forces led by Mao Zedong and retreated to the island of Taiwan. Truman was blamed for "losing China" to the communists.

That same year, the Soviet Union tested its first atomic weapon, leading many Americans to believe that U.S. atomic secrets had been leaked to the Soviets. The second Red scare (a color associated with communists; the first Red scare had occurred just after World War I) heated up with the trials of Alger Hiss and Ethel and Julius Rosenberg. Fear that the government had been infiltrated by communists spread through the nation.

Senator Joseph McCarthy picked up on this fear and made himself a name with it. He charged, without substantiation, that many government agencies, including the State Department, were filled with communists and communist sympathizers. Truman and the Democratic party were quickly labeled as "soft on communism."

Truman's quick response to the communist invasion of South Korea in 1951 did little to help him politically. By 1952 the war was at a stalemate. Truman then fired Douglas MacArthur, who had led the U.S. and allied forces in Korea, for insubordination after the popular general publicly advocated all-out war with the communist People's Republic of China. Truman's decision did not sit well with the American people, who wanted the hostilities in Korea ended quickly and the soldiers returned home. Truman announced in March 1952 that he would not seek reelection.

Truman remained active in politics for the rest of his life, writing his memoirs and speaking out on the issues of the day. Although he was rarely very popular during his years in the White House and was often seen as undignified and erratic, most historians now contrast his blunt frankness favorably against the contrived deviousness of many of his successors and rate him as one of the strongest, most decisive postwar Presidents.

SEE ALSO

Employment Act of 1946; Fair Deal; McCarthyism; National Housing Act of 1949; Rosenberg case

FURTHER READING

Ferrell, Robert H. *Harry S. Truman: A Life.* Columbia: University of Missouri Press, 1994.

Ferrell, Robert H. *Harry S. Truman and the Modern American Presidency.* New York: HarperCollins, 1995.

Hamby, Alonzo L. *Man of the People: A Life of Harry S. Truman.* New York: Oxford University Press, 1995.

Leavell, Perry. *Harry S. Truman.* New York: Chelsea House, 1988.

McCullough, David. *Truman.* New York: Simon & Schuster, 1992.

Truman, Harry S. *The Autobiography of Harry S. Truman.* Edited by Robert H. Ferrell. Boulder: Colorado Associated University Press, 1980.

25th Amendment

On February 10, 1967, the 25th Amendment to the Constitution of the United States was ratified. Written to address issues of Presidential succession, it states that in the event of the "removal of the President from office or of his death or resignation, the Vice President shall become President."

In addition, if the President becomes "unable to discharge the powers and duties of his office," the Vice President becomes Acting President. Finally, it mandates that if the office of the Vice President becomes vacant, the President is to nominate a Vice President, who must then be confirmed by a majority vote of both houses of Congress. This procedure was used in 1973 after Vice President Spiro Agnew resigned and was replaced by Gerald Ford. It was also used after President Richard Nixon's resignation, when President Ford nominated Nelson Rockefeller to replace himself as Vice President.

SEE ALSO

Ford, Gerald Rudolph; Nixon, Richard Milhous

FURTHER READING

Abrams, Herbert L. *"The President Has Been Shot": Confusion, Disability, and the 25th Amendment.* Stanford, Calif.: Stanford University Press, 1994.

Feerick, John D. *The Twenty-Fifth Amendment: Its Complete History and Applications.* Bronx, N.Y.: Fordham University Press, 1992.

Gilbert, Robert E. *The Mortal Presidency.* New York: Basic Books, 1992.

A U-2 reconnaissance plane like this one went down inside the Soviet Union during a spying mission in 1960.

U-2 crisis

On May 1, 1960, a U-2 high-altitude U.S. reconnaissance plane went down about 1,300 miles inside the Soviet Union. U.S. officials quickly told the public that it was a weather plane that had flown off course, but Dwight Eisenhower's administration was caught in an embarrassing lie when the Soviets produced the American pilot, Francis Gary Powers, who confessed to espionage.

President Eisenhower, who was in Paris for a summit conference with the Soviet premier, Nikita Khrushchev, took full responsibility but refused to apologize for the flights. An infuriated Khrushchev prematurely ended the summit conference and withdrew an invitation to Eisenhower to visit the Soviet Union. In 1962 Powers was returned to the United States in exchange for a Soviet spy.

SEE ALSO

Cold war

FURTHER READING

Brune, Lester H. *The Missile Crisis of October 1962: A Review of Issues and References.* Claremont, Calif.: Regina Books, 1985.

Beschloss, Michael R. *Mayday: Eisenhower, Khrushchev, and the U-2 Affair.* New York: Harper & Row, 1986.

Powers, Francis Gary. *Operation Overflight: The U-2 Spy Pilot Tells His Story for the First Time.* New York: Holt, Rinehart and Winston, 1970.

United States Senate Committee on Armed Services. *Francis Gary Powers: Hearing before the Committee on Armed Services.* Washington, D.C.: U.S. Government Printing Office, 1962.

United Automobile Workers (UAW)

In the years immediately following World War II, Walter Reuther led the United Auto Workers (UAW) in securing landmark contracts from the United States's largest car companies. In 1948 General Motors agreed to automatic wage increases whenever production was boosted or the cost of living rose. In 1953 the Ford Motor Company agreed to supplement government unemployment benefits for its own workers by paying laid-off employees two-thirds of their regular earnings. The UAW, moreover, attempted to push U.S. politics toward a more genuine social democracy, fighting for full employment and civil rights.

The United Automobile Workers adopted this logo in 1959.

As president of the Congress of Industrial Organizations (CIO) from 1952 to 1955, the UAW's Reuther fought strenuously to rid unions of corruption and communism and was instrumental in merging that organization with the American Federation of Labor (AFL) in 1955. Because of disagreements with the more conservative George Meany, president of the new AFL-CIO, especially over the war in Vietnam and President Lyndon B. Johnson's War on Poverty program, Reuther took the UAW out of that organization in 1968 and the following year joined forces with the International Brotherhood of Teamsters in the Alliance for Labor Action.

Reuther died in an airplane crash on May 9, 1970, and his successors as president of the UAW—Leslie Woodcock, Douglas Fraser, and Owen Bieber—each tried and failed to halt the loss of power experienced by unions during the more conservative swing in politics from the 1970s through the 1990s.

SEE ALSO

Labor movement

FURTHER READING

Barnard, John. *Walter Reuther and the Rise of the Auto Workers.* Boston: Little, Brown, 1983.

Boyle, Kevin. *The UAW and the Heyday of American Liberalism, 1945–1968.* Ithaca, N.Y.: Cornell University Press, 1995.

Lichtenstein, Nelson. *The Most Dangerous Man in Detroit: Walter Reuther and the Fate of American Labor.* New York: Basic Books, 1996.

United Farm Workers of America (UFW)

Founded in 1961 by Cesar Chavez, a Mexican American from California, the United Farm Workers of America (UFW) organized a strike against California grape growers from 1965 to 1970 in order to gain both recognition of its union and increased wages and benefits for its members. When traditional picketing by farm laborers proved unsuccessful, Chavez and the UFW followed the nonviolent model of Martin Luther King, Jr., and organized mass rallies and marches to promote a public boycott of grapes picked by nonunion workers (Chavez himself also fasted in protest).

By framing the strike as part of the larger struggle for civil rights, the UFW was successful in publicizing the poor working and living conditions faced by farm laborers. As a result, the union rallied sufficient national consumer support for the boycott to force the grape growers to the bargaining table.

Later, the UFW organized a tougher strike against lettuce growers and successfully promoted voter registration and the passage of laws to protect migrants' rights. In addition to improved working conditions, the UFW did much to enhance ethnic consciousness among Mexican Americans.

Two buttons from the UFW's crusades to secure better working conditions and wages for migrant workers. The button at left refers to a grape strike in Delano, a town north of Los Angeles; the button above says in Spanish, "Yes, you can!"

SEE ALSO

Chavez, Cesar; Civil rights movement; Hispanic Americans; Labor movement

FURTHER READING

Ferriss, Susan, and Ricardo Sandoval. *The Fight in the Fields: Cesar Chavez and the Farmworkers Movement.* Edited by Diana Hembree. Orlando, Fla.: Harcourt Brace, 1997.

Garcia, Mario. *Mexican Americans: Leadership, Ideology, and Identity.* New Haven, Conn.: Yale University Press, 1989.

Mooney, Patrick H., and Theo J. Majka. *Farmers and Farm Workers' Movements: Social Protest in American Agriculture.* Twayne's Social Movements Past and Present Series. Old Tappan, N.J.: Macmillan, 1995.

Rodriguez, Consuelo, and Ruperto Garcia. *Cesar Chavez.* Hispanics of Achievement Series. Broomall, Pa.: Chelsea House, 1991.

United Nations

The United Nations was formally organized on June 26, 1945, at a conference in San Francisco, where its basic charter was drafted. Like the earlier failed League of Nations, the United Nations sought to promote international peace and security.

The main organ of the United Nations is the General Assembly, at which every member nation is represented. The Security Council, which has primary responsibility for the maintenance of international peace and security, includes six member nations elected for two-year terms and five permanent members (the United States, Russia, China, France, and Britain) each of which has veto power on any matter of substance.

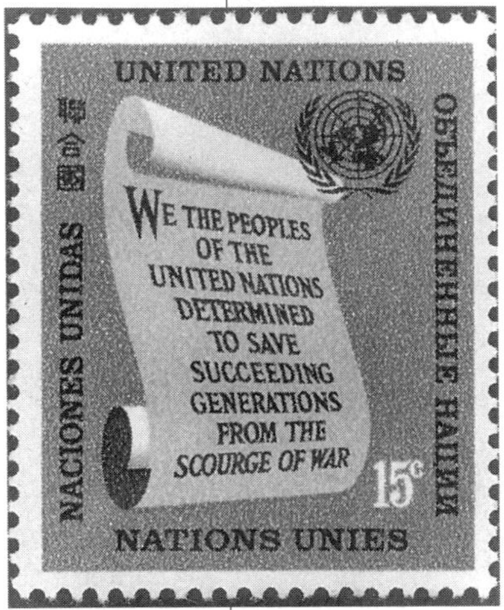

This UN stamp bears the opening lines of the UN charter.

In 1949 the United Nations moved into its permanent headquarters in New York City. Among its major actions since then, the Security Council voted to defend South Korea, in 1950; to condemn the Iraqi invasion of Kuwait and to permit the use of force against Iraq if it did not withdraw, in 1990; to halt the bloodshed in Bosnia and Somalia with U.N. peacekeeping troops, in 1991 and 1993; and to mediate an agreement between Salvadoran rebels and their government to end a civil war, in 1992. The U.N. has also played a peacekeeping role in the Middle East and helped to end civil wars in Mozambique and Guatemala. During the Balkan crisis in 1999, the U.N. resisted pressure from the United States to send ground troops into Kosovo to force an end to the civil war, but did endorse air raids on the Yugoslavian capital of Belgrade.

The U.N., which is a huge organization, has a number of smaller organizations that focus on specific goals. Among the best-known of these smaller groups are the U.N. Children's Fund, better known as UNICEF, which is devoted to promoting the long-term survival, protection, and development of children; UNESCO, the United Nations educational, scientific, and cultural organization, which promotes education for all, cultural development around the world, protection of the world's natural and cultural heritage, international cooperation in science, and freedom of the press and of communication; and WHO, the World Health Organization, which tries to solve health problems around the world.

U.S. opponents of the U.N., nevertheless, criticize it as being too expensive and inefficient and as an infringement on U.S. sovereignty.

SEE ALSO

Korean War; Persian Gulf War

FURTHER READING

Carpenter, Ted Galen. *Delusions of Grandeur: The United Nations and Global Intervention.* Washington, D.C.: Cato Institute, 1997.

Forsythe, David P., Roger A. Coate, and Thomas George Weiss. *The United Nations and Changing World Politics.* Boulder, Colo.: Westview, 1997.

Patterson, Charles. *The Oxford Fiftieth Anniversary Book of the United Nations.* New York: Oxford University Press, 1995.

United Nations. *Basic Facts About the United Nations.* New York: United Nations, 1996.

United States Civil Rights Commission

The U.S. Civil Rights Commission was established by the Civil Rights Act of 1957 to collect information on civil rights and report its findings to Congress and the President. The six-member bipartisan commission was charged with studying any failure to provide equal protection under the Constitution. Although it was initially scheduled to disband after two years, the commission's life has been repeatedly extended by subsequent Congresses. In 1983 a new commission was established under that year's new Civil Rights Act. The new commission's reports have focused mainly on issues of civil rights and equal opportunities in education.

SEE ALSO

Civil rights movement

FURTHER READING

Davidson, Scott. *The Inter-American Human Rights System.* Brookfield, Vt.: Dartmouth Publishing Co., 1997.

Dulles, Foster Rhea. *The Civil Rights Commission, 1957–1965.* East Lansing: Michigan State University Press, 1968.

Walton, Hanes. *When the Marching Stopped: The Politics of Civil Rights Regulatory Agencies.* Albany: State University of New York Press, 1988.

United States v. *Richard M. Nixon* (1974)

In late July 1974 the Supreme Court, in *United States* v. *Richard M. Nixon,* rebuffed President Nixon's claim to executive privilege. Citing the President's obligation to provide evidence necessary for the due process of law, a unanimous Court ordered Nixon to turn over tapes of White House conversations to a special prosecutor and the House Judiciary Committee as part of the Watergate investigation.

The tapes were crucial to this investigation of a 1972 break-in at Democratic party campaign headquarters at the Watergate apartment and office complex in Washington, D.C.

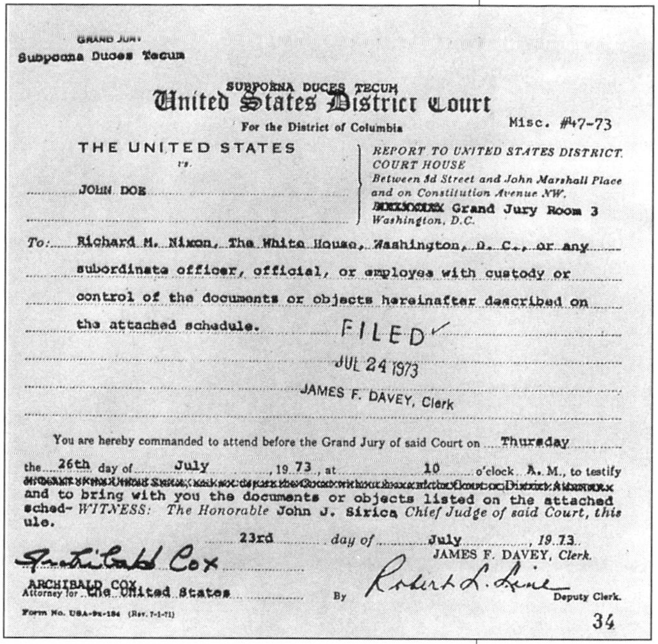

GRAND JURY
Subpoena Duces Tecum

SUBPOENA DUCES TECUM
United States District Court
For the District of Columbia

Misc. #47-73

THE UNITED STATES
vs.
JOHN DOE

REPORT TO UNITED STATES DISTRICT COURT HOUSE
Between 3d Street and John Marshall Place and on Constitution Avenue NW.
[illegible] Grand Jury Room 3
Washington, D.C.

To: Richard M. Nixon, The White House, Washington, D. C., or any subordinate officer, official, or employee with custody or control of the documents or objects hereinafter described on the attached schedule.

FILED
JUL 24 1973
JAMES F. DAVEY, Clerk

You are hereby commanded to attend before the Grand Jury of said Court on Thursday the 26th day of July, 19 73, at 10 o'clock A. M., to testify [illegible] and to bring with you the documents or objects listed on the attached schedule.

WITNESS: The Honorable John J. Sirica Chief Judge of said Court, this 23rd day of July, 19 73.

JAMES F. DAVEY, Clerk.

Archibald Cox
ARCHIBALD COX
Attorney for the United States

By Robert L. [illegible]
Deputy Clerk.

Form No. USA-9x-184 (Rev. 7-1-71)

34

This subpoena commands President Richard Nixon to supply tapes of his White House conversations to the grand jury investigating the Watergate scandal. The Supreme Court refuted Nixon's claim that he did not have to provide the tapes because of executive privilege.

The burglars had connections to the Nixon administration. The tapes contained evidence that linked Nixon to a conspiracy to obstruct justice by covering up the scandal, and he resigned within three weeks of their release.

This decision established the limits of Presidential immunity, that is, how much the President can be beyond reach of the laws that are applied to ordinary citizens.

SEE ALSO

Nixon, Richard Milhous; Watergate

Vance, Cyrus

- *Born: Mar. 27, 1917, Clarksburg, W. Va.*
- *Accomplishments: Secretary of U.S. Army, 1962–64; Deputy Secretary of Defense, 1964–67; U.S. Secretary of State, 1977–80*

Secretary of State for President Jimmy Carter, Cyrus Vance advocated the protection of human rights abroad, but he was attacked by critics who felt that

Carter's administration was inconsistent in applying that standard. Attacks also came from critics who feared that it sacrificed U.S. national interests to vague moralizing.

Carter's national security advisor, Zbigniew Brzezinski (who was the first national security advisor to hold cabinet rank), particularly scorned Vance's human-rights emphasis and his desire to extend détente, the lessening of international tensions. Vance won out over his rival in negotiating the treaties to give control of the Panama Canal to the government of Panama and in concluding a peace agreement between Israel and Egypt, but Brzezinski trumped the secretary of state in convincing Carter to shelve the Strategic Arms Limitation Treaty (SALT II) talks and détente following the Soviet invasion of Afghanistan in 1979.

When 52 Americans were taken hostage in Iran that year, Vance advised Carter to negotiate, whereas Brzezinski advocated strong military action. Frustrated by the failure of peaceful means to win the release of the kidnapped hostages, Carter finally authorized a risky rescue attempt by U.S. commandos in 1980. It was a terrible failure, resulting in the deaths of eight Americans, and Cyrus Vance resigned in protest. He had been kept in the dark about the raid and thus not been able to keep his promise to the Senate to brief it in advance of any military action.

In 1980 Vance returned to private legal practice, and occasionally he served as a personal envoy to United Nations fact-finding and peacekeeping missions in the 1990s.

SEE ALSO

Brzezinski, Zbigniew; Camp David peace talks; Carter, James Earl, Jr. ("Jimmy"); Iranian hostage crisis (1979)

FURTHER READING

McLellan, David S. *Cyrus Vance.* Lanham, Md.: Rowman & Littlefield, 1985.

Vandenberg, Arthur

- *Born: Mar. 24, 1884, Grand Rapids, Mich.*
- *Accomplishments: U.S. senator (Republican–Mich.), 1928–51*
- *Died: Apr. 18, 1951, Grand Rapids, Mich.*

Formerly an avowed isolationist, Senator Arthur Vandenberg of Michigan responded to changing world conditions after 1945 to become the leading Republican advocate of a bipartisan and interventionist foreign policy. He is best known as the author of the Vandenberg Resolution, passed by Congress on June 11, 1948.

Concerned about Soviet expansion in Europe and other parts of the globe, Vandenberg introduced a plan by which the United States could participate in regional security agreements, such as the Brussels Pact, a European mutual security agreement, without a congressional treaty. The resolution proposed that the United States participate in these security agreements within the framework of the U.S. role in the United Nations.

The resolution had no legal force, but it gave assurance to U.S. allies that the United States would respond against aggression and offer aid to countries that were attacked. Vandenberg also developed bipartisan support for the United Nations, the Marshall Plan in 1948, and the North Atlantic Treaty Organization (NATO) in 1949.

SEE ALSO

Cold war; Marshall Plan; North Atlantic Treaty Organization (NATO); Truman, Harry S.

FURTHER READING

Tompkins, C. David. *Senator Arthur H. Vandenberg: The Evolution of a Modern Republican, 1884–1945*. Lansing: Michigan State University Press, 1970.

Vietcong (VC)

SEE National Liberation Front (NLF)

Vietnamization

To fulfill his campaign pledge to achieve "peace with honor" in Vietnam, President Richard M. Nixon began the withdrawal of U.S. ground troops in 1969, as part of his program known as Vietnamization—reducing U.S. military actions on the ground and having the South Vietnam army do more of the fighting. The withdrawals continued steadily for the next three years so that from a peak of more than 540,000 in 1969 the number of American soldiers in Vietnam dwindled to some 60,000 in 1972.

Vietnamization did nothing to break the stalemate in the negotiations with the North Vietnamese to end the war, so Nixon broadened U.S. involvement by greatly intensifying the bombing of North Vietnam and the Ho Chi Minh Trail and by beginning to bomb enemy sanctuaries in Cambodia and Laos.

SEE ALSO

Nixon, Richard Milhous; Vietnam War

Vietnam War

The United States's longest war and its first military defeat, the Vietnam War divided the country more than any other event of the 20th century. In keeping with cold war policy-making, the United States first intervened in Vietnam in the 1950s as part of a worldwide strategy to contain communism. By the early 1970s, however, government officials who had grown much more concerned with containing the domestic upheaval caused by the war finally ended U.S. involvement in Southeast Asia, but only after 58,000 Americans and millions of Vietnamese had died.

At the end of World War II, the United States participated in ceremonies marking Vietnam's declaration of independence from France. President Franklin D. Roosevelt had been opposed to recolonization after the war, and the freedom of colonial peoples had been implied in the Atlantic Charter, the war aims agreed upon by the United States and Britain.

President Harry S. Truman, however, made the containment of communism in Europe a higher priority. In exchange for France's approval of the admission of Germany to the North Atlantic Treaty Organization (NATO), Truman agreed to aid France in the reassertion of its position in Indochina. By the early 1950s, U.S. funding covered 80 percent of the French military expenses in Vietnam.

In 1954 France suffered a decisive defeat at Dien Bien Phu in northwest Vietnam. In the peace settlement at Geneva, negotiators (who did not include Americans) agreed to partition Vietnam at the 17th Parallel until 1956, when democratic elections could be held and the country reunited. But Dwight Eisenhower's administration immediately moved to undermine this settlement.

The so-called domino theory informed the Eisenhower administration's decision. Fearing that a democratic election would be likely to result in victory for the communist nationalist leader Ho Chi Minh, and that his win might cause neighboring countries to fall, like dominoes, to communism, Eisenhower had the CIA help to establish an independent government in South Vietnam under President Ngo Dinh Diem.

The Army of the Republic of Vietnam (ARVN), also known as the South Vietnamese army, was formed after Ngo Dinh Diem became president of the new nation in 1954. The CIA worked with the new regime to train its armed forces and to block the scheduled election. Although ARVN personnel were largely trained by U.S. military advisors, they remained undisciplined and often corrupt, which caused them to fare poorly against the North Vietnamese in the early years of the war. Forces from the North began guerrilla attacks on the South in 1957 and in 1960 helped organize the National Liberation Front of South Vietnam (NLF; also known as the Vietcong) in opposition to Diem. Later, when President Richard Nixon began the process of Vietnamization, or shifting the responsibility for fighting the ground war from the withdrawing U.S. forces back to the ARVN, the ARVN forces again performed miserably.

An upper-class Catholic with a French education, Diem had quickly alienated much of the poor Buddhist population of Vietnam by refusing to institute land reform or eliminate government corruption. The NLF capitalized on this and attracted wide support in the South.

President John F. Kennedy's advisors Walt Rostow and General Maxwell Taylor recommended increased military support and a commitment of 8,000 U.S. troops to aid the South Vietnamese. Kennedy opted instead to send more military advisors, ultimately increasing their number to 16,000.

In 1963, despite pressure from the Kennedy administration to institute reforms to try to marshal more support, Diem brutally put down demonstrations by those who opposed him. After Buddhist monks began publicly burning themselves to death in protest, Kennedy decided that a new government was needed in Saigon. U.S. policymakers approved a military coup that resulted in Diem's death just three weeks before Kennedy himself was assassinated.

Diem's successors (there would be nine new governments in the next five years) also proved unable to defeat the NLF as it increased its attacks on the South in 1964. President Lyndon B. Johnson was hesitant to expand U.S. involvement. He knew that it would undermine his domestic efforts to achieve his Great Society program. But fearing the spread of communism as much as his predecessors had, and not wanting to be labeled "soft on communism" by his Republican opponents, Johnson expanded U.S. intervention.

Johnson appointed Maxwell Taylor, still an outspoken proponent of wider U.S. involvement, as ambassador to South Vietnam. Then, after receiving a blank check from Congress in 1964 in the form of the Gulf of Tonkin Resolution, Johnson boldly escalated the war.

Between 1965 and 1968, U.S. planes dropped 800 tons of bombs on North Vietnam every day as part of Operation Rolling Thunder. This tonnage was equivalent to three times that which was dropped by all nations in all of World War II. By the end of 1967,

Near Saigon, South Vietnamese wait to be picked up by U.S. helicopters and taken into battle against the Vietcong.

moreover, nearly 500,000 U.S. soldiers were stationed in South Vietnam.

As the war escalated, television cameras brought grisly battle scenes into American homes almost nightly. A credibility gap developed as military leaders, including the U.S. commander General William Westmoreland, optimistically cited body count statistics and suggested that victory was "just around the corner."

When the cease-fire that had been called every year to celebrate Tet, the Vietnamese New Year, began on January 30, 1968, approximately 86,000 Vietcong and North Vietnamese army soldiers simultaneously attacked all of the major cities and towns in South Vietnam. This surprise offensive struck the six largest cities in South Vietnam as well as 36 provincial capitals, 64 district capitals, 12 U.S. bases, and the U.S. embassy in Saigon.

Although the U.S. and South Vietnamese forces quickly recovered and routed the invading enemy, the massive scope of the offensive convinced many Americans that they could no longer believe their own government's estimates that the North Vietnamese would soon be defeated. Even though the U.S. forces recovered territory initially lost and went on to inflict devastating casualties on the enemy, the nation came to see in the North Vietnamese a strong, aggressive enemy that appeared nowhere near defeat. The tide of public opinion began to shift and on March 31, after an embarrassing showing in the New Hampshire primary against peace candidate Eugene McCarthy, President Johnson bowed out of the Presidential race.

Republican Richard M. Nixon defeated Vice President Hubert Humphrey and became President in part because he pledged to achieve "peace with honor" in Vietnam. In his first term, Nixon reduced the number of U.S. troops in Vietnam to fewer than 30,000 and sent Henry Kissinger to negotiate with the North Vietnamese. But at the same time, Nixon dramatically increased the bombing of North Vietnam and secretly began bombing the Ho Chi Minh Trail and other supply routes in the neighboring neutral countries of

At the Vietnam Veterans Memorial in Washington, D.C., the name of every U.S. soldier who died is engraved on the wall, which is black and shiny, and reflects the images of its visitors. During the conflict, 58,000 Americans were killed.

Laos and Cambodia. Targeting the trail did little to stem the flow of supplies into South Vietnam, however, because the roads were small and virtually invisible under the canopy of leafy trees and low clouds.

In April 1970 Nixon announced that U.S. and South Vietnamese troops would invade Cambodia to attack North Vietnamese staging areas there. Militarily the invasion was successful, but it ended Cambodia's neutrality and widened the war. Massive protests—including those ending in violence at Kent State University in Ohio and Jackson State University in Mississippi—took place across the United States.

After further bombing campaigns in 1972 (most notably the Christmas bombing of Hanoi and Haiphong), U.S. and North Vietnamese negotiators announced a settlement in Paris. The Paris peace accords, which ended U.S. involvement in the war but did not include a final political settlement between North and South Vietnam, were signed on January 27, 1973.

On April 30, 1975, North Vietnam conquered Saigon, thus defeating the South Vietnamese and unifying Vietnam 30 years after the country declared its independence from France.

The war inflicted considerable damage on the United States. The U.S. government spent more than $150 billion, and 58,000 lives were lost fighting in Vietnam; 300,000 others were wounded. Some veterans, disillusioned during their tours of duty in Vietnam, turned to drugs, deserted, or committed atrocities. Often they felt unwelcome and alienated when they returned to the United States.

Many other Americans felt frustrated when protest did not immediately end the war. The war became a source of cynicism about the honesty of government officials. Coupled with the Watergate scandal that toppled President Nixon, the war caused many to abandon their faith in government. The American optimism of the 1950s and early 1960s died a slow, painful death in the rice paddies of Vietnam.

SEE ALSO

Antiwar movement; Cambodia, bombing and invasion of; Geneva Conference (1954); Gulf of Tonkin Resolution (1964); Hawks and doves; Laos, bombing of; National Liberation Front (NLF); Paris peace talks (1968–72); Vietnamization; Westmoreland, William C.

FURTHER READING

Braestrup, Peter. *Big Story: How the American Press and Television Reported and Interpreted the Crisis of Tet 1968 in Vietnam and Washington.* New Haven, Conn.: Yale University Press, 1983.

Clodfelter, Mark. *The Limits of Air Power.* New York: Free Press, 1989.
Halberstam, David. *The Best and the Brightest.* New York: Random House, 1972.
Herring, George. *America's Longest War: The United States and Vietnam, 1950–1975.* New York: Knopf, 1986.
Isaacs, Arnold R. *Without Honor: Defeat in Vietnam and Cambodia.* Baltimore: Johns Hopkins University Press, 1983.
Karnow, Stanley. *Vietnam: A History.* New York: Viking, 1983.
Kolko, Gabriel. *Anatomy of a War: Vietnam, the United States, and the Modern Historical Experience.* New York: Pantheon, 1986.
Moss, George Donnelson. *Vietnam: An American Ordeal.* 2nd ed. Englewood Cliffs, N.J.: Prentice Hall, 1994.
Oberdorfer, Dan. *Tet! The Turning Point in the Vietnam War.* New York: Doubleday, 1971.
Sheehan, Neil. *A Bright Shining Lie: John Paul Vann and America in Vietnam.* New York: Random House, 1988.
Spector, Ronald. *After Tet: The Bloodiest Year in Vietnam.* New York: Free Press, 1993.
Stevens, Richard. *Mission to the Ho Chi Minh Trail: Nature, Myth, and War in Vietnam.* Norman: University of Oklahoma Press, 1995.

Voting Rights Act (1965)

Introduced by President Lyndon B. Johnson in March 1965, passed by Congress, and signed into law by the President in early August, the Voting Rights Act guaranteed the voting rights of all U.S. citizens "without distinctions of race, color, or previous condition of servitude." The law was aimed at striking down a web of statutes and practices in southern states that had prevented the vast majority of African Americans from voting there, especially laws requiring prospective voters to read and interpret sections of the state constitution and to provide written answers to a test that could be as long as 20 pages.

The act restricted literacy testing, forbade intimidation of voters, authorized the attorney general to dispatch

Black voters in Arlington, Virginia, line up with their white neighbors at the polling place in 1968. Because of the reforms guaranteed by the Voting Rights Act, three-fifths of southern blacks had registered to vote by 1969.

federal registrars and observers to counties that tried to resist the act, and empowered the Justice Department to clear in advance changes in state electoral rules that might unfairly burden African-American voters.

Along with the 24th Amendment to the Constitution, which had been ratified the previous year and prohibited the poll tax in federal elections, and a Supreme Court decision that prohibited poll taxes in all elections, this landmark legislation gave the vote back to southern blacks. By 1969 approximately three-fifths of adult African Americans in the South had registered to vote. The most sweeping gains came in Mississippi, where black registration leaped from 7 percent in 1964 to 60 percent in 1968, and in Alabama, where African-American voter enrollment jumped from 23 percent to 53 percent.

SEE ALSO

Civil Rights Act of 1964; Civil rights movement; Johnson, Lyndon Baines

FURTHER READING

Davidson, Chandler, and Bernard N. Grofman, eds. *Controversies in Minority Voting: The Voting Rights Act in Perspective.* Washington, D.C.: Brookings Institute, 1992.

Hamilton, Charles V. *The Bench and the Ballot: Southern Federal Judges and Black Voters.* New York: Oxford University Press, 1973.

Lawson, Steven F. *Black Ballots: Voting Rights in the South, 1944–1969.* New York: Columbia University Press, 1976.

Thompson, Kenneth H. *The Voting Rights Act and Black Electoral Participation.* Washington, D.C.: Joint Center for Political & Economic Studies, 1984.

Wallace, George Corley

- *Born: Aug. 25, 1919, Clio, Ala.*
- *Accomplishments: Governor of Alabama (Democrat), 1962–72, 1982–87; Presidential candidate, 1968, 1972*
- *Died: Sept. 14, 1998, Montgomery, Ala.*

Best known for his staunch opposition to desegregation in the 1960s and his third-party Presidential bid in 1968, George Wallace symbolized white backlash against the civil rights movement and helped shape the agenda of social conservatism that dominated the politics of the 1970s and 1980s.

After serving as assistant attorney general, state legislator, and district judge in Alabama, Wallace won his second bid for the governorship in 1962, vowing "Segregation now! Segregation tomorrow! Segregation forever!" The next year he gained nationwide notoriety when he stood in a doorway at the University of Alabama to block the enrollment of two black students, Vivian Malone and James Hood. Although the federal government enforced the integration of the campus, Wallace's stand gained him popularity among whites who supported segregation.

In 1968 Wallace broke from the Democratic party to launch a third-party bid for the Presidency. Running as the candidate of the American Independent party, he denounced school integration, welfare, and radical protestors; he called for law and order, and pledged to keep the domestic peace through military force if necessary. The message appealed to many Americans disturbed by desegregation, campus protests against the Vietnam War, and race riots in urban ghettos.

Wallace garnered more than 10 million votes, 14 percent of the popular vote. In a second bid for the Presidency in 1972, this time within the Democratic party, he emphasized opposition to court-ordered school busing and a "get tough with protestors" policy, but the campaign was cut short by an assassination attempt by Arthur Bremer. Wallace was paralyzed and confined to a wheelchair. He successfully ran again for governor in 1982, publicly recanting his opposition to desegregation and capturing an overwhelming number of black votes. Because of ill health, Wallace retired from politics in 1987.

FURTHER READING

Carter, Dan T. *The Politics of Rage: George Wallace, the Origins of the New Conservatism, and the Transformation of American Politics.* New York: Simon & Schuster, 1995.

Lesher, Stephan. *George Wallace: American Populist.* Reading, Mass.: Addison-Wesley, 1994.

War on Poverty

The War on Poverty was a major component of President Lyndon B. Johnson's Great Society program, a legislative agenda that stands as one of the farthest-reaching federal reform movements of the 20th century. Declaring "unconditional war on poverty" in 1964, Johnson proposed a wide array of training programs and support services for the 40 million poor people in the United States.

The War on Poverty was anchored by four programs. The first was the Economic Opportunity Act of 1964, which established the Office of Economic Opportunity to fund and coordinate public-works projects and a Job Corps that would train young people in marketable skills.

Second was VISTA (Volunteers in Service to America), a domestic Peace Corps to work in poverty areas. Project Head Start, which provided education for preschoolers from disadvantaged families, was the third major part of the War on Poverty.

The last piece of the effort, the Community Action Program, encouraged the "maximum feasible participation" of the poor themselves in the policy decisions that affected them. Overall, the War on Poverty programs provided opportunities rather than simply giving relief checks; its slogan was "a hand up, not a handout."

Other aspects of the Great Society program also sought to eliminate the barriers that stood in the way of the poor. This was accomplished by fighting for equal economic opportunities for racial minorities; supplying legal services and a food stamp program for the poor; and extending aid for education and medical insurance for welfare recipients and the elderly (Medicaid and Medicare, respectively).

Other programs provided housing assistance; funded highway construction, health centers, and resource devel-

A New York City block of slums was cleared to make way for a public housing project in 1962. Part of Lyndon Johnson's War on Poverty was ensuring that people had adequate, affordable housing.

opment in depressed areas of the Appalachian Mountains; gave scholarships to needy college students; and established a Model Cities program in an effort to redevelop urban slums. But increasing political opposition to the community action programs and diminishing financial support caused by the escalation of the Vietnam War brought the War on Poverty to an end before it could achieve more than a modest victory.

SEE ALSO

Great Society; Johnson, Lyndon Baines

FURTHER READING

Goldman, Eric F. *The Tragedy of Lyndon Johnson.* New York: Knopf, 1969.

Harrington, Michael. *The Other America: Poverty in the United States.* New York: Macmillan, 1962.

Katz, Michael B. *The Undeserving Poor.* New York: Pantheon, 1989.

War Powers Act of 1973

In 1973 Congress overrode a Presidential veto to pass the War Powers Act, which required the President to inform Congress within 48 hours of the deployment of troops overseas. In addition, the new law forced the President to withdraw troops from overseas within 60 days if Congress refused to authorize the operation. Although this legislation was sought to make sure that the country never again slid into a war without a full congressional debate (as had happened in Vietnam), no President has acknowledged the constitutionality of the War Powers Act.

Warren Commission

Just days after the assassination of President John F. Kennedy on November 22, 1963, his successor, Vice President Lyndon B. Johnson, appointed a seven-man commission, headed by Chief Justice Earl Warren, to investigate the assassination. The commission also included Gerald R. Ford, a Republican congressman from Michigan who would later become President, and Allen W. Dulles, former director of the Central Intelligence Agency.

In September 1964 the panel concluded that Lee Harvey Oswald, who was psychologically disturbed, had acted "alone and without advice or assistance" when he shot and killed the President. Some people felt that the commission's report failed to answer all of the questions surrounding the assassination, however, and conspiracy theorists have continued to argue that Oswald was part of a larger plan, which may have included other gunmen and perhaps anti-Castro or pro-Castro Cubans, the Mafia, and U.S. government officials opposed to Kennedy's policies. The report has remained controversial and its findings have been under attack since it was issued.

SEE ALSO

Kennedy, John Fitzgerald; Oswald, Lee Harvey; Warren, Earl

FURTHER READING

Achenbach, Joel. "JFK Conspiracy: Myth vs. the Facts." *Washington Post,* February 28, 1992.

Meagher, Sylvia. *Accessories after the Fact: The Warren Commission, the Authorities, and the Report.* New York: Vintage, 1976.

Posner, Gerald. *Case Closed: Lee Harvey Oswald and the Assassination of JFK.* New York: Random House, 1993.

Warren Court

In the mid-1950s the Supreme Court veered leftward under the leadership of its new chief justice, Earl Warren, addressing individual rights in the way that earlier courts had stressed property rights. Formerly a conservative Republican governor of California, Warren led the court that outlawed racial segregation, established the "one person, one vote" principle in legislative apportionments, bolstered the rights of the accused in the criminal justice system, prohibited prayer in public schools, and extended the right of free speech.

Conservatives bitterly opposed the Warren Court's decisions. Many called for the chief justice's impeachment. Eventually President Dwight D. Eisenhower, who appointed Warren because Warren had helped him secure the Republican Presidential nomination in 1952, came to regret his choice.

The Court's most momentous decision came in 1954 when it ruled unanimously in *Brown* v. *Board of Education of Topeka, Kansas,* that "separate educational facilities are inherently unequal" and therefore that segregation in public schools was unconstitutional. Although most southern states initially resisted desegregation, the *Brown* decision helped catalyze a massive civil rights movement in the South.

In the 1957 case of *Yates* v. *United States,* the Court overturned convictions of Communist party members and extended free speech protection to the teaching of general revolutionary ideology. After Presidents John F. Kennedy and Lyndon B. Johnson appointed four more liberal judges in the 1960s, the Court recognized new personal rights. For instance, it ruled in *Gideon* v. *Wainwright* (1963) that individual defendants in criminal proceedings had the right to have a lawyer represent them.

In *Mapp* v. *Ohio* (1961), the Court barred the use of illegally seized evidence, and in *Miranda* v. *Arizona*

The Supreme Court headed by Chief Justice Earl Warren. Seated: Tom Clark, Hugo Black, Earl Warren, William Douglas, John Marshall Harlan. Standing: Byron White, William Brennan, Potter Stewart, Abe Fortas.

(1966) it insisted that the police must advise suspects of their constitutional rights upon arrest, including the rights to counsel and to a court-appointed lawyer if they could not afford to hire one.

The Warren Court continued to attack discrimination based on race. It upheld the civil rights laws passed by Congress, gave constitutional protections to African-American protesters, and in 1967 struck down laws that prohibited interracial marriages. In *Engel* v. *Vitale* (1962) the Court banned prayer in public schools and in *Abington* v. *Schempp* (1963) it prohibited Bible reading in public schools. *Jacobellis* v. *Ohio (1963)* extended the 1st Amendment protection of free speech to include sexually explicit material, and *New York Times* v. *Sullivan* (1964) limited libel suits against the press.

SEE ALSO

Brown v. *Board of Education of Topeka, Kansas* (1954); *Engel* v. *Vitale* (1962); *Miranda* v. *Arizona* (1966); *New York Times* v. *Sullivan* (1964); Supreme Court; Warren, Earl

FURTHER READING

Schwartz, Bernard. *Super Chief: Earl Warren and His Supreme Court*. New York: New York University Press, 1983.

Warren, Earl

- *Born: Mar. 19, 1891, Los Angeles, Calif.*
- *Accomplishments: Governor of California (Republican), 1943–53; Chief Justice of the United States, 1953–69*
- *Died: July 19, 1974, Washington, D.C.*

After serving as the Republican governor of California from 1943 to 1953 and running for Vice President on the Republican ticket with Thomas Dewey in 1948, Earl Warren was appointed Chief Justice of the United States in 1953 and held that position until 1969. Warren also chaired the Warren Commission, which investigated the assassination of President John F. Kennedy.

Earl Warren, the controversial Chief Justice of the United States, poses in his book-lined office in 1963. He was 73 years old, and would serve for another six years.

Under Warren, who was the most liberal chief justice in Supreme Court history, the Court outlawed racial segregation, bolstered the rights of the accused in the criminal justice system, prohibited prayer in public schools, and extended the right of free speech. While President Eisenhower regarded his appointment of Warren as "the biggest damn fool mistake I ever made," a fellow liberal on the court, Justice Abe Fortas, hailed Warren's judicial accomplishments as "the most profound and pervasive revolution ever achieved by substantially peaceful means."

SEE ALSO

Supreme Court; Warren Court

FURTHER READING

Patrick, John J. *The Young Oxford Companion to the Supreme Court of the United States*. New York: Oxford University Press, 1998.
White, G. Edward. *Earl Warren: A Public Life*. New York: Oxford University Press, 1972.

Watergate

In the summer of 1971, following a series of leaks to the press about secret U.S. military operations in Cambodia and the publication of the Pentagon Papers, the secret documentary history of U.S. involvement in Vietnam, President Richard M. Nixon ordered his special counsel, Charles Colson, to create the White House Special Investigations Unit. This group, nicknamed the "plumbers" because their mission was to plug the leaks within the executive branch as well as to engage in covert, or secret, action against the President's opponents, was headed by former CIA operative E. Howard Hunt and G. Gordon Liddy, an ex-FBI agent. To try to find information to discredit Daniel Ellsberg, who had leaked the Pentagon Papers, they burglarized his psychiatrist's office and conducted similar activities against other presumed enemies of the White House.

Although Nixon, a Republican, was almost assured of victory in the Presidential election that was coming in 1972, he continued to seek an extra edge, using the millions of dollars of contributions to CREEP (the Committee to Re-Elect the President) to finance a special internal espionage unit to spy on his opponents, the Democrats. He also wanted the unit to play "dirty tricks" on them.

In 1972, Jeb Stuart Magruder, a former White House aide and the assistant director of CREEP, approved a plan presented to him by G. Gordon Liddy, who was then the counsel to CREEP's finance committee. The plan called for CREEP operatives to break into the office of Lawrence O'Brien, who was the Democratic party's national chairman and who worked at the Watergate apartment and office complex in Washington, D.C., and to tap his phones. On April 17, 1972, five men were arrested at the Watergate as they attempted to install the taps. One of the five carried an address book that linked them with Liddy and Hunt, who was then working for the President. These arrests started a chain of events that resulted in criminal proceedings against some 50 people, prison sentences for a former attorney general and leading members of the White House staff, and President Nixon's resignation from office.

Immediately after the foiled break-in, a White House cover-up began. Nixon's aides removed Hunt's name from the White House telephone directory and took his papers out of a White House safe. Nixon said "categorically" that "no one in the White House staff, no one in this administration, presently employed, was involved in this bizarre incident." He sought to buy the silence of those arrested with hush money and directed the CIA to halt the FBI's investigation of Watergate, citing national security. And Liddy immediately destroyed all the incriminating evidence in his possession and offered himself as a sacrifice, even volunteering to stand at a given street and time if the White House wished to have him assassinated. Although he was in California at the time of the arrest, Magruder quickly called his assistant in Washington and had him destroy materials in his files. Later, afraid that he might be made a scapegoat, Magruder confessed to a grand jury that had been convened on the Watergate affair and testified to Sam Ervin's Senate committee that Attorney General John Mitchell had approved and helped plan the Watergate break-in.

The President's press secretary, Ronald Ziegler, disavowed any White House association with the affair when he said, two days after the arrests, "I'm not going to comment from the White House on a third-rate burglary attempt." In fact, the story of the initial arrests was of such small interest to the media that it received only a brief mention on page 30 of the June 18 issue of the *New York Times.*

At first the White House cover-up went well. The five men who were arrested kept their silence, as did Hunt and Liddy. Nixon won the 1972 election overwhelmingly, with nearly 61 percent of the popular vote. But gradually details of the spreading scandal were revealed by two *Washington Post* reporters, Carl Bernstein and Bob Woodward, and by James W. McCord, a former CIA agent and chief of security for CREEP, who was one of the men arrested at the Watergate. McCord confessed that the White House had known about the break-in before it happened.

The trial of the seven defendants—the five "plumbers," E. Howard Hunt, and Gordon Liddy—began in January 1973 before John J. Sirica, chief judge of a U.S. district court. Living up to his nickname "Maximum John," Sirica threatened the defendants with long prison terms unless they told what they knew. His relentless prodding led McCord to break his silence and reveal that the White House had paid him hush money and promised a pardon if he kept quiet. Outraged, Sirica convened a grand jury to investigate Watergate further.

In February 1973, the Senate established the Special Committee on Presidential Campaign Activities to investigate the alleged election misdeeds; folksy 76-year-old Senator Sam Ervin, a North Carolina Democrat who was an expert on constitutional law, chaired the committee. It began its work on May 17, 1973, and soon the testimony given to its members, and to the nation, included information about the existence of a White House "enemies list," the President's use of government agencies to harass his opponents, and administration favoritism in return for illegal campaign donations. As the trail of revelations led closer to the Oval Office, President Nixon fired his special counsel, John Dean, and announced the resignations of his two top aides, H. R. Haldeman and John Ehrlichman.

After he was fired by Nixon, Dean agreed to cooperate with the Ervin Senate committee as it investigated the cover-up. Dean's revenge came when he testified for five days during the televised hearings and revealed that Nixon had authorized the payment of hush money to those arrested in the Watergate break-in and had personally directed the cover-up. Another Presidential aide, Alexander Butterfield, testified that Nixon had installed a secret, voice-activated taping system in the White House that recorded all conversations and meetings held in the Oval Office, and all phone calls made there. This was another bombshell.

Nixon denied any wrongdoing, and because it was the President's word against Dean's, proving the truth of Dean's testimony became essential to the Ervin committee. The committee wanted access to the tapes; they could have proven irrelevant, but they also could have shown Nixon to be innocent or been the "smoking gun" necessary to find the President guilty. The President, citing executive privilege, refused to surrender the tapes.

Nixon did give in to Senate demands that he appoint a special Watergate prosecutor with broad powers of investigation and subpoena. In May 1973 Elliot Richardson, Nixon's attorney general, chose Archibald Cox, a Democrat and Harvard Law School professor, for that post. Working closely

As chairman of the Senate committee investigating the Watergate scandal, Senators Sam Ervin (center) and Howard Baker (left) listen to testimony. The televised hearings riveted the country for months.

with a federal grand jury, Cox subpoenaed the secret Oval Office tapes.

In October 1973, when Cox sought a court order to obtain the tapes, Nixon ordered Elliot Richardson to fire Cox. The attorney general refused and resigned in protest, as did the deputy attorney general. Although Nixon's order was finally carried out by Solicitor General Robert Bork, the furor resulting from this Saturday Night massacre sent Nixon's public-approval ratings plummeting.

Leon Jaworski, Cox's replacement as special prosecutor, and the House Judiciary Committee, which was considering impeachment proceedings, both then subpoenaed the President for the tapes. Still trying to maintain the cover-up, Nixon released edited transcripts of the tapes in April 1974. They would not suffice, and in late July the Supreme Court rejected Nixon's claim of executive privilege and ordered the President to hand over the 64 unedited tapes being sought.

Three days later, the House Judiciary Committee adopted the first article of impeachment, charging Nixon with obstruction of justice, and then voted two additional articles, for the President's abuse of power and for his contempt of Congress in refusing to obey a congressional subpoena. On August 5, Nixon conceded in a televised address that he had withheld relevant evidence from the special prosecutor and the Judiciary Committee, and he surrendered the subpoenaed tapes. They proved that Nixon had ordered the cover-up, obstructed justice, used the CIA to prevent a FBI investigation, and had lied about his role in Watergate for more than two years.

The certainty of an impeachment trial and conviction forced Nixon to resign from office on August 9, 1974. His Vice President, Gerald Ford, was then sworn in as President. The very next month, Ford unconditionally pardoned Nixon for any and all crimes he might have committed while he was in office. Many Americans reacted to the pardon with outrage, while others expressed relief that what President Ford called "our long national nightmare" was finally over.

SEE ALSO
Ford, Gerald Rudolph; Nixon, Richard Milhous; Pentagon Papers

FURTHER READING

Ambrose, Stephen. *Nixon: Ruin and Recovery. 1973–1990.* New York: Simon & Schuster, 1989.
Bernstein, Carl, and Bob Woodward. *All the President's Men.* New York: Simon & Schuster, 1994.
Dabney, Dick. *A Good Man: The Life of Sam J. Ervin.* Boston: Houghton Mifflin, 1976.
Dean, John. *Blind Ambition.* New York: Simon & Schuster, 1976.
Hoff, Joan. *Nixon Reconsidered.* New York: Basic Books, 1994.
Kurland, Philip B. *Watergate and the Constitution.* Chicago: University of Chicago Press, 1978.
Kutler, Stanley. *The Wars of Watergate: The Last Crisis of Richard Nixon.* New York: Knopf, 1990.
Liddy, G. Gordon. *Will: The Autobiography of G. Gordon Liddy.* New York: St. Martin's, 1996.
Schell, Jonathan. *A Time of Illusion.* New York: Knopf, 1975.

Water Quality Act of 1965

Touted by supporters as a "major new weapon to combat water pollution," the Water Quality Act of 1965 was designed to prevent water pollution before it occurred. The act required states to set standards of purity for all interstate waterways within their boundaries. If a state failed to do so, or if it set weak standards, the federal government would step in and set federal standards.

The act also created the Water Pollution Control Administration, to be housed within the Department of Health, Education, and Welfare.

SEE ALSO

Environmental movement

FURTHER READING

Bowden, Charles. *Killing the Hidden Waters.* Austin: University of Texas Press, 1977.

Water Quality Improvement Act of 1970

The Water Quality Improvement Act of 1970 was passed in response to a number of devastating oil spills in 1969. The act made petroleum companies liable for up to $14 million to clean up oil spills. The act also outlawed the flushing of raw sewage from boat toilets into waterways and strengthened regulations on thermal pollution from nuclear power plants.

SEE ALSO

Environmental movement

FURTHER READING

Nader, Ralph, et al., eds. *Who's Poisoning America: Corporate Polluters and Their Victims in the Chemical Age.* San Francisco: Sierra Club Books, 1981.
Rosenbaum, Walter. *The Politics of Environmental Concern.* New York: Praeger, 1973.

Watts riot (1965)

Black residents of the Watts section of Los Angeles rioted for six days in August 1965, looting shops, firebombing white-owned businesses, sniping at law enforcement officials and firefighters, and leaving in their wake 34 dead, 900 injured, and $30 million in property damages. The disorder, like many during the "long, hot summers" from 1964 to 1968, was precipitated by a confrontation between police and blacks.

An estimated 50,000 blacks participated in the Watts upheaval, and 4,000 were arrested before the Nation-

A police officer aims in the direction of a sniper's bullet in Watts during the riots of 1965.

al Guard finally quelled the riot. Although the Kerner Commission assigned to study this and other riots concluded that the root causes were racism, poverty, and police brutality, and called for increased social spending, most white Americans blamed African-American militancy, fueling a "white backlash" and undermining support for President Lyndon B. Johnson's Great Society programs.

SEE ALSO

Detroit race riot (1967); Kerner Commission (National Advisory Commission on Civil Disorders); Race riots

Weathermen

The most radical group to split off from the Students for a Democratic Society (SDS), the Weathermen, bitterly opposed to the war in Vietnam and to what they saw as the overwhelming hypocrisy and corruption of the capitalist system and American life, advocated violent confrontation with police and sought full-scale revolution in the late 1960s and early 1970s. The group's name was taken from the Bob Dylan lyric, "You don't need a weatherman to know which way the wind blows"; soon it was changed to the Weather Underground because some members found that Weathermen was sexist.

The Weathermen first came to the attention of the public during what they called the "days of rage," when approximately 200 Weathermen dressed in full combat gear went on a vandalism spree and battled police. Later, the movement went underground (echoing its name) and hoped to undermine "the establishment" through random bombings of its institutions. After several members were killed in a Manhattan townhouse when the bomb they were manufacturing detonated, the Weather Underground bombed about 20 sites (including a bathroom in the U.S. Capitol) during the next few years before fading into obscurity.

SEE ALSO

Students for a Democratic Society (SDS)

FURTHER READING

Alpert, Jane. *Growing Up Underground.* New York: Morrow, 1981.

Jacobs, Harold, ed. *Weatherman.* Berkeley: University of California Press, 1970.

Weaver, Robert C.

- *Born: Dec. 29, 1907, Washington, D.C.*
- *Accomplishments: Secretary of Housing and Urban Development, 1966–69*
- *Died: July 17, 1997, New York, N.Y.*

Robert C. Weaver became the first African American to hold a cabinet post when Lyndon B. Johnson appointed him secretary of the Department of Housing and Urban Development (HUD) in 1966. Weaver, a prolific scholar, had held positions in President

Franklin D. Roosevelt's administration and was considered a member of that President's unofficial "black cabinet."

Weaver also served as administrator of the federal Housing and Finance Agency in John Kennedy's administration. After leaving HUD in 1969, he served as president of Baruch College in New York City for two years.

Westmoreland, William C.

- *Born: Mar. 16, 1914, Spartanburg, S.C.*
- *Accomplishments: Superintendent of West Point (1960–64); Army general; Commander of American troops in Vietnam (1964–68); Army Chief of Staff (1968–72)*

A 1936 graduate of West Point, William Westmoreland served as an army officer in World War II and Korea before he was promoted to the rank of general in the 1950s. In 1964 he became head of the Military Assistance Command (MACV); he was in charge of all U.S. forces in South Vietnam. In that role he presided over the U.S. escalation of the war from 1964 to 1968.

Westmoreland based his military decisions on a strategy of attrition, which he believed would wear down North Vietnamese and Vietcong troops until they would ultimately surrender. He suffered strong criticism at home from those who were skeptical of his optimistic predictions of imminent victory, especially after he made a request for an additional 206,000 troops in February 1968.

Westmoreland served as army chief of staff from 1968 to 1972, when he retired. In later years, he claimed that the United States could have won the war if he had been allowed to attack communist strongholds in North Vietnam, Laos, and Cambodia after the Tet offensive.

SEE ALSO

Vietnam War

FURTHER READING

Westmoreland, William C. *A Soldier Reports.* New York: Doubleday, 1976.

Wilkins, Roy

- *Born: Aug. 30, 1901, St. Louis, Mo.*
- *Accomplishments: Executive secretary, National Association for the Advancement of Colored People, 1955–65; Executive director, 1965–77*
- *Died: Sept. 8, 1981, New York, N.Y.*

Roy Wilkins served as executive secretary and director of the National Association for the Advancement of Colored People (NAACP) during its most successful years, from 1955 to 1977. A journalist by trade, Wilkins served as editor of that organization's magazine, *The Crisis,* and as an assistant to Walter White before he ascended to the leadership in 1955.

Under Wilkins, the organization fought a series of successful legal battles in the Supreme Court and lobbied successfully for federal laws guaranteeing voting, civil, and employment rights for African Americans. Wilkins retired and was replaced by Benjamin Hooks in 1977.

SEE ALSO

National Association for the Advancement of Colored People (NAACP)

FURTHER READING

Wilkins, Roy, with Tom Mathews. *Standing Fast: The Autobiography of Roy Wilkins.* New York: Viking, 1982.

Women's Liberation Movement

SEE Feminism

Woodstock Festival (1969)

The ultimate celebration of the 1960s counterculture of sex, drugs, and rock and roll, the Woodstock Festival took place on a farm near Bethel, New York, from August 15 to 17, 1969. For three days, more than a quarter of a million young people celebrated peacefully while listening to dozens of the era's top musicians, including Jimi Hendrix, Janis Joplin, and the Jefferson Airplane. They swam nude in a nearby lake, took drugs, and good-naturedly condemned the materialism of their parents and the establishment's war in Vietnam. Some hailed the festival as the sign of a new era of peace and love, but later attempts to repeat the Woodstock experience proved unsuccessful, and violent deaths at an Altamont, California, festival in December 1969 dimmed the luster of the "Woodstock nation."

Janis Joplin performs at Woodstock. The huge audience got to see some of the most popular and influential rock n' rollers around; no festival using the name Woodstock since has ever been able to match the mystique and power of the first one.

Hippies at Woodstock wore "Flower power" and peace-sign buttons such as these to demonstrate their opposition to the war in Vietnam.

SEE ALSO

Counterculture

FURTHER READING

Reich, Charles. *The Greening of America.* New York: Random House, 1970.

Roszak, Theodore. *The Making of a Counter Culture.* Garden City, N.Y.: Doubleday, 1969.

World Wide Web

The World Wide Web is a mesh of hyperlinked, or connected, pages that exists on the Internet. The Internet is the global network that links millions of computers and local networks; the Web is one of the technologies that uses the Internet to provide information. The Web, which first ran in 1990 in CERN (the European Laboratory for Particle Physics in Switzerland), was created by Tim Berners-Lee, an English computer scientist now at M.I.T., as a way to make information available to as many people as possible. Web sites consist of text and graphics that are stored on a computer called a server. They are retrieved by user software called a browser and sent over the Internet's cable connections when the user selects a link on his or her own computer screen. The Web allows a user, safely at home or in the office, to connect to servers anywhere in the world for access to almost any kind of information.

The Web is growing very quickly—by the end of August 1998 there were 300 million Web pages in existence, and 1.5 million pages were being added every day—and that growth is making individual users, companies, and governments confront ethical questions about free speech, hate speech, ownership of intellectual property, and the effects of unsupervised Web surfing on children. Meanwhile, people are developing new ways to use the Web to make money, to reach more people, and to communicate ideas effectively.

SEE ALSO

Computers; Internet, The

FURTHER READING

Berners-Lee, Tim, and Mark Fischetti. *Weaving the Web: The Creator of the World Wide Web Reveals Its Origins, Its Problems, and Its Untapped Potential.* San Francisco: Harper, 1999.
Burke, James. *The Knowledge Web: From Electronic Agents to Stonehenge and Back, and Other Journeys Through Knowledge.* New York: Simon & Schuster, 1999.
Jefferis, David, and Mat Irvine. *Cyber Space: Virtual Reality and the World Wide Web.* New York: Crabtree, 1999.

Wounded Knee (1973)

For 71 days during the spring of 1973 in the tiny village of Wounded Knee in the Pine Ridge Reservation of South Dakota, federal law enforcement officials faced off against members of the American Indian Movement (AIM). On February 27, some 200 armed supporters of AIM had occupied the village—the site of a notorious massacre of 300 Lakotas by the U.S. Army in 1890—to call attention to the federal government's treaty violations and what they considered to be its persecution of local activists as well as to demand free elections of tribal leaders and a government investigation into the workings of the Bureau of Indian Affairs. The raiders took supplies and ammunition from the Wounded Knee trading post and barricaded themselves in a church.

Indians stand guard outside of the Church of the Sacred Heart in South Dakota as they confronted federal law enforcement officials at Wounded Knee.

The following day, federal law-enforcement officers sealed off the village, beginning the long siege. It ended on May 8, after the government agreed to investigate charges of broken treaties and the uncompensated expulsion of the Sioux from lands ceded to them. In 1974 a federal district court judge dismissed charges of assault, conspiracy, and larceny brought by the government against AIM leaders Dennis Banks and Russell Means, criticizing the prosecution for misleading the court and the FBI for suppressing evidence. In following years, Indian tribes throughout the United States benefited from the activism at Wounded Knee and other Native American protests of the period.

SEE ALSO

American Indian Movement (AIM); Native Americans

FURTHER READING

Churchill, Ward, and Jim Vander Wall. *Agents of Repression: The FBI's Secret Wars against the Black Panther Party and the American Indian Movement.* Boston: South End Press, 1988.

Yalta Conference

In early February 1945, when World War II was almost over and it was clear that the Allies would win, British prime minister Winston Churchill, Soviet premier Joseph Stalin, and President Franklin D. Roosevelt of the United States met at Yalta in the Soviet Union. They approved plans to establish a United Nations for collective security and decided to accept only an unconditional surrender from Germany. They also agreed to divide postwar Germany into four military zones—each of their countries would administer one zone, and the fourth would be run by France.

President Franklin Roosevelt meets with British prime minister Winston Churchill (left) and Soviet premier Joseph Stalin (right) at Yalta.

Stalin agreed to enter the Pacific war against Japan after the end of the war in Europe and vaguely promised to allow free elections to determine the future government of Poland. In return, the Soviet Union was promised concessions in Manchuria and the return of lands lost in the Russo-Japanese War of 1904–5. Although Roosevelt's critics later charged him with selling out to the Soviets at Yalta, the agreements reached there reflected both the United States's wartime priorities and the 1945 balance of power in Europe.

FURTHER READING

Clemens, Diane S. *Yalta.* New York: Oxford University Press, 1970.

Youth International party (Yippies)

Founded by Jerry Rubin and Abbie Hoffman, the largely anarchistic Youth International party (Yippies) sought to mock the U.S. establishment through small- and large-scale guerrilla theater. Although they were less influential in the antiwar movement than were other, more serious organizations, the Yippies often received a disproportionate share

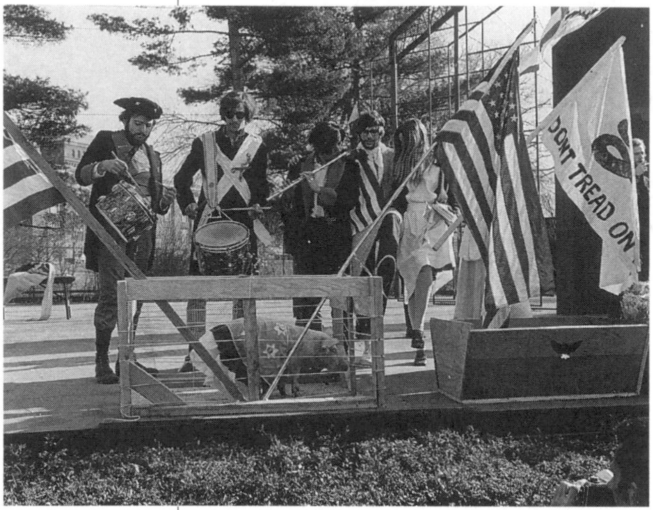

On the grounds of the Washington Monument, Yippies hold a demonstration to introduce their "pig queen"—one of their many attempts to mock U.S. culture with guerrilla theater.

of the media attention because of the flamboyant personalities of Hoffman and Rubin, who excelled at publicizing their offbeat activities.

In 1968 the Yippies planned a Festival of Life to counter the Democratic National Convention being held in Chicago. They presented a pig as their presidential nominee and titillated the press with threats to pour LSD into the city water supply and to seduce the wives and daughters of convention delegates.

SEE ALSO

Democratic National Convention (Chicago, 1968)

FURTHER READING

Hoffman, Abbie. *Revolution for the Hell of It.* New York: Dial, 1968.

Hoffman, Jack. *Run, Run, Run: The Lives of Abbie Hoffman.* New York: Putnam, 1994.

Rubin, Jerry. *Do It!* New York: Simon & Schuster, 1970.

Yuppies

While the *y* in "yuppie" is generally used to mean "young" and the *p* stands for "professional," the *u* in the middle can be either "urban" or "upwardly mobile." The term is used loosely to refer to people whose styles of life are more materialistic than idealistic. They may be any age from early adulthood to middle age, they are not necessarily professional but most often are white collar, and they may be found living in the suburbs as well as in cities. "Yuppie" was a disparaging term almost from the time it first appeared in the late 1970s. *Newsweek* magazine called 1984 "the Year of the Yuppie," noting the visibility of a generation preoccupied by a concern with their careers and personal lives, seemingly to the point where they cared about little else. They tended to work out often, dress expensively, eat exotically, and vacation flashily. Although liberal on social issues, such as abortion and gay rights, many were conservative on economic issues and supported Ronald Reagan's Presidency. The booming economy of the 1980s made money available even to people just out of college, and while Ronald Reagan was President, greed was to some extent socially acceptable. The movie that best describes yuppies is possibly Oliver Stone's 1987 *Wall Street*, where the reptilian Gordon Gecko insinuatingly tells his audience that "greed is good"; and people were not self-conscious about flaunting what they had. Because yuppies were always more a vague trend than they were a definable movement, it is hard to say when they ceased to be a strong cultural force, but by the end of the 1980s their time had passed.

FURTHER READING

Lasch, Christopher. *The Culture of Narcissism: American Life in an Age of Diminishing Expectations.* New York: Norton, 1979.

Schur, Edwin. *The Awareness Trap: Self-Absorption Instead of Social Change.* New York: Times Books, 1976.

Sewall, Gilbert T., ed. *The Eighties: A Reader.* New York: Perseus, 1997.

APPENDIX

IMPORTANT DATES IN THE HISTORY OF THE UNITED STATES SINCE 1945

1946
- ENIAC, the first electronic computer, begins operation
- Dr. Benjamin Spock, *Baby and Child Care*

1947
- Levittown, New York, suburban development started
- Truman Doctrine
- Taft-Hartley Act

1948
- Marshall Plan
- Alfred C. Kinsey, *Sexual Behavior in the Human Male*
- Harry S. Truman elected President

1950
- Joseph McCarthy launches his anti-communist crusade
- Korean War begins
- Ethel and Julius Rosenberg arrested as spies for the Soviet Union

1951
- J. D. Salinger, *The Catcher in the Rye*
- William Buckley, *God and Man at Yale*
- *Dennis* v. *United States*

1952
- Dwight D. Eisenhower elected President

1953
- Korean War truce signed
- Earl Warren appointed to the Supreme Court position of Chief Justice of the United States

1954
- Army-McCarthy hearings
- *Brown* v. *Board of Education of Topeka, Kansas*

1955
- AFL-CIO merger
- Montgomery bus boycott begins

1957
- Jack Kerouac, *On the Road*
- Little Rock school-desegregation crisis
- 40 million TV sets in the U.S., up from 17,000 in 1946

1958
- National Defense Education Act

1960
- Sit-ins to protest segregation
- U-2 incident
- Birth-control pill marketed
- John F. Kennedy elected President
- 22.2 percent of Americans living in poverty

1962
- Rachel Carson, *Silent Spring*
- Michael Harrington, *The Other America*
- Cuban missile crisis

1963
- Civil rights demonstrations in Birmingham and March on Washington
- Betty Friedan, *The Feminine Mystique*
- Kennedy assassinated; Lyndon B. Johnson becomes President.

1964
- "Freedom Summer" in Mississippi
- Civil Rights Act
- Berkeley Free Speech Movement
- War on Poverty begins
- Johnson elected President

1965
- Voting Rights Act
- Watts riot in Los Angeles
- Immigration Reform Act

1966
- National Organization for Women (NOW)
- Black Panthers

1967
- Major race riots in Detroit, Newark, and other cities
- March on the Pentagon

1968
- Tet Offensive
- Martin Luther King, Jr. assassinated; Robert F. Kennedy assassinated
- Democratic convention in Chicago marred by violence
- Richard M. Nixon elected President

1969
- *Apollo 11* lands first Americans on the moon
- Warren Burger appointed to the Supreme Court position of Chief Justice of the United States
- Woodstock Festival

1970
- U.S. invades Cambodia
- Environmental Protection Agency established
- Earth Day celebrated

1971
- *New York Times* publishes Pentagon Papers
- First American trade imbalance in modern era

1972
- Nixon visits China and the Soviet Union
- Strategic Arms Limitation Treaty (SALT I)
- Break-in at the Democratic National Committee headquarters in Watergate
- Nixon reelected President

1973
- Vietnam cease-fire agreement signed
- *Roe* v. *Wade*
- Arab oil boycott; major rise in OPEC prices
- Vice President Spiro Agnew resigns; Gerald Ford appointed Vice President

1974
- House Judiciary Committee votes to impeach Nixon
- Nixon resigns; Ford becomes President

1975
- South Vietnamese government falls to North Vietnamese troops
- Birth rate declines to 14.6 per 1,000 people in population, lowest in 20th century

1976
- Jimmy Carter elected President

1980
- Iran hostage crisis
- Ronald Reagan elected President
- 12.2 percent of Americans living in poverty

1981
- AIDS disease documented

1983
- U.S. invasion of Grenada
- Reagan proposes Strategic Defense Initiative (Star Wars)

1984
- Geraldine Ferraro chosen as Vice Presidential nominee by Democrats
- Reagan reelected President

1986
- Immigration Reform and Control Act
- William Rehnquist appointed Chief Justice of the United States
- Explosion of the *Challenger* space shuttle

1987
- Iran-Contra scandal hearings

1988
- U.S. and U.S.S.R. sign INF Treaty
- George W. Bush elected President

1989
- U.S. invasion of Panama; Manuel Noriega arrested
- Communist governments in Eastern Europe collapse; Berlin Wall dismantled

1990
- Germany reunified
- Iraq invades Kuwait
- Hispanics constitute 9 percent of U.S. population; Asians 3 percent; African Americans 11.5 percent

1991
- Persian Gulf War (Operation Desert Storm)
- Sovet Union ceases to exist; fragments into many separate nations
- Communist rule in Russian Republic ends
- Despite Anita Hill's charges of sexual harassment, Senate confirms appointment of Clarence Thomas to Supreme Court

1992
- William J. Clinton elected President

1993
- World Trade Center bombed
- North American Free Trade Agreement (NAFTA)
- Special prosecutor appointed to investigate so-called Whitewater affair

1994
- Republicans win control of Congress for first time since 1952 elections
- 15 percent of Americans living in poverty
- 15 percent of American labor force is unionized; down from 35.5 percent in 1945
- 8.7 percent of U.S. population is foreign-born, the most since 1940

1995
- Newt Gingrich elected Speaker of the House of Representatives
- Republicans enact major proposals in their "Contract With America"
- Bombing of Oklahoma City federal building kills 169 people
- Budget impasse between Clinton and Congress leads to government shutdown
- U.S. sends peacekeeping troops to Bosnia

1996
- Welfare Reform Act ends most federal entitlements
- Clinton reelected President

1998
- House of Representatives votes to impeach Clinton on the grounds of obstruction of justice and perjury

1999
- Senate votes not to remove Clinton from office

DOING RESEARCH ON THE UNITED STATES SINCE 1945: FURTHER READING

Many entries in this volume include references to books dealing with that specific subject. The reader may find the following volumes a bit more general in scope. They provide vital ideas, interpretations, and information for your further study of the history of the United States since the end of the Second World War. Many also include comprehensive bibliographies, guides to sources and archives, and references to websites and internet resources.

Anderson, David L., ed. *Shadow on the White House: Presidents and the Vietnam War, 1945–1975*. Lawrence: University Press of Kansas, 1993.

Anderson, Terry. *The Movement and the Sixties: Protest in America from Greensboro to Wounded Knee*. New York: Oxford University Press, 1995.

Ashmore, Harry. *Civil Rights and Wrongs: A Memoir of Race and Politics, 1941–1994*. New York: Pantheon, 1994.

Barnouw, Erik. *Tube of Plenty: The Evolution of Television*. New York: Oxford University Press, rev. ed., 1982.

Baughman, James L. *The Republic of Mass Culture: Journalism, Filmmaking, and Broadcasting in America Since 1941*. Baltimore: Johns Hopkins University Press, 1992.

Berman, Ronald. *America in the Sixties: An Intellectual History*. New York: Free Press, 1968.

Bernstein, Irving. *Guns or Butter: The Presidency of Lyndon Johnson*. New York: Oxford University Press, 1996.

Bernstein, Irving. *Promises Kept: John F. Kennedy's New Frontier*. New York: Oxford University Press, 1991.

Bloom, Alexander and Winifred Breines, eds. *Takin' It to the Streets: A Sixties Reader*. New York: Oxford University Press, 1995.

Boyer, Paul. *Promises to Keep: The United States Since World War II*. Lexington: D. C. Heath, 1994.

Breines, Wini. *Young, White, and Miserable: Growing Up Female in the Fifties*. Boston: Beacon, 1992.

Brennan, Mary C. *Turning Right in the Sixties: The Conservative Capture of the GOP*. Chapel Hill: University of North Carolina Press, 1995.

Carter, Dan T. *The Politics of Rage*. New York: Simon and Schuster, 1995.

Carroll, Peter. *It Seemed Like Nothing Happened: America in the 1970s*.New Brunswick: Rutgers University Press, 1990.

Chafe, William H. *Paradox of Change: American Women in the 20th Century*. New York: Oxford University Press, 1991.

Chafe, William H. *Unfinished Journey: America Since World War II*. New York: Oxford University Press, rev. ed., 1999.

Chalmers, David. *And the Crooked Places Made Straight: The Struggle for Social Change in the 1960s*. Baltimore: Johns Hopkins University Press, 1991.

Crawford, Alan. *Thunder on the Right: The "New Right" and the Politics of Resentment*. New York: Pantheon, 1980.

DeBenedetti, Charles and Charles Chatfield. *An American Ordeal: The Antiwar Movement of the Vietnam Era*. Syracuse: Syracuse University Press, 1990.

Dickstein, Morris. *Gates of Eden: American Culture in the Sixties*. New York: Basic Books, 1977.

Diggins, John Patrick. *The Proud Decades: America in War and Peace, 1941–1960*. New York: Norton, 1988.

Echols, Alice. *Daring to Be Bad: Radical Feminism in America, 1967–1975*.

Minneapolis: University of Minnesota Press, 1989.

Ellwood, Robert S. *The Sixties Spiritual Awakening: American Religion Moving from Modern to Postmodern.* New Brunswick: Rutgers University Press, 1994.

Epstein, Barbara. *Political Protest and Cultural Revolution: Nonviolent Direct Action in the 1970s and 1980s.* Berkeley: University of California Press, 1991.

Farber, David. *The Age of Great Dreams: America in the 1960s.* New York: Hill & Wang, 1994.

Fried, Richard. *Nightmare in Red: The McCarthy Era in Perspective.* New York: Oxford University Press, 1990.

Gardner, Lloyd C. *Pay Any Price: Lyndon Johnson and the Wars for Vietnam.* Chicago: Ivan R. Dee, 1995.

Garfinkle, Adam. *Telltale Hearts: The Origins and Import of the Vietnam Antiwar Movement.* New York: St. Martin's Press, 1995.

Giglio, James. *The Presidency of John F. Kennedy.* Lawrence: University Press of Kansas, 1991.

Gilbert, James B. *Another Chance: Postwar America, 1945–1968.* Philadelphia: Temple University Press, 1981.

Gitlin, Todd. *The Sixties: Years of Hope, Days of Rage.* New York: Bantam Books, 1987.

Graham, Hugh Davis. *The Civil Rights Era : Origins and Development of a National Policy, 1960–1965.* New York: Oxford University Press, 1990.

Goldfield, David. *Black, White, and Southern: Race Relations and Southern Culture 1940 to the Present.* Baton Rouge: Louisiana State University Press, 1990.

Halberstam, David. *The Fifties.* New York: Villard Books, 1993.

Harrison, Cynthia. *On Account of Sex: The Politics of Women's Issues, 1945–1968.* Berkeley: University of California Press, 1988.

Hartmann, Susan. *From Margin to Mainstream: American Women and Politics since 1960.* Philadelphia: Temple University Press, 1989.

Herring, George. *America's Longest War: The United States and Vietnam, 1950–1975.* New York: Knopf, rev. ed., 1994.

Hodgson, Godfrey. *America In Our Time.* New York: Random House, 1976.

Hunter, James Davidson. *Culture Wars: The Struggle to Define America.* New York: Basic Books, 1991.

Jones, Landon Y. *Great Expectations: America and the Baby Boom Generation.* New York: Coward, McCann and Geoghegan, 1980.

Kaiser, Charles. *1968 in America: Music, Politics, Chaos, Counterculture, and the Shaping of a Generation.* New York: Weidenfeld and Nicolson, 1988.

Karnouw, Stanley. *Vietnam: A History.* New York: Penguin, rev. ed., 1991.

Leffler Melvyn P. *A Preponderance of Power: National Security, the Truman Administration, and the Cold War.* Stanford: Stanford University Press, 1992.

Lomperis, Timothy. *The War Nobody Lost—and Won: America's Intervention in Vietnam's Twin Struggles.* Baton Rouge: Louisiana State University Press, 1984.

London, Herbert. *Closing the Circle: A Cultural History of the Rock Revolution.* Chicago: Nelson-Hall, 1985.

Marling, Karal Ann. *As Seen on TV: The Visual Culture of Everyday Life in the 1950s.* Cambridge: Harvard University Press, 1994.

Matusow, Allen. *The Unraveling of America: A History of Liberalism in the 1960s.* New York: Harper & Row, 1984.

May, Larry. *Recasting America: Culture and Politics in the Age of the Cold War.* Chicago: University of Chicago Press, 1989.

May, Elaine Tyler. *Homeward Bound: American Families in the Cold War Era.* New York: Basic Books, 1988.

Murray, Charles. *Losing Ground: American Social Policy, 1950–1980.* New York: Basic Books, 1984.

Meyerowitz, Joanne, ed. *Not June Cleaver: Women and Gender in Postwar America, 1945–1960.* Philadelphia: Temple University Press, 1994.

Olson, James and Randy Roberts. *Where the Domino Fell, America and Vietnam, 1945 to 1990.* New York: St. Martin's Press, 1991.

O'Neill, William L. *America High: The Years of Confidence, 1945–1960.* New York: Free Press, 1986.

Oshinsky, David. *A Conspiracy So Immense: The World of Joe McCarthy.* New York: Free Press, 1983.

Patterson, James T. *America Since 1941: A History.* Fort Worth: Harcourt Brace, 1994.

Perrett, Geoffrey. *A Dream of Greatness: The American People, 1945–1963.* New York: Coward, McCann & Geoghegan, 1979.

Sale, Kirpatrick. *The Green Revolution: The American Environmental Movement, 1962–1992.* New York: Hill and Wang, 1993.

Sayre, Nora. *Running Time: Films of the Cold War.* New York: Dial Press, 1982.

Schwartz, John. *America's Hidden Success: Twenty Years of Public Policy.* New York: Norton, 1983.

Silk, Mark. *Spiritual Politics: Religion and America since World War II.* New York: Simon & Schuster, 1988.

Sitkoff, Harvard. *The Struggle for Black Equality, 1954–1992.* New York: Hill & Wang, rev. ed., 1993.

Steigerwald, David. *The Sixties and the End of Modern America.* New York: St. Martin's Press, 1995.

Steinberg, Stephen. *Turning Back: The Retreat from Racial Justice in American Thought and Policy.* Boston: Beacon, 1995.

Stern, Mark. *Calculating Visions: Kennedy, Johnson and Civil Rights.* Brunswick: Rutgers University Press, 1992.

Unger, Irwin, and Debi Unger. *The Movement: A History of the American New Left, 1959–1972.* 1974. Reprint, Lanham, Md.: University Press of America, 1988.

Unger, Irwin, and Debi Unger. *Turning Point: 1968.* New York: Scribners, 1988.

Urgo, Joseph R. *Novel Frames: Literature as Guide to Race, Sex, and History in American Culture.* Jackson: University Press of Mississippi, 1991.

Van Deburg, William L. *New Day in Babylon: The Black Power Movement and American Culture, 1965–1975.* Chicago: University of Chicago Press, 1992.

Wells, Tom. *The War Within: America's Battle Over Vietnam.* Berkeley: University of California Press, 1994.

Young, Marilyn B. *The Vietnam Wars, 1945–1990.* New York: HarperCollins, 1991.

INDEX

References to illustrations are indicated by page numbers in *italics*. References to main article entries are indicated by page numbers in **boldface**.

PICTURE CREDITS

The American Indian Movement/Dick Bancroft: 20; Archive Photos: 31, 32, 33, 90, 130, 137, 168; Archives of Labor and Urban Affairs, Wayne State University: 56, 245, 254; Dick Bancroft: frontispiece, 200; George Bush Library: 45, 106, 215; Cable News Network: 213; The Carter Center: 52; Jimmy Carter Library: 51; Chicago Historical Society, Photographer Betty Hulett: 197; Corbis/Bettmann: 108, 139, 151, 164, 188, 211, 226, 276; The D'Arcy Collection of the Communications Library of the University of Illinios at Urbana-Champaign: 267; The Detroit Free Press/Frank Williams: 268; Dwight D. Eisenhower Library: 94; Gerald R. Ford Library: 54, 84, 107; © 1992 Greenpeace/Culley: 100; Hake's Americana: 166, 233, 255; Ilke Hartmann: 127, 199; Reprinted by permission of International Creative Management, © Toni Morrison: 189; Japanese American History Archives: 25; John F. Kennedy Library: 81, 142, 145; Elliott Landy: 275; Library of Congress: 8, 9, 16, 27, 29, 34, 35, 41, 42, 43, 44, 47, 49, 50, 55, 58, 59, 60, 61, 73, 77, 79, 80, 83, 85, 86, 88, 91, 96, 98, 99, 105, 109, 110, 111, 114, 117, 118, 119, 125, 126, 127, 129, 132, 133, 134, 139, 148, 150, 160, 163, 170, 179, 184, 185, 195, 202, 203, 206, 208, 209, 214, 225, 229, 230, 231, 233, 234, 236, 239, 240, 241, 243, 247, 251, 254, 261, 265, 268, 273, 277, 278, 289; Library of Virginia: 107; Maryland State Police Dept.: 93; Metro-Goldwyn-Mayer (Museum of Modern Art): 191; Museum of Modern Art: 216; National Archives: 10, 11, 18, 19, 22, 71, 141, 146, 152, 155, 157, 158, 159, 162, 171, 172, 180, 211, 214, 223, 232, 257, 263; National Archives/ Nixon Papers: 204; Courtesy National Endowment for the Arts, photo by Vernon Lujan: 196; National Park Service: 262; Picture Collection, New York Public Library, Astor, Lenox and Tilden Foundation: 40; Panopticon, Inc., photo by Whithers: 166, 187; Ronald Reagan Library: 76, 207, 219, 221; Reuters/Mike Theiler/Archive Photos: 115; Reuters/Win McNamee/Archive Photos: 69; Photographs and Print Division, Schomburg Center, New York Public Library, Astor, Lenox and Tilden Foundation: 36, 37, 39, 74; Senate Historical Office: 175, 271; Sophia Smith/Boston Women's Health Collective: 105; Sophia Smith Collection, Smith College/Reprinted by permission of *Ms.* Magazine, © 1972: 193; Collection of the Supreme Court of the United States: 267; Nancy Toff: 130; Temple University Archives, Urban Archives: 14, 217; From the collection of Carl Van Vechten, Department of Special Collections, Syracuse University: 223; Photo by Richard A. Wandel, The Lesbian and Gay Community Services Center, National Archive of Lesbian and Gay History: 238; Copyright Washington Post, reprinted by permission of the D.C. Public Library: 101, 113; Courtesy Sarah Weddington, 225; The White House Photo Office: 271, 273; United Nations: 275; UPI/Corbis Bettman: 276, 277.

Harvard Sitkoff, Professor of History at the University of New Hampshire, earned his Ph.D. from Columbia University. He is the author of *A New Deal for Blacks* and *The Struggle for Black Equality, 1954–1992*, the editor of several books on 20th-century U.S. history, and the author of numerous articles in professional journals. He has also lectured on American history in some 100 universities in Africa, Asia, and Europe, and been the recipient of the Fulbright Commission's John Adams Chair in American Studies in the Netherlands and Mary Ball Washington Chair in American History in Ireland.

William H. Chafe is Alice Mary Baldwin Distinguished Professor of History and Dean of the Faculty of Arts and Sciences at Duke University. His numerous publications include *Civilities and Civil Rights: Greensboro, North Carolina and the Black Struggle for Freedom* (winner of the Robert F. Kennedy Book Award); *A History of Our Time: Readings in Postwar America* (edited with Harvard Sitkoff); *The Unfinished Journey: America Since World War II; The Paradox of Change: American Women in the Twentieth Century; Never Stop Running: Allard Lowenstein and the Struggle to Save American Liberalism* (winner of the Sidney Hillman Book Award); and *The Raod to Equality: American Women Since 1962*. Professor Chafe is currently the president of the Organization of American Historians.